The Cold War

John Lamberton Harper is Professor of American Foreign Policy and European Studies at the Bologna Center of the Johns Hopkins University School of Advanced International Studies. He is the author of *America and the Reconstruction of Italy* (1986), winner of the Marraro prize from the Society for Italian Historical Studies, *American Visions of Europe: Franklin D. Roosevelt, George F. Kennan, and Dean G. Acheson* (1994), winner of the Ferrell prize from the Society for Historians of American Foreign Relations, and *American Machiavelli: Alexander Hamilton and the Origins of U.S. Foreign Policy* (2004).

The Cold War

JOHN LAMBERTON HARPER

OXFORD
UNIVERSITY PRESS

OXFORD

UNIVERSITY PRESS

Great Clarendon Street, Oxford OX2 6DP
United Kingdom

Oxford University Press is a department of the University of Oxford.
It furthers the University's objective of excellence in research, scholarship,
and education by publishing worldwide. Oxford is a registered trade mark of
Oxford University Press in the UK and in certain other countries

© John Lamberton Harper 2011

The moral rights of the author have been asserted

First published 2011
Reprinted 2013

British Library Cataloguing in Publication Data
Data available

Library of Congress Cataloging in Publication Data
Data available

ISBN 978-0-19-923701-2

In memory of Maria

ACKNOWLEDGEMENTS

As a sophomore at Haverford College, I read works by Louis J. Halle and George F. Kennan that stirred my curiosity about the origins of the Cold War. Around the same time, John P. Spielman of Haverford and Richard A. Fletcher of the University of York taught me lessons about writing history. For their support over the years, I am also grateful to friends and colleagues (past and present) at the Johns Hopkins University School of Advanced International Studies. They include David P. Calleo, David Ellwood, Simon Serfaty, Pierre Hassner, Robert W. Tucker, and Michael Mandelbaum. A number of Bologna Center students helped me with this book: Alton Buland, Ross Campbell, Melissa Chadbourne, Mehtab Dere, Thomas Field, Anthony Mansell, Donatello Osti, Campbell Palfrey, Matthew Tidwell, Abby Wakefield, Ian Warthin, and Joanne Yao. Barbara Wiza, the faculty secretary, and Gail Martin, Ludovica Barozzi, and John Williams of the Bologna Center Library were efficient and quick to lend a hand. Finally, I am grateful to Christopher Wheeler of Oxford University Press, who suggested the project to me, Matthew Cotton of OUP, who was unfailingly helpful along the way, and Emma Barber and Veronica Ions who assisted in the final stages of the book.

CONTENTS

LIST OF MAPS AND ILLUSTRATIONS

Maps

Illustrations

ABBREVIATIONS

ABM	anti-ballistic missile
ARVN	Army of the Republic of Vietnam
CCP	Chinese Communist Party
CDE	Conference on Disarmament in Europe
CDU	Christlich Demokratische Union: Christian Democratic Union (West Germany)
CFE	Conventional Forces in Europe
CFM	Conference of Foreign Ministers
CIA	Central Intelligence Agency (USA)
CMEA	Council for Mutual Economic Assistance (Soviet bloc)
CPD	Committee on the Present Danger (USA)
CPSU	Communist Party of the Soviet Union
CSCE	Conference on Security and Cooperation in Europe
CWIHP	Cold War International History Project
DPRK	Democratic People's Republic of Korea (North Korea)
DRV	Democratic Republic of Vietnam (North Vietnam)
ECA	Economic Cooperation Administration (Marshall Plan)
EDC	European Defense Community
EE	Division of Eastern European Affairs (U.S. State Department)
EEC	European Economic Community

ERP	European Recovery Program
FLN	Front de Libération Nationale (Algerian National Liberation Front)
FNLA	Frente Nacional de Libertação de Angola: National Front for the Liberation of Angola
FRG	Federal Republic of Germany (West Germany)
FRUS	*Foreign Relations of the United States*
GDR	German Democratic Republic (East Germany)
GRU	Glavnoye Razvedyvat´noye Upravleniye: Soviet military intelligence
ICBM	intercontinental ballistic missile
INF	intermediate-range nuclear forces
IRBM	intermediate-range ballistic missile
JCS	Joint Chiefs of Staff (USA)
KGB	Komitet gosudarstvennoy bezopasnosti: Committee for State Security (USSR)
KKE	Kommounistikó Kómma Elládas: Greek Communist Party
KPD	Kommunistische Partei Deutschlands: [East] German Communist Party
MAAG	Military Assistance and Advisory Group (USA in South Vietnam)
MAD	mutual assured destruction
MBFR	Mutual Balanced Force Reduction talks
MFN	Most Favored Nation
MIRV	multiple independently targetable re-entry vehicle
MIT	Massachusetts Institute of Technology
MO	Mezhdunarodnyi otdel: International Department of the CPSU Central Committee (USSR)
MPLA	Movimento Popular de Libertação de Angola: Popular Movement for the Liberation of Angola

MRBM	medium-range ballistic missile
NATO	North Atlantic Treaty Organization
NEP	New Economic Policy (USSR)
NKVD	Narodnyy komissariat vnutrennikh del': People's Commissariat for Internal Affairs (secret police, USSR)
NLF	National Liberation Front (South Vietnam)
NSC	National Security Council (USA)
OPC	Office of Policy Coordination (USA)
OPEC	Organization of Petroleum Exporting Countries
PCF	Parti Communiste Français: French Communist Party
PCI	Partito Comunista Italiano: Italian Communist Party
PDPA	People's Democratic Party of Afghanistan (Afghan Communist Party)
PKI	Partai Komunis Indonesia: Indonesian Communist Party
PLA	People's Liberation Army (China)
PPS	Policy Planning Staff (U.S. State Department)
PRC	People's Republic of China
PSB	Psychological Strategy Board (USA)
PSIUP	Partito Socialista Italiano di Unità Proletaria: Italian Socialist Party
PZPR	Polska Zjednoczona Partia Robotnicza: Polish United Workers Party
ROC	Republic of China
ROK	Republic of Korea (South Korea)
RSA	Republic of South Africa
RSVN	Strategic Rocket Forces (USSR)
RVN	Republic of Vietnam (South Vietnam)
SAC	Strategic Air Command (USA)
SALT	Strategic Arms Limitation Talks
SDI	Strategic Defense Initiative

SED	Sozialistische Einheitspartei Deutschlands: Socialist Unity Party of [East] Germany
SPD	Sozialdemokratische Partei Deutschlands: [West] German Social Democratic Party
START	Strategic Arms Reduction Talks
SWAPO	South West Africa People's Organization
UN	United Nations
UNITA	União Nacional para a Independência Total de Angola: National Union for the Total Liberation of Angola
USSR	Union of Soviet Socialist Republics
VRYaN	Vnezapnoe raketno-yardenoe napadenie: Surprise Nuclear Missile Attack (Soviet intelligence operation)

INTRODUCTION

What was the Cold War? In what sense was it a war? Does the adjective "cold" accurately describe international relations from the close of World War II until the Soviet empire's collapse? After all, if for Europe, the scene of centuries of carnage, 1945–89 was a kind of "long peace," millions died in wars and insurgencies in Africa, the Middle East, and Asia.[1] Why did the conflict begin? Why did it vary in intensity and focus but still continue? Why did it end? These are the basic questions this book will address.

In simplest terms, the Cold War was a contest for supremacy between the United States, which saw itself as the leader of a "Free World" of capitalist and liberal democracies (even though many who aligned themselves with Washington were far from democratic) and the Union of Soviet Socialist Republics (USSR), claiming to lead a Communist or socialist camp (even though some of its followers fitted that description in name only).[2] It was a struggle for physical control of places considered vital to both, above all, Germany, the Middle East and its approaches, and Northeast and Southeast Asia. Simultaneously, it was a contest to prove the superiority of contending political and economic systems in generating power and well-being, and as "models of development" for the post-colonial and non-aligned nations. The two sides were divided not only by irreconcilable security requirements, but by conflicting ideologies. Like the split in Christianity at the time of the Reformation, the ideological rift could be seen as a clash between branches of the same broad European civilization. But in the Cold War, each side advanced a *secular* religion purporting to provide the path to material progress. Each

1

claimed universal validity for its outlook and believed its system would prevail.[3]

A protracted struggle to the death between ideologically opposed coalitions was nothing new under the sun. A fine early account saw the Cold War as the latest episode in a never-ending drama whose players had included Athens and Sparta, Napoleonic France and its enemies, as well as Nazi Germany and the Grand Alliance of 1941–45.[4] But a *cold* war was a historical novelty. The main contenders did not come to blows on the battlefield, preferring to engage each other through proxies, via their intelligence services, using economic and psychological warfare, and in the arena of world public opinion. This is because the post-1945 struggle took place in a novel context. Raymond Aron captured it when he spoke of "paix impossible, guerre improbable." Peace was impossible because of the seemingly irreconcilable world-views and interests of the "super-powers" and their respective followers. But all-out war was improbable because of the technological reality unforgettably displayed at Hiroshima and Nagasaki in August 1945.[5]

For all its trenchancy, Aron's description ignored an essential psychological fact: leaders and ordinary people *feared* that war involving nuclear weapons might well happen and consequently *hoped* some kind of settlement or modus vivendi was not beyond the wit of statesmen. The story of the Cold War is the story of a contest for supremacy by means other than general war, but also of attempts to define minimum common interests and reach agreements that would prevent a catastrophic end to the world.

In addition to nuclear weapons, there are at least three other basic factors that set the Cold War's parameters and influenced its direction. The first was the new and ambiguous position of the protagonists of earlier struggles for mastery. Defeated, occupied, and disgraced, Germany, Italy, and Japan became prizes in the great-power contest. France and Britain, although on the winning side in 1945, and not lacking military power, found themselves dependent on the United States and with their empires undermined. But the older powers were not passive bystanders. They were determined to retain (in the cases of Germany, Italy, and Japan, to regain) their freedom of action and restore themselves economically. Their indispensability as allies gave them leverage in dealing with the Americans. By the same token, the Soviet Union's allies and clients attempted (with varying degrees of success) to act independently. In relations with its "satellites," Moscow was continuously reacting to events.

The second factor is the emergence of the newly independent states of Asia and Africa. The anti-colonial "revolt against the West" had begun early in the twentieth century,[6] but received decisive impetus from World War II. Proclaiming, *believing*, themselves true anti-imperialists and champions of progress, the United States and the USSR embarked on a frenetic and costly competition to replace European influence and gain strategic and economic advantage in the "*tiers monde*" or "third world."[7] Asia, Africa, and Latin America became proving grounds for the notion, indispensable to the prestige and self-esteem of each superpower, that "the bandwagon of international politics" was under its control.[8]

A final, closely related, factor is the rise, if not of a third superpower, of a third geopolitical and ideological pole: the People's Republic of China (PRC). After a century of internal decay and penetration by European and Japanese imperialism, China recovered its unity under the Communists and sought an international role commensurate with its size and history. Chinese assertiveness not only conditioned U.S. policy but at times aggravated the U.S.–Soviet confrontation. The Soviet involvement in Latin America, Africa, and Asia that produced clashes with the United States was connected to the competition, beginning in the late 1950s, for the mantle of Communist leadership between Moscow and Beijing.

The Cold War world, in short, was not really "bipolar," a term suggesting a globe neatly divided between a pair of adversaries. Contemporaries saw, as Aron wrote in 1956, that the "unity of the planet [was] manifestly tending to disintegrate." New "centers of force," outside the boundaries of the U.S. and Soviet blocs were "due to rise."[9] Actors other than the United States and the USSR were active from the beginning, sometimes managing to convert vulnerability into strength. The Cold War world appeared to contemporaries as something other than tidy, stable, and frozen. On the contrary, it seemed to be constantly changing and prone to war.

"Bipolarity" is also misleading insofar as it suggests that the United States and the Soviet Union possessed *equal* power. The Cold War playing field was never a level one, nor seen to be by the big powers. In November 1944, shortly after the U.S. presidential elections, British Prime Minister Winston Churchill wrote to President Franklin D. Roosevelt reminding him that at the end of the fighting:

> You will have the greatest navy in the world. You will have, I hope, the greatest air force. You will have the greatest trade. You have all the gold. But these things do not oppress my mind with fear because I am sure the American people under your reclaimed leadership will not give themselves over to vainglorious ambitions, and that justice and fair play will be the lights that guide them.[10]

If anything, Churchill understated the disparity. The war had cost Britain 25 percent of its national wealth and left it deeply in debt to its sterling bloc allies and the United States. It had laid waste to the western regions of the USSR and cost the lives of some 25 million Soviet soldiers and civilians.[11] The U.S. economy, meanwhile, had scaled new technological heights and dramatically raised its output. If Churchill had been writing Roosevelt nine months later, moreover, he could have added: "You alone have the atomic bomb."

Reading between the lines, and in light of recent tensions over how to deal with Moscow, Britain's bloody suppression of a Communist uprising in Athens, and post-war economic arrangements, it is clear that Churchill was anything but sure the Americans would use their power wisely. There is no analogous message from Joseph Stalin because he was not in the habit of pointing out his country's inferiority by every measure of power except ground forces. (And, awesome as it was, the Red Army could not be kept on a war footing indefinitely in view of post-war reconstruction needs.) But Stalin was as aware as Churchill of the gap between America and the rest, and even more worried about its implications. As Nikita Khrushchev recalled, victory did not stop Stalin "from trembling inside."[12] Stalin's fear, in effect, of the *lack* of bipolarity, and assumption that the capitalists would add Germany and Japan to their power-base, was an important factor, although not the only one, conditioning his behavior after 1945.

Paradoxically, what worried Moscow—the basic, enduring fact of U.S. superiority—rarely reassured Washington. As the war ended, U.S.

leaders wondered whether America's power could be translated into effective policies. How could the United States maintain its preponderance and rebuild the world if the public demanded (as it had after 1918) a quick withdrawal from Europe and return to "normalcy," namely, demobilization of the armed forces and a drastic reduction in federal taxes and spending? How would Germany and Japan be stabilized and prevented from reverting to extremism? How would the West deal with the Soviet army in the middle of Europe and strong Communist parties in France and Italy? It could be argued that the Russians were better placed to consolidate control over the enormous war-making potential of Europe in 1945 than the Nazis had been at the height of their success in 1940–2. Despite, or partly because of, their huge power, the Americans were afflicted during the Cold War by the sensation that they were acting from a position of declining strength.

If the Cold War's setting was not bipolar, and the United States and the USSR never had equal power, this does not mean they were not the key players. On the contrary, the U.S.–Soviet ideological and geopolitical competition lay at the heart of the conflict and perpetuated it over time. What kind of countries were they? What historical baggage did they carry when their armies met at the Elbe River in Germany in April 1945? Were they bound to clash once their common enemies had been defeated? Or were there other possibilities? Some of these questions will be addressed in the early chapters of the book.

*   *   *

A word is necessary on the author's focus and method. Writing a compact book on a large subject requires what may seem an arbitrary and rather brutal selectivity. The Cold War was waged simultaneously at several levels, but the reader will not find a detailed treatment here of the important cultural, economic, and espionage theaters of the conflict. This is pre-eminently a political and diplomatic history. It focuses on what decision-makers in the major countries thought and did.

As for method, the outcome of the Cold War may have discredited Marxism, but not one of Karl Marx's basic insights. "Men," the German philosopher wrote, "make history, but they do not make it just as they please; they do not make it under circumstances chosen by themselves, but under circumstances directly encountered, given and transmitted from the past."[13] One must keep both parts of that statement in mind to explain a set of events as complex as the Cold War. The first part—"men make history"—points to human will and agency, the capacity to decide and act. History is composed of a tangled skein of decisions, some far more consequential than others. Isaiah Berlin stretches Marx's argument, but not excessively: "at crucial moments, at turning points, when factors appear more or less equally balanced, chance, individuals and their decisions . . . can determine the course of history."[14]

The story recounted here bears this out. The Cold War contained moments when individual decisions made the difference between life and death on an enormous scale. Berlin's fellow philosopher of history R. G. Collingwood argued that, "All history is the history of thought."[15] He reminds us that an essential part of the historian's task is to re-enact what people thought and consequently did at crucial moments, and to try to recapture their motives. When the evidence is imperfect and/or incomplete (as it frequently is), seekers of truth must rely on historical imagination, or intuition, to put themselves in their subjects' shoes, or rather in their minds.[16]

The second part of Marx's statement refers to the underlying structural elements, or "givens," that condition thought and action. Like children born in a certain family, neighborhood, and historical period, collectivities are subject to circumstances largely beyond their control. Nations, and the people who run them, operate in physical surroundings partly determined by nature and in the confines of institutional orders and political cultures "given and transmitted from the past." To a considerable degree, they are creatures of outlooks and patterns of behavior difficult (although, as the story reveals, *not impossible*) to change in the near term. The "Documentary Traces" and Chapter 1 will suggest how this applies to the main actors of the Cold War.

DOCUMENTARY TRACES

Preparing themselves for the worst

The subject of David Low's cartoon (Figure 1) published in a London newspaper, the *Star*, on October 17, 1925, is the now-forgotten "Campbell Case." In 1924 the Communist newspaper editor J. R. Campbell had published a letter urging British servicemen to turn their weapons on their class oppressors rather than the workers. Prime Minister Ramsay MacDonald's minority Labour Party government had decided to drop the prosecution of Campbell, opening it to charges from the Conservatives and Liberals that Labour was in the hands of backbench subversives. The MacDonald government lost a vote of no confidence and resigned. Shortly before the subsequent general elections, the *Daily Mail* newspaper published a letter forged by anti-Bolshevik White Russians but purporting to be from the head of the Communist International (Comintern), Grigory Zinoviev, to the British Communist Party. The message was that the rapprochement between Britain and Soviet Russia pursued by MacDonald would help in revolutionizing the British working class. The "Zinoviev letter" contributed directly to Labour's defeat on October 29, 1924. Sir William Joynson-Hicks (nicknamed "Jix"), Home Secretary in the new Conservative government, was the British analogue of U.S. Attorney General Mitchell Palmer, who had gained notoriety for his pursuit of radicals. In October 1925, at Jix's urging, Campbell and eleven other Communists were tried and convicted under the Incitement to Mutiny Act of 1797.

Low is satirizing the political use of anti-Communism. His point is that the threat was exaggerated to gain power. Indeed, at no point in the

Figure 1. "The Empire is Saved," by David Low, the *Star*, October 17, 1925.

twentieth century did domestic Communists threaten the stability of Western countries.[1] Nor did the USSR plan to launch an unprovked war on the West. But as the Labour government discovered, the "Red Menace" was no laughing matter. In post-1945 Western Europe, many dreaded a gradual Communist take-over or sudden Soviet offensive. In the United States, fear of subversion from within, Communist gains abroad, and nuclear surprise attack from the air, was a fact-of-life that politicians attempted to exploit and ignored at their peril.

On February 4, 1931, Joseph Stalin spoke to industrial managers in Moscow. After consolidating power, Stalin had launched the USSR on a brutal quick march to heavy industrialization and agricultural collectivization in pursuit of a defensive strategy known as "socialism in one country." It was now Year 4 in an ambitious Five-Year Plan. At stake in exceeding the plan's targets, Stalin said, were the Soviet Union's "obligations to the working class of the whole world." But not only:

To slacken the tempo would mean falling behind. And those who fall behind get beaten...One feature of the history of old Russia was the continual beatings she suffered because of her backwardness. She was beaten by the Mongol khans. She was beaten by the Turkish beys. She was beaten by the Swedish feudal lords. She was beaten by the Polish and Lithuanian gentry. She was beaten by British and French capitalists. She was beaten by the Japanese barons. All beat her—because of her backwardness: because of her military backwardness, cultural backwardness, political backwardness, industrial backwardness, agricultural backwardness. They beat her because it was profitable and could be done with impunity...We are 50 or 100 years behind the advanced countries. We must make good this distance in 10 years. Either we do it or they will crush us.[2]

Sound as Stalin's analysis may have been, his paranoia-driven purges in the late 1930s weakened the military, and his 1939 non-aggression pact with Hitler proved a near-fatal miscalculation. Stalin was unprepared for the German invasion and the USSR lost 6 million killed, wounded, or captured in the first six months of the war. By the same token, 1930s

Figure 2. Red Army soldiers, November 1941.

industrialization left the country strong enough to survive and counter the Nazi onslaught. In 1945 the USSR deserved the lion's share of the credit for defeating one of the greatest war machines ever seen. The Soviet Union's performance left an indelible impression. Depending on their political viewpoints, millions of Europeans either feared or hoped the Red Army would continue its advance westward. For the USSR, preventing another attack like the one on June 22, 1941, and securing the fruits of victory, became overriding imperatives. This meant holding the territories that had been "won for socialism" at enormous cost.

Handmaidens of History

In October 1913 President Woodrow Wilson addressed businessmen in Mobile, Alabama, on the subject of Latin America. The Panama Canal had recently opened and many anticipated new commercial opportunities. But Wilson's was a rather different vision:

The future...is going to be very different for this hemisphere from the past. These States lying to the south of us, which have always been our neighbors, will now be drawn closer to us by innumerable ties, and, I hope, chief of all by the tie of a common understanding of each other....It is a spiritual union which we seek...

Human rights, national integrity, and opportunity as against material interests—that, ladies and gentlemen, is the issue which we now have to face. I want to take this occasion to say that the United States will never again seek one additional foot of territory by conquest. She will devote herself to showing that she knows how to make honorable and fruitful use of the territory she has, and she must regard it as one of the duties of friendship to see that from no quarter are material interests made superior to human liberty and national opportunity. I say this, not with a single thought that anyone will gainsay it, but merely to fix in our consciousness what our real relationship with the rest of America is. It is the relationship of a family of mankind devoted to the development of true constitutional liberty....We know that this is a cause which we are making in common with our neighbors, because we have had to make it for ourselves.

For Latin America (and by implication all of what would be called the third world), the United States was guide and protector against unwanted interference along the path to "true constitutional liberty." Out of a sense of duty and interest in promoting democracy (rather than base commercial motives), the United States would *itself* interfere when necessary to safeguard the common cause. The context of the speech included the Mexican revolution. Wilson had refused to recognize the brutal Victoriano Huerta, who had taken control of Mexico City in February 1913. In the months following the speech, Wilson took steps to force Huerta to surrender power.[3]

In his final lines, Wilson hinted at both his plans for Huerta, and his basic view of history:

> We dare not turn from the principle that morality and not expediency is the thing that must guide us and that we will never condone iniquity because it is most convenient to do so. It seems to me that this is a day of infinite hope, of confidence in a future greater than the past has been, for I am fain to believe that in spite of all the things that we wish to correct the nineteenth century that now lies behind us has brought us a long stage toward the time when, slowly ascending the tedious climb that leads to the final uplands, we shall get our ultimate view of the duties of mankind. We have breasted a considerable part of that climb and shall presently, it may be in a generation or two, come out upon those great heights where there shines unobstructed the light of the justice of God.[4]

Events belied hopes for democracy's early victory, but U.S. entry into the World War allowed Wilson to proclaim his vision for all humanity.[5] Like Moses, he did not reach the final destination. But after 1945, his followers would seize the opportunity to try to complete the tedious climb.

Like Wilsonianism, Marxism–Leninism purported to explain history's dynamics, proposed a path to salvation, and promised a kind of kingdom of God on earth. In his "Letter to American Workers" (August 20, 1918), the Bolshevik leader Vladimir Lenin expressed his fundamental certainty about the future:

> We are banking on the inevitability of the world revolution, but this does not mean that we are such fools as to bank on the revolution inevitably

11

coming on a *definite* and early date. We have seen two great revolutions in our country, 1905 and 1917, and we know revolutions are not made to order, or by agreement. We know that circumstances brought *our* Russian detachment of the socialist proletariat to the fore not because of our merits, but because of the exceptional backwardness of Russia, and that *before* the world revolution breaks out a number of separate revolutions may be defeated.

In spite of this, we are firmly convinced that we are invincible, because the spirit of mankind will not be broken by the imperialist slaughter. Mankind will vanquish it. And the first country to *break* the convict chains of the imperialist war was *our* country. We sustained enormously heavy casualties in the struggle to break these chains, but we *broke* them. We are *free from* imperialist dependence, we have raised the banner of struggle for the complete overthrow of imperialism for the whole world to see.

We are now, as it were, in a besieged fortress, waiting for the other detachments of the world socialist revolution to come to our relief. These detachments *exist*, they are *more numerous* than ours, they are maturing, growing, gaining more strength the longer the brutalities of imperialism continue...Slowly but surely the workers are adopting communist, Bolshevik tactics and are marching towards the proletarian revolution, which alone is capable of saving dying culture and dying mankind. In short, we are invincible, because the world proletarian revolution is invincible.[6]

Like Wilson, Lenin died in early 1924. By then the Bolsheviks had secured their position and begun to transform the country. While the "besieged fortress" mentality remained, Lenin's successors saw the USSR as a redoubt from which to export revolution, and a beacon to the world.

Late in life, Lenin expressed qualms about Stalin's brutality. The first foreign Communist leader to question Stalin's claim to be Lenin's rightful heir and the head of international Communism was Yugoslavia's Josip Broz Tito in 1948. Stalin's eventual successor Nikita Khrushchev managed to settle the dispute with Tito but, as Low suggests, a more formidable challenger, Mao Zedong, was waiting in the wings (Figure 3).

THE MANTLE OF LENIN

Figure 3. "The mantle of Lenin," by David Low, published in the *Manchester Guardian*, April 30, 1958.

By the mid-1960s, the Cold War was a three-sided contest, with China gradually becoming a de facto ally of the United States.

The necessity to coexist

On September 11, 1945, shortly after Japan's surrender, the retiring secretary of war, Henry L. Stimson, wrote President Harry S. Truman on the most vexing issue of the moment:

> The advent of the atomic bomb has stimulated great military and probably even greater political interest throughout the civilized world.... In many quarters it has been interpreted as a substantial offset to the growth of Russian influence on the [European] continent. We can be certain that the Soviet Government has sensed this tendency and the temptation will be

strong for the Soviet political and military leaders to acquire this weapon in the shortest possible time . . . Accordingly, unless the Soviets are voluntarily invited into partnership upon a basis of cooperation and trust, we are going to maintain an Anglo-Saxon bloc over against the Soviet in the possession of this weapon. Such a condition will almost certainly stimulate feverish activity on the part of the Soviet toward the development of this bomb in what will in effect be a secret armament race of a rather desperate character . . . [I]f we fail to approach them now and merely continue to negotiate with them, having this weapon rather ostentatiously on our hip, their suspicions and their distrust of our purposes and motives will increase. It will inspire them to greater efforts in an all-out effort to solve the problem. If the solution is achieved in that spirit, it is much less likely that we will ever get the kind of covenant we may desperately need in the future. The risk is, I believe, greater than the other, inasmuch as our objective must be to get the best kind of international bargain we can— one that has some chance of being kept and saving civilization not for five or for twenty years, but forever.

The chief lesson I have learned in a long life is that the only way you can make a man trustworthy is to trust him; and the surest way to make him untrustworthy is to distrust him and show your distrust.[7]

Whether Stimson's lesson would have applied to dealings with Stalin on atomic weapons is unknown because Truman preferred to retain U.S. control rather than seriously pursue a deal.[8] But the secretary's prediction about Soviet behavior proved accurate and his advice that the USSR be treated as something other than a deadly adversary became, if anything, more valid once both sides had the bomb.

The USSR tested its own bomb in 1949, leading the United States to develop the next generation of nuclear weapons. In August 1953, Soviet premier Georgi Malenkov announced something that would not have surprised Stimson:

The trans-Atlantic enemies of peace have of late found a new solace: The United States is in possession of a still more powerful weapon than the atomic bomb and has the monopoly of the Hydrogen bomb . . . . But this is not so. The Government deems it necessary to report to the Supreme Soviet that the United States has no monopoly in the production of the hydrogen bomb either. As you see, convincing facts are shattering the wagging tongues about the weakness of the Soviet Union.

But in an arresting passage Malenkov had solace for those who thought the nuclear threat necessitated dialogue:

> We firmly believe that at the present moment there is no disputable or outstanding issue that could not be settled in a peaceful way on the basis of mutual agreement between the countries concerned. This refers also to those issues under dispute that exist between the U.S.A. and the U.S.S.R. We stood and stand for a peaceful co-existence of two systems. We consider that there is no objective grounds for a collision between the U.S.A. and the U.S.S.R. The interests of the security of both countries, as well as international security, the interests of the development of trade between the U.S.A. and the U.S.S.R. can be safeguarded on the basis of normal relations between the two countries.[9]

How U.S.–Soviet relations would have developed if Malenkov had consolidated power will never be known because he was shunted aside by more ruthless competitors. "Peaceful coexistence" remained an ambiguous policy. But Stimson's and Malenkov's words expressed a hope that remained alive even, or rather especially, in the tensest moments of the Cold War.

CHAPTER 1
RUSSIA AND THE WEST
DESTINED TO COLLIDE?

On the last page of *Democracy in America* Alexis de Tocqueville left a striking prophecy:

> There are, at the present time two great nations in the world which seem to tend towards the same end, although they started from different points: I allude to the Russians and the Americans. Both of them have grown up unnoticed . . . The American struggles against the natural obstacles which oppose him; the adversaries of the Russian are men; the former combats the wilderness and savage life; the latter, civilization with all its weapons and its arts: the conquests of the one are therefore gained by the plough-share; those of the other by the sword. The Anglo-American relies upon personal interest to accomplish his ends, and gives free scope to the unguided exertions and common-sense of the citizens; the Russian centres all the authority of society in a single arm: the principal instrument of the former is freedom; of the latter servitude. Their starting-point is different, and their courses are not the same; yet each of them seems to be marked out by the will of Heaven to sway the destinies of half the globe.[1]

The French aristocrat was a gifted but sometimes glib observer. Russia had been an organized state for a millennium. To say the Americans had renounced the sword, and ignore slavery, was to paint a distorted picture to say the least. But Russia and America *were* on their way to becoming continent-sized powers, and the conditions in which they grew had a decisive impact on their institutions and outlooks. As to whether they were destined to clash, Tocqueville was intriguingly silent. His famous coda begs a look at the characters of the two *frères-ennemis*.

Hobbesian Fatalism

Long before Thomas Hobbes, Russia's rulers had absorbed the lesson that life in the "state of nature," the unregulated world of feuding princes and marauding nomads, was "nasty, brutish, and short." Such was Stalin's view when exhorting his countrymen in 1931.[2] From one angle, Russian history was indeed a string of crushing defeats and near-escapes from disaster. The small state based in Kiev that emerged in the ninth century lacked natural borders and was hemmed-in by enemies.[3] In 1240 the Mongols overran Kiev. Around the same time Alexander Nevsky, hero of the republic of Novgorod, defeated German invaders in a legendary battle, but he and Moscow-based princes paid tribute to the Mongols until the late fifteenth century. During the dynastic crisis (the "Time of Troubles") of the early seventeenth century, Roman Catholic Poles occupied Moscow's Kremlin fortress and laid siege to the Monastery of the Holy Trinity, seat of the Eastern Orthodox Church. Napoleon captured Moscow in 1812. Britain, France, and Turkey occupied the Crimean peninsula in 1856. In 1905, Russia lost a costly war to Japan.

These setbacks were nothing compared to the catastrophes of 1917–20 and 1941–2. World War I ended the Romanov dynasty and cost Russia its possessions in Poland, Finland, and on the Baltic. A Polish army, advised by France, occupied Kiev in 1920. By the Treaty of Riga (1921) Poland kept much former Russian territory in the Ukraine. In 1941–2, German armies reached Stalingrad on the lower Volga, near the old headquarters of the Golden Horde. Life in such an environment gave rise to a kind of Hobbesian fatalism: an unshakable assumption of the worst about the outside world, and reliance on territorial expansion to keep enemies at bay. Constant vigilance and the mobilization of power, in turn, required an exacting and suffocating polity. Over time, the existence of external enemies became the rationale for an arbitrary and oppressive state.

A war psychosis in 1927 helped Stalin to consolidate absolute power. The devastating attack of June 22, 1941 marked a generation of leaders. A 1980s reformer recalled: "It was widely argued that the people would forgive the leadership anything but a repetition of the tragedy of the beginning of World War II and that this was the primary political priority. We remained under the spell of such arguments under [Yuri] Andropov and even for some time after [Mikhail] Gorbachev came to power." Indeed, throughout the 1980s, the defense ministry maintained a secret illegal biological weapons program on the grounds the Americans must be doing likewise.[4] During the Cold War, military budgets represented 15 to 20 percent of the USSR's gross domestic product. The armed forces and defense industry became, if not a great beast, a potent pressure group demanding to be fed.

From another angle, Russian history looks like the Herculean effort to break the encirclement of enemies and establish an empire from the Danube to the Pacific, the Baltic to the Black Sea, and with an eye toward the Mediterranean. The milestones include Ivan III's defiance of the Mongols in 1480, fusion with part of the Ukraine in the mid-seventeenth century, Peter the Great's conquest of the Baltic coast and construction of St Petersburg in the early eighteenth century, and Catherine the Great's seizure of the Crimea in 1783. Russian armies fought the French in Italy in 1799, watered their horses in the Place de la Concorde in 1814, and intervened to suppress an uprising in Budapest in 1848. By 1900, Russia had extended its sway to the Balkans, subdued the Caucasus, and penetrated Manchuria. In 1918–20, the Bolsheviks defeated "White" counter-revolutionary armies financed by France and Britain in a vicious civil war. In 1945 Soviet soldiers raised their blood-red flag over the ruins of the Reichstag in the center of Berlin.

Russia's historical predicament was that reality had too often confirmed its hyper-Hobbesian preconceptions. There was no disputing Stalin's 1931 statement, and enemies like Nazi Germany were unlikely to give quarter. But this outlook became a self-fulfilling prophecy. Russia lived in a neighborhood where survival meant arming to the teeth and lording it over surrounding areas. But in resorting to these tried and true methods, the Russian state tended to exhaust itself and its people, while giving its neighbors an interest in cutting it down to size. From this basic pattern—more reminiscent in the end of the labors of Sisyphus than Hercules—the Soviet Union's situation offered no clear avenue of escape.

America's historical predicament seems almost ridiculously tame by comparison. With ocean barriers, weak neighbors, and a thinly populated hinterland, its rise to continental supremacy was far less prolonged and traumatic than Russia's. It was no accident that not Hobbes, the theorist of absolute monarchy, but John Locke, the advocate of political pluralism, was associated with the American experiment in limited government and free enterprise. It seems reasonable to conclude that America's insularity, along with its experience with colonial self-government, allowed it to develop free institutions rather than be condemned to create a garrison state typical of continental Europe, and of which Russia's was the extreme case.

There is truth in this Tocquevillian version of American history, but it is a partial view. The Americans, too, acquired a kind of Hobbesian outlook. It was not inculcated with the same punishing regularity as in Russia, but it was a salient fact. American Hobbesianism arose from contact with the fickle, brutal world of nature, and with Native Americans who fought with ruthlesness and skill. A strain of visceral nationalism developed during 1775–1814, when the infant nation struggled to secure its independence and post-war territorial integrity. A revealing motto, emblazoned below the image of a coiled rattlesnake on a Revolutionary War battle flag, was "Don't tread on me."

Alexander Hamilton, the leading strategic thinker of the American founders, taught that men were "ambitious, rapacious and vindictive." "Universal monarchy" on the European continent was a threat to America as well as Britain. The United States must have professional forces, the capacity to manufacture weapons and munitions, and an executive able to wage war without outside interference. Thomas Jefferson and James Madison taught the opposite lesson: the people must be on constant guard against presidential power-grabbing. But the view that the state must cultivate the art and science of war, and that the executive must know (as Machiavelli had put it) how "to be not good" to protect the polity, was as American as the Lockean point of view.[5]

In the mid-nineteenth century, the United States provoked war with Mexico to extend the border of Texas and take California. The Civil War (1861–5) put on display the "American way of war": the exploitation of industrial might and overwhelming fire-power to annihilate the enemy.[6] In 1898, the United States fought another war of conquest, ousting Spain from Cuba and the Philippines. Once Britain had withdrawn its fleet, the Caribbean became an "American lake." The tsars and their Soviet successors had a harder time turning the Black Sea into a "Russian lake" and securing the Turkish straits, a waterway at least as vital to Russia as the Suez canal was to Britain and the Panama canal to America. Russian efforts were foiled not only by Turkey but at various times by France, Britain, Austria, Germany, and after 1945, the United States.

Around 1900, commentators turned attention to Britain's relative decline and Russia's rise. In *America's Economic Supremacy*, Brooks Adams observed that Britain's future efforts "could hardly be expected to equal those of the past, and Society must be prepared to face the loosening of the bond which from beyond the limit of human memory, has been the containing power of the world." From now on, "America must fight her own battles whether she wills or no. From the inexorable decree of destiny she cannot escape.... All signs now point to the approaching supremacy of the United States." America would have to step into Britain's shoes, or at least assist it, as the "containing power of the world."[7]

In his seminal 1904 essay "The Geographical Pivot of History," the British geographer Halford Mackinder argued that European Civilization had emerged from a struggle between Asiatic landpower and Western sea power. The base of the former was the so-called "pivot area" of Siberia and Mongolia, a kind of impregnable fortress inaccessible to the West (see Map 1). During the "Columbian Age," sea power had gained the upper hand by developing bases invulnerable to land power. Mackinder called these the "Outer Crescent": Britain, North America, South Africa, Australia, and Japan. His central message was that sea power's four hundred-year advantage was ending. With the railway, Russia could mobilize the pivot area's immense wealth. "The oversetting of the balance of power in favor of the pivot state, resulting in its expansion over the marginal lands of East Asia, would permit the use of vast continental resources for fleet building and the *empire of the world* would thus be in sight. This might happen if Germany were to ally herself with Russia" or if one were to dominate the other and combine the power of the two.[8]

In *Democratic Ideals and Reality* (1919), Mackinder renamed the pivot "Heartland" and redefined it to include areas where Western sea power

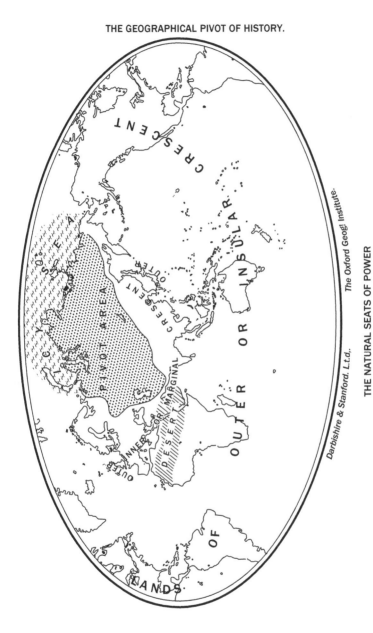

Darbishire & Stanford. L.t.d.,   The Oxford Geogl Institute.

THE NATURAL SEATS OF POWER

Pivot area—wholly continental.   Outer crescent—wholly oceanic.   Inner crescent—partly continental, partly oceanic.

Map 1. "The Geographical Pivot of History/The Natural Seats of Power," by Halford Mackinder (1904).

might "be refused access" like Eastern Europe and the Black and Baltic Seas. Indeed, he argued, Eastern Europe was now the focal point of struggle for the Heartland between the Germans and the Slavs. "Who rules Eastern Europe commands the Heartland: who rules the Heartland commands the World-Island: who rules the World-Island commands the world." Mackinder recommended creating a "middle tier" of states including Czechoslovakia, Poland, and Hungary as a "complete territorial buffer between Germany and Russia." During the Western intervention in the Russian civil war, Mackinder was British high commissioner for South Russia and pushed for an independent state there as well as in White Russia, Georgia, Armenia, and the Ukraine.[9]

Not all readers endorsed Mackinder's geographical determinism. But the Russian "bear" (an image already current) *had* moved southward and eastward, threatening (or so some believed) British interests in India, and China. Mackinder's advice to build up the natural barriers on Russia's periphery struck a responsive chord to many. According to this perspective, a successful war of containment, the Crimean War of 1854–56, had already been fought. Another application of this view was Secretary of State John Hay's Open Door Notes (1899 and 1900) declaring a U.S. interest in China's territorial integrity. The 1902 Anglo-Japanese alliance allowed Japan to attack Russia and defeat the latter's plans to dominate Manchuria. American animosity toward Russia arose not only from the clash of Far Eastern interests. Anti-Jewish pogroms in western Russia and exposure of inhuman conditions in Russia's Siberian penal colonies inflamed public opinion. An American authority on Siberia, George Kennan, saw the Russo-Japanese War as a contest between barbarism embodied by Russia and civilization represented by Japan. Kennan later became an ardent supporter of the campaign to roll back the Bolshevik regime.[10]

After World War I, the custodian of this "proto-containment" outlook, onto which was grafted a vigorous anti-Communism, was the State Department's Division of Eastern European Affairs (EE). In the late 1920s, EE acquired the talented newcomers Charles E. Bohlen, later Franklin D. Roosevelt's Russian interpreter, and U.S. ambassador to Moscow, and George F. Kennan, son of a first cousin of the Siberia expert, and the theorist of "containment" in 1946–9. In Britain, the anti-Bolshevik view was associated (in addition to Mackinder) with Lord Curzon, foreign secretary after 1918, and Winston Churchill (born 1874), war minister (1919–21) and driving force behind the Allied intervention.[11] Proto-containment had fierce critics. But from 1900 onward the view that Russia and the West were destined to collide was well-embedded in Britain and the United States.

*　　*　　*

World War I showed off America's enormous strength, even though the fighting ended before its potential had been achieved. The "American way of war" was further developed in 1941–5. World War II confirmed another feature of the American approach to security: keeping enemies at bay by extending the frontier. Around 1900, anti-imperialists had argued that occupying Hawaii and the Philippines would provoke attack and forfeit the protection of the Pacific.[12] In 1940–1, the grass-roots organization "America First" argued that entry into the European conflict would cast American power to the wind. Although an attack of the very kind predicted brought the United States into the war, few dared make such arguments after "the day of infamy," December 7, 1941. Isolationism, the vision of the United States as "Fortress America," or an outsized Switzerland, became synonymous with defeatism and naïveté. Pearl Harbor gave rise to a kind of surprise-attack syndrome analogous to the Soviets' after June 22, 1941. Followed by the use of strategic bombing and the atomic weapon, it "generated an enormous sense of vulnerability and called for defense in depth."[13] A basic lesson of the war was that the United States must deter and defeat its enemies at a distance. Plans prepared by the Joint Chiefs of Staff (JCS) for a world-wide network of air and naval bases were implemented during or soon after the war.

America's Hobbesian fatalism produced a predicament less acute but analogous to Russia's. Experience showed that enemies were not imaginary. But defensive expansion antagonized potential opponents. A Soviet official noted: "There is no corner of the world in which the USA cannot be seen. The US has air bases everywhere: in Iceland, Greece, Italy, Turkey, China, Indonesia and other places and an even greater number of air and naval bases in the Pacific Ocean ... This is evidence of a real expansionism and expresses the striving of certain American circles towards an imperialist policy."[14] Maintaining an expanded security sphere also implied, if not a garrison state, concentrating power in the executive and levels of military spending unknown in times of peace. Indeed, thanks to World War II and the Cold War the United States developed something akin to the peacetime "military-industrial complex" Hamilton had imagined. It was composed of a loose alliance of groups with an interest in rising defense budgets, and hence in the existence of outside threats. Scholars would speak of an "iron triangle" of the armed services, private defense contractors, and members of Congress eager to have money spent in their districts.[15] Less noticed by historians, but equally consequential, was a kind of "iron law" of the U.S. political system. In most presidential elections after 1945, the two-party democratic competition biased policy toward greater preparedness and/or provocative action because politicians sought to use or avoid the dread charges of "appeasement," "softness on Communism," and weakening the country. The law can be summarized: "your opponent will make you pay if you look weak."[16]

Messianic Genes

Organized societies have not engaged in war and expansion simply because they feared for their survival or coveted their neighbors' goods. At least they have not *believed* they have. They have shown extraordinary ingenuity in devising nobler reasons for self-serving behavior. A historian tellingly observes,

> We make history ourselves though we are under the inspiration of grace. The modern world, to a greater extent than we may appreciate, has been motivated by this kind of conviction, whether its form is Christian apocalypticism or "Marxist dialectic"; both set forth predictions and general guides, both call for the most strenuous efforts to destroy the opposition and to progress toward the happy time sure to come, by a path marked out in advance.[17]

The American Puritans cultivated "the sense of being a 'separated' nation which God was using to make a new beginning for mankind."[18]

24

This did not necessarily mean redeeming all humanity, but Protestant theology also encouraged the view that events were moving toward an end-state when Good would triumph and that America was the agent of this design. The idea of America as a messianic nation received new impetus from the belief that in founding a state dedicated to protecting inalienable rights, the Americans were acting for everyone: their cause was "the cause of all mankind."[19] In the 1840s the journalist John O'Sullivan spoke of "the right of our manifest destiny to overspread and to possess the whole of the continent which Providence has given us."[20] "Manifest destiny" thrived again in the 1890s. According to Senator Albert Beveridge, God had "marked the American people as His chosen nation to finally lead in the regeneration of the world."[21]

Woodrow Wilson (born 1856; president, 1913–21) deserves pride of place in the history of American messianism. In the preface to the Fourteen Points (January 8, 1918), his program for peace and a new world order, he declared that "the day of conquest and aggrandizement is gone by." America, as he later put it, "had the infinite privilege of fulfilling her destiny and saving the world."[22] Assuredly there was much in the Fourteen Points of benefit to others—autonomous development for the peoples of Austria-Hungary, an independent Poland, and a "general association of nations" to secure "mutual guarantees of political independence and territorial integrity to great and small states alike." An equally significant effect of Wilson's program would have been to reinforce U.S. supremacy. Point two, freedom of navigation, aimed to reduce Britain's sea power. Point three, removal of economic barriers, consolidated America's position as the world's leading exporter and creditor. Point five, the adjustment of colonial claims in the interests of the inhabitants and the powers concerned weakened Europe's empires and garnered influence for the United States.

Wilson also played a central role in U.S–Soviet relations. His administration was confronted with the collapse of the Tsarist regime in March 1917, and seizure of power by the Bolsheviks (the majority faction of the Russian Social Democratic Party) in November, 1917. The Bolsheviks called on the warring peoples to begin "open negotiations for peace" and condemned annexations violating self-determination.[23] When this "Decree on Peace" was ignored, they began peace talks with Germany.

Wilson announced his Fourteen Points during a breakdown in these negotiations and aimed to give Russia an alternative to a separate peace that would endanger the Western front. Point six spoke of "the evacuation of all Russian territory and such a settlement of all questions affecting Russia as will secure the best and freest cooperation of the other nations of the world in obtaining for her an unhampered and unembarrassed opportunity for the independent determination of her own political development and national policy and assure her of a sincere welcome into the society of free nations under institutions of her own choosing".[24] But the Bolsheviks spurned Wilson's offer and concluded the Treaty of Brest-Litovsk. In so doing they ceded Finland, Russian Poland, the Baltic states, and the Ukraine to the Tsar's enemies, but made good their promise of peace to the Russian people and bought time to consolidate their position. They assumed that revolutions would soon occur in Germany and elsewhere, rendering the treaty inoperable. Like Wilson, they were sure History was on their side.

According to "Marxism–Leninism," the Communist Party, vanguard of the exploited proletariat, was the agent of humanity's liberation. Some Bolsheviks, including Vladimir Lenin (born 1870), were cosmopolitans with an intimate knowledge of the West. But this imported secular religion did not put down roots in a historical vacuum. Russia was fertile terrain for numerous varieties of messianism. The philosopher Nikolai Berdiaev remarked that "Messianic consciousness [was] more characteristic of the Russians than any other people except the Jews."[25] The poet Pushkin extolled Russia's unique sacrifices on behalf of civilization in opposing the Mongols, while Gogol believed the Russians had been appointed to prepare the world for the Christian millennium. The "Pan-Slav" intellectuals called on Russia to liberate the Slavs from Austria and Turkey and unite them under Russia. Stalin would tell the Yugoslav Communists, "Give them [the Germans] twelve to fifteen years and they'll be on their feet again. And this is why the unity of the Slavs is important." Slavic solidarity under Moscow's leadership was a constant theme.[26]

A venerable notion with consequences after 1917 was that Moscow was the successor to Rome and Constantinople. According to Orthodox and secular authorities based in the Grand Duchy of Muscovy, those capitals had proved unfit to lead Christianity. Grand Duke Ivan III declared the Russian church independent of Constantinople. He married the niece of the last Byzantine emperor and took the Byzantine title of Tsar, or Caesar. Later churchmen and tsars (notably Peter the Great, who abolished the position of Moscow Patriarch) rejected the doctrine of "Moscow the Third Rome." But the idea persisted that it was not only Russia's interest but duty and destiny to liberate Constantinople. Even as they stamped out the Orthodox religion, the Communists inculcated the belief that Russia was the agent of humanity's liberation. Although they killed or deported Westernized intellectuals and professionals, they welcomed into their ranks xenophobic nationalists who viewed them as saviors of the Russian state.[27]

The Beginning of the Cold War?

In 1918 the Wilson administration and the Bolsheviks proclaimed their respective programs. Both envisioned the sweeping away of the Europe-centered state system and the end of imperialism. Wilson's millennium was based on self-determination, liberal democracy, a capitalist world economy, and collective security enshrined in the League of Nations; Lenin's, on the overthrow of democracy and capitalism and their replacement by the dictatorship of the proletariat and the international solidarity of the working masses. Each side had thrown down the gauntlet. Had the Cold War, in effect, begun?

The answer requires a look at policies as well as words. In July 1918, after pressure and cajoling from the French and British, Wilson agreed to place a small U.S. force in northern Russia. Its mission was to support efforts to renew an eastern front and guard Allied supplies supposedly at the port of Archangel.[28] The force became marginally involved in the town's defense against Reds. Somewhat more enthusiastically, Wilson approved sending a larger force to Vladivostok to secure the Trans-Siberian railroad and facilitate the evacuation of the Czechoslovak Legion, a unit composed of deserters and prisoners of war from the Austro-Hungarian army whom the Allies wished to send to the western front. Unlike some of his advisers, Wilson understood that outside intervention to try to change Russian events was foolish: it discredited local forces who accepted help and reinforced Bolshevik animosity. David Lloyd George (born 1863; prime minister, 1916–22) came to share this opinion. But Wilson did not really try to stop intervention and the Bolsheviks could be forgiven for thinking they faced a united western front.[29]

During the 1919 peace conference, Wilson and Lloyd George were prepared to deal with the Bolsheviks as the de facto government, and tried to organize talks among the Russian factions. But the French premier Georges Clemenceau opposed a conference and encouraged the White factions to stay away. The French were stung by the Bolsheviks' removal of Russia from the war and repudiation of the previous regime's debts. In April 1919 Wilson and Lloyd George authorized a mission to Moscow by the progressive journalist Lincoln Steffens and a young member of the U.S. delegation at Paris, William C. Bullitt. The Americans came back with Lenin's offer "for a cessation of hostilities between the various existing governments and factions in Russia, for a raising of the Allied blockade, for the opening up of the channels of communication, for a withdrawal of Allied troops and a termination of Allied military support for any Russian groups. Most important of all, it promised a general amnesty for those who had supported the Allies."[30]

Distracted by other issues and in poor health, Wilson declined to see Bullitt when he returned. This gave Lloyd George, under attack from the Conservative Party and *The Times* because of the "Bolshevik menace," a pretext to disavow the mission. In one authority's view, an important opportunity may have been missed.[31] This is possible, although France would almost surely have blocked a deal. Moreover, Western public opinion was agitated over the reported spread of Bolshevism "like a prairie-fire." A Communist uprising had been suppressed in Berlin in early 1919 but the situation there remained uncertain. Red regimes appeared briefly in Hungary and Bavaria. During the spring 1920 "red scare" in America, Attorney General Palmer ordered the round-up of hundreds of suspected subversives. With presidential elections in November, the Wilson administration declined to recognize the Bolshevik government on the grounds that it was "determined and bound to conspire against our institutions." The "iron law" of U.S. politics was in effect.[32]

It would be misleading to say 1919–20 events marked the beginning of the Cold War between America and Russia. Britain, center of the world's greatest empire, was still the Bolsheviks' "ultimate enemy."[33] But Wilson's ambiguous policy reinforced Bolshevik hostility. And there was no denying the impact of words as well as deeds. Each side's dramatically proclaimed messianism gave the confrontation a life or death quality. Periods of truce were possible, even necessary, but could not last indefinitely. Lenin wrote, "As long as capitalism and socialism exist, we cannot live in peace; in the end, one or the other will triumph—a funeral dirge will be sung either over the Soviet Republic or over world capitalism." Wilson's statement that "the world must be made safe for democracy" suggested that, until the entire world had become democratic, the Western system was not secure.[34]

To Live and Let Live ...

Hobbesian fatalism, the search for security through expansion, and messianism, positing a monopoly on truth and the inevitable triumph of one's way of life, explain much about Tocqueville's titans. But their behavior was also conditioned by participation in a broader international system. Usually traced to the Peace of Westphalia (1648), the system was based on respect for members' territorial integrity and the control of each over internal matters. In the seventeenth and eighteenth centuries, authorities on the "law of nations" elaborated rules governing every conceivable interaction between sovereign states.

As members of this system, Russia and the United States traded goods, negotiated treaties, and joined alliances. Peter the Great turned to Western Europe for a model of development. He made Russia a member of "the European power game," a distant precursor of what would be called a "common European home."[35] Although it resisted Peter's reforms, the Russian aristocracy came to see the West as a cultural model and preferred French to their native tongue. Russia allied with Austria and Venice against Turkey, and with Austria and France against Prussia in the Seven Years War. It played a distinguished part against Napoleonic France and was a decisive factor in its defeat. Tsars Alexander I and Nicholas I made Russia a pillar of the post-1815 European order.

In the 1890s Russia allied with France against Germany. In 1907, only three years after Mackinder's warning, Russia reached an accord with Britain settling disputes over Persia and Afghanistan and paving the way for the "Triple Entente" of 1914–17.

Despite the myth that it matured in isolation, America was also part of the broader state system. Its independence was made possible by an alliance with France, and it was a mercantile power from its youth. During a "parenthesis" after 1815, the United States, like Russia, concentrated on conquering its hinterland. With that task completed, it once again became active in world politics. Theodore Roosevelt (born 1858; president, 1901–9), seeing the importance of a Far Eastern balance of power, mediated an end to the Russo-Japanese War. In 1919–20 Republican senators opposed Wilson's League of Nations because it allegedly abridged U.S. sovereignty. But rejection of League membership did not signify withdrawal from the world.

After 1917, whether to adopt a hostile attitude toward the existing state system emerged as a long-standing Soviet dilemma. The answer became "yes and no, depending on circumstances," but more "no" than "yes." On one hand, the Bolsheviks boldly challenged the principle of noninterference:

> They challenged it by the universality of their own ideological pretensions—by the claim, that is, to an unlimited universal validity of their own ideas as to how society ought to be socially and politically organized. They challenged it by their insistence that the laws governing the operation of human society demanded the violent overthrow everywhere of governments which did not accept the ideological tenets of Russian communism, and the replacement of these governments by ones that did.[36]

In March 1919 the Bolsheviks convened the first meeting of the Third International, or Comintern, an organization of Communist parties that Moscow would use to foment revolution and undermine foreign governments as it saw fit.

But the story did not end there. In 1919 the Bolsheviks also tried to make a deal to end Western intervention and normalize relations.[37] A turning point occurred in 1921. The civil war, the Polish war, and the

Allied interventions had ended a year earlier. March 1921 witnessed the German Communists' failure to seize power through general strike. Just as the early Christians had suspended hopes for Jesus's imminent return, the Bolsheviks were forced to revise their schedule for Communism's triumph. The fledgling Soviet Union faced a devastating famine and a shattered economy. Hoping to increase production, Lenin launched the New Economic Policy (NEP), allowing individuals to sell food at a profit. March 1921 saw the conclusion of an accord with the evil empire: the Anglo-Soviet Trade Agreement. The path to full diplomatic ties was strewn with obstacles. In 1924 the "Campbell case," followed by the "Zinoviev letter," led to Labour's defeat.[38] Anglo-Soviet relations remained tense, but the two countries exchanged ambassadors in 1930, three years before the USSR and the United States.

Lenin and Stalin never ceased to demonize the big powers. States run by rival gangs of robbers competed to control the world's markets and resources. Imperialism was the highest stage of capitalism. The result was war, leading to a new pecking order and division of the spoils. Intra-capitalist war was not only inevitable, it was the "mother" (or, as one analyst puts it, "crowbar") of revolution. Such wars were to be encouraged because they would undermine the capitalists vis-à-vis their colonies, trigger revolution inside the losers, and strengthen the position of Soviet Russia.[39]

But war might *also* occur if the capitalists banded together against Russia. The most important goal of Bolshevik foreign policy was to preserve the Soviet state as the bastion of Communism by preventing such a coalition. This meant remaining at peace with some of the capitalists for extended periods. Stalin observed in 1927:

We must not forget Lenin's statement that as regards our work of construction very much depends upon whether we succeed in postponing war with the capitalist world, which is inevitable, but which can be postponed either until the moment when the proletarian revolution in Europe matures, or until the moment when the colonial revolutions have fully matured, or until the moment when the capitalists come to blows over the division of the colonies. Therefore the maintenance of peaceful relations with the capitalist countries is an obligatory task for us. Our relations with the capitalist countries are based on the assumption that the co-existence of two opposite systems is possible.[40]

For a decade after 1918, the face of Soviet diplomacy belonged to the aristocrat Georgi Chicherin. As foreign minister he was an architect of the treaty between the USSR and the German Weimar Republic made at Rapallo in 1922. The treaty was an attempt to break "capitalist encirclement" and prevent a united front including Germany against Russia.[41] But it is hard to imagine a tsarist government behaving differently at the time.

The same cannot be said of 1928–34. Capitalizing on the 1927 "war scare," Stalin eliminated his rivals, abandoned the NEP, and launched the first Five-Year Plan. Contemporaneously, he forbade the German Communist Party (KPD) to collaborate with the Social Democrats (SPD) in opposing the Nazis, and facilitated Hitler's 1933 take-over. According to one view, Stalin felt an ideological solidarity with his fellow despot and sought a long-term alliance.[42] Undoubtedly, he welcomed the prospect that Hitler would end Foreign Minister Gustav Stresemann's policy of reconciliation with France and Britain, and put the capitalists at loggerheads. And he shed few tears when Hitler destroyed the KPD.

This is partly because Stalin, although committed to world revolution, was ambivalent toward foreign Communists. Joseph Djugashvili (the nickname "Stalin" meant "man of steel"), born in Gori, Georgia, in 1878, was a cobbler's son. While an assiduous student of Marxism, his formal education had been confined to the Tbilisi Orthodox seminary. As a political renegade he had been more at home in the company of criminals than intellectuals, and distrusted the refined socialists of the West.[43] In opposition, and dependent on him, foreign Communists were useful. But Stalin did not welcome revolutions installing independent leaderships who might inspire internal opposition to his tyrannical rule in the Soviet Union. According to the Yugoslav Communist Milovan Djilas, Stalin "felt instinctively that the creation of revolutionary centers outside of Moscow could endanger its supremacy in world Communism. . . . That is why he helped revolutions only up to a certain point—up to where he could control them—but he was always ready to leave them in the lurch whenever they slipped out of his grasp."[44]

It is mistaken, in any case, to think Stalin strongly preferred Nazi Germany as an ally. Like others, he saw short-term advantages in Hitler's rise and misread the threat. When Hitler began to reveal his aims, the Soviet Union shifted course. Moscow encouraged Communist parties to form popular fronts with socialists (as in France, 1936–8). It signed alliances with France and Czechoslovakia and aided the Spanish republic after the military uprising against it in 1936. Moscow joined the League of Nations and preached "collective security" against aggression. This policy tack is associated with another polished, Western-oriented foreign minister, Maxim Litvinov.

The drawbacks of this approach were evident. Using the Franco-Russian alliance as a pretext, Hitler re-occupied the Rhineland. Paris and London stood by as Hitler carried out the *Anschluss* with Austria. The culmination of "appeasement" was the 1938 Munich agreement allowing Hitler to absorb the Sudetenland. Only after Hitler took all of Czechoslovakia in March 1939, did Britain give a guarantee to Poland. But there was reason to doubt Britain's ability and intention to stop Hitler's next move to the east.

Stalin probably saw that France and Britain were unreliable as early as 1936. If so, his choice was to fight Germany alone or make a deal postponing war. In the meantime, Stalin hoped, the capitalists would tear each other apart as in 1914–18. One reason for the "great purges" of 1936–8, the seemingly wanton bloodbath in which at least 700,000 died, was Stalin's determination to eliminate anyone who might be part of a fifth column in case of war. The purges targeted "former kulaks, active anti-Soviet elements and criminals"; "counter-revolutionary national contingents" of Poles, Germans, Latvians, Estonians, Finns, and others seen to be plotting with their countries of origin; and officers and party officials thought to be in league with foreign powers or opposition elements in the West. It may be that the purges also reflected Stalin's realization that he would have to make "cynical and shabby compromises" with Hitler, and internal enemies might use this against him.[45] Stalin's deal with Germany came in August 1939, when the Red Army was engaged against Japanese forces on the Mongolian–Manchurian border. The non-aggression pact and subsequent secret protocol defining German and Soviet spheres of influence allowed the USSR to avoid a two-front war, and to reoccupy former possessions seen as vital to its western defenses: southern Finland, eastern Poland, and the Baltic states.

Although it shocked the world, the pact did not mean Moscow assumed permanent co-operation. Nor for Stalin and his new foreign minister Viacheslav Molotov (born 1890) did it have much to do with advancing Communism. In October 1939 Churchill called Stalin's action "a riddle wrapped in a mystery inside an enigma." Perhaps, he said, there was a key: "Russian national interest."[46] He was partly right. Djilas spoke later of the Soviet leadership's "unconcealed concern primarily with the interests of their own state." This certainly applies to 1939. It is revealing that Moscow re-annexed the Baltics and Bessarabia only in mid-1940 after the shocking defeat of France. Stalin tried to appease Hitler in spring 1941 by offering to join the three-power pact of Germany–Italy–Japan because he continued to suspect a British plot to embroil him with the Germans, or a British–German alliance. It was also a desperate attempt to delay a war for which the Soviet Union was unprepared, and whose outbreak would show that Stalin had seriously miscalculated in 1939.[47]

The one sense in which Moscow preferred a deal with Germany was that Berlin had endorsed a degree of Soviet territorial revision, while London and Paris had refused. But this changed after Hitler launched his war of annihilation against the Soviet Union on June 22, 1941. Explicitly or not, Britain and the United States would eventually recognize the same territorial changes to consolidate an alliance with the USSR.

*   *   *

The notion that Russia was *not* the culprit of the century and might prove a suitable long-term ally of Britain and America did not suddenly arise as Stalin's armies battled Hitler's. Following Russia's defeat in 1905, Theodore Roosevelt had written: "I have never been able to persuade myself that Russia was going to conquer the world at any time near enough for us to be justified in considering it... In a dozen years the English, Americans and Germans, who now fear one another as rivals in the trade of the Pacific, will have each to dread the Japanese more than they do any other nation."[48] While not renouncing the alliance with Japan, Britain settled its differences with Russia in view of the rising German threat. Progressive Republican followers of Theodore Roosevelt favored U.S. entry into the war in 1914 alongside the Triple Entente, a harsh peace for Germany in 1919, and non-recognition of Japan's conquests in China in the 1930s. Franklin Roosevelt (born 1882; president 1933–45) was eager for diplomatic relations with the USSR because he hoped it would help to contain Japan. After concluding negotiations with Litvinov, Roosevelt sent William Bullitt, accompanied by 30-year-old George F. Kennan, as ambassador to Moscow in 1934.

In 1943 the influential journalist Walter Lippmann popularized an interpretation of history that turned Mackinder's on its head. "The enduring element in Russian–American relations is that in critical times each nation has always been 'for the other a potential friend in the rear of potential enemies.'"[49] During the War of Independence the Continental Congress had sought Russian help and Catherine II had practiced an armed neutrality favoring America. In 1863, during the Civil War, Washington had refused to condemn Russian suppression of a Polish uprising while St Petersburg had called the preservation of the United States an "imperative necessity" for Russia. It had dispatched warships to New York and San Francisco, the message to London and Paris being that those governments should not assist Poland or the Confederacy.

The pattern had emerged even more clearly in World Wars I and II. Lippmann summarized: "Historic experience shows, then, that Russia and the United States, placed 'on opposite sides of the globe,' have always been antagonistic in their political ideology...Yet each has always opposed the dismemberment of the other. Each has always wished the other to be strong. They have never had a collision which made them enemies. Each has regarded the other as a potential friend in the rear of its potential enemies."[50] In September 1945 Secretary of War Stimson drew on the argument when trying to persuade Truman to make a private approach to Stalin on the international control of atomic energy. Stimson referred to the Russians as "our traditional friends."[51]

The thesis of Theodore Roosevelt, Lippmann, and Stimson was geopolitical: Russia, given its location, had interests in common with the West. Not only was Mackinder mistaken, trying to contain Russia only served to confirm its fears. Liberals and left-wing supporters of the USSR took the argument several steps further. Lincoln Steffens famously remarked after visiting Soviet Russia: "I have seen the future and it works." Western Communists and fellow travellers looked to the USSR for guidance. Many non-Communists believed that the blame for Soviet hostility should be laid at the doorstep of those (Wilson, Clemenceau, Churchill) who had cold-shouldered the Bolsheviks in 1919 and intervened in the civil war.

During the 1930s some believed the two systems were growing less antagonistic if not actually converging.[52] A complementary argument was that one should do business with the Soviets. As early as February 1920, Lloyd George had told parliament: "We have failed to restore Russia to its sanity by force. I believe we can save her by trade...Trade, in my opinion, will bring an end to the ferocity, the rapine, and the crudity of Bolshevism surer than any other method."[53] If this proved an illusion in the twenties, the view persisted that the Soviet Union was a vast market for Western goods and technology. Commerce would foster friendlier relations. Constituencies would develop in the USSR economically dependent on the West.

U.S., and to a lesser extent British, policy toward Moscow in 1941–5 was based on a combination of these optimistic assumptions. The Soviet Union was a natural partner. Its animosity was partly the West's fault and could be assuaged by satisfying Moscow's security interests and treating it with the respect it craved and deserved. The Russians could be co-opted into a post-war security system. Roosevelt spoke in 1942–3 of the "Four Policemen"—the United States, USSR, Britain, and China— who would keep the peace.[54] Given their ideological preconceptions, not to mention their practical experience, Soviet leaders had reason to doubt the feasibility of co-operation. But the war years had shown there were "live and let live" tendencies in Soviet policy. Litvinov, after his replacement by Molotov, went not to Siberia but Washington as Soviet ambassador, 1941–3. Stalin himself was convinced that collaboration held considerable advantages, if satisfying Moscow's terms.

By the same token, the Western policy adopted in 1946–7 was based on the "proto-containment" view of Russia fused with an abhorrence of

Communism. Containment assumed that "What Stalin was really after was the expulsion of American influence from the Eurasian land mass generally, and its replacement by that of his own regime."[55] Containment aimed to create a defensive line using the strength of Germany, Turkey, Japan, and other peripheral nations, and backed by U.S. and British power. It also included the positive aim of organizing the West according to Wilsonian principles, and enlarging the so-called Free World until it incorporated the entire globe. The question why the Cold War began has much to do with why a Western policy resting on the optimistic assumptions was replaced by one based on a starkly different set.

CHAPTER 2
THE END OF ILLUSIONS, 1945-1946

The Cold War began in Europe, along the Middle East's "Northern tier", and in East Asia where Soviet and Western interests and ambitions collided. Gradually, each camp came to see confrontation as unavoidable, and naturally blamed the other. But no one desired or deliberately started it, and on both sides rising tensions produced not only anger but surprise and disappointment. Was the Cold War inevitable? Given the natures of the Soviet Union, the United States, and Britain, and of the situation facing them, it is hard to argue otherwise. But this does not mean that the conflict was destined to develop as it did. Avoidable errors and miscalculations marked its beginnings as well as its later vicissitudes. Who was responsible for the coming of the Cold War? The answer is all sides.

Roosevelt and Stalin: Post-war Plans Compared

Franklin D. Roosevelt was an inspiring but elusive leader, a self-described "juggler" whose right hand, he admitted, sometimes did not know what the left was doing. Contemporaries were puzzled about his post-war intentions; historians have debated them ever since. In fact, his vision was simple and rather brutal in its implications. FDR admired Jefferson, the denouncer of Old World power politics. Roosevelt's notion of the post-war world resembled a Palladian temple, Jefferson's favorite architectural form. At the "ground level," the main culprits would be disarmed, denuded of their empires, and in Germany's case dismembered and partially de-industrialized. Under State and War

Department pressure, Roosevelt distanced himself from Treasury Secretary Henry Morgenthau's radical "Morgenthau Plan," a summary version of which he had endorsed. (The September 1944 plan called for the wholesale destruction of German mines and factories.) But he wanted a harsh peace. This time the Germans would know they had lost the war and be unable to start another. France, too (although nominally a winner), was an irresponsible troublemaker in light of its egoistic behavior after 1918 and ignominious wartime performance. It would lose its overseas bases and colonies and, like Italy, be reduced to third-rate status. Continental Europe, in sum, would be retired from its checkered international career, no longer able to wreak havoc on itself and the world.[1]

Towering over the continent would be two regional pillars, Britain and the Soviet Union. Roosevelt did not foresee a long-term European role for America. Its attention would be devoted to the Western Hemisphere, and to replacing the influence of Japan and the declining European powers in the Far East and Middle East. As the over-arching structure of world politics, FDR foresaw the Four Policemen—the United States, Britain, the USSR, and China (in whom FDR put stock as the rightful leader of Asia). They would monopolize military power, consult on vital matters, and punish transgressors. Under pressure from Wilsonian opinion, FDR retreated from this hierarchical scheme and accepted a United Nations based on the sovereign equality of nations. But he never abandoned the notion that peace depended on the co-operation of the strong.

Roosevelt's central premise, in effect, was the Grand Alliance's continuation. For this many considered him foolish. FDR's enemies were particularly scathing about his alleged sell-out of Eastern Europe. But such criticisms missed the considerations underlying his cultivation of Stalin and failed to offer a realistic alternative. Roosevelt and his top military adviser, General George C. Marshall (born 1880), recognized that between Hitler's invasion of the USSR in June 1941 and the Anglo-American invasion of France in June 1944, the Russians bore the brunt of the war. It was mere prudence to assume that unless they were given U.S. "lend-lease" aid and rewarded for their sacrifices, they might be defeated or seek a separate peace. U.S. military experts also assumed that Soviet help would later be useful, if not indispensable, to defeat Japan.[2]

Roosevelt realized that the Russians would occupy Eastern Europe in the course of beating Germany, just as the Americans and British had occupied Italy, excluding Moscow from a role there, in 1943. This could not have been prevented unless the United States and Britain had been prepared to assume a far greater burden of the fighting and/or to confront the Russians militarily. Roosevelt was both practical and resigned. In September 1943 he told Archbishop Spellman of New York that he expected Soviet control of much of Europe. He hoped the Russians would observe democratic forms, but he expected their domination to be harsh. The U.S. Ambassador to Moscow Averell Harriman remarked in late 1944, "The President consistently shows very little interest in Eastern European matters except as they affect sentiment in America." FDR had no sympathy for Hitler's allies, Romania, Hungary, and Bulgaria, and little for the Poles, who, he thought, had behaved badly before the war.[3]

But Roosevelt's endorsement of a Soviet sphere did not arise simply from military necessity and personal indifference. Recognizing the gains to which Russia's efforts entitled it was the only way to forge an understanding that would bring wartime and post-war dividends. Indeed, the ultimate in cynical and probably self-defeating Realpolitik would have been, having benefited from the staggering Soviet expenditure of lives necessary to break the back of the Third Reich, to try to prevent the Russians from occupying Eastern Europe and Berlin. FDR believed inviting the USSR to sit at the "high table" as a permanent UN Security Council member was more likely to moderate its behavior than was treating it as a pariah state.

At the Tehran (November 28–December 1, 1943) and Yalta (February 4–February 11, 1945) conferences, Roosevelt basically accepted Stalin's demands for new Polish borders (giving the USSR eastern Poland and compensating Poland at Germany's expense), and a Polish cabinet broadened to include non-Communists but in which the Communists would predominate. Roosevelt gave way on Poland, an issue affecting Soviet but not vital U.S. interests and where Western influence was limited. In return, Stalin renewed his pledge to enter the Pacific war and endorsed the details of the UN project, issues of far greater importance to FDR. The UN would be the means for keeping the peace and a vehicle for sustaining the American people's support of an active U.S. role. Roosevelt's assumptions were open to question, but the United States did not lack leverage in dealing with Moscow. The Russians needed post-war reconstruction assistance. As they licked their wounds from the titanic struggle with Germany, they would prefer America's friendship to its wrath.

What relation did Roosevelt's plans bear to Stalin's? After Tehran, Roosevelt's interpreter Bohlen observed:

Germany is to be broken up and kept broken up. The states of eastern, southeastern and central Europe will not be permitted to group them-selves into any federations or associations. France is to be stripped of her colonies and strategic bases beyond her borders and will not be permitted to maintain any appreciable military establishment. Poland and Italy will remain approximately their present territorial size, but it is doubtful if either will be permitted to maintain any appreciable armed force. The result will be that the Soviet Union will be the only important political and military force on the continent of Europe. The rest of Europe will be reduced to political and military impotence.[4]

With the benefit of hindsight, we can see that this was a perceptive view, although needing corrections and additions. Moscow, as Stalin told Foreign Secretary Anthony Eden in December 1941, foresaw British bases in northwest Europe and in the Mediterranean. Like Washington and London, it favored Germany's break-up as late as Yalta, but when the Western allies shifted their position in spring 1945, the Russians followed suit. They did not want to be seen to favor dismemberment if the others did not, and imagined the possibility of a united Germany (minus cessions to Poland, Czechoslovakia, and themselves) under Communist influence. In several respects, Bohlen's assessment was incomplete or premature. It did not mention Stalin's intention to keep the territories obtained through the 1939 pact with Hitler, to create a sphere based on Slav unity, and to obtain massive German reparations. It left out Moscow's Far East objectives: acquisition of the Kurile Islands, and return of the southern half of Sakhalin Island and the Manchurian ports and rail lines lost to Japan in 1905. Nor did it include demands Moscow would make for a UN trusteeship over one or more of Italy's former colonies, revision of the 1936 Montreux Convention to give it, as well as Ankara, control of the Turkish Straits (including a Soviet base on the Mediterranean), and a role in the occupation of Japan.

Thus amended, the Soviet program suggests Molotov was too modest when he said his job had been "to expand the borders of the fatherland." Stalin considered it essential to take advantage of the unique opportunity presented by the defeat of Germany and Japan to strengthen his country on a permanent basis. The Russian state's Hobbesian fatalism was alive and well. On another occasion Molotov recalled: "Stalin often said that Russia wins wars but doesn't know how to avail itself of the fruits of victory . . . It was my main task as minister of foreign affairs to see that we would not be cheated." Added to security considerations were a sense of entitlement and determination to have what Moscow considered its "just rewards"—its fair share of the spoils.[5]

Equally striking is that Stalin's program was basically compatible with Roosevelt's. At Yalta FDR consented tacitly to the Eastern European sphere and explicitly to Moscow's Far Eastern agenda.[6] It is not clear what position Roosevelt would have taken on the Mediterranean questions, but in June 1945 Secretary of State Edward Stettinius wrote Soviet ambassador to the United Nations Andrei Gromyko supporting in principle a Soviet trusteeship over a former Italian colony.[7] Even Churchill, who generally took a harder line than FDR, favored revising the Montreux Convention. FDR would presumably have resisted demands concerning Japan, but an occupation zone there was probably not at the top of Stalin's priorities. But here another question arises: with booty in hand would Stalin want to continue cordial relations? Did the "live and let live" element of Russian foreign policy figure in his approach?

On the one hand, this seems inherently implausible. Stalin's Marxist–Leninist world-view and habit of deducing the future from the past told him World War III would surely follow World War II. According to Molotov, Stalin believed World War I had "wrested one country from capitalist slavery; World War II [had] created a socialist system; and the third [would] finish off imperialism forever."[8] The Allies' behavior, including their procrastination in invading France, had done little to inspire confidence. Even Litvinov, well-disposed toward the West, believed it "beyond doubt that the military calculations of both powers [the United States and Britain] are based on the striving for the maximum exhaustion and wearing down of the forces of the Soviet Union in order to diminish its role in deciding postwar problems." After telling Molotov in May 1942 that he hoped for and expected a second front in Europe that year, FDR supported "Operation Torch," the landings in Morocco and Algeria. At Casablanca in January 1943, the Allies decided to invade Sicily, delaying the invasion of France once again. According to Stalin, "Churchill is the kind who, if you don't watch him, will slip a kopek out of your pocket... Roosevelt is not like that. He dips in his hand only for bigger coins." He made this remark on June 5, 1944, waiting skeptically for news of the second front.[9]

Yet the evidence confirms that Stalin *did* want and expect post-war co-operation.[10] Concern about the Soviet military situation ran deep and anti-Allied resentment left its mark. But one should not exaggerate the impact of the second front controversy. Molotov departed Washington in 1942 realizing that shipping shortages and a negative British attitude would probably make a cross-Channel operation impossible that year. The Russians grasped that the front's delay, and the impression it created of unequal sacrifice, gained them political capital in the West. When "D-Day" finally arrived, Stalin was grateful, and impressed by its massive scale.[11]

In fact, Stalin wanted to continue the alliance for some of the reasons Roosevelt believed and hoped he would. The Soviet Union needed help and made a loan request to Washington at the end of the war. While many Soviet demands (control of the Baltics, for example) would be satisfied by force, others (German reparations from current production; revision of Montreux) depended on Allied approval.[12] In a speech on November 6, 1944, Stalin said that the wartime alliance was based not on "accidental or transitory motives, but vitally important and long-lasting interests," especially "preventing new aggression or a new war, if not forever, then at least for an extended period of time." After hearing of FDR's Four Policemen idea, Stalin wired Molotov, "Roosevelt's considerations about peace protection after the war are absolutely sound."[13] Not only was a big-power concert necessary, it was gratifying. The "just rewards" Stalin desired included respect and recognition for the Soviet Union and himself personally. FDR's scheme provided both.

Stalin's hopes for a period of good relations rested on his own remarkably optimistic assumptions: Washington would adopt a relatively detached attitude toward Europe, and the United States and Britain would compete with each other rather than combine against the USSR. The Roosevelt administration did much to encourage these assumptions. At Yalta, as the British and Russians argued over Poland, FDR remarked that the United States viewed the question as the inhabitant "of another hemisphere."[14] He reminded Stalin and Churchill that U.S. troops would have to leave Europe within two years of the end of the war. American public hostility toward the British Empire was well known. Washington attempted to tie lend-lease and post-war aid to Britain to the dismantling of the "imperial preference system." Roosevelt went out of his way on occasion to distance himself from Churchill and avoid the impression of Anglo-American collusion. FDR's attitude toward Britain dovetailed with Marxist–Leninist premises, and appears to have had its effect.[15]

A final question glossed over in Bohlen's assessment was the weight of Communist messianism in Soviet policy. Did the abolition of the Comintern in 1943 and exaltation of Russian nationalism during the "Great Patriotic War" mean Stalin had postponed or abandoned the goal of spreading Communism and, in effect, adopted the foreign policy of the monarchy?[16] Stalin admired Ivan the Terrible and Peter the Great as centralizers and modernizers. He identified with Alexander I, who had pushed Russian power to the west.[17] But he did not see himself as simply the latest tsar. The evidence indicates he *did* wish to spread Communism and foresaw its ultimate triumph. But to respect local sensibilities and avoid an early break with the Allies, his chosen vehicle in Eastern Europe was the "national front." Communist parties would ally themselves with other progressive groups and work gradually within parliamentary institutions to transform society. Stalin insisted to Eastern European Communists that there were national paths differing from the creation of soviets and the dictatorship of the proletariat. The Bolshevik model need not apply.[18]

This was even truer for Western Europe. Stalin's first priority was to build democratic, anti-fascist systems, and he knew the United States and/or Britain were in a position to intervene. This was obvious after the

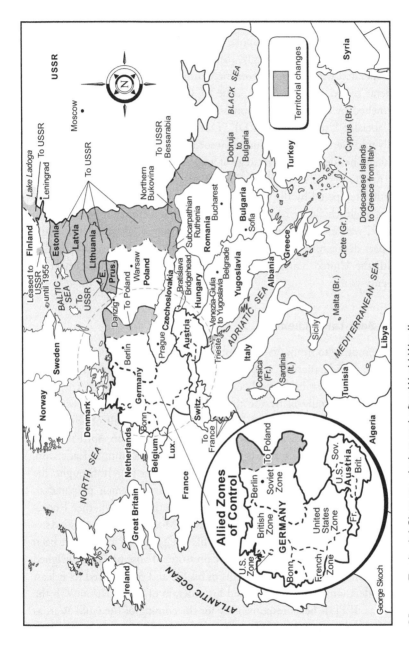

Map 2. Territorial Changes during and after World War II.

British suppressed a Communist uprising in Athens in December 1944. (The Italian Communists spoke thereafter of *la prospettiva greca*, the "Greek lesson.") Accordingly, the French and Italian Communists co-operated with social democratic, Christian democratic, and classical liberal parties. In the Soviet zone of Germany a national front was launched by fusing the Communist and social democratic parties into a "Socialist Unity Party" (SED). "During 1945 and 1946, Stalin repeatedly told German Communists that socialism was not on the agenda." In general, he "demanded a strategy of long-term gradual build-up of power in the bourgeois states."[19] Stalin's Western European ambitions were further tempered by the possibility that independent-minded Communists might challenge Moscow. In any case, the national or popular front model was another source of optimism. Europe's leftward shift would respect democratic forms and be gradual enough to allow co-operation with the United States and Britain to continue for perhaps fifteen to twenty years.

The Best-Laid Schemes...

It is tempting to think that if Roosevelt had remained in good health and able to decide matters with Stalin, the Cold War might have been delayed, and less intense when it began. This may well be true. But FDR was mortally ill by the time of Yalta. Harry Hopkins, who was there, doubted the president "had heard more than half of what went on."[20] He died from a massive cerebral hemorrhage on April 12, 1945. Roosevelt's death mattered. It led to a temporary vacuum of leadership, an internal debate, and a new pattern of behavior. It brought the retirement of Hopkins, Morgenthau, and Stimson, men prepared to conciliate the Russians. It raised Soviet concerns as to whether Roosevelt's policies would continue and inclined Moscow to hedge its bets.

But even if Roosevelt had survived, his foreign policy would have been increasingly constrained by domestic pressures. Those pressures weighed heavily in the last eighteen months of his life and contributed to at least three decisions that compromised his program of co-operation with the Soviets. If FDR bears responsibility for the coming of the Cold War, as he surely does, it is mainly here that it lies.

The first was to insist to Churchill and Stalin that U.S. troops must depart Europe quickly. The American people would demand it, and Roosevelt assumed that doing otherwise might produce a backlash that would undermine an internationalist foreign policy. But the effects of bowing to this political "fact of life" were pernicious and counter-productive. Although there is little direct evidence, Stalin's reaction was probably ambivalent. U.S. withdrawal would mean a Europe more open to Soviet influence, but also a more hostile, defensive Britain, and less outside help in dealing with the Germans. The prospect of U.S. departure meant that Moscow could—and must—act more boldly and unilaterally to secure its ends.

The message to Britain was a stark one. With German power gone and France a shadow of its former self, Churchill asked: "What will be left between the white snows of Russia and the White Cliffs of Dover?"[21] A feeling of growing vulnerability prompted him to try to reach a bilateral deal with Stalin to limit Soviet expansion in Eastern Europe, the Balkans, and the Mediterranean.[22] But the thrust of his policy was to provoke a showdown. When Moscow dragged its feet after Yalta over the inclusion of non-Communists in the Polish cabinet, Churchill publicly denounced it. As resistance in western Germany faded, he urged the Americans to drive for Berlin and hold territory assigned by prior agreement for occupation by the Russians, pending Soviet good behavior. The Allies should "march as far east into Germany as possible" and "if open to us" into Poland. Roosevelt and the Supreme Allied Commander, General Dwight D. Eisenhower, rejected this advice, but Britain's cards were on the table. On June 4, 1945, Churchill informed Roosevelt's successor of his "profound misgivings [at] the retreat of the American army to our line of occupation in the central sector, thus bringing Soviet power into the heart of Western Europe and the descent of an iron curtain between us and everything to the Eastward."[23]

A second important decision (or set of decisions) was to veil Washington's understandings with Moscow. In his private dealings with Stalin, FDR showed "his temperamental inclination to settle things with fellow princes around a conference table."[24] As one prince to another, he considered Eastern Europe's "loss" a price worth paying for Soviet co-operation and evinced little regard for the area's alleged strategic value. In his public presentation, and that of his "Yalta sales-man," the Democratic Party notable James Byrnes, however, the February 1945 agreements spelled "the end of the system of unilateral action and exclusive alliances and spheres of influence and balances of power and all the other expedients which have been tried for centuries—and have failed."[25]

Roosevelt's views were closer to Theodore Roosevelt's (especially the notion of great-power co-operation) than to Wilson's, but he had wrapped himself in a Wilsonian mantle. Never did this seem more necessary than in 1944-5. FDR and his advisers feared a reaction led by Republicans like Senator Arthur H. Vandenberg, who announced that his support of the UN would be conditional on its capacity "to review protested injustices" to Eastern Europe.[26] Everyone remembered the Senate's rejection of the League in 1919-20. FDR's prized project depended on the backing of Wilsonian liberals. For their consumption, he sugar-coated his agreements with Stalin. When the Soviets did not act like Wilsonians, there was dismay and disillusion. Roosevelt's approach struck many not as cold-blooded and realistic but craven and naïve.

A third decision, also dictated by domestic considerations, was Roosevelt's handling of his own succession. As running mate in 1944, Roosevelt chose the Missouri senator Harry S. Truman, dropping vice president Henry A. Wallace. FDR sensed the country was moving rightward. Wallace, a spokesman for the Democratic Party left, had become a divisive figure. The other obvious choice, Byrnes of South Carolina, nicknamed the "assistant president," and overseeing domestic mobilization, appealed mainly in the southern states. FDR and Democratic insiders believed Truman, a plain-spoken mid-westerner, would unite the party and prove valuable in gaining Senate passage of the United Nations. But in the likely event Truman became president, the problems were obvious. Truman had no foreign policy experience. He was a loyal but literal-minded believer in the UN and had never sub-scribed to the view that Soviet Russia and America were natural partners. He lacked the flexibility, self-confidence, and guile FDR had relied on to square circles at home and abroad. According to one historian, "he judged men by their reliability in keeping agreements, and it was the standard by which he, in turn, wanted to be judged."[27] The "man from

Independence" had his virtues—honesty, courage, unpretentiousness—but was ill-suited to manage the complicated foreign policy enterprise he inherited in April 1945.[28]

Roosevelt may have assumed Byrnes would take responsibility for foreign policy, and that is why he took the South Carolinian to Yalta. Indeed, Truman appointed Byrnes secretary of state on July 1, 1945, with a broad mandate to act in his name. Byrnes was a more senior and wily operator than the new president, but he too lacked foreign policy experience. As executors of FDR's testament, Byrnes and Truman were initially like the blind leading the blind. But for this FDR bore much of the blame. At Yalta, he had excluded Byrnes from the controversial Far Eastern discussions so that he would put a positive, Wilsonian gloss on what had happened.[29] Despite, or because of, the fact that Roosevelt had tapped Truman for domestic reasons, he made no effort to educate him. Many factors beyond his control conspired to prevent Roosevelt's conciliatory approach from surviving his death, but by personalizing foreign policy, and failing to prepare Truman, he made his own contribution to that result.

Trying to fill the shoes of someone who had become a legend in his own time, the Missouri amateur faced a dilemma. He wished to show he was his own man and capable of making hard decisions. He also wanted to be seen as FDR's worthy successor. These desires pulled him in opposite directions with respect to the Russians. The result was not a prompt reversal of Roosevelt's policies, but mixed messages and zigzag diplomacy. The pattern reflected the fact that Roosevelt's advisers were themselves divided. In line with growing public concern about Soviet behavior, Ambassador Harriman, Secretary of State Stettinius, Under Secretary Joseph Grew, and General John Deane, head of the U.S. military mission to Moscow, wanted to hold the Russians to the letter of Yalta on broadening the cabinet and free elections in Poland. Marshall, Stimson, Morgenthau, Hopkins, and former U.S. ambassador to Moscow Joseph Davies counselled a conciliatory approach.

By instinct, Truman and Byrnes stood with the former camp. According to Truman's account of his April 23, 1945, meeting with Foreign Minister Molotov, he lectured the Russian in no uncertain terms. "'I have never been talked to like that in my life'", said Molotov.

"'Carry out your agreements and you won't get talked to like that'", snapped Truman. There is some doubt about the authenticity of this exchange (it does not appear in the U.S. or Soviet memos of the conversation). But even if Truman did embroider his version, there was a new attitude and a new tone. According to Truman's interpreter Bohlen, the conversation ended with:

> Truman firmly and briskly [saying] that he was not interested in propaganda; he merely wished that Molotov would inform Stalin of his concern over the failure of the Soviet government to live up to his agreements at Yalta. Molotov turned a little ashy and attempted to steer the discussion back to the Far East, but Truman cut him off and said, 'That will be all Mr Molotov, I would appreciate it if you would transmit my view to Marshal Stalin. Having been dismissed, Molotov quickly left.

In lecturing Molotov, Truman had followed Eden's suggestion that he play "tough cop" on the Polish question. It is inconceivable that Roosevelt would have taken coaching from the Tory foreign secretary or dealt with Molotov so bluntly. After Germany's surrender several weeks later, Truman abruptly cut off lend-lease aid to the USSR.[30]

Not surprisingly, the Soviets showed no signs of giving in to pressure. To avoid a break with Moscow and pro-Roosevelt opinion in America, Truman tacked in a new direction. Heeding the advice of Marshall, Stimson, Davies, and Hopkins, he sent Hopkins to Moscow to prepare a meeting between himself and Stalin. Hopkins struck a deal (providing for the inclusion of a handful of non-Communists in the Polish cabinet) that essentially settled the question on Stalin's terms and removed it from the agenda. In a flight of cynicism parodying FDR's, Truman noted he had told Hopkins to tell Stalin that "Poland ought to have 'free elections,' at least as free as Hague, Tom Pendergast, Joe Martin, or Taft would allow."[31] In two months, Truman had managed to provoke the Russians with nothing to show for it, while indicating that holding firm might elicit a softening on the U.S. side.

This pattern repeated itself in the second half of 1945. At the Potsdam Conference (July 17–August 2, 1945; attended by Truman, Stalin, Churchill, and after the latter's defeat in the general election, Prime Minister Clement Attlee) a tough line re-emerged. Truman and Byrnes were determined to stop the spread of Soviet power and drive bargains that would be popular at home. Byrnes insisted that the first charge on exports from the occupied western zones of Germany would be to pay for essential imports. The United States had no intention of subsidizing Germany so that it could finance reparations to Moscow. The Russians, who had received a pledge of $10 billion in German reparations at Yalta, would have to take the lion's share from their poorer eastern zone. In return, the United States and Britain recognized Soviet annexation of part of northern East Prussia, accepted the Oder–Neisse Rivers as the provisional German–Polish border (giving substantial German territory to Poland), and backed down on a demand that Western monitors supervise elections in Hungary, Romania, and Bulgaria.[32]

But the United States and Britain did not intend to give Moscow carte blanche in the East. In late August Washington and London informed Moscow that they would not recognize Communist-dominated governments in Romania and Bulgaria until reorganized on a broader democratic basis. To support their policy they attempted to provide covert help to pro-Western groups and individuals on the ground.[33] Byrnes's policy aimed, in effect, to foster internal freedom in Eastern European states while conceding Soviet influence over their foreign policies. Such an arrangement, later called "Finlandization," or an "open" sphere, appeared eminently reasonable in the West and had the added virtue of testing Moscow's real intentions.[34] At the the first session of the Council of Foreign Ministers (CFM), the body created at Potsdam to prepare peace treaties for the defeated nations, in London in September 1945, Byrnes floated an idea that would become the centerpiece of his open-sphere diplomacy: a twenty to twenty-five-year treaty demilitarizing Germany and gradually dismantling the occupation. The purpose was "to induce the Soviets to relent in Eastern Europe by removing their fears of a revanchist Germany—or else force them to show by rejection of the instrument [the proposed treaty] that 'security' was only a pretext for prolonging the occupation of Eastern Europe." As Truman put it after the Soviets had rejected the idea, Moscow's bluff had been called.[35]

The new toughening in U.S. policy, and the events of July–September 1945, were closely connected to a seminal moment in the Cold War. On July 16, at Alamogordo in the New Mexico desert, U.S. and British scientists working on the ultra-secret "Manhattan project" witnessed the successful test of their handiwork, an atomic blast. Concealing his elation, Truman spoke to Stalin on July 24 of a new and terrible weapon. Feigning satisfaction, the Soviet dictator hastened to enter the Far Eastern war to secure the territories promised him at Yalta and a direct role in Japan. An American B-29 dropped the first bomb on Hiroshima on August 6. The USSR declared war on August 8, and began a massive offensive against Japanese forces in Manchuria. A second bomb obliterated Nagasaki on August 9. After a bitter internal debate, Tokyo accepted the Allied demand for an unconditional surrender on August 15, and ordered its armies to cease fire the next day.

The decision to use the bomb and reject Grew's and Stimson's advice to demonstrate it in advance (or warn Japan and/or reassure it concerning the emperor's survival) to induce surrender did not cost Byrnes and Truman sleep. It arose from three considerations: the desire to save thousands of U.S. lives expected to be lost in the invasion of Japan, scheduled for November 1, 1945; the need to avoid the charge, in the case the bomb were not used, of having wasted not only lives but billions in public funds spent to develop it; the hope that the bomb would serve as a diplomatic instrument. Ideally, the bomb would make Soviet entry into the Pacific war unnecessary. More realistically, it might limit Moscow's gains on the ground and its post-war political leverage. Significantly, it *appeared* to the Americans to have done just that: Tokyo surrendered before the Soviets could carry out a planned invasion of Hokkaido, decisively weakening their bid for a major role in the occupation. In reality—and ironically—it was probably the Soviet move into Manchuria that delivered the shock leading the Emperor and his close advisers to sue for peace. In any case, Washington assumed that the bomb's political weight would be enhanced if its military value had been demonstrated. This was a reason why the administration wanted to end the war through the use of the bomb rather than in some other way.[36]

The tendency to invest the bomb with a kind of magical persuasiveness was understandable. Churchill's reaction to the news from Alamogordo was, "It's the Second Coming... It has just come in time to save the world." For the Americans, facing a sudden vacuum of charismatic leadership and with their armies slated for demobilization, there was a similar tendency to place exaggerated hopes in the bomb. Stimson referred to it, even before it had been tested, as a "master card," part of a "royal straight flush," and a "badly needed equalizer"[37] Byrnes, too, felt buoyed by the bomb. Unlike Stimson, who came to fear an arms race, or Roosevelt, who had leaned toward discussing the question with Stalin, Byrnes dismissed the notion that the Russians would soon obtain it.[38] Shortly before the London CFM, he told one of Stimson's deputies, John J. McCloy, "the Russians were only sensitive to power and all the world, including the Russians, were cognizant of the power of this bomb, and with it in his hip pocket he felt he was in a far better position to come back with tangible accomplishments even if he did not threaten anyone expressly with it." Byrnes's hope to practice "atomic diplomacy" was an open secret in Washington. In a lame attempt at humor, Molotov asked Byrnes in London if he were carrying "an atomic bomb in his side pocket."[39] For Molotov's boss, however, the bomb was no laughing matter. It was a vivid symbol of how his schemes had gone awry.

Stalin's Fading Assumptions

Although Stalin did not share the failing president's implicit belief in his own immortality, his picture of the post-war world was nearly as rosy as FDR's. The Soviet dictator's misreading of the future is less surprising when it is remembered that he had once before mistakenly placed his conditional trust in the "class enemy." Stalin was a man of steel but not a seer.

His growing anger with the West fed Western hostility, which in turn confirmed his view that a new and dangerous phase had started. For a pair of Russian historians, two events—both eminently predictable— "dramatically altered Stalin's view of the diplomatic landscape and loosed his demons of suspicion: the first was the death of Roosevelt; the second was America's dropping of the A-bomb on Hiroshima."[40] Soviet doubts had begun to deepen after Yalta when the Allies seemed intent on quibbling over Poland. Molotov commented, "Poland—a big deal! But how governments are being organized in Belgium, France, Greece, etc., we do not know...We have not interfered because it is the Anglo-American zone of military action." The "Berne affair," secret Allied contacts with the Germans in Switzerland, seemed to herald a dreaded separate peace. Still, Stalin counted on FDR and the "progressive element" of the bourgeoisie to stick to a conciliatory policy. Having put his eggs in the Roosevelt basket, he was genuinely dismayed by his death.[41]

According to a Soviet physicist, not only Stalin but the whole Soviet government "interpreted [Hiroshima] as atomic blackmail against the U.S.S.R., as a threat to unleash a new, even more terrible and devastating war." Instead of a relatively distant, benign America, Moscow now faced a more hostile U.S. leadership equipped with a weapon it could try to use to deny the USSR its rewards and counter its conventional military advantage. On August 18, Truman rejected Stalin's request for an occupation zone on Hokkaido. In September, the United States deployed 50,000 Marines in northeast China to block a possible Soviet or Chinese Communist advance southward from Manchuria. The Anglo-American message on the Bulgarian and Romanian governments and the emerging partnership of Byrnes and British Foreign Secretary Ernest Bevin, a hard-bitten former trade unionist, signalled the demise of another assumption. Rather than drifting toward conflict as capitalist rivals, the Anglo-Americans were beginning to coalesce.[42]

Simultaneously, the rather facile premises of Stalin's "national front" strategy began to crack. In Czechoslovakia, a victim of Western betrayal in 1938, the Russians remained relatively popular and Soviet troops withdrew in 1946. Poland was different. Where, Stalin lamented at one point, were the reasonable bourgeois Poles one could talk to?[43] Part of the answer was that he had ordered the execution by pistol shot in the back of the neck of thousands of captured Polish officers in the Katyn Forest, and other locations, in March 1940, to eliminate opposition to the annexation of eastern Poland. Although conditions in each occupied country were different, the frequently brutal and arrogant behavior of Soviet soldiers, administrators, and intelligence personnel undermined what regard the USSR and local Communist parties enjoyed as liberators, and fed nationalist reactions. In the case of Germany and its allies, such behavior, including the rape of hundreds of thousands of women, was not simply wanton; it was revenge for the untold brutalities visited on the Soviet people. Aside from the moral censure it brought, however, it was profoundly counter-productive. Instead of allying with

Moscow-sponsored groups, non-Communists adopted a defiant attitude which "soon found strong support from the United States and Britain." That support "emboldened many opposition leaders and persuaded them that they did not really need to come to terms with the Soviets or local Communists." This, in turn, fed Soviet and Eastern European Communist suspicion of the Anglo-Americans, and encouraged them to impose Communism by force and fraud. The result (although not definitively until 1947–8), was that "Stalin succeeded in bringing socialism to Eastern Europe, but sooner than he had planned, by methods different from those he had preferred, and at a cost he had hoped not to pay."[44]

Stalin's reaction to Hiroshima was to order a crash program to obtain the bomb, under the supervision of his fellow Georgian Lavrenti Beria, head of the security organ, the NKVD. In the meantime, Molotov, supervised (and at times browbeaten) by Stalin, practiced a sort of "reverse atomic diplomacy."[45] The Russians were determined to disabuse the Americans and British of the notion that they could use the bomb to cheat the USSR or rewrite prior agreements. In London, Molotov pressed the Soviet claim to a trusteeship over Tripolitania and refused to give on the Romanian and Bulgarian governments. When Stalin learned that his foreign minister, in a departure from procedures decided at Potsdam, had agreed to a request to let French and Chinese delegates discuss the Finnish and Balkan treaties, he ordered Molotov to return to the Potsdam rules. On another occasion he cabled: "The Allies are pressing on you to break your will and force you into making concessions. It is obvious that you should display complete adamancy." Molotov showed an interest in Byrnes's German treaty but Stalin smelled a rat: the purpose was to divert attention from Japan where the Americans were monopolizing the occupation. He also suspected an Anglo-American bid to control Germany by removing the Red Army from the Soviet zone and ending the rationale for its presence in Eastern Europe. Other Soviet officials agreed. Marshal Georgi Zhukov, the conquerer of Berlin, believed that "[t]he Americans would like to finish the occupation . . . as soon as possible and to remove the armed forces of the USSR from Germany, and then to demand a withdrawal of our troops from Poland, and finally from the Balkans." Even Litvinov believed the treaty might bring a premature end to the occupation and a revival of the German threat.[46]

The London conference ended in acrimony but Stalin thought he had made his point. In fact, in a repetition of May 1945, the Americans changed tack again. Mistakenly believing the obstacle to agreement was Molotov, Byrnes proposed direct talks in Moscow with Stalin. At the December CFM, the Western allies agreed to recognize the Romanian and Bulgarian governments after cosmetic changes. Bowing to reality, Moscow agreed to sit on an Allied Control Commission for Japan in a purely advisory status. Stalin accepted Byrnes's proposal to create a UN Commission of Atomic Energy. Since they could not be cowed by the bomb, perhaps the Soviets "could be lured into a favorable agreement to regulate the future of atomic energy."[47] Once again, the Americans had provoked Soviet anger, then signalled that intransigence might bring concessions. Stalin told Molotov: "It is obvious that in dealing with such partners as the US and Britain we cannot achieve anything serious if we begin to give in to intimidation or betray uncertainty. To get anything from this kind of partner, we must arm ourselves with the policy of tenacity and steadfastness."[48]

The statement suggests Stalin had not decided to break with the Anglo-Americans. There were deals to be done including peace settlements with the smaller powers, and then Germany where he still hoped for a united country friendly to the USSR. He was capable of gestures such as removing troops from Czechoslovakia and Manchuria, and gave reassuring interviews to cultivate Western opinion.[49] But the fading of his original assumptions meant the strengthening of the Hobbesian fatalist tendency in his policy. Stalin would talk but also *take* what he could to secure the Soviet Union, based on the accurate assumptions that the window of opportunity to do so was closing, there would be no Western gifts (quite the opposite), and he had less to lose in terms of Western good will than six months earlier. This approach has struck some historians as vacillating and incoherent, but from Stalin's perspective it must have made perfect sense.[50]

Having launched an all-out atomic program, Stalin also began to prepare his war-weary people for what he called in a February 9, 1946 speech "another powerful upswing of our national economy." The speech was erroneously seen in the West as the declaration of an anti-U.S. offensive. Stalin did not say war was imminent and drew a distinction between the two world wars. (The latter had been an anti-fascist struggle fought together with other "freedom-loving countries.")[51] But its basic analysis, positing inevitable war due to intra-capitalist rivalry, reflected classic Marxism–Leninism. It is no doubt true that Stalin needed an external enemy to justify an iron control over his people. Soviet actions in Eastern Europe were themselves a basic source of Western suspicion and hostility, for which the Russians had mainly themselves to blame. Such considerations aside, Stalin's fear was not feigned and not without justification. It is hard to disagree with Hans Morgenthau: "Once we had allowed the Soviet armies to advance to a point one hundred miles east of the Rhine, the verbal attempts to roll them back were not only futile but pernicious, for they provided empirical proof for Stalin's suspicions." Stalin's assumption that a new conflict was inevitable can only have been reinforced by the developments of April–September 1945.[52]

The Mackinderian Moment: 1946

The post-Roosevelt zigzag pattern ended in late 1945–early 1946. In September, Truman rejected Stimson's advice on atomic energy.[53] His Navy Day speech (October 27, 1945), reflecting the views of Navy Secretary James Forrestal and Stimson's replacement, Robert Patterson, announced that the United States would try to lock in its position of global military supremacy. Possession of the bomb was a "sacred trust" in a "lawless world" and there would be no "compromise with evil." The same month, the Joint War Plans Committee of the Joint Staff identified the USSR as the most likely future enemy.[54] Although they saw political advantages in public negotiations, Truman and his military advisers considered a deal whereby the United States would give up its atomic monopoly under an international regime to be impractical and unwise. The relatively cheap—as opposed to conventional forces—bomb appealed for financial as well as military reasons. After winning the Senate and House of Representatives in the November 1946 elections, the Republicans called for slashing taxes and the federal budget. Until 1950 Truman himself was stubbornly committed to a ceiling on defense spending to channel investment into the civilian economy. When Under Secretary of State Dean Acheson and former Tennessee Valley Authority head David Lilienthal devised a plausible plan for UN control of atomic energy, Truman allowed it to be transformed into the more radical "Baruch Plan" (after the Democratic Party financier Bernard Baruch), calling for "swift and sure punishment" of offenders, something Moscow was sure to reject.[55]

Truman's late-1945 mood was affected by his simmering resentment of Byrnes's secretive modus operandi and patronizing manner. In a January 5, 1946 letter, he complained that he had been kept "completely in the dark" during the recent Moscow talks.[56] But in a parallel with Stalin's earlier anger with Molotov, Truman was upset with the substance of his subordinate's approach as well as the form.[57] He voiced dismay over reported police-state conditions in Bulgaria and Romania and called the Oder–Neisse border "a high handed outrage." The president (in another parallel with Stalin) did not want an immediate rupture, and left Byrnes to finish the treaty-writing task. (Byrnes would resign, ostensibly for health reasons, in January 1947.) Breaking with the Soviets also meant breaking with the Democratic Party left wing. Truman hesitated to do this until Byrnes and Henry Wallace forced him to choose between them in September 1946.[58] And although his administration had not written off Eastern Europe, there was little for now that could be done in that part of the world.

But Truman was determined to draw a line against *further* Russian expansion. Uppermost in his mind was the so-called Northern Tier. The Soviets had failed to leave Iran within six months of the war's end as per a 1941 agreement with Britain, and were angling to create an autonomous zone in the oil-endowed Azerbaijani region of the country. In June 1945 Moscow had told Turkey it wanted the retrocession of the Kars and Ardahan districts (Russian-owned between 1878 and 1921), and revision of Montreux. Truman was steeped in the view that Russia was engaged in an inexorable drive toward the edges of Eurasia. His missive to Byrnes ended: "Unless Russia is faced with an iron fist and strong language another war is in the making...I'm tired of babying the Soviets."[59] Truman's letter was part of a conditioned Mackinderian reflex and cry of alarm in Western circles that went up in 1946.

U.S. analyses of the Straits question rested on self-serving logic. The Joint Chiefs of Staff acknowledged that the USSR believed it needed the Straits to protect itself, just as Britain needed the Suez Canal and the Straits of Gibraltar, and the United States the Panama Canal. However, the JCS concluded, the Anglo-Saxons were defensive-minded whereas Soviet demands indicated designs on the Middle East. Soviet penetration of the Mediterranean would force the British to fight to hold the "vital Suez Canal–Aleppo–Basra triangle." A British defeat "would eliminate from Eurasia the last bulwark of resistance between the United States and Soviet expansionism." Washington and London drew up a joint plan for war against the USSR. It called for the temporary withdrawal of ground forces from Central Europe to Spain and Italy (and perhaps from the continent altogether), military support of Turkey, and a devastating atomic bombing campaign against Soviet territory from bases in Britain and Egypt.[60]

On February 22, 1946, a middle-level U.S. diplomat in Moscow cabled home a lengthy analysis of Soviet behavior. George F. Kennan's simmering resentment was due to what he saw as the Rooseveltian illusions still guiding policy (witness Byrnes's recent "zag"). According to Kennan, Stalin's regime was a "political force committed fanatically to the belief that with [the] US there can be no permanent modus vivendi and that it is desirable and necessary that the internal harmony of our society be disrupted, our traditional way of life be destroyed, the international authority of our state be broken, if Soviet power is to be secure."[61] In a *Foreign Affairs* magazine essay in July 1947, published under the pseudonym Mr. "X," Kennan gave a name to the policy he advocated: "firm containment" of the USSR.[62]

Kennan's telegram and article included a second essential argument: Soviet power "unlike that of Hitlerite Germany, is neither schematic nor adventuristic . . . It does not take unnecessary risks. Impervious to the logic of reason, it is highly sensitive to the logic of force." The threat to Western Europe was political, not military, and consisted of the appeal of local Communist parties. Compared to the West, the Soviets were "by far the weaker force." By virtue of its recent expansion and the burden of controlling Eastern Europe, the USSR faced strains that had "once proved a severe tax on Tsardom." Not only that, the Soviet system had yet to prove itself "as a form of internal power."[63] Kennan's point about Soviet caution and vulnerability was lost on those whose image of the USSR was based not on study and first-hand experience but the performance of the Red Army, the Russians' brutal record in Eastern Europe, and the fact of Stalinism's appeal in the West. Kennan had been behind what he thought was the Potemkin village—the rickety façade—of Soviet power. His audience had not. For the moment, however, such distinctions had limited importance. Forrestal circulated the "long telegram" in Washington. Its unmistakable message about Soviet hostility reinforced the view that it was time to draw a line.[64]

At Westminster College in Fulton, Missouri, Winston Churchill, in the United States to lobby for a major loan to Britain, played the Mackinderian theme to the hilt. "From Stettin in the Baltic to Trieste in the Adriatic an iron curtain has descended across the continent." Not only did the Russians behave as barbarians on their side of the line, their fifth columns constituted a "growing challenge and peril to Christian Civilization." Echoing Kennan's analysis, the ex-prime minister argued that the Russians did not seek war, only the indefinite expansion of their power and ideology. But Churchill then blurred Kennan's crucial distinction between the Hitler and Stalin regimes by warning against 1930s-style appeasement. This emotive argument would frequently prove a rhetorical trump card during the Cold War. Truman avoided endorsing the opposition leader's opinions. Privately, he agreed with every word.[65]

As a practical matter, containment was first applied in northern Iran. Washington encouraged Iran to resist Soviet inroads and took the matter to the United Nations. In April–May 1946, Tehran and Moscow reached a compromise on the exploitation of oil in northern Iran. Soviet troops withdrew, and did not return when the Iranian parliament failed to ratify the agreement. A crucial test occurred over Turkey in August. Following a Soviet military build-up in Bulgaria and Romania, Moscow renewed its demands on Ankara for bases and a revision of the Montreux Convention (although not concerning Kars and Ardahan). Believing that Soviet penetration of the Mediterranean might lead to an Anglo-Soviet war and wishing to deter a Soviet attack, the Truman administration took decisive action. It rejected Moscow's demand for joint control of the Straits, warned the USSR against aggression, and decided it would go to war, if necessary, to defend the Turks. With a U.S. aircraft carrier group en route to the area, and U.S. resolve clear thanks to a Soviet spy in the British Embassy in Washington, Moscow relaxed its pressure. The Straits crisis converted Under Secretary Acheson, until now agnostic about Russia, to a hard-line position. Political expediency, and loyalty to Truman, drew him in that direction. So did his conviction that British power was in decline and the moment Brooks Adams had predicted was approaching. The United States was due to become "the containing power of the world."[66]

Stalin's motives in Iran and Turkey are not a mystery. He had no new grand design and was essentially reacting to events. Churchill's speech, which deeply angered him, and Kennan's dispatch, obtained by Soviet intelligence, made obvious the drift in Western policy. In May 1946 the U.S. occupation authorities in Germany ended reparations payments to the USSR from current industrial production. Moscow's request to Washington for a major loan was inexplicably misplaced. It was clear that U.S. public opinion was shifting rightward. Around the time Truman dismissed Henry Wallace, Nikolai Novikov, Soviet ambassador to Washington, accurately reported that U.S. policy was no longer controlled by Rooseveltians but an alliance of conservative Democrats and Republicans.[67] This shift had more to do with taxes and labor unrest than with international politics, and the Republican sweep in November 1946 was not a mandate for a showdown with Moscow. But the losers were those inclined to give the benefit of the doubt to the Russians. In the circumstances, it was reasonable for Stalin to think he had less to gain through deference, and less to lose by playing rough. Perhaps he believed tensions between Washington and London could be exploited and/or that Ankara could be induced to fold in a game of intimidation. It is extremely unlikely that he ever intended to attack Turkey. Rather, he raised the stakes and then backed down when his bluff was called.[68]

Any objective observer could see that the USSR had vital interests in the Turkish Straits. But just as no action was more likely to trigger Soviet suspicions of double-dealing than Western efforts to dilute Soviet control over Eastern Europe, nothing was surer to set off Anglo-American alarm bells than probes toward the Mediterranean and Persian Gulf.

Along with the massacre of the Poles in 1940, these actions in 1946 probably did more than any others to compromise the post-war strategy that Stalin himself had favored. For once, Molotov's judgment is eloquent: "It [the demand on the Turkish Straits] was an inopportune, impossible affair. I consider Stalin an outstanding politician, but he too made mistakes."[69]

CHAPTER 3
THE CONSOLIDATION OF THE BLOCS, 1947-1949

The Cold War began in 1945, escalated in 1946, was unofficially "declared" in 1947, and congealed into a system in 1948–9. Moscow's climb-down in Iran and the defusing of the Turkish affair offered a respite along the Northern Tier. But Soviet intentions there remained threatening in the minds of Western leaders, and a third crisis was about to explode. Encouraged by Yugoslavia, the Greek Communist Party (KKE) embarked on the romantic, foolhardy course that led to its defeat in the remote north of the country in 1949. In September 1946 the KKE decided to raise a guerrilla force to overthrow the royal government and expel British troops. In February 1947 it opted for "all out war."[1] Stalin, who had taken little interest in Greece since his October 1944 deal with Churchill, gave a "faint 'green light'" to the uprising in May 1947. Although the KKE had taken the initiative and Stalin's support was half-hearted, the Anglo-Americans and anti-Communist Greeks saw the renewal of the civil war as another flagrant challenge to Western control of the approaches to the Middle East.[2]

The Greek crisis, together with the Labour government's February 1947 message that it could no longer afford to help Athens and Ankara, galvanized the Truman administration and led it to take direct responsibility for the situation. Simultaneously, the United States and local pro-Western forces faced what they considered an even more serious opportunity for the Soviet Union to spread its influence: the deteriorating situation in Western Europe. The precarious state of the Northern Tier and need to secure the Mediterranean led to the Truman Doctrine of

March 1947. The parlous condition of Western Europe prompted the announcement in June of what became the Marshall Plan.

The Truman Doctrine

On March 12 President Truman delivered a dramatic appeal to a joint session of Congress. After describing the crises facing Greece and Turkey and requesting $400 million in aid, he laid down a basic principle: "It must be the policy of the United States to support free peoples who are resisting attempted subjugation by armed minorities or by outside pressures." Although Truman did not mention the USSR (the new secretary of state, George C. Marshall, was in Moscow, talking about Germany), the speech left no doubt that Communist subversion and Soviet pressure were at the root of the problems faced by the "free" societies of the West.[3]

The significance of Truman's pronouncement was threefold. First, although Britain would remain an important player in the region, it marked America's assumption of the main burden of defending the lines of communication between the Levant and the West. The Doctrine was a milestone along the road of progressive U.S. entanglement in the Middle East. Second, the speech defined America's role in a sweeping fashion and set a precedent for commitments to other areas considered marginal before 1945. The administration did not intend to issue a blank check and said it would consider aid requests on a case-by-case basis. But Acheson, department speech-writer Joseph Jones, and their colleagues chose to cast the Greek–Turkish question as a challenge not only to Western security but to the survival of "free peoples" everywhere. According to the speech's Wilsonian logic, the failure to counter aggression or subversion anywhere would embolden evil-doers and lead to general war.

The administration defined the issue thus because it wanted to appeal to Wilsonian opinion, and sincerely believed in what it said. The problem, as critics quickly pointed out, was that, having appointed itself the defender of universal principle (the United Nations now assumed a subordinate role), Washington would be faced with other requests that it would be difficult to turn down. Kennan's companion-piece to the

Truman speech, published in July 1947, defined containment as "the adroit and vigilant application of counterforce at a series of constantly shifting geographical and political points corresponding to the shifts and manoeuvres of Soviet policy that cannot be charmed or talked out of existence." Walter Lippmann called such a reactive and undiscriminating approach a "strategic monstrosity."[4] Ironically, both Kennan and Marshall harbored doubts about the implications of Truman's language at the time.

Third, the speech and campaign to win approval for Greek and Turkish aid determined the type and tone of argument the administration would use to persuade the budget-slashing Republicans who controlled Congress in 1947–9. While Kennan and Marshall preferred an appeal to enlightened self-interest, Acheson favored stronger medicine. As he later put it: "Qualification must give way to simplicity of statement, nicety and nuance to bluntness, almost brutality...If we made our points clearer than truth we did not differ from most other educators and could hardly do otherwise."[5]

Acheson tested the melodramatic approach at a famous White House meeting on February 26, 1947. When Marshall's low-key presentation failed to impress the gathering, including Senate Republican leader Vandenberg, the under-secretary took the floor: "Like apples in a barrel infected by one rotten one, the corruption of Greece would affect Iran and all to the east. It would also carry infection to Africa through Asia Minor and Egypt and to Europe through Italy and France...The Soviet Union was playing one of the greatest gambles in history at minimal cost."[6] In fact, the Soviet Union had retreated in Iran and Turkey, and the French and Italian Communist parties (the PCF and PCI) were still bending over backwards to co-operate. But sober appeals fell flat according to what Acheson himself had called a "Gresham's law of politics and words."[7] The stakes were high, and making matters "clearer than truth" proved effective. Unfortunately, just as over-selling the notion that the "Soviet Union had changed" contributed to a reaction against Roosevelt's policy, preaching that the Soviet Union was the cause of the world's problems entailed its costs. It encouraged a black and white view of reality and an anti-Communist backlash that would complicate the lives of Truman and Acheson after 1948.

Spring 1947: *Doppiezza*, the Dollar Gap, and the *Deutsche Frage*

The overall Western European crisis comprised three distinct, although interrelated, crises. They came to a head simultaneously during the first six months of 1947. On the political mood after 1945, a commentator wrote: "Nobody in Europe believes in the American way of life—that is, in private enterprise." People "want Socialism, but they also want the Rights of Man."[8] For many, free-market capitalism had been discredited by the depression and extreme nationalism by the war. In Britain, the Labour Party launched a program to create a welfare state and control the economy's "commanding heights" in the collective interest. The PCF and PCI basked in the reflected glory of Stalin and the Red Army. But they had also garnered prestige and popularity by spearheading the resistance to Nazi occupiers and collaborationist governments. Millions of non-Communists were sympathetic to the defense of national sovereignty and defiance of American political and cultural domination— "cocacolization"—that the Communists claimed to represent. In France, the newly founded daily *Le Monde* adopted an influential neutralist position in the Cold War. A U.S. embassy official would later comment that it was "poisoning the mind" of the French.[9]

PCI membership increased from about 5,000 in 1943 to 1.7 million by the end of 1945. In elections for a constituent assembly in June 1946, the PCI and its ally, the socialist party (PSIUP), received 38 percent of the vote. In November 1946 legislative elections, the PCF won 28 percent, and a plurality of seats in parliament. In line with Moscow's strategy, the two parties focused on consolidating democracy and building alliances. The PCI steered clear of nationalizations and even a modest patrimonial tax proposal that might alienate the middling classes. As minister of justice in a government headed by the Christian Democrat Alcide De Gasperi, Palmiro Togliatti, the PCI's cautious, cerebral leader, presided over an amnesty benefiting tens of thousands of Fascists. To widespread disbelief, the PCI voted in early 1947 to include the Lateran Pacts in Italy's new constitution. This was the 1929 accord between Mussolini and the Vatican, making Catholicism the state religion and paying a large subsidy to the church.

The problem for Washington and local anti-Communists, however, was the Communists' apparent *doppiezza*, or duplicity: the PCF and PCI were believed to be playing a double game. While behaving moderately and building up strength in the ministries, trade unions, and the world of culture (universities, publishing houses, cinema), the parties were thought to be planning to take power either legally or, if the opportunity arose, by force. In reality, neither Togliatti nor his French counterpart Maurice Thorez seriously considered following the KKE's example. During the fiercely fought 1948 Italian election campaign, in response to an inquiry from Togliatti, Molotov secretly conveyed the Kremlin's opinion that, barring an armed attack on the PCI, an insurrection would be a "dangerous misadventure."[10] At the same time, the PCF and PCI kept stocks of weapons and each had its "insurrectionary" minority. Many hoped or feared (as the case might be) that the Red Army or Yugoslav Communists would somehow help to bring the PCI and PCF to power. A popular Roman saying was *ha da venir baffon*—"wait till the man with the big mustache gets here!"

Fear of what the Communists *might* do affected the French and Italian economies. Unsure whether their property would be taxed or confiscated, entrepreneurs funneled capital abroad. Although they proposed no radical overhauls, the Communists used their clout in government, the unions, and factory councils to try to defend the jobs and living standards of their base. This too constituted an obstacle to recovery along capitalist lines, and the Communists themselves were proposing no basic alternative. Italian (like German) industrial plant had suffered surprisingly light damage (destruction of roads, bridges, railroads, harbors, and housing was a more serious problem) but factories were badly in need of retooling and rationalization.[11] This meant hundreds of thousands of workers in the car, mechanical-engineering, steel, and ship-building sectors would find themselves redundant. But, many feared, if workers were thrown into the streets, or living standards collapsed owing to food and fuel shortages and inflation, the Communists would benefit and pose an even greater threat.

The British had taken the lead in trying to engage U.S. power in Europe. As early as March 1944, a Foreign Office memo had lucidly outlined what should be done:

It must be our purpose not to balance our power against that of America, but to make use of American power for purposes which we regard as good ... If we go about our business in the right way we can help to steer this great unwieldy barge, the United States, into the right harbour ... We must use the power of the United States to preserve the Commonwealth and the Empire, and, if possible, to support the pacification of Europe.[12]

In 1945–7, the British continued their efforts, while able continental leaders like De Gasperi and the Frenchman Léon Blum, did the same. Although the PCF and PCI exerted a moderating influence, anti-Communists discovered that emphasizing the Communist threat was a sure-fire way to fix American attention on the need for assistance. When the Prince of Monaco jokingly offered to take in some Italian Communists, De Gasperi quipped: "I need every Communist I can get."[13] But conservatives and moderate socialists genuinely believed that the Communists and their Soviet backers would try to exploit economic chaos. French and Italian leaders also recognized that the presence of Communist ministers in their governments generated anxiety in America and was an obstacle to sustained support.

The political and the economic crises converged and reinforced each other in early 1947. Much ink has been spilled trying to determine the true state of affairs. Acheson set out one view in his memoirs:

In Europe no one could remember such a winter as January 1947 ushered in. The one before had been bad enough, a winter of freezing drought. This was one of freezing blizzards. Since the surrender of Germany, the life of Europe as an organized industrial community had come well-nigh to a standstill and, with it, so had production and distribution of goods of every sort.

Assistant Secretary of State Will Clayton, reflecting the tenor of countless reports, wrote on May 27, 1947: "Europe is steadily deteriorating. Millions of people in the cities are slowly starving ... Without further and substantial aid from the United States, economic, social, and political disintegration will overwhelm Europe."[14] The economic historian Alan Milward later painted a different picture. Europe had faced a structural balance of payments deficit aggravated by the war, that is, a shortage of dollars to pay for the wheat, coal, cotton, and industrial equipment that only the United States could supply in abundance. This "dollar gap" was reaching a critical juncture, threatening economic regression, but not because Europe's economies were at a standstill. It was the rapid pace of recovery that had augmented Europe's appetite for dollars. Far from a Lazarus in need of revival by America, Europe resembled a healthy athlete who was running out of breath.

Indeed, industrial production and exports had recovered impressively in many parts of Europe and much infrastructure had been repaired.[15] But the situation *seemed* dire to those without the gift of prophecy. The $2.75 billion British loan (approved by Congress in 1946) was quickly exhausted when sterling became convertible to the dollar. A U.S. Export–Import Bank loan to France was soon spent. Milward's own figures indicate that production fell in the first quarter of 1947, even if rising again over the rest of the year. The harsh weather did close factories and slow the distribution of goods, in places leaving trains frozen in their tracks. Millions scraped by on meager food rations and little coal to heat their homes. Passage of the Greek–Turkish bill did not mean Congress would soon again reach into its pockets. U.S. embassy officials in Rome made it clear that Italy would first have to begin "to put its house in order." If the message was not so explicit, U.S. expectations with regard to France were the same.[16] In May 1947, when the Communists chose to support Renault car workers striking for higher pay in defiance of a government wage freeze, Premier Paul Ramadier expelled PCF ministers from the cabinet. When the Italian government fell the same month, De Gasperi formed a government without Communist and Socialist ministers and adopted painful measures to rein in inflation. But with the left now in opposition, the political battle intensified in parliament and the streets.

Significantly absent from the general upswing in 1945–6 was Europe's largest economy. This was partly because U.S. policy (embodied in Joint Chiefs of Staff directive 1067) and the Potsdam agreement limited German industrial production, and the decision to treat the four occupation zones as a single economic unit had not been implemented. Nor had the occupying powers made basic decisions about what kind of state would rise from the ashes of the Third Reich. Frustrated by Soviet and

French policy, including the rejection of their proposed treaty, the Americans decided to break the logjam, and win German "hearts and minds." In a speech at Stuttgart in September 1946, Byrnes offered to merge the U.S. zone with other zones and called for a "German National Council" to act as a provisional government and draft a new constitution. This soon led to "bizonia" (the combined U.S. and British zones). By the end of 1946, U.S. officials were convinced that reviving Germany was necessary to prevent a resurgence of extremism and to spur broader recovery. Germany was an indispensable market and supplier of raw materials and equipment for Europe. Without the recovery of the rest of Europe, Communism's advance appeared inevitable. The United States could live, if necessary, without the European market, but Communism's triumph was tantamount to placing Eurasia's enormous warmaking potential in the hands of a hostile power. That was exactly what America had fought World War II to avoid. In March–April 1947 the European political and economic crises coincided with the geopolitical moment of truth for the United States.

Secretary of State Marshall's first task after his appointment was to attend a CFM session in Moscow. With peace treaties for the smaller powers completed, the German question topped the agenda. The United States and Britain proposed a decentralized, federal state as an antidote to dictatorship. The Kremlin appears to have seen three options. Stalin's preference continued to be a united Germany with strong central institutions allowing a government friendly to the Soviet Union to administer the entire country. This position also reflected Stalin's view that the incorrigibly nationalist Germans would look favorably on the USSR if it supported unity, and unfavorably on the Western Allies if they could be shouldered with the responsibility for partition.[17] A second option was the compromise later agreed to for Austria: a united, demilitarized, nonaligned state without foreign troops. Molotov saw merit in this and would propose it in 1952 and after Stalin's death. The third option was Germany's division into two unequal pieces. Although it ensured Communism in the Soviet zone and ensconced the Red Army in the heart of Europe, this was not Stalin's first choice for obvious reasons. Not surprisingly, the Western powers took the initiatives leading to this result.

At Moscow, Stalin stuck to his first choice and the conference ended in deadlock. Marshall and Bevin drew a consequential, but questionable, conclusion: Stalin was in no hurry to resolve the German question and assumed the Communists would profit from economic distress and political uncertainty. Returning home, Marshall told a national radio audience, "The patient is sinking while the doctors deliberate," and ordered the State Department to prepare a major initiative. A newly created Policy Planning Staff (PPS) under George Kennan took up the task. On June 5, 1947, Marshall made his famous, although vaguely defined, offer of aid to Europe. In July 1947 the Truman administration overhauled its foreign policy bureaucracy, consolidating the departments of the army and navy under a Secretary of Defense, creating the National Security Council (NSC) to coordinate high policy, and a Central Intelligence Agency (CIA) to collect foreign intelligence. Congress approved the European Recovery Program (ERP) in April 1948.[18]

The Marshall Plan: Intended and Other Consequences

At Congress's insistence, the ERP had four official objectives: to increase production, expand foreign trade, enhance internal financial stability, and foster European economic co-operation. Participating nations signed bilateral agreements with Washington, pledging to pursue these aims. The ERP's *unofficial* objectives were also fourfold: to deal with the dollar gap, Western European Communism, and the festering German question, and to encourage change in the "satellite area." Between mid-1948 and the end of 1951, the plan transferred $12.6 billion (approximately $110 billion in 2010 dollars) to seventeen countries, 90 percent as grants. The bulk of the aid took the form of American wheat, coal, cotton, capital goods, and transportation equipment necessary to continue the recovery that had stalled in early 1947, but had resumed when the plan began. Although the ERP did not end the payments deficit, it sent a clear message of U.S. interest in Europe, and had helped to alter the psychological climate even before shiploads of goods arrived. It provided a cushion of resources (equal to 2 percent of the combined gross national products of the participants in 1948–51) allowing governments to limit to varying degrees the austerity measures necessary to deal with inflation and the dollar shortage. Through local-currency "counter-part funds," the plan financed thousands of individual projects. Via its educational and propaganda arms, European businessmen, trade union-ists, and housewives learned U.S. management techniques and the consumption-based "American way of life." The message was "you too can be like us."[19]

Germany was not a major recipient compared to Britain, France, and even Italy.[20] The German "economic miracle" owed more to the new currency (the Deutsche Mark) introduced in 1948, and orders generated by Western rearmament during the Korean War. At the same time, one of the plan's architects wrote of "the decisive emphasis placed on the rehabilitation of the German economy and the introduction of the concept of German recovery as a vital component of the recovery of Europe as a whole."[21] The plan was the lever Washington used to begin to change the hostile French attitude toward German recovery. The French were obliged to accept German recovery if they, too, wished to participate. The ERP's launching provided a favorable context for the so-called London Program initiated by the allies in early 1948, the creation of a federal West German state.

The Marshall Plan was also the point at which Washington placed a bet on European integration. A single European market would first of all pave the way to the removal of economic barriers on a global basis. Eliminating economic blocs had been the hobby-horse of Secretary of State Cordell Hull. Needless to say, the removal of barriers would also serve the interests of the world's most competitive exporter. Secondly, the Americans believed a single market along U.S. lines would make Europe more productive and prosperous and hence resistant to Com-munism and Fascism. Finally, an integrated Europe would make war unlikely and provide a framework for Germany's revival. And it would be more cohesive and self-reliant vis-à-vis the Soviet Union. The original rationale for unity was that it would allow Europe to wean itself from dependency on the United States and obviate yet another American intervention in the Old World.

Although the plan promoted a considerable degree of co-operation and trade liberalization, here it fell short of its goal. To administer the ERP and oversee adherence to its objectives, Congress created the

Economic Cooperation Administration (ECA). The ECA zealously promoted integration and pushed Britain to take the lead. But when Attlee, Bevin, and their colleagues refused to cede sovereignty to a newly created Organization of European Economic Cooperation, the State Department declined to try to force them. It was France, facing the prospect that the Americans would remove limits on German production, which decided to embrace its historic enemy and devise a structure perpetuating a degree of supervision over the Ruhr's war-making capacity. The European Coal and Steel Community (1952) was the result. The Americans gradually faced a paradox with respect to their initial objectives. The Western Europeans did not see unity as an *alternative* to U.S. protection. Indeed, they feared that it might become exactly that, and were prepared to accept more integration only in return for U.S. promises to stay in Europe as a guarantor against German and Russian aggression. Such an attitude turned Washington's logic on its head.[22]

For the typical U.S. congressman, fighting Communism was the Marshall Plan's overriding goal. Indeed, the ERP was approved in the climate of fear and uncertainty generated by the Communist take-over of Czechoslovakia in February 1948. Here again, results were mixed. The plan did not save Western Europe from Communism because it did not need to be saved. With the PCF and PCI already on the defensive, the U.S. initiative turned a retreat into a rout. Told by Moscow to try to wreck the plan, the PCF and PCI resorted to strikes and violent propaganda. But with popular expectations for U.S. aid high and Moscow in no position to help Western Europe (the USSR was taking reparations from Germany and Italy), the Communists were in a political cul de sac. Marshall's statement that a Communist–Socialist victory in the April 1948 elections would be interpreted to mean Italy did not wish to participate in the ERP probably contributed as much to the left's defeat as the "un-vouchered funds" given the pro–Western parties by the United States.[23]

The PCI, in effect, had served De Gasperi's purposes. It had been strong and provocative enough to alarm the Americans and the Italian middle classes, but co-operative and fragile enough not to pose a threat to the new political system. Still, the PCF and PCI gradually recovered from the setbacks of 1947–8. They profited from the widespread perceptions that the ERP's benefits were not equally distributed across the social spectrum, that U.S. diplomats, intelligence agents, and labor union officials meddled in French and Italian politics, and that the U.S.-sponsored rearmament of Western Europe during the Korean War might provoke World War III.

The ERP's fourth unofficial aim is sometimes forgotten. Marshall made his initial offer to *all* Europe. To be sure, the gesture to Moscow was a gamble that the Russians (once they had understood the strings attached to U.S. aid) would refuse, putting the onus of rejection on themselves.[24] Among other problems, Soviet participation would have seriously complicated Congressional approval. But the offers to Poland, Czechoslovakia, and other states under Soviet influence were genuine. If they managed to take part, they would be pulled out of the Soviet orbit. If Moscow blocked their participation, it would face the anger and material plight of those denied the plan's benefits. After Moscow's refusal, the plan remained a means of "building up the hope and vigor of western Europe to a point where it [came] to exercise the maximum attraction" to Eastern Europe.[25] Washington aimed not to divide Europe but to lure the satellites westward as soon as circumstances would permit.

Convinced that Europe's division was dangerous and unnecessary, Kennan was especially keen on this aspect of the plan. But he was not alone in insisting the ERP should be part of an offensive strategy. When Defense Secretary Forrestal requested a comprehensive statement of policy toward the Soviet Union, Kennan responded that U.S objectives should be "a. To reduce the power and influence of Moscow to limits in which they will no longer constitute a threat to the peace and stability of international society; and b. To bring about a basic change in the theory and practice of international relations observed by the government in power in Russia." As for Eastern Europe specifically, the U.S. aim in peacetime should be "to place the greatest possible strain on the structure of relationships by which Soviet domination of this area is maintained and gradually...to maneuver the Russians out of their position of primacy."[26] These general objectives and specific aims were included in National Security Council document 20/4 (NSC 20/4, November 23, 1948), the Truman administration's basic statement of its Cold War goals.[27]

Given Stalin's earlier reaction to efforts to dilute Soviet control over Eastern Europe, it is not surprising that the U.S. initiative was a failure. What *is* surprising is that Moscow initially hoped U.S. aid might be unconditional and was at pains to explore Marshall's intentions. In June 1947 Molotov and a large delegation attended the conference in Paris organized by France and Britain in response to Marshall's speech. But it was soon clear that the Americans intended to create an integrated economic area including Germany and (if possible) the satellites, and supervise the policies of participants. Molotov departed Paris, and Moscow ordered Poland and Czechoslovakia not to attend a second conference called by France and Britain. The Czechs, who were seriously interested in the plan, had little choice but to comply. "For Stalin," Geoffrey Roberts observes, "the Marshall Plan was the breaking point in relations with the United States."[28] Together with the Truman Doctrine and Kennan's article, the plan triggered a basic reassessment of U.S. aims and a new phase in Soviet policy. It was now obvious that FDR's approach was dead and buried, and that the United States was seeking not just to contain but to push back and undermine the USSR.[29]

Stalin's answer was to abandon "popular fronts" and "national roads" to socialism, a strategy that had assumed a Rooseveltian policy in the West and had proved ineffective on the ground. In September 1947 the major European Communist parties met secretly at the Polish resort town of Szklarska Poreba. The Leningrad party chief Andrei Zdhanov delivered Moscow's counter-declaration of the Cold War. The world was now divided into "two camps," one "imperialist and anti-democratic," the other "anti-imperialist and democratic." Whereas the old Comintern had grown obsolete in a phase of "national roads" and looser control from Moscow, a new organization, the Communist Information Bureau (Cominform) would now coordinate Communist activities. PCF and PCI delegates sat astonished as Yugoslav comrades denounced their "parliamentary illusions" and timidity in defending their countries' sovereignty. The message they took was to destabilize capitalism and topple pro-U.S. governments (although not to renounce the parliamentary path to power).[30] The advice only played into the hands of Marshall Plan supporters. Stalin cynically and angrily used the PCF and PCI as cudgels against the West, and the parties allowed themselves to be used.

In Eastern Europe Soviet officials began to give local Communists what they had been requesting: a green light to eliminate the non-Communist opposition by means fair or foul. If in France and Italy anti-Communists had expelled Communists, in Eastern Europe Communists repaid the favor with interest. Rather than different paths, there was now the Soviet path: "communist monopoly of political power, crash industrialization programs, class struggle, and the dictatorship of the proletariat." In early 1948, Moscow signed treaties of friendship with Romania, Hungary, Bulgaria, and Finland. Since Moscow respected the Finns' capacity for resistance and hoped to avoid additional trouble with the West at the time of the Czech affair, it granted Helsinki internal political and economic autonomy in return for a friendly foreign policy. Others on the Soviet periphery were not so fortunate. The end of Stalin's hopes for co-operation with the West, and his fear of Western penetration of the satellites, precipitated the Sovietization of the East.[31]

The ERP and London Program inevitably provoked a shift in Moscow's approach to Germany. While Soviet officials continued to debate German policy, under SED pressure they began to push socialization. In late 1947 they authorized creation of paramilitary units and an anti-opposition intelligence body under the "Directorate of the Interior," the police apparatus in the Soviet zone. In September 1948 SED leaders took the bit in their mouth and (without orders from Moscow) abandoned the concept of a special German road to socialism. Even so, Stalin "still saw a united, neutral, and demilitarized German state as preferable to complete separation. In his view, the latter condition would be neither durable nor beneficial for Soviet interests in the long run."[32] Only after the birth of the Federal Republic (May 23, 1949) did Moscow authorize the declaration (October 7, 1949) of the German Democratic Republic (GDR). Although destined to become the Kremlin's favorite son, at its birth the GDR was "Stalin's unwanted child."[33]

To Each his Third Choice

The emerging division of Europe, Charles S. Maier observes, did not represent the first, or even the second-best, solution for either side. The preferred solution for both would have been to have all Europe under friendly or subordinate governments. The second-best solution was the one prevailing from roughly 1945 to 1947, in which each side retained some influence in the still-inchoate sphere of the other. The third-best solution was the division of the continent into rigid, mutually hostile blocs, rendering unlikely the conversion or takeover of one by the other, and heightening the chance of war.[34]

Who, in the final analysis, was responsible for this state of affairs? World War II created the basic parameters in which the two sides operated. At its end, each pursued an expansive definition of security and was influenced by ideological considerations. The West's attempts to weaken the Soviet grip on Eastern Europe, while taking the initiative to consolidate control over the most important parts of Germany and reduce Communist influence in France and Italy, provoked Stalin's angry and defiant reaction. By the same token, the Russians' brutal behavior in Eastern Europe and Germany, and probes toward sensitive areas beyond those occupied by the Red Army, triggered alarm and reinforced the determination of Washington and London to draw a line and push back. The list of provocative and counter-productive moves by both sides in 1945–7 is a long one. It includes U.S. "atomic diplomacy," unilateral moves in Germany, and deliberate mobilization of domestic anti-Communism. On the Soviet side, it includes attempts to intimidate Iran and Turkey, and unleashing the PCI and PCF against the Marshall Plan. New moves would be added to the list.

Was the freezing of the blocs still reversible in early 1948? Kennan, for one, saw the possibility of "a new situation" in which Moscow, having failed to control Western Europe, might be prepared "to do business seriously with us." He recommended secret discussions with Stalin to convince the Russians that it would "be worth their while (a) to reduce communist pressure elsewhere in Europe and the Middle East to a point where we can afford to withdraw all our armed forces from the continent and the Mediterranean; and (b) to acquiesce thereafter in a prolonged period of stability in Europe."[35] Kennan's suggestion was partly inspired by Lippmann, who had criticized Mr. "X" for seeming to rule out a settlement in Germany. "The history of diplomacy," Lippmann wrote, "was the history of relations among rival powers...There would be little for diplomats to do if the world consisted of partners, enjoying political intimacy, and responding to common appeals."[36]

Kennan had seen the "Czech coup" as defensive, and Moscow had neither issued direct orders to the Czech party nor offered to move troops to the border to intimidate the non-Communists. He correctly believed the Soviets neither wanted nor expected war "in the foreseeable future."[37] But General Lucius Clay, head of the U.S. occupation in Germany, saw Czech events differently. "War," he said, "could come with dramatic suddenness." An early 1948 "war scare" fed support for a step few had imagined six months earlier: a transatlantic alliance. In December 1947 London and Paris launched a defense pact they hoped the Americans would eventually join. The initiative is evidence for the later thesis that the budding American protectorate was an "empire by invitation."[38] It is also true that the Europeans issued their "invitation" with the State Department's blessing and after indications Washington would respond positively. Following the signature of the Brussels Treaty (March 17, 1948), the United States and the pact's adherents (Britain, France, Belgium, the Netherlands, and Luxembourg) negotiated what became the North Atlantic Treaty in April 1949.

For Kennan, an alliance was a gift on a silver platter to the Soviets looking for ways to legitimize their presence in the satellites. And it was the beginning of the end of the policy that assumed European recovery and unity would allow the Americans to withdraw. Other U.S. officials were increasingly convinced that Soviet aggressiveness and Western Europe's eagerness for protection obliged the United States to remain. For Bevin and the French foreign minister Georges Bidault, a transatlantic alliance was a way to kill several birds with one stone. Its main objectives were to deter and, if necessary, repel an attack, and to involve the United States from the start. The alliance had an additional, unstated, rationale: to contain Germany while using it for defensive purposes. Hence the famous remark that the North Atlantic Treaty's aim was "to keep the Americans in, the Russians out, and the Germans down."[39]

For Stalin, the London program and nascent alliance were a strategic nightmare. An initial reaction was to avoid further provocation. Moscow told Yugoslavia to drop plans to annex Albania and call off support for the Greek Communists. Disagreement on these issues, and Stalin's wish to cut the proud, popular Tito down to size, were behind the break between the two in early 1948. Stalin made his next move, reminiscent of the unleashing of the PCF and PCI, from a position of growing weakness. As the allies completed the London Program and introduced the new German currency in Berlin, the Russians cut ground communications between Western Germany and the capital. Stalin hoped to compel the Allies to reopen negotiations on Germany or, failing that, to force them out of Berlin. The Allies replied with the legendary "Berlin airlift," using transport planes to bring in coal, bread, milk, and chocolate for months on end. Discussion of the Atlantic pact moved forward in the charged atmosphere of the blockade. West Berliners rallied around their charismatic socialist mayor, Ernst Reuter, in defying the Soviets and expressing gratitude to their U.S. and British rescuers. Seeing the game was up, Stalin ended the blockade on May 9, 1949. From his actions, it is obvious that Stalin had felt more threatened by, and resisted more vigorously, the consolidation of the blocs than had the Western powers. The division not only defeated his original aims. It left the West in control of the lion's share of Europe's wealth. But his "aggressive crudeness," albeit defensive in purpose, had served to accelerate the process.[40] Thanks to Stalin, Hitler's capital managed to rebrand itself as the symbol of Western freedom and resistance to the barbarians from the East.[41]

On June 28, 1948, early in the blockade, Truman ordered sixty long-range B-29 bombers to forward bases in Britain. The planes were not configured to carry atomic weapons, but the message to Moscow was unmistakable: if war came, the United States would launch an atomic attack on the Soviet Union. The outcome of the crisis suggested a pair of lessons. The first was that, although U.S. possession of the bomb had not produced political or territorial concessions from the Soviets, it had presumably helped to deter them from trying to take West Berlin. The existence of the bomb had reinforced the status quo. Some observers drew another lesson which, although far more dubious, was pregnant with consequences for the near future: if the Soviet Union had possessed its own bomb, it would probably have moved on West Berlin. Indeed, when technically able to do so, it might well launch a preventive nuclear attack on the United States.[42]

*   *   *

In Kennan, Stalin had a kind of odd analogue as well as a keen student. Kennan persisted in thinking Europe's division was avoidable, but his favored policies tended to reinforce the split. After Tito's break with Moscow, Kennan supported patient cultivation of Belgrade and promotion of "Communist heresy" elsewhere.[43] Mistakenly assuming U.S. efforts had decisively influenced the 1948 Italian elections, Kennan and others supported "a 'directorate' for overt and covert political warfare." An Office of Policy Coordination (OPC) began operations in September 1948. In 1948–9, Kennan helped to inspire and supervise its projects including recruitment of Eastern European refugees for intelligence and paramilitary activities, and the launching of Radio Free Europe and Radio Liberty.[44] But encouraging Titoism elsewhere and stepping up covert action proved counter-productive. Tito's break may have been "as important for Communism as Martin Luther's proclamation was for the Roman Catholic Church," but Stalin and his allies conducted a ruthless counter-reformation.[45] When Kennan wrote later that the results of statesmanship never "bear anything other than an ironic relation to what the statesman in question intended to achieve and thought he was achieving," he might have been referring to the OPC.[46]

Meanwhile, under Kennan's supervision, the State Department prepared a possible alternative to the London Program. Known as "Program A," it foresaw a reunited, demilitarized Germany, and the withdrawal of occupying forces to peripheral garrison areas.[47] Like Stalin, Kennan believed the Germans *themselves* were unalterably opposed to partition. Forcing them to swallow it would play into the hands of the Communists and/or give rise to a new revanchism.[48] Uniting and demilitarizing Germany through agreement with Moscow would give the Red Army a graceful exit from Central Europe just as the Tito virus seemed to be making its presence problematical. The possibility could not be excluded that without such an exit, Moscow might provoke hostilities. Program A would also gracefully remove the Western powers from their precarious perch in Berlin, a problem dramatically evident in 1948–9.

Stalin, had he known of Program A, might have been interested. But practically everyone on the Western side was opposed.[49] In May 1949 the

New York Times revealed that Washington was still considering reunification and disengagement. The article, and the hostile, panicky reactions of the British and French it provoked, sank Program A.[50] Konrad Adenauer, the elderly but vigorous Christian Democratic Union (CDU) leader, also opposed the plan. According to his "policy of strength," the pressure and attraction exerted by a robust West Germany on East Germany would eventually bring reunification on Western terms. Time would tell if Adenauer was right, but it was clear by mid-1949 that the view of Germany underpinning Program A was too rooted in history to capture the novelty of the situation. Like Stalin, Kennan overestimated the appeal of pan-German nationalism, as opposed to hunger for economic well-being and political tranquility. Neither had foreseen how anti-Communism and the experience of the blockade would help to forge an emotional bond between the Germans and the Allies.[51]

THE COLD WAR AS HISTORY

Why was there a Cold War? Historians, memoirists, and commentators took up the question soon after World War II. Intentionally or otherwise (and to varying degrees), contributions to the scholarly debate about causes have always been linked to the contemporaneous debate about the foreign and security policies of the United States and Europe. With rare exceptions, Cold War historiography was politicized from the start.

Three or four tendencies, or schools of thought, emerged in the vast English-language literature. According to the influential "orthodox" account, the conflict was unavoidable owing to the nature of Soviet objectives and Stalin's character. It was an illusion to believe that the "Uncle Joe" of pro-Soviet wartime propaganda corresponded to reality. Stalin was no horse-trading statesman or American-style political boss, but a ruthless dictator determined to extend his totalitarian system— identical in its basic features to Hitler's—far beyond the strict requirements of Soviet security. Nothing the United States and Britain might have done would have persuaded him to moderate his designs.

Members of the orthodox school were mainly liberal internationalists, or at least backers of the official Western line. They believed in the necessity of American leadership and the prospect of a harmonious world based on the spread of democracy and capitalism. They were not uncritical of U.S. behavior: the retreat to isolationism after 1918, and failure to confront the dictators in the 1930s, were grave errors, and the United States bore some responsibility for the avoidable catastrophe of World War II. For the orthodox historians, and liberal internationalists in general, the post-1945 period represented a second chance to accomplish America's historic mission. Thanks to the lessons of 1918–39, and a generation of tough-minded, far-sighted leaders (Truman, Marshall, Acheson; on the British side, Churchill and Bevin), the United States and its allies managed to contain Communism and build a lasting peace.[1]

A fundamental weakness in the orthodox account was its difficulty in admitting, or even seeing, the elements of self-interest and ambition in Western policies. The United States did aim to perpetuate its post-war position of economic and military supremacy. Its liberal economic program was tailored to U.S. needs. It was determined to deny Soviet influence over the Turkish Straits, northern Iran, and elsewhere of the sort it exercised over its Western Hemisphere "near abroad." A related weakness was the orthodox account's simplistic and mechanical view of Soviet policy (as if Moscow's actions were ideologically pre-programmed and unconnected to Western actions and the USSR's war experience), and of Moscow's relations with other parts of the Communist world (as if the Soviet Union were always dictating events in its sphere and developments there unfolded according to a master-plan).

By the early 1960s, the orthodox interpretation was ripe for revision. Stalin had died in 1953, and East–West tensions subsided after the Cuban missile crisis of 1962. The 1960s cultural climate encouraged the jettisoning of dogma and the defiance of authority. Above all, the Vietnam War led scholars to focus on the roots of America's "arrogance of power" and imperial excesses. A new generation of historians, writing from a variety of left-wing perspectives, began an assault on the orthodox position around 1965.

According to the basic New Left or "revisionist" account, the Cold War was the inevitable result of *American* expansionism. U.S. behavior (officially sanctioned by the turn-of-century "Open Door" doctrine, point three of Wilson's Fourteen Points, and the war aims of FDR) was driven by American capitalism's hunger for new markets and investment opportunities. The U.S. capitalist and foreign policy elites were interchangeable. Marx, after all, had said that the state was the general staff of the bourgeoisie. The only way to bring an end to America's predatory policies was a radical redistribution of wealth and power *within* the United States. Post-war Soviet policy had been essentially defensive. If Roosevelt's progressive government had leaned toward recognition of Moscow's legitimate security requirements, Truman's had behaved aggressively, causing the Russians to react. In France, Italy, Greece, and elsewhere, the Americans helped reactionary forces to defeat the left, frustrating hopes for reform.[2]

Revisionism provided a needed correction to orthodoxy but replaced one stereotypical view of the USSR with another, while failing to admit (or see) that Soviet actions had raised legitimate fears in the West. It also advanced a simplistic view of capitalism and its connection to foreign policy. Some influential businessmen were outward-looking and expansionist, but others were domestic-oriented and isolationist. Interestingly, the outward-looking and expansionist sectors of American capitalism tended to favor improved relations with the Soviet Union. The "liberal accommodationist" camp within, or close to, the Roosevelt administration had included W. Averell Harriman (Brown Brothers, Harriman bank), Edward Stettinius (U.S. Steel Corp.), Will Clayton (Anderson, Clayton and Co., the world's biggest cotton exporter), and Thomas Lamont (J. P. Morgan bank). Small and medium-sized businessmen (Main St. as opposed to Wall St.) were more inclined to support the Republicans and the notion of an anti-Communist crusade. Revisionism provoked indignant reactions by some of the protagonists of U.S. policy, seeking to "set the record straight," as well as replies by established and emerging orthodox historians.[3]

At the dawn of containment, a third group of scholars and observers tried to stake out a more detached position and view the East–West contest from a longer-term perspective. According to the so-called realists, international political life was essentially a struggle for power in a world of limited resources and lacking central authority. The Cold War was the latest in a never-ending cycle of struggles to dominate the European continent. Since World War II led to a power vacuum in Europe, it was inevitable that the United States and the USSR would try to fill it and collide in the process. But the realists were harshly critical of the quality of recent statesmanship. The intellectually rigorous practitioners of the eighteenth century had (allegedly) waged wars for limited ends and heeded the requirements of a balance of power. The pseudo-statesmen of the twentieth had (allegedly) succumbed to the influence of vindictive publics and universalist ideologies (Wilsonianism and Communism) and been pulled into the vortex of "total war." The world wars and the Cold War were throwbacks to the pernicious religious conflicts of the sixteenth and seventeenth centuries in which each side had attempted to impose its way of life.

Writing of America's demonization of the enemy and utopian war aims in 1917–19, George Kennan observed: "History does not forgive us our national mistakes because they are explicable in terms of our domestic politics...A nation which excuses its own failures by the sacred untouchableness of its own habits can excuse itself into complete disaster."[4] As Kennan suggested, for the realist, as well as orthodox and revisionist interpretations, Woodrow Wilson was a seminal figure. For the orthodox, he was the prophet of a new world order based on collective security and U.S. leadership; for the revisionist, spokesman-in-chief of American liberal imperialism; for the realist, a Don Quixote seeking to abolish war and spread Anglo-American values throughout the world.[5]

Of the realists skeptics asked: how realistic were they? Without a magic wand it was impossible to banish what had made the twentieth century radically different from the eighteenth—democratic politics, powerful mass media, all-embracing ideologies, the technical and industrial capacity for total war. Kennan, at least, was willing to face up to this problem and let the chips fall where they might. If the U.S. system was not suited to the conduct of power politics, the United States, he believed, should either stick to cultivating its own garden, or else neutralize the influence of public opinion and Congress by placing foreign policy in the hands of a small elite (or both).

Signs of a cross-fertilization among outlooks were evident by the 1970s. For the prominent orthodox historian Arthur M. Schlesinger Jr., "The Cold War could have been avoided only if the Soviet Union had not been possessed by convictions both of the infallibility of the Communist world and of the inevitability of the Communist world. These convictions transformed an impasse between national states into a religious war..." But he was prepared to admit: "It seems hard to deny...that American postwar policy created genuine difficulties for the Russians and even assumed a threatening aspect for them. All this the revisionists have rightfully and usefully emphasized."[6] In the early 1980s, orthodoxy's younger standard-bearer, John Lewis Gaddis, declared the emergence of a "post-revisionist synthesis" incorporating insights from both points of view.

The post-revisionist interpretation, according to Gaddis, acknowledged that the United States had created a kind of empire after World War II. The American elites had wielded the weapon of economic assistance abroad and manipulated public opinion (i.e. by fanning the flames of anti-Communism) at home to advance their cause. But, contrary to revisionist claims, the American empire was neither driven by economic imperatives nor imposed on unwilling and helpless victims. It was a defensive empire, driven by national security anxieties and actively solicited by its "subjects" in Europe and elsewhere because it provided protection against the Communist menace. "Post-revisionism" accepted revisionism's claim that Stalin did not operate from a masterplan in an attempt to conquer Eurasia. He was "a cagey and insecure opportunist, taking advantage of such tactical openings as arose to expand Soviet influence but without any long-term strategy for or even very much interest in promoting the spread of communism beyond the Soviet sphere."[7] The USSR did, however, bear final responsibility for the Cold War. Stalin had lacked a sense of limits, and frightened and provoked the West.[8]

There was much to be said for incorporating revisionist insights into the orthodox interpretation, and focusing on the complex relations between the superpowers and their respective clients. The Cold War was full of instances where weak and vulnerable actors were able to exert influence on the strong. But carried too far, post-revisionism posited a vacuum of American ideas and ambitions. Moreover, it would have surprised millions of left-wing and neutralist Europeans, Asians, and Latin Americans to learn that U.S. overlord-ship was an "empire by invitation." Some critics dismissed post-revisionism as "orthodoxy plus archives," and denied the existence of a new synthesis.[9] Indeed, the next phase of the debate, coinciding with the end of the Cold War and the gradual opening of Soviet, Chinese and Eastern European archives, showed that talk of consensus was premature.

Much of the so-called new history of the Cold War that poured forth after 1989 constituted not so much new interpretations as fresh attempts to advance familiar arguments (or weave them together in novel ways) using previously unavailable evidence. What was genuinely new in the debate was that former Communist-bloc historians, many writing in English, had joined the fray. Based on Soviet evidence, a pair of Russian historians argued (as post-revisionists had suggested) that Stalin did not have a grand design or timetable to conquer Europe, and had sought post-war co-operation with the West. Breathing new life into orthodoxy, however, they concluded (as some realists and post-revisionists had suggested) that he was not simply pursuing a tsarist foreign policy but driven by ideological assumptions and objectives: the capitalists would never tolerate the USSR's existence over the long run, and Communism was destined to triumph across the globe. Stalin's aggressiveness and miscalculations, for example in the Turkish Straits, were a basic cause of the Cold War.[10] In the mid-1990s, Gaddis crafted a narrative claiming to summarize how recent scholarship had added to knowledge of the Cold War's origins and development. His conclusion was that the post-revisionists had been correct to advance the notion of "empire by invitation" as opposed to the Soviets' "empire by imposition." Using new evidence of Stalin's ideological motives, and emphasizing the excesses of Soviet soldiers in Germany, Gaddis also revived the view that the Soviet dictator was not a cause, but essentially *the* cause of the Cold War. Gaddis's book foreshadowed his triumphalist overview appearing in 2005.[11]

The neo-orthodoxy of Gaddis and others was challenged by a sophisticated inheritor of the revisionist mantle, Melvin Leffler. Leffler (reflecting post-revisionist thinking) stressed less the economic determinants of American behavior than U.S. leaders' expansive definition of security, and determination to keep the "preponderance of power" inherited from World War II. His argument showed the ways in which U.S. policy toward Eastern Europe, Germany, the Turkish Straits, and elsewhere had alarmed Moscow and suggested hostile American intentions.[12] In research complementing Leffler's, Eduard Mark cast further light on the Soviet side of the story. His work helped to establish a point made earlier by the post-revisionists: Stalin had preferred to advance his objectives gradually and pragmatically (he had envisioned the indefinite participation of Communists in coalition governments), rather than in a way that would compromise ties with the West. A number of factors (including U.S. attempts to dilute Soviet influence in Eastern Europe and the lack of non-Communist interlocutors) prompted him to change his approach. Other historians portrayed an at times reckless and impulsive Stalin, determined to reap the fruits of victory and advance Communism, but indignant and alarmed by Western moves. There were also path-breaking, multi-archival works on Chinese foreign policy, and on the complex Stalin-Mao relationship that left a legacy of distrust eventually exploitable by the West.[13]

Studies appearing several decades after 1989 clearly indicated that the manner in which the conflict had ended, and new archival evidence, did not serve to bury the old controversies. An Australian-born historian took Roosevelt and Truman to task for their attempts to conciliate the USSR in tones echoing conservative Republican attacks on the Democrats in the late 1940s. A major biography of Acheson offered a vindication of its subject's "uncomplicated strategy of amassing countervailing power," embodied in the controversial analysis *cum* strategy, NSC 68. Enterprising historians shed new light on Soviet espionage activities in the United States. But they also used newly declassified documents to reveal U.S. plans and covert activities aiming to subvert Communist control over Eastern Europe and destabilize the Kremlin. Another study departed from the vogue of multi-archival "international history" to remind readers how U.S. domestic politics deeply conditioned foreign policy. Meanwhile, a British historian offered the most favorable Western portrait of Stalin in forty years: not only had the Soviet dictator been a great war leader, he had assiduously tried to make the Grand Alliance work. A Russian historian's balanced and well documented overview of Soviet foreign policy left no doubt that Stalin was the captive of a schematic world-view, but also of the illusion that cordial relations with the United States might continue. If any conclusion could be drawn from post-1989 scholarship, it was that both East and West had behaved provocatively and furnished the other side with abundant reasons for alarm.[14]

CHAPTER 4
THE GLOBALIZATION AND MILITARIZATION OF THE CONTEST, 1949–1953

If a historical perspective blinded George Kennan to the novelty of the post-war German situation, it allowed him to see other events with an unusual degree of detachment. In September 1952 he wrote of a "sort of cosmic misunderstanding." Stalin's moves in 1948 had been defensive reactions to the Marshall Plan and London Program. "Nevertheless, a firm opinion crystallized in Western circles that there was a danger of a Soviet attack." The North Atlantic Treaty initiative, accompanied by exaggerations of Soviet capabilities, must have convinced Moscow that the West probably intended to start a war as soon as the requisite strength had been created. Mutual misunderstanding had been "considerably heightened" by the outbreak of the Korean War on June 25, 1950. Although there was no evidence that the North Korean invasion "was part of any global pattern of projected Soviet military moves," that is how some interpreted it. By the same token, Western steps in late 1950–early 1951 (General Douglas MacArthur's bid to "liberate" North Korea, the U.S. proclamation of a national emergency and massive rearmament, the decision to raise German units, the appointment of a U.S. supreme commander for Europe, and transfer of four divisions to Germany) were presumably seen in Moscow as suggesting a Western-initiated war.[1]

Kennan would not have been surprised to learn that Stalin had secretly summoned Eastern European leaders to the Kremlin in January 1951. He ordered them to launch a build-up for completion in three years, to coincide with Soviet rearmament. Accounts of the three-day meeting differ. According to the Czech defense minister, Stalin spoke of an invasion of Western Europe in 1954. According to his Romanian colleague, Stalin said preparations were necessary because of "the imperialists' way of thinking: they habitually attack unarmed or poorly armed countries...but they stay clear of well-armed countries." It may be that Stalin viewed a war started by the West as inevitable and wanted to be ready. World Wars I and II had advanced Communism. Under the right circumstances, so would World War III.[2]

Kennan's 1952 analysis practically ignored several developments and their impact on Western perceptions. On August 30, 1949, the heads of the Soviet nuclear program informed Stalin that the previous day, in the remote steppes of Kazakhstan, "there was obtained the explosion of the U.S.S.R.'s first atomic bomb."[3] On October 1, 1949, Mao Zedong, Communist leader in the civil war with the Nationalists of Chiang Kai-shek, declared the founding of the People's Republic of China (PRC). Stalin had tried not to antagonize the Americans in China, and discounted Mao's chances. But he now had a major ally in the Far East. In late 1949, moreover, thanks to a tip-off to Moscow by Kim Philby, a British spy, Stalin's ally Enver Hoxha foiled U.S. and British attempts to overthrow the Communist regime in Albania. Rollback was failing on the ground.

Kennan did not inflate the significance of the Soviet atomic test. In early 1950 he reminded the public that Moscow preferred to triumph thanks to "the inner contradictions of the capitalist system" rather than military action.[4] He intuitively grasped Moscow's reason for rushing to get the weapon. "Had it taken another year or year and a half for us to develop the bomb," Stalin told those who had made it, "we would have probably 'tasted' it on ourselves."[5] For Stalin, the bomb was not an offensive weapon but a deterrent. As for China, Kennan discounted the backward giant's importance compared to its highly industrialized neighbor, Japan, now under U.S. control. Nor was he ready to admit that covert action in the satellites only encouraged ferocious repression. The West, in sum, was not losing the Cold War and remained much stronger than the East.

But the reigning outlook was far more pessimistic. The Truman administration reacted to the Soviet test and the "fall of China" in ways that compounded the "cosmic misunderstanding" Kennan later identified. Simultaneously, domestic trends pushed the United States toward deeper entanglement in Asia. The result was a set of world-spanning commitments few had imagined in 1945.

Washington's Strategic Assessment

The U.S. response came first with Truman's decision (January 30, 1950) to develop the fusion or hydrogen bomb. In February–March, a panel of State and Defense Department officials followed with a deeply alarmist assessment. They submitted their top secret report, known as NSC 68, to Truman on April 14, 1950. Its main author was Paul H. Nitze, a former Wall Street banker and protégé of Forrestal and Acheson who had replaced Kennan as Policy Planning Staff head at the end of 1949. Nitze (born 1911) combined his generation's abiding angst about vulnerability to surprise attack with an anti-Soviet zealotry and faith in military might.[6]

A pair of preoccupations animated NSC 68. The first, incorporating the conclusions of an earlier Joint Intelligence Committee report (JIC 502) was the looming risk of an atomic Pearl Harbor. Once the Soviet Union had 200 bombs and the means to deliver them, it might well see the advantages Nitze and some others thought would accrue to the initiator of an atomic war, and carry out a devastating strike on the mobilization base of the United States. NSC 68 predicted the Soviets would have that capacity in mid-1954. The second fear concerned the impact of the changing military balance on Western Europe. With the United States *itself* vulnerable to atomic attack, its willingness to defend Europe would be questioned. Moscow could then use its conventional superiority either to carry out piecemeal aggression, or intimidate the Europeans into accepting neutrality or Soviet domination. Present trends might force the United States to surrender Europe and retreat into a beleaguered isolation:

> The risk that we may...be prevented or too long delayed in all needful measures to maintain the integrity and vitality of our system is great. The risk that our allies will lose their determination is greater. And the risk that in this manner a descending spiral of too little too late, of doubt and recrimination, may present us with ever narrower and more desperate alternatives, is the greatest risk of all.[7]

To avert this Mackinderian nightmare, NSC 68 called for a massive conventional build-up (requiring a tripling of the current defense budget of $13 billion). The purpose would be to deter, and if necessary defeat, a Soviet attack, while reducing reliance on nuclear weapons. The build-up would also buy time and serve as a shield for a "vigorous political offensive" designed to roll back Soviet gains, reduce the Kremlin's power inside the U.S.S.R., and compel it to abandon its supposed design for world conquest. Among other steps, NSC 68 recommended intensified covert "economic and political and psychological warfare with a view to fomenting and supporting unrest and revolt in selected strategic satellite countries." The document put the misleading term "containment" in quotation marks and frankly defined it as "a policy of calculated and gradual coercion." NSC 68, in effect, recommended a program for victory in the near term. In its quasi-apocalyptic view that time was working against the United States, that the choice was between a dramatic expansion of power-in-being or retreat and submission, NSC 68 is the purest expression of Hobbesian fatalism in the annals of American statecraft. NSC 68's was the logic of the frontier struggle transposed onto the world stage: win or die.[8]

NSC 68's authors did not invent "roll back," a goal since NSC 20/4 (November 1948). Nor was one of NSC 68's core concerns, the conventional military imbalance, imaginary. In 1950 there were perhaps twenty-five combat-ready Soviet divisions in Eastern Europe, compared to two U.S. divisions in West Germany. Germany's own military power was non-existent. The French army's best cadres were engaged in a *guerre sale* in Indochina gainst the Communist-nationalist Viet Minh. Britain's World War II army had stood down. Kennan later compared the situation to that of an unarmed man facing a dog inside a walled-in garden.[9] His advice, in effect, was let sleeping dogs alone. But those less familiar with the animal preferred to have a stick, even if brandishing it was bound to provoke the dog. Kennan's fable, moreover, neglected to mention the garden's nervous European inhabitants. To feel reassured, pro-Western leaders and publics wanted to see what Acheson called "situations of strength" on the ground.[10]

NSC 68 was nonetheless a flawed analysis and recommended an approach that would prove unsustainable and self-defeating. As Bohlen argued, Soviet leaders were cautious men unlikely to risk a war that might undermine their internal power. As long as Stalin was alive, atomic weapons were not assigned to forces or integrated into military doctrine. NSC 68 also inflated Soviet capabilities. The estimation of 200 atomic bombs by 1954 was inaccurate, and the USSR did not have an intercontinental bomber until 1955. Of a total of 175 Soviet divisions estimated by the United States, many existed only on paper, or at partial strength.[11]

It is doubtful whether NSC 68's authors consciously intended "symmetrical" or indiscriminate worldwide containment.[12] But in its assumptions that Soviet ambitions were unlimited, that "a defeat of free institutions anywhere is a defeat everywhere," and that its interests thrust on America "the responsibility of world leadership," NSC 68's was the logic of global interventionism.[13] Finally, in its fixation with a preponderance of power as the basis on which to pursue an offensive strategy, NSC 68 excluded the option of compromise. Negotiations could only take the form of unilateral Soviet concessions. As if to flaunt the point, Acheson publicly laid out ten preconditions for talks that Moscow was sure to reject.[14]

Asia and the Domestic State of Siege

It was not only the Democratic administration's ample conception of U.S. responsibilities that pulled it toward entanglement beyond Europe and the Northern Tier. It was pushed and prodded in that direction by its domestic enemies. America had been a Pacific power since the acquisition of Hawaii and the Philippines, and declared an interest in China's territorial integrity and equal access to its market in the Open Door notes of 1899–1900. After Pearl Harbor, elements of the army and navy, and Republican politicians, opposed the Anglo-American decision to focus on Germany before Japan. This Europe versus Asia tension persisted after 1945. "Asia-firsters" demanded more aid to the historic enemy of the Chinese Communists, Generalissimo Chiang Kai-shek. Since early in the century, moreover, businessmen, missionaries, military officers, and journalists with ties to the country had promoted a China myth:

The myth spoke of great riches to be had in China and millions of souls to be saved for Christ. It described a barbarian people who labored diligently and exhibited a remarkable cleverness and aptitude for Western learning. Most importantly, it referred to the dark oppressions that [European] imperialism visited upon the unfortunate heathen and extolled America's virtuous self-restraint. The American people...were, in fact, great friends of China. The United States, a nation above such base behavior, never indulged in territorial or economic exploitation of the Chinese. Moreover, the United States had helped to protect China from dismemberment with its Open Door policy, for which the Chinese felt boundless gratitude. Sino-American relations had always been good and, if preserved from the evil influences of alien ideologies [e.g., Communism], would continue to prosper.[15]

In the 1940s subscribers to these views coalesced into an informal alliance known as the "China lobby." Members included Henry Luce (born Penglai City, China), publisher of *Life*, *Time*, and *Fortune* magazines, the columnists Joseph and Stewart Alsop, Air Force General Claire Chennault, Senator William Knowland of California, Congressman Walter Judd of Minnesota, Frederick McKee, a Pittsburgh manufacturer, Alfred Kohlberg, a New York-based lace importer, and William Loeb, editor of the *Manchester* [NH] *Morning Union*. Backed by the Nationalist government, they portrayed the Methodist Chiang as the champion of Christian Civilization. The lobby became a potent force thanks to two developments in 1948–9.[16]

The first was the growing militancy of the Republican right wing, with which the lobby overlapped. The catalyst for the right's rise was Truman's victory, notwithstanding a divided Democratic Party, in November 1948.[17] Many Republicans blamed their party's centrist candidate, Thomas Dewey, his adviser, the Wall St. lawyer John Foster Dulles, and Senate leader Vandenberg, who had refrained from attacking the administration's foreign policy. In the name of "bipartisanship," they had let Truman off the hook. Frustrated conservatives now went on the warpath against "passive" and "immoral" containment. The Democrats, they charged, had lost Eastern Europe thanks to something worse than incompetence—treachery. House and Senate investigations, some of which degenerated into anti-Communist "witch hunts," followed. Under political pressure, the Truman administration had already begun reviews of federal employee loyalty. Several hundred were fired and thousands pressured to resign.[18]

The second reason for the lobby's rise was the outcome of the civil war in China. Despite their initial superiority, the Nationalists were on the verge of collapse, and Chiang had fled to Taiwan by early 1949. The lobby blamed this latest disaster on the State Department. China experts who had predicted a Communist victory and/or favored exploring the possibility of using Mao as an "Asian Tito," were the particular objects of their wrath. The Chiang loyalists were right that FDR had made a deal with Stalin behind the Nationalists' back at Yalta. It restored Russian control of the warm-water base of Port Arthur (Lushun), in Manchuria, and its rail connection to Siberia. But the Nationalists themselves had endorsed the arrangement (by which Moscow recognized them as the legitimate government) in the Soviet–Chinese Treaty of August 1945.[19] The lobby was also right that Truman had been less than wholehearted in backing Chiang, and had sent Marshall to try to mediate the Nationalist–Communist conflict in 1946. But he had also sent marines to northern China in September 1945 to deter the Communists. During Marshall's mission, and after the outbreak of civil war in 1946, Washington continued to aid Chiang.[20]

Chiang's failure lent credence to the journalist Theodore White's observation that his regime had combined the cruelty of the Spanish Inquisition with the corruption of Tammany Hall (the Democratic Party political machine in New York).[21] He could have added the military ineptitude of Fascist Italy. After mid-1949, Washington pursued an ambiguous, "wait and see" policy. In its China White Paper (August 5, 1949), the State Department washed its hands of Chiang, arguing that no amount of U.S. aid could have saved his cause.[22] But unlike the British, concerned with retaining Hong Kong, the Americans were not yet prepared to recognize the Communists, and did not interfere with the Nationalists' illegal naval blockade of mainland ports.

Washington remained alert to the possibility that PRC–Soviet tensions (caused, most recently, by Stalin's deal with Chiang) might be exploited. In late 1949 Acheson persuaded Truman to reject U.S.

military advice to aid Chiang on Taiwan. Defending Taiwan against a probable Communist attack would incur Chinese hatred and undermine a policy of trying to detach Beijing from Moscow.[23] In January 1950 Washington signaled that it was open to a strategic relationship with Beijing. Truman reiterated the position dating from the 1943 Cairo conference that Taiwan should be returned to China. In a January 12 speech at the Washington Press Club, Acheson warned China of Soviet designs on Manchuria. Answering a question, he said the U.S. defense perimeter included Japan and the Philippines but did not mention South Korea, Indochina, or Taiwan.[24]

Why, despite Acheson's valiant effort to disentangle the United States from Chiang, did Washington decide to defend Taiwan and forswear attempts to woo "Red China."? There were two reasons. Either would have sufficed. The first was the lobby's furious reaction to the White Paper and evident aim to write off Taiwan. Matters took a turn for the worse on February 9, 1950. In a speech in Wheeling, West Virginia, a gifted demagogue and former marine, Senator Joseph McCarthy of Wisconsin, made his national debut. McCarthy claimed Acheson was shielding 205 Communists in the State Department. Although unable to produce the list, McCarthy would continue his investigations until 1954, with considerable public backing. His favorite targets were intellectuals and policymakers considered by many to be part of a treasonous cabal that had infiltrated government, the press, and academia. McCarthy was particularly popular among fellow Irish Catholics who had suffered discrimination at the hands of Protestants. The Irish-American millionaire Joseph Kennedy (although a Democrat) was a prominent supporter and his son Robert ("Bobby") Kennedy worked for McCarthy for a time.

Soviet intelligence *had* penetrated the British and U.S. governments, recruiting idealistic Communists and "fellow travellers," even if the KGB's networks had been dealt a serious blow in 1945.[25] A notorious case concerned former State Department official Alger Hiss, pursued by Republican Congressman Richard M. Nixon in 1948. Although Hiss and his supporters insisted he was innocent, evidence coming to light in the 1990s established he had worked with the GRU, Soviet military intelligence. Hiss's conviction for perjury in January 1950 coincided with the exploding Taiwan controversy. After the verdict, Acheson announced:

"I do not intend to turn my back on Alger Hiss." The statement reflected Acheson's loyalty to Alger's brother, his former law partner Donald Hiss, and contempt for the administration's tormentors. But Acheson was now a target. His effectiveness was compromised just as it was needed to defend the administration's policy on Taiwan.[26]

Immediately after North Korea's offensive, Truman ordered the Seventh Fleet to the Taiwan Strait to defend the island.[27] But he had already moved in that direction in March–April 1950. To lower the political heat, Acheson had put Deputy Under-Secretary Dean Rusk in charge of the Far Eastern Bureau and brought John Foster Dulles into the department as an adviser. Rusk favored making Taiwan a United Nations trusteeship and defending it against the Communists. With its back to the wall politically, the administration would have been hard-pressed to abandon Taiwan even if the Korean War had not begun. Indeed, it is hard to believe that the composers of NSC 68 were unaffected by the poisoned Washington atmosphere in which they deliberated. Consciously or not, the Truman administration's offensive strategy was shaped by the need to break the domestic state of siege.

It Takes Two to Tango: Mao, Stalin, and the Coming of the Korean War

Acheson recalled: "between the bungling incompetence" of Chiang and "the intransigence of Mao," U.S. choices "were small indeed."[28] He was right that an "Asian Tito" policy required a Chinese partner. The second reason for the fatal turn in relations is that there was no such partner. Mao had been open to co-operation in 1944, but Washington continued to aid Chiang until 1949. Mao had also been forced to adapt himself to Stalin's shifting line. Stalin had rarely shown confidence in Mao's prospects and wanted to avoid a showdown with the Americans. This explains his decision to secure the USSR's "just rewards" through a deal with the Nationalists. Thereafter he zigzagged in response to U.S. policy. When the Americans assisted Chiang in controlling northern China and made clear they would exclude the Russians from Japan, the Red Army increased its aid to the Communists in the northeast. When this threatened to provoke a confrontation, the Soviets desisted. After a brief thaw coinciding with Byrnes's December 1945 trip to Moscow, Washington embraced containment. On February 12, 1946, it published the secret Yalta Far East agreement, triggering an anti-Soviet outcry in China. In response, the Red Army announced its withdrawal from Manchuria, and handover of the area to the forces of the Chinese Communist Party (CCP).[29]

With the Communist victory in sight in early 1949, Anastas Mikoyan (born 1895), a rising Politburo member of Armenian origin, visited CCP headquarters. Mao explained his principles of "making a fresh start" and "cleaning house before entertaining guests." The latter referred to the hated unequal treaties imposed by foreigners, and exclusive enclaves carved from Chinese territory. The Communists refused to recognize the status of diplomats accredited to the Nationalists. The elderly U.S. consul in Mukden, Angus Ward, and members of his staff, were held incommunicado, tried on various charges, and deported in late 1949. In June 1949 Mao's number two, Liu Shaoqi, visited Moscow. Stalin promised help and encouraged the Chinese to sponsor (under the USSR's overall leadership) revolutions in the Far East. On June 30, shortly after Liu's arrival in Moscow, Mao dispelled any doubt about the CCP's position: China must "unite in a common struggle with those nations of the world that treat us as equal . . . that is, ally ourselves with the Soviet Union . . . We must lean to one side."[30] The stage was set for Mao's own trek across Siberia to Moscow in December 1949.

Mao and his comrades were driven by a burning sense of victim-hood and ambition vis-à-vis the West. They were determined to liquidate the subordinate relationship with the great powers and restore China to its rightful place in the international system. They planned a revolutionary transformation of China's state and society, requiring high levels of popular mobilization and vigilance. Before the "lean to one side" pronouncement, there had been several secret meetings between the U.S. ambassador John Leighton Stuart and CCP officials, but they had done nothing to assuage Mao's hostility or alter his preference for a Soviet connection. The United States had been part and parcel of China's humiliation. It was the lone-surviving capitalist great power and might well attack China and/or try to subvert it. The last thing Mao intended or expected was to live and let live with America. The United States was a useful as well as a natural enemy, just as the Soviet Union (or so it seemed) was a useful and natural friend.[31]

For Stalin, the Soviet atomic bomb and the Nationalists' defeat signaled a favorable shift in the international correlation of forces, but he proceeded with "characteristic caution."[32] He had no intention of allowing a rival center of Communist influence.[33] He was especially reluctant to give up the gains from his treaty with Chiang Kai-shek. When Mao requested an invitation and arrived in Moscow determined to scrap the patently unequal treaty, he discovered that Stalin was prepared to revise but not replace it. Mao showed his own steely resolve and the mission risked collapse. Following Mikoyan's advice that a new treaty would not necessarily be harmful, and not wishing to break with Mao, Stalin changed his mind. The Sino-Soviet treaty of friendship, alliance, and mutual assistance, signed on February 14, 1950, provided for $300 million in credits to China, and the return of Lushun after a peace treaty with Japan.[34] But before agreeing, Stalin seems to have surmised that he could have his cake and eat it: an accord consolidating ties to the PRC and giving the lie to Soviet designs on Manchuria, but also alternatives to Lushun serving to deter Japanese aggression. The alternatives were the southern Korean ports of Pusan and Inchon.[35] Whether Stalin's object was Manchuria or southern Korea, the rationale was the same: expand to secure.

After the breakdown of a tenuous Soviet–U.S. agreement to create a single government under a United Nations Trusteeship, and the withdrawal of occupying troops, Korea was a tinderbox.[36] Kim Il Sung, the former anti-Japanese partisan leader and strongman of the Soviet-sponsored Democratic People's Republic of Korea (DPRK), was eager to unite the country. His southern counterpart, the Princeton-educated Methodist minister Syngman Rhee, had the same idea. The forces of his U.S.-backed Republic of Korea (ROK) provoked frequent shooting incidents along the 38th parallel division line and battled Communist guerrillas in the south.[37] In September 1949 the Kremlin rejected Kim's request to support the seizure of the Ongjin peninsula and Kaesong region of South Korea on the grounds that conditions were not ripe for a southern uprising and war would "give the Americans an excuse" to interfere. In late January 1950 however, Stalin told Kim he was prepared to help. The Soviet leader had studied Acheson's January 12 warning to China about Soviet designs on Manchuria. This part of the speech strengthened the case for a treaty returning Lushun to China, and therefore increasing Korea's importance as an alternative. Acheson's remarks on South Korea suggested the risks involved in seizing it were lower than anticipated. Mao also encouraged Stalin to think the Americans would remain passive. After all, they had failed to intervene in China despite Communist anxieties. In April 1950, Kim secretly visited Moscow and received the green light for an invasion of the south.[38]

Stalin assumed the Americans would not get involved, or at least that the war would be over before they had time to do so. But he also told Kim, "If you should get kicked in the teeth, I shall not lift a finger. You have to ask Mao for all the help."[39] The North Koreans were told to seek China's advance approval. The Chinese were planning to take Taiwan and Tibet in 1950 and opposed North Korean actions that might prove a costly distraction. When Kim went to Beijing, Mao and foreign minister Zhou Enlai did not at first believe him when he said he had Stalin's backing. In answer to their query, Moscow cabled that "in light of the changed international situation" it had endorsed the attack, pending Chinese approval.[40] Since Moscow had agreed, Beijing saw little choice, even if the operation served North Korean and Soviet but not Chinese interests. Thus Stalin not only forced Mao's hand but limited Soviet liability. If necessary, it would be China which rescued Kim.

Washington's decision to send forces to South Korea immediately after June 25, 1950, and to organize a coalition under U. N. Security Council auspices, was an unpleasant surprise to Moscow and Beijing.[41] On July 13, Beijing created the Northeast Border Defense Army and began to deploy 260,000 troops on the Yalu River (the Chinese-Korean border). Once the North Koreans were in a war with the Americans, the Chinese acquired a significant stake in their success, above all in preventing U.S. forces from installing themselves in the vicinity of the Yalu. The memory of Japanese aggression against the industrial heartland of Manchuria in the 1930s, using Korea as a staging area, was fresh in their minds.

The Chinese received Soviet weaponry and Stalin's pledge to try to provide air cover should their forces move into Korea. When hopes for a quick victory faded (U.S. and ROK forces managed to hold the "Pusan perimeter" in southeast South Korea), Stalin reflected on the advantages of a prolonged Chinese–American conflict. In a late August message to the Czech leader Klement Gottwald, he noted that U.S. attention and resources would be diverted to Asia. A third world war would be postponed indefinitely, "and this would give the time necessary to consolidate socialism in Europe."[42] But after the landing of 70,000 U.S. marines at Inchon in mid-September, outflanking and then routing the North Korean army, Stalin changed his tune. His October 1, 1950, message urging China to send five or six divisions into battle did not mention Soviet backing.[43] After U.S. and ROK forces crossed the 38th parallel and drove north, Beijing and Moscow faced off in a tense, high-stakes negotiation. Although Mao was strongly inclined to intervene, he gave Stalin a provisional negative answer. Part of the leadership feared a lack of preparation and an "open conflict" with the United States, "as a consequence of which the Soviet Union can also be dragged into war."[44] Mao wanted concrete assurances of aid and sent his colleagues Zhou and Lin Biao to see Stalin at his vacation compound on the Black Sea.

A vexed Stalin reiterated his reasoning to Mao, including the point that the Americans were "not ready at present for a big war" and that by intervening China could gain favorable outcomes in both Korea and Taiwan. He added:

> Of course, I took into account [the possibility] that the USA, despite its unreadiness for a big war, could still be drawn into a big war out of [considerations of] prestige, which, in turn, would drag China into the war, and along with this draw into the war the USSR, which is bound to China by the Mutual Assistance Pact. Should we fear this? In my opinion, we should not, because together we will be stronger than the USA and England, while the other European capitalist states (with the exception of Germany which is unable to provide any assistance to the United States now) do not present serious military forces. If a war is inevitable, then let it be waged now, and not in a few years when Japanese militarism will be restored as an ally of the USA and when the USA and Japan will have a ready-made bridgehead on the continent in a form of the entire Korea run by Syngman Rhee.[45]

This message suggests that, although Stalin did not seek war or think it probable in the near future, he probably feared it less now that he had the atomic bomb and, like the Americans, saw dangers in a policy of appeasement.[46] But his purpose was to reassure the Chinese and convince *them* to save his gamble, while keeping the USSR in a supporting role. Stalin's reassurance seems to have had some effect. Mao gained the leadership's support to dispatch nine divisions to Korea, and informed Stalin on October 7. But the decision was not for immediate execution. By October 13 Stalin had given up hope of Chinese intervention and ordered Kim to evacuate his army to China and/or the USSR. Only on October 18, when Mao was convinced (thanks to the Zhou-Lin mission) that Moscow would furnish substantial aid, including air defense of Chinese cities and air cover for Chinese troops in Korea, did he order Chinese troops into the war.[47]

War of Delusions, 1950–53

Stalin's assumption that the Americans would remain detached in the Far East had discounted growing evidence to the contrary. The Truman administration had inched toward defending Taiwan, and proposed aid packages for South Korea (approved by Congress in February) and French Indochina (approved in May 1950) before the Korean War. Nor did Stalin see that the United States would consider it necessary to defend South Korea to retain its credibility as the leader of NATO. By the same token, Washington concluded in light of the Korean War that shoring up Europe's defenses, including the mobilization of German forces, could no longer be avoided. This was the opposite of what Stalin had suggested to Gottwald. The United States would not only fight in Korea, it would strengthen the "central front."

The second phase of the war had begun with Inchon, followed by the decision to push north. Reflecting the administration's previously adopted aim of destroying the North Korean army, the JCS prepared orders authorizing operations north of the 38th parallel, but only if there had been "no entry into North Korea by major Soviet or Chinese Communist forces, no announcement of intended entry, nor a threat to counter our operations militarily in North Korea." Approved with minor changes by Truman, these orders were transmitted to the commander of U.S. forces in the Far East, General Douglas MacArthur, on September 27, 1950. Defense Secretary Marshall advised MacArthur in a separate cable that he should "feel unhampered tactically and strategically to proceed north of the 38th parallel."[48]

Halting the war at this juncture would have required defying the "iron law" of American politics. The Republicans, and (polls suggested) public opinion in general, supported the north's "liberation." Along with opportunism, the decision reflected a deluded view of China. The delusion consisted in thinking the Chinese were unlikely to intervene in force because they did not feel sufficiently threatened by an offensive in the direction of their main industrial region, they lacked air and naval support, their Kremlin "masters" would not permit them, and above all because they would be unwilling to pay the cost of a major war.[49] The tendency to minimize the threat persisted despite Chinese troop movements into Manchuria and across the Yalu, Zhou's unequivocal (October 2, 1950) statement the day after ROK troops crossed the parallel that, if U.S. troops followed, China would intervene, and subsequent warnings in the Chinese press.

MacArthur and his entourage argued that China was bluffing, and even if it was not would intervene on a small scale and be vulnerable to air attacks.[50] Anyone who remembered the Japanese invasion of Manchuria, and realized the Chinese had little reason to believe U.S. pledges to stop at the Yalu, took a different view. The Americans had declared at the end of June that their military action was "solely for the purpose of restoring the Republic of Korea to the status prior to the invasion." During the summer U.S. planes, albeit accidentally, hit targets in Manchuria, MacArthur visited Chiang, raising the possibility of a U.S.–Nationalist alliance, and Navy Secretary Francis Matthews spoke of "a [preventive] war to compel cooperation for peace."[51] Matthews had been repudiated but was still at his post.

The Chinese sprang their trap in late November. Despite growing alarm over the presence of People's Liberation Army (PLA) troops, the advancing X Corps and Eighth Army were unprepared for the size and ferocity of the Chinese offensive. Seoul fell to the PLA on January 4, 1951. The longest retreat in U.S. military history caused shock and disbelief. The Republican right reflexively blamed a "crimson clique" in high circles. Truman's initial reaction was to blame Republican news-papers who, by attacking his administration, had shown the country was divided.[52] Acheson and Rusk argued that the counter-offensive was unconnected to U.S. action, could only have been planned long in advance, and must be part of a Soviet design.[53]

The mistaken belief that China was merely Moscow's puppet was in one way fortunate. It induced caution during the debate over whether to attack Chinese territory. MacArthur and some Republicans pressed for a wider war (as to a lesser degree did the JCS and even Marshall). Truman and Acheson were later prepared to approve limited air strikes on China and the transfer of atomic weapons to the Far East as a warning. But they feared that MacArthur's approach (captured in his phrase "There is no substitute for victory") would bring Soviet intervention. By the same token, they rejected British advice to end the fighting by conceding Taiwan to China. Washington adopted the middle course of "limited war": confined to Korea, aiming to restore the status quo ante bellum, and open to negotiations. When he publicly challenged this policy, MacArthur was fired and recalled to the United States.[54]

In early 1951, it was Beijing's turn to delude itself by thinking it could expel U.S. forces from Korea. In January Mao over-ruled his more cautious field commander Peng Dehuai and insisted on total victory. But the Eighth Army regrouped and counter-attacked the over-extended Chinese. After the failure of a final offensive, and punishing losses in April–May 1951, Mao contented himself with his late-1950 gains and sought a peace preserving the original border. Although bitter fighting continued, the front stabilized near the 38th parallel. With Stalin's approval, the Chinese began armistice discussions in July 1951.

The talks proved more tortuous than either side had expected. The United States and South Korea insisted that Communist prisoners of war not wanting repatriation be allowed to stay in the south. The Commu-nist side had no intention of letting captured soldiers be used for propaganda purposes and insisted on their return. A question of face for both sides prolonged the war by several years. Stalin, who saw obvious advantages in having the United States bleed, backed Beijing's line and provided planes, pilots, and anti-aircraft units to allow China to continue the war along the 38th parallel. The main losers were the the Koreans, whose country was in ruins by 1953.[55] After Stalin's death in March 1953, the Soviet leadership was ready to end the war and open a new chapter in relations with the West. By the same token, and despite threats by both sides to escalate the war in early 1953, neither Washington nor Beijing saw much advantage in prolonging the deadlock. A compromise (despite Rhee's attempt to sabotage it by releasing 25,000 North Korean prisoners) was finally reached and an armistice signed on July 27, 1953.[56]

Live and Let Live, Again

The Korean conflict was an important Cold War milestone. The United States extended its defense umbrella not only to Korea, but Taiwan, Japan, and Indochina. Although a formal U.S.–ROC (Republic of China) alliance was not signed until December 1954, Washington decided to defend Taiwan in 1950. With the U.S.–Japan peace treaty and defense pact of September 1951, Japan became an American military protectorate. It was in the context of Korea that Washington defined holding Indochina to be "essential to the security of the free world," and by late 1952 was paying much of France's bill for the war.[57]

The war reinforced the two-bloc system in Europe. As late as mid-1949, Acheson had denied that the North Atlantic alliance meant additional U.S. troops on the continent. Even NSC 68 had not called for a more direct U.S. role. It was the fear after June 25, 1950, that GDR and/or Soviet forces might attack that prompted the decisions to create West German units, appoint Eisenhower supreme commander, and adopt the risky strategy of "forward defense," with major U.S. forces on the central front. German rearmament (attempted first through an integrated European Defense Community, or EDC) was part of the price the Americans demanded of their allies in return for sending soldiers to help hold a line east of the Rhine.

The war also generated serious transatlantic tensions. Although initially concerned about a Soviet offensive, many Europeans worried that U.S.-sponsored German rearmament would provoke the war it was supposed to deter. The British Conservative government elected in

1951 quickly displayed its preference for the economical alternative of nuclear deterrence. The NATO build-up decided at the 1952 Lisbon Conference proved an illusion. German units were delayed indefinitely when the French National Assembly rejected the EDC in August 1954.[58] Truman formally approved NSC 68 in September 1950. U.S. defense appropriations reached $56.9 billion in 1952, compared to $13 billion in 1950. Beneficiaries included the nuclear weapons production program and the Strategic Air Command (SAC), whose mission was to attack the USSR. In line with NSC 68's call for Communism's rollback by 1954, the supposed "year of maximum danger," the administration created a Psychological Strategy Board (PSB) to oversee an intensified program of covert warfare.[59] While the State Department and CIA fought over the PSB's mandate, the CIA's existing body, the OPC, vastly expanded "plausibly deniable" activities.[60] The OPC's post-1950 history remains to be written, but enough is known of its activities to say they were mostly exercises in futility. Although the Truman administration avoided public calls for liberation, its covert operations confirmed Stalin's view that the West aimed to destroy Communism, and provoked repression rather than a weakening of the Eastern bloc.

By 1952 a war in which 37,000 Americans ultimately perished had become deeply unpopular in the United States.[61] Paying for it provoked partisan rancor.[62] Efforts to achieve a "situation of strength" from which to pursue a Cold War-winning strategy were unsustainable. Facing a stalemate, the administration conducted a lengthy internal debate. Bohlen (State Department representative on the NSC senior staff) disputed NSC 68's assumptions that Moscow would seriously risk war and might strike first if the nuclear balance were in its favor. The result of his effort, NSC 135/3 (September 1952), did not deny the possibility of a nuclear attack, but argued it could be deterred if the West's strength meant war would "result in serious risk to the Soviet regime."[63] The utility of Nitze's prized but quixotic goal of preponderance was called into serious question. In effect, the USSR of NSC 135/3 was more prudent than Nitze's, as depicted in NSC 68, and more robust than Kennan's, as depicted in his famous memos. As Bohlen had written to Kennan in 1945, "[W]hat is clear is that the Soyuz [Soviet Union] is here to stay, as one of the major factors in the world."[64]

Before the 1948 elections, Lippmann had written that the public wanted a conservative president and might have "something like a nervous break-down if it is frustrated much longer."[65] The anti-Communist hysteria of the early fifties was a fulfillment of Lippmann's prediction. A final result of Korea was the election of a conservative war-hero with a winning personality. Eisenhower and his secretary of state-designate Dulles had lambasted the Democrats for allegedly appeasing Communism and forsaking rollback.[66] But Western publics were in no mood for an aggressive strategy, and economic circumstances did not allow one. A period of live and let live had arrived

With the help of biology—Stalin's death from a cerebral hemorrhage on March 5, 1953—the same was true in the East. The Soviet bloc was then in the middle of its own costly rearmament. Moscow had increased investment in its war, naval, and arms-producing ministries by 60 percent in 1951 and 40 percent in 1952.[67] NSC 68 and U.S. rearmament, based on the dubious premises of growing Soviet power and aggressiveness, had helped to trigger Soviet rearmament. But Stalin's support of North Korea had provoked European, including German, rearmament. It is hard to say which side had been more severely punished by the law of unintended consequences in 1950–3.

Just as Korea accelerated the FRG's integration into the West, it led Stalin to embrace his "unwanted child," the GDR. The prospect of war against an enemy enjoying nuclear superiority increased the strategic importance of East Germany as a base in which to prepare a powerful conventional offensive able to deter, and if necessary counter, an attack by the West. The episode of the March–April 1952 Soviet notes is understandable in this light. On March 10, 1952, the Soviet Foreign Ministry proposed a peace treaty providing for a reunited, non-aligned Germany. Historians have long debated Moscow's intentions and whether the Western allies were correct to reject the proposal, as they did, in effect, in a March 26 reply. It is clear today that Molotov and elements of his ministry saw advantages in what later became the "Austrian solution." Stalin's own thinking is evident from what he told GDR leaders in early April 1952: "You need to create an army." "You too need to organize an independent state." The notes were at least partly designed to encourage Social Democratic and nationalist opposition in the FRG to German rearmament. Stalin had assumed a negative reaction to the notes (the Americans, he said, needed troops in West Germany to control Europe) and he had come to see the value of a strong East Germany. GDR leaders were eager to oblige and embarked on a course of accelerated sovietization. One consequence was the tension in East German society (120,000 emigrated in early 1953) that exploded after Stalin's death.[68]

If the Korean War had a beneficiary, it was China. The 1950–3 trial by fire cost the PRC the chance to take Taiwan, and at least 400,000 casualties, but gained it prestige in the eyes of the second (Communist) and third (decolonizing) worlds.[69] Although making his share of mistakes, Mao had fought the planet's leading power to a standstill. In his own eyes, he was a full-fledged international figure, equal if not superior in revolutionary spirit and acumen to the Soviet leaders who followed Stalin. The war tightened Chinese-Soviet ties but also sowed the seeds of conflict. The Chinese would remember Stalin's ambiguous behavior, and that he demanded hard currency for the supplies sent in 1950–3. Stalin's legacy included NATO rearming in the West and "Tito-ism" germinating in the East.

CHAPTER 5
THE AGE OF BRINKMANSHIP, 1953–1963

Aron's classic description ("impossible peace, improbable war") says much about the climate and dynamics of the 1950s and early 1960s.[1] War was unlikely because both sides, even as they stocked their arsenals with new "warheads" and "delivery vehicles," came to see that a conflict would mean untold devastation. Events, moreover, were to demonstrate further the simple truth that possession of nuclear weapons served to hold territory but not to take it. By the same token, a mutually satisfactory solution was impossible because both sides' messianism, reinforced by internal political pressures, was alive and well.

Much ink has been spilled over the prospects for ending the Cold War after the installation of new U.S. and Soviet leaderships. The fact was that neither side was ready to renounce its aims.[2] In his inaugural address on January 20, 1953, Eisenhower spoke of a world in which the "forces of good and evil are massed and armed and opposed as rarely before in history." In a campaign statement, Dulles had called for threatening "to retaliate instantly...by means of our choosing" against aggression, together with a political offensive to go beyond the "negative, futile, and immoral" policy of recent years.[3]

Following Stalin's death, the presidential adviser C. D. Jackson, a former *Time* editor, and M.I.T. Professor Walt Rostow recommended a bizarre psychological warfare plan supposed to induce the Red Army to overthrow the regime, accompanied by a presidential speech offering to settle the Korean and German questions. State Department officials countered that this might backfire by seeming to pounce even before Stalin's corpse had been buried, and negotiations on Germany would undermine support for the EDC. Eisenhower was impatient with this disagreement, and had an open mind on the possibility of change in the Soviet Union. But he had sought and received the Republican right's support in the elections. Even if so inclined, the administration was in no position to make serious concessions.[4] In an April 16, 1953 speech Eisenhower stated that the new Soviet leaders had "a precious opportunity... to help turn the tide of history". But there must be an end to the Korean War followed by "free elections in a united Korea." The United States was ready to strive for a "broader European community" including a fully independent Eastern Europe. If the Cold War ended, it would be on Western terms.[5]

Moscow initially seemed readier than Washington to turn over a new leaf. A collective leadership composed of the premier and Presidium chairman Georgi Malenkov,[6] Internal Affairs minister Beria, CPSU chairman Nikita Khrushchev, and Foreign Minister Molotov, promptly released a million prisoners from Siberian camps, banned routine use of torture, and dropped Stalin's paranoid charges against a group of Jewish physicians. In his funeral oration (March 9, 1953), Malenkov pledged "a policy based on the Lenin–Stalin premise of the possibility of the prolonged coexistence and peaceful competition of two different systems." A week later he stated: "At the present time there is no disputed or unresolved question that cannot be settled peacefully..."[7] Moscow hastened to end the Korea deadlock and ordered East Germany to reverse the Stalinization program that was provoking unrest and mass emigration.[8] Malenkov bluntly informed SED leaders that the overriding priority was "the restoration of German unity" and Germany's transformation into a peaceful country. Under present circumstances, such a Germany could only be "a bourgeois-democratic state."[9]

But two events reinforced the new leaders' caution. On June 16, 1953 East Berlin construction workers struck against higher work quotas. On June 17 hundreds of thousands took to the streets and assaulted regime buildings in Berlin, Halle, Gorlitz, and Magdeburg. At least fifty-five died in clashes with Red Army tanks and the paramilitary *Volkspolizei*. Soviet and SED leaders believed Western agents were responsible. Negotiating the end of East Germany under pressure was unacceptable. Khrushchev, in particular, took a stand in support of "Stalin's child," and opposed compromises he believed would only encourage the West German imperialists.

The second event was Beria's sudden fall. His fellow oligarchs feared the cunning, brutal Georgian and decided to preempt his suspected bid for power. In late June Presidium members denounced him as "a bourgeois renegade." Beria was subsequently arrested, tried, and shot.[10] One charge raised against him was that he had been in league with the capitalists against East Germany. Indeed, Beria had been even keener than Malenkov to liquidate the failing GDR as part of a settlement with the West. That idea was now associated with the disgraced secret police chief. Moreover, while the anti-Beria group wrongly assumed the West had instigated the riots, the Americans did try to exploit the situation. On June 29, 1953 Eisenhower approved NSC 158, calling for action to "nourish resistance to communist oppression throughout satellite Europe, short of mass rebellion." Steps included the establishment of "secure resistance nuclei," intensification of "defection programs," and emphasizing "U.S. support for German unity based on free elections."[11] The Soviets were unwilling to settle on such terms.

The sociologist C. Wright Mills would write later in the fifties: "The drift and thrust toward World War III is now part of the contemporary sensibility—and a defining characteristic of our epoch."[12] The unstable division of Europe nourished this dread of war. Washington remained committed to freeing the satellites and reunifying Germany according to West German conditions (free all-German elections creating a government that would bring a united Germany into the EDC or NATO). But it worried that the collapse of one or more satellites might trigger a superpower conflict. Khrushchev worried that another *17. Juni 1953* might precipitate FRG intervention, leading to a kind of Korean War in reverse, or worse. "What we fear," he later said, "is the ability of an armed Germany to commit the United States by its own actions. We fear the ability of Germany to start a world atomic war."[13]

Another factor nourishing fear was the arms race and alleged prospect of a Soviet surprise attack. On November 1, 1952, on Eniwetok Atoll in the Marshall Islands, the Americans conducted the first test of a hydrogen device. The explosion yielded 450 times the energy of the Nagasaki bomb. On August 12, 1953 the Soviets tested their own thermonuclear weapon. Technological advances in the 1950s included small, "tactical" nuclear weapons, and delivery systems such as the B-52 intercontinental bomber and the intercontinental ballistic missile (ICBM). Moscow showed its scientific prowess in October 1957 by launching "Sputnik," a crude satellite carried into orbit by an ICBM. A series of studies fed anxiety about U.S. vulnerability. These included the 1955 Killian Commission report ("Meeting the Threat of Surprise Attack"), the 1956 "Vulnerability Study" by the RAND Corporation expert Albert Wohlstetter, and the 1957 Gaither Report ("Deterrence & Survival in the Nuclear Age"). The last predicted that 1959–62 would be a "very critical period" when Soviet ICBMs might be able to destroy America's B-52s on the ground, denying the United States a "second-strike" (retaliatory) capability. In 1958 National Intelligence Estimates predicted the USSR would have 500 ICBMs by 1961. The United States had none at the time. Military officers, defense contractors, politicians, and serial alarmists like Paul Nitze and the columnist Joseph Alsop touted a "missile gap."[14]

A third source of fear were the frequent big-power confrontations in Europe and Asia. The crises over the tiny Nationalist Chinese islands of Quemoy and Matsu (1954–5; 1958), the Suez Canal (1956), Hungary (1956), Iraq (1958), Berlin (1958–62), and Cuba (1962) revealed a pattern. Each side believed it was acting defensively or responding to provocation. A considerable degree of initiative lay in the hands of local actors, with Washington and Moscow acting partly to retain prestige and credibility. The crises ended in ways that reinforced the existing situation. The risk of nuclear war led Washington and Moscow to choose stability over trying to change the status quo.

If both sides' abiding messianism, and fear of displaying weakness, ruled out a settlement of the Cold War, there were also powerful incentives to compromise. On August 8, 1953 Malenkov revealed Soviet possession of the H-bomb and warned against viewing the USSR as "a colossus with feet of clay." But the same speech called for "the drastic upsurge in the production of consumer goods" and "further development and upsurge of agriculture." While brandishing the bomb, Soviet leaders were eager to shift resources and raise living standards. According to Malenkov, there was "no objective grounds for a collision between the USA and the USSR." In March 1954 he declared that nuclear war would

mean "the end of world civilization." His rivals would use this unortho-
dox statement against him, but Khrushchev, at least, was under no
illusions as to the point.[15]

The double incentive to avoid catastrophe and reallocate resources was
also at work in the West. Publics were heartily sick of rearmament. Prime
Minister Churchill called for a four-power summit.[16] For Eisenhower,
reducing the risk of war and safeguarding solvency were favorite themes.
"Under the cloud of threatening war," he lamented, "it is humanity
hanging from a cross of iron." He told Republican leaders he "'would
follow a new policy which would continue to give primary consideration
to the external threat but would no longer ignore the internal threat.'"[17]
The latter arose from budget deficits requiring higher taxes or diverting
savings from civilian investment. Eisenhower, too, was looking for ways
to pursue a credible, dynamic Cold War policy but at a far lower cost.

Trying to Square the Circle, 1953–1956

Eisenhower's strategy emerged from a series of intense discussions, and
in response to events. Following the debate over how to respond to
Stalin's death, Eisenhower ordered a review known as the "Solarium
Project." It created three task forces, each to elaborate a distinct
approach. Task Force A, led by Kennan, was to design a policy produc-
ing the "diminution and progressive retraction" of Soviet power but
without "materially increasing the risk of general war." Its report was a
reprise of NSC 20/4 (1948), calling for gradual rollback, combined with
negotiations to reunify Germany.[18] Task Force B explored drawing a
line beyond which a Communist military advance would mean war.
Task Force C proposed aggressive rollback to end Communist rule in the
USSR and China, accepting "a substantial risk of general war." Its report
reprised NSC 68's argument that a military build-up must cover a covert
and political offensive, combined with MacArthur's post-November
1950 preferences: victory in Korea using atomic weapons, and air and
sea attacks on the PRC.[19]

While rejecting option B, Eisenhower favored psychological warfare
and saw merit in parts of C. But he and Treasury Secretary George
Humphrey were also in sympathy with a JCS report calling for a partial

redeployment home of U.S. forces. Those who "really studied foreign and military problems," Eisenhower said, had always considered stationing U.S. troops abroad "a temporary expedient." Even before the Soviet H-bomb test, moreover, he had developed doubts "about how much we should poke the animal through the bars of the cage," an obvious criticism of option C.[20] Dulles initially leaned toward a combination of B and C. In September 1953, however, he mused that the "NATO concept" was "losing its grip" because the Europeans felt "U.S. vulnerability is becoming such that we might stay out if Europe were attacked first," while troop withdrawals would further undermine allied confidence. He moved toward option A, even suggesting a kind of amalgam of Kennan's moribund Program A for Germany and Byrnes's "open" sphere: withdrawals of U.S. and Soviet forces, a "Finlandized" Eastern Europe, and international control of nuclear weapons. The Presbyterian minister's son was the bane of progressives for his sanctimonious rhetoric and failure to confront McCarthy, and the butt of jokes for his cold demeanor. Bohlen is said to have coined the epithet, "dull, duller, dulles." But he was more flexible than he seemed.[21]

The administration's at-times agonized discussions produced a "Basic National Security Policy" (NSC 162/2, October 30, 1953). Eisenhower oversaw a compromise between those who emphasized reducing U.S. over-extension while also sustaining pressure on the Communists, and those who feared the effects in Europe and Asia of troop withdrawals and had concluded that, short of war, negotiated agreements with Moscow were the only way of substantially reducing the Russian threat.[22] NSC 162/2 outlined a fourfold approach. While rejecting immediate pullbacks, Eisenhower was determined to cut spending and did not believe U.S. forces could remain in Europe indefinitely. The administration's view of the Soviet bloc as a "vast central land mass" recalled Mackinder's.[23] Like the British geographer's, it emphasized building up the natural barriers. Eisenhower hoped that European integration underway in the 1950s would lead to "a third great-power bloc."[24]

Secondly, as Dulles declared, the United States sought "maximum deterrent at bearable cost." The way to avoid new Koreas was "to be willing and able to respond vigorously at places and with means of our own choosing." Local defenses "must be reinforced by the further deterrent of massive retaliatory power."[25] The administration believed (plausibly) that such a policy might have prevented the Soviet–North Korean miscalculation leading to war, and (on the basis of scant evidence) that the conflict had ended because of veiled threats to use atomic weapons. In March 1955, after Chinese shelling of Quemoy and Matsu, Dulles declared that the United States was considering a nuclear strike. When Beijing suspended attacks and Zhou Enlai declared China's willingness to negotiate, nuclear "brinkmanship" appeared to have worked again.[26]

Thirdly, NSC 162/2 called for "feasible political, economic, propaganda, and covert measures designed to create and exploit troublesome problems for the USSR."[27] Although some were reluctant to exclude incitement of revolution, the administration shifted toward promotion of evolutionary change. Answering JCS criticism in December 1954, Dulles observed that he could only sympathize with their views because he, too, had called for liberation. "However, experience indicated that it was not easy to go very much beyond the point that the administration had reached in translating a dynamic policy into courses of action." Trying to overthrow satellite regimes would mean war. Even if attempts succeeded, the Soviet nuclear threat would remain, and allied support would have been lost.[28]

Ironically, in view of its initial, loudly proclaimed position, the Eisenhower administration phased out overt and covert attempts to roll back Communism beyond the Iron Curtain. But it had no intention of retrenching in what it considered the vital regions of Latin America, the Middle East, and Southeast Asia. Its reputation for using covert action to wage the struggle "on the cheap" was acquired outside Europe. Under its director Allen Dulles, the CIA helped to overthrow the nationalist prime minister of Iran, Mohamed Mossadeq, in 1953, and the leftist president of Guatemala, Jacobo Arbenz Guzmán, in 1954. The "agency" built up the regime of Ngo Dinh Diem in South Vietnam after France withdrew in 1955. Probably following Eisenhower's August 1960 oral authorization, Dulles and his assistant, the former Yale economist Richard Bissell, gave orders to engage the Italian-American Mafia in a plot to assassinate Fidel Castro. Confident that it had the right and capacity to make or break third world governments, Washington began to plan what became the Bay of Pigs landing by Cuban exiles in 1961.[29]

Finally, the administration was prepared to negotiate on specific issues. The Korea armistice was a major goal. Although deeply worried about a Communist victory in Indochina—in April 1954 he invoked the "the 'falling domino' principle"—Eisenhower rejected U.S. intervention to save the French stronghold at Dien Bien Phu. Congress was in no mood for Asian adventures, the British wanted a settlement, and Eisenhower realized it would be difficult to save the French.[30] Washington (with Paris, London, Moscow, and Beijing) participated, albeit reluctantly, in the May–July 1954 Geneva conference that ended the Indochina war on the basis of Vietnam's temporary division along the 17th parallel.

The German impasse continued. Chancellor Adenauer, a Rhineland Catholic, was in no hurry to re-embrace the traditionally socialist east, and opposed a compromise settlement. Khrushchev, now running Soviet foreign policy, insisted on a separate GDR. After Paris had torpedoed the EDC in August 1954, Washington and London insisted on bringing West Germany into NATO. Moscow replied by embedding East Germany in a counter-alliance known as the Warsaw Pact. In this more settled context, Khrushchev was ready to overrule Molotov's insistence on linking the Austrian and German questions, and respond positively to an invitation from Vienna to negotiate.[31] In May 1955 the four powers agreed to the Austrian State Treaty, providing for Austria's demilitarization and neutralization, and the withdrawal of occupying forces. In July, in a climate of détente, the leaders of the four gathered at Geneva for the first summit meeting since Potsdam. They discussed Germany and a U.S. proposal to allow reconnaissance flights over each other's territory, known as "Open Skies." As the "spirit of Geneva" lingered, Adenauer visited Moscow in September. Although the FRG refused to recognize the GDR, Moscow and Bonn exchanged ambassadors at the end of 1955.

A Game More than One can Play

In 1956 Dulles expounded on the technique that had become associated with his tenure: "The ability to get to the verge without getting into war is the necessary art. If you cannot master it, you inevitably get into war. If you try to run away from it, if you are scared to go to the brink, you are lost."[32] But the efficacy of "brinkmanship" was called into serious question before Dulles's retirement and death from stomach cancer in 1959. Browbeating China with nuclear weapons, together with the U.S.–Taiwan alliance concluded in December 1954, seemed to have worked in 1955. But the Chinese inaugurated a second Taiwan Strait crisis with week's of artillery bombardment of Quemoy in August–September 1958.

Mao was preparing an internal mobilization called the Great Leap Forward in which millions of peasants were shunted to communes, while others abandoned farming to build backyard blast furnaces. An estimated 35 to 50 million would starve to death as a result.[33] The Great Helmsman hoped to use a crisis to raise the level of revolutionary fervor, teach the American bullies (in 1957 they had put tactical nuclear weapons in Taiwan) a lesson, and show off his anti-imperialist credentials. When U.S. aircraft carrier groups escorted Nationalist ships resupplying Quemoy, Mao ordered his forces to avoid hitting the Americans. But as premier Zhou Enlai avowed to Soviet foreign minister Andrei Gromyko, the PRC was "ready to take all the hard blows, including atomic bombs." This echoed Mao's November 1957 statement that Communists should not fear nuclear war, and frequent references to the atomic bomb as a "paper tiger."

In the end, the Chinese leadership decided it was wiser to keep Quemoy and its U.S. protector in a "noose" that could be periodically tightened than to fight the Americans, and the shelling tapered off. Dulles appeared to have won again. But China's attitude raised the possibility that Beijing might someday call the Americans' bluff. If the United States failed to act, its credibility would be destroyed, but using nuclear weapons would provoke international outrage. Although prepared to fight for Quemoy, Washington conceded (September 30, 1958) that a cease-fire could lead to the removal of Nationalist forces from the offshore islands. Moscow publicly supported Mao, but was privately alarmed by his deliberate assault on "peaceful coexistence." Beijing's brinkmanship had forced it to take a position toward Washington it would have preferred to avoid.[34]

A different kind of challenge to the Eisenhower-Dulles policy had occurred in Eastern Europe. It was an unintended effect of Khrushchev's accumulation of power and de-Stalinization campaign of 1955–6. The

CPSU first secretary proved to be the toughest and wiliest member of the new ruling clique. He saw Malenkov as weak, and disagreed with his emphasis on consumer goods, preferring further development of heavy industry and cultivation of virgin lands.[35] In February 1955 Khrushchev formed an alliance with Molotov and Marshal Nikolai Bulganin. Bulganin replaced Malenkov as premier and Khrushchev became Presidium chairman. He then out-maneuvered Molotov, winning Presidium support for the Austrian treaty and a rapprochement with Yugoslavia. In June 1957, with the backing of defense minister Zhukov, the KGB, and a Central Committee majority, he reversed a no-confidence vote engineered by Malenkov, Molotov, and others fed up with his arbitrary methods. After sending this "anti-party group" into internal exile, firing the independent-minded Zhukov, and elevating protégés like Leonid Brezhnev (born 1906), Khrushchev was practically unchallenged for seven years.

Proud, emotional, and insecure, Khrushchev, compared to Stalin, was both a more promising and a more provocative interlocutor for the West. He had a famous wit (after meeting Senator John F. Kennedy in 1959, he wrote to him, "perhaps this card will help you get out of jail after the revolution comes") and a capacity for self-restraint.[36] He knew the USSR shared responsibility for Cold War tensions, aimed to reduce military spending, and believed in peaceful competition.[37] In a February 1956 address to the 20th CPSU congress, he stunned his audience by condemning Stalin's "cult of the individual" and crimes against the party and the military.[38] The "children of the 20th party congress," a generation of intellectuals and officials in their twenties, would mature in a relatively open climate. During the post-1956 "thaw," research and training centers became "oases of creative thought."[39] At the same time, however, Khrushchev was more committed than Stalin to advancing anti-colonial "national liberation" movements. He was also more impulsive, and prone to actions whose consequences were difficult to control.

A case in point was the 1956 "secret speech" itself. Obtained by Western intelligence agencies, it was published and broadcast back to Eastern Europe. On June 28, 1956, economic distress in Poland boiled over in a worker's revolt in Poznań, brutally suppressed by the regime.

On October 19, under popular pressure, the Polish Communist Party restored Wladyslaw Gomulka (born 1905) to the position of first secretary he had lost during Marshall Plan-era purges. Khrushchev's de-Stalinization did not cause the "Polish October," but it emboldened the Poles and conditioned the Soviet reaction. When Khrushchev and other Presidium members confronted Gomulka in Warsaw, he told them "If you talk with a revolver on the table you don't have an even handed discussion."[40] The Kremlin decided it could live with Gomulka, a loyal Communist as well as a nationalist, and dropped the threat of intervention. The Poles were allowed to remove Konstantin Rokossovski (the Red Army marshal imposed by Stalin as defense minister) and adopt reforms. Gomulka had gone to the brink and won.

Polish events triggered a spontaneous rebellion by anti-Stalinist Communists and nationalists in nearby Budapest on October 23. During the next week, some 15,000 insurgents, mainly young and working-class, used stolen arms and "Molotov cocktails" to battle the Red Army and regime security forces. The Hungarian party recalled the popular anti-Stalinist leader Imre Nagy (a Malenkov protégé, removed in February 1955). After initially vacillating, Nagy embraced the uprising and declared a multi-party system. The Presidium, advised by two of its members on the spot, Khrushchev's savvy ally Mikoyan, and Mikhail Suslov, decided the same day, October 30, 1956, to accept a "Polish solution" and withdraw Soviet forces from Budapest. A declaration published on October 31 affirmed the Eastern European states' right to greater autonomy and Moscow's willingness to negotiate the removal of its troops from Hungary, Poland, and Romania. Tragically, the Presidium reversed this remarkable decision in less than twenty-four hours. On October 31 it ordered Soviet forces to restore order. Nagy declared Hungary's withdrawal from the Warsaw Pact and appealed to the world for assistance. By November 4 Budapest was in Red Army hands.[41]

The Presidium's change of heart was not, as sometimes claimed, a reaction to Nagy's declaration of neutrality (Nagy was reacting to Moscow's decision).[42] Rather, the Russians had learned that a mob had assaulted municipal Communist headquarters on October 30, and hanged secret policemen and party workers from lampposts. Nagy, unlike the sure-handed Gomulka, was not in control of events. The hard-liner Suslov (although not Mikoyan) favored a crackdown, as did the Soviet ambassador to Hungary, Yuri V. Andropov. The Chinese comrades, who had had blamed Moscow's "big power chauvinist" policy for the Polish troubles, advised Moscow to keep its troops in Budapest. Even Tito (who may have preferred his position as Europe's sole national communist) agreed. Finally, and perhaps fatally, Budapest events on October 30 happened to coincide with the final phase of the Suez crisis. It had begun when Egypt's president Gamal Abdel Nasser nationalized the British- and French-owned Suez canal in July. Executing a plan hatched with Israel, France and Britain launched an operation to seize the canal and, or so it appeared, topple Nasser's Arab nationalist regime. Khrushchev, who backed Nasser and had agreed to finance his pharaonic Aswan dam irrigation project, spelled out to his colleagues a Soviet version of the "falling domino" theory: "If we leave Hungary, this will encourage the Americans, the English and the French—the imperialists. They will interpret it as our weakness and take the offensive. Then we will reveal the weakness of our positions. Our party will not understand us. Then we will add Hungary to Egypt for them. We have no other choice."[43]

The Hungarian crisis showed that U.S. brinkmanship was unusable to change the status quo. Taken totally by surprise, and preoccupied by the November presidential elections, the Eisenhower administration had no intention of risking war and assured Moscow that it did not see Poland or Hungary as potential allies. Nor, despite its commitment to libera-tion, did it offer practical advice to Nagy or incentives to Moscow (such as talks on the mutual withdrawal of forces) to encourage Soviet tolera-tion. Finally, far from encouraging caution in hopes of a "Polish out-come," the Americans allowed their Munich-based Radio Free Europe to urge the rebels not to compromise with the "Stalinist" Nagy. The Hungarian debacle belied talk of de-Stalinization and cost the USSR the support of hundreds of thousands of sympathizers and Communist Party members in Western Europe. It exposed U.S. policy as ineffectual and hypocritical. It was a sad performance all around.[44]

*   *   *

In December 1954 Dulles privately suggested that he had taken on board Kennan's view of Russia: "The verdict of history was that the Soviet leaders had been rather cautious in exercising their power. They were not reckless, as Hitler was; but primarily they rely not on military force but on methods of subversion."[45] The most serious problem with U.S. brinkmanship and reliance on nuclear weapons as a policy was that, with Khrushchev's consolidation of power, the Kennan–Dulles analysis temporarily lost some (fortunately not all) of its validity. The blunt, burly son of peasants was due to emerge as the boldest brinksman of them all.

"A Bone in my Throat", 1958–1960

Not long after Hungary, Khrushchev told a group of Western diplomats in Warsaw: "Whether you like it or not, history is on our side. We will bury you." The remark revealed his fierce competitiveness and faith that Communism would surpass capitalism in the realm of production.[46] Less than a year later, Sputnik fed missile and education gap hysteria in the West. Americans felt not only vulnerable to Soviet ICBMs, but bested in the technological arena. Sputnik also nourished European doubts about the U.S. nuclear protectorate. France's President Charles de Gaulle would later declare that no one, not even the Americans themselves, could say if, when, and under what circumstances U.S. nuclear weapons would be used to defend Europe.[47]

In fact, Khrushchev had few illusions about his country's present inferiority. Catching up required far more investment. One of his basic objectives, as he repeated to Westerners, was to wind down the Cold War and shift competition to the area of economics.[48] In 1958, this policy faced two serious obstacles. The first was a deepening conflict with China. Having decided to reject de-Stalinization, Mao lectured Moscow that despite Stalin's mistakes, his career had been "70 percent" one of positive achievement. When Khrushchev visited China after a 1959 trip to America, he angered Mao by recommending that he release U.S. prisoners, and attacked his aggressive policy toward Taiwan and India (the latter a key developing country friendly to the USSR). Mao tried to end the visit on a conciliatory note, but increasingly saw China as the lodestar of Communism. Later in 1959 Moscow reneged on a 1957 agreement to provide a nuclear weapons design to Beijing, and in 1960 removed most of its advisers from China.[49] Chinese competition reminded Khrushchev that deals with the Americans must be seen to advance the anti-imperialist cause, and limited his flexibility in trying to live and let live with the West.

A second ominous cloud was growing German power. The FRG was in the middle of a stunning economic boom. Conventional rearmament was underway and Adenauer, after winning elections in 1953 and 1955, was riding high. His "German Gaullist" defense minister Franz Josef Strauss believed Germany should have nuclear weapons to enhance deterrence. In March 1958 the Bundestag passed a law permitting the acquisition of tactical nuclear arms.[50] The Adenauer government (reflecting the sentiments of millions who had fled territories ceded to Poland and Czechoslovakia) refused to recognize the Oder–Neisse border. Meanwhile, the GDR regime under the SED leader Walter Ulbricht struggled to cope with the loss of workers and professionals who entered West Berlin and then flew to the FRG.[51] Moscow, in sum, faced the prospect of a nuclear-armed, revanchist Germany that might intervene in a faltering GDR and/or trigger a U.S.–Soviet conflict. Soviet anxieties were clear to discerning observers from the West.[52]

But, despite his awareness of Soviet vulnerability, Khrushchev was confident, even cocky, about his ability to play a winning hand of poker. He noted the panicky reaction to Sputnik and thought encouraging the illusion of a "missile gap" would enhance his leverage. He boasted to Mao in July 1958, "Now that we have the transcontinental missile, we hold America by the throat." In December 1958 he warned a visiting U.S. senator, "We have rockets, too." In November 1959 he told journalists, "[I]n one year two-hundred and fifty rockets with hydrogen warheads came off the assembly line in the factory we visited."[53] In reality, the USSR was able to deploy four vulnerable, liquid-fueled R-7 ICBMs in December 1959. It was no coincidence that Khrushchev was opposed to disarmament proposals including on-site inspections, and angered by flights over Soviet territory by American U-2 spy aircraft.[54]

Khrushchev was apparently emboldened as well by the Middle East crises of 1956 and 1958. After the Anglo-French landing in the Suez canal zone, Moscow had threatened London and Paris with a nuclear attack. The USSR had had no missiles to make good the threat, but when the British and French retreated, Khrushchev believed the ploy had worked.[55] In fact, Prime Minister Anthony Eden and Premier Guy Mollet had abandoned the operation for a different reason. Furious that he had not been consulted, and sure gunboat diplomacy would play into Communist hands, Eisenhower had demanded they desist.[56]

In July 1958 anti-Western officers led by Brigadier Abd al-Karim Qasim carried out a violent coup against the Hashemite monarchy of Iraq, a member of the British-sponsored "Baghdad Pact."[57] The Eisenhower administration sent Marines to Beirut to shore up pro-Western Lebanon, while London dispatched paratroops to protect the Hashemite king of Jordan. Khrushchev sent signals that intervention in Iraq would mean war. Although Washington and London had not intended to attack Baghdad, Khrushchev again concluded that his bluff had been successful. In late 1958, the Russians did deploy twelve medium-range (1,200 kilometer) R-5m missiles capable of hitting London and Paris from sites north of Berlin.[58] But Khrushchev had yet to grasp the real lesson of Quemoy and Hungary (and of Suez, if one assumed the British and French *had* acted for the reasons he believed): nuclear weapons could be used to preserve but not change the status quo. This was a fundamental flaw in his approach to the German question, specifically what he called a "bone in his throat," the Allied presence (11,000 troops plus numerous spies) in West Berlin.[59]

On November 27, 1958 the Soviet Foreign Ministry delivered a note to the Western powers proposing that West Berlin become a demilitarized "free city." This would terminate U.S., British, and French rights to station troops there, and to travel to and from the city across GDR territory. If, after six months, they had not agreed, the USSR would sign a treaty with the GDR ceding its own rights and giving the East Germans control of three air corridors used by their citizens to leave Berlin. This ultimatum represented a watering down under Mikoyan's pressure of Khrushchev's original plan to cede Soviet rights immediately.[60] As clarified by Mikoyan himself on a visit to Washington, and by Gromyko in talks in Geneva, the Soviets wanted a settlement that contained West German power and salvaged the GDR. Along with the "free city," Moscow proposed treaties with the two Germanies ending the state of war, outlawing German production of atomic arms and missiles, and guaranteeing the existing borders.[61] Khrushchev was prepared to live with the free city idea (presumably more palatable to the Allies than giving West Berlin to the GDR) and extend the deadline. But he insisted Western rights must end and GDR control over its territory be respected. He told Averell Harriman in June 1959: "If you want to perpetuate or prolong your rights this means war."[62]

Here was the rub for the Allies. West Berlin had no military value and would be quickly overrun in case of hostilities. But no Cold War episode better illustrates the superpowers' obsession with prestige and credibility. It was impossible to renounce rights (and promises to protect 2 million West Berliners) at gunpoint. As Eisenhower told Khrushchev, "Berlin had become a symbol." The United States's "whole position" was involved.[63] And lest Eisenhower and Dulles's replacement, Congressman Christian Herter, falter under pressure, Bonn was quick to warn them against appeasement. De Gaulle endorsed the Oder–Neisse border, and hoped eventually to dismantle the two-bloc "Yalta system." But he

PATTERNS OF FEAR

Figure 4. "Patterns of Fear," by David Low, published in the *Manchester Guardian*, June 16, 1959.

did not intend to be pushed out of Berlin and was eager to show that France was a truer friend than the Anglo-Saxons. He backed Adenauer to the hilt.[64]

By inviting Khrushchev to the United States, the Americans hoped to induce flexibility in his position. Indeed his September 1959 visit was not without this effect. Despite tough exchanges, Khrushchev gained a favorable view of Eisenhower. He concluded that the president, although pressured by reactionaries, also wanted to defuse the conflict.[65] This was not simply wishful thinking. In the face of severe criticism, the former general resisted calls for big rises in defense spending, dismissed the "missile gap," and would later warn against the unwarranted influence of a "military-industrial complex." He told Khrushchev: "We do not want to perpetuate the present situation in Berlin and keep our Occupation Troops forever. We hope to find a way out with honor." Prime Minister Harold Macmillan was even more eager for a compromise.[66] Khrushchev dropped his time-limit in exchange for Eisenhower's acknowledgment that the Berlin situation was abnormal, and acceptance of a four-power summit. They also agreed to shift the focus of negotiations to disarmament, setting the stage for a new Soviet démarche. Khrushchev's thirteen-day tour of American factories and farms drove home to him that, despite impressive economic growth the fifties, Soviet living standards and production levels lagged far behind.[67]

Khrushchev left America, according to his son Sergei, feeling "euphoric." At Moscow airport he declared, "I have gained the impression that he [Eisenhower] sincerely wishes to see the end of the cold war."[68] Preparations began for the president's return visit in June 1960, including constructing the USSR's first golf course. In December 1959 the Presidium agreed to Khrushchev's proposal to reduce the armed forces by 1.2 million men. Simultaneously the Kremlin created the Strategic Rocket Forces (RVSN), but deployment of new R-9 and R-16 ICBMs was perhaps six years away.[69] Even as columnists like Alsop, and Democratic senators Stuart Symington, Lyndon Johnson, and John Kennedy bemoaned alleged U.S. weakness, the USSR faced a real and growing gap. With the United States deploying "Atlas" and "Titan" ICBMs, the Soviet Union would be vulnerable for several years to an American first strike.

It is tempting to believe that, but for a reckless American decision, 1960 might have brought a historic breakthrough. The downing of a U-2 spy plane over Soviet territory on May 1, 1960, cast a pall over the up-coming summit in Paris. Khrushchev was deeply embarrassed and offended by the incursion, and suspected the CIA had acted on its own. But to his horror, not only had Eisenhower authorized the flight, once Moscow revealed that it held the pilot, he refused to distance himself. When they faced each other at the Elysée Palace, a livid Khrushchev insisted Eisenhower condemn the flight, punish the guilty, and promise there would be no further missions. An indignant president was prepared to consider only the last of these demands. Khrushchev departed Paris in a huff, and with his strategy in ruins.[70]

The moral of the fiasco was that Eisenhower and Khrushchev were not in a position to end the Cold War single-handedly. Ironically, one of Eisenhower's reasons for risking the flight was to acquire evidence against those who charged him with weakening the country.[71] But his domestic critics were insistent, and if the Paris summit had made progress would have done their best to derail the result. At the same time, while Soviet bluster had encouraged the "missile gap" myth, the disarmament proposal Moscow had prepared for Paris stood little chance of acceptance. Abolishing nuclear delivery vehicles without on-site veri-fication was a non-starter, but the Russians opposed inspections that would reveal their abject weakness. Disarmament would also have pro-voked resistance from the generals, bureaucrats, and missile designers who had been rewarded with the rocket program. In May 1960, more-over, the two sides were no closer on Berlin than they had been the previous September. Even in the unlikely event de Gaulle and Adenauer had been flexibile, it is not clear how Eisenhower and Khrushchev could have agreed on the question of Western rights.

Raising the Ante, 1961

Moscow's decision in late 1958 to force a solution to the central geopo-litical issue of the Cold War coincided by chance with a dramatic development on the "periphery": the fall of the pro-U.S. dictator Ful-gencio Batista and triumphal entry of Fidel Castro, Che Guevara, and their comrades of the 26th of July Movement into Havana on January 1, 1959. By early 1960 Washington had decided not to tolerate a radical (if not yet avowedly Marxist–Leninist) government that might infect Latin America. It proceeded to isolate Cuba by cutting its sugar quota (July 1960) and plotted the regime's elimination.[72] The firebrand Castro signed a trade-and-aid agreement with Moscow (February 1960), denounced the United States after the destruction in Havana harbor of a ship carrying Belgian rifles to the Cuban army (March 1960), and expropriated American-owned sugar-mills, utilities, and oil refineries (October 1960). On January 3, 1961 the United States broke diplomatic relations with Cuba. With the election of the new president, John Kennedy, both Washington and Moscow were under growing pressure to resolve the Berlin and Cuba questions on their terms.

The 43-year-old son of an Irish-American millionaire cut a dashing figure but his mettle was anything but certain. Not only was Cuba seen by the U.S. and regional governments as an intolerable challenge, Kennedy had used the issue to discredit his opponent, Richard Nixon, and was expected to take strong action. One of his first decisions was to approve the Bay of Pigs operation in April. The landing by a CIA-trained brigade of Cuban exiles failed to spark an internal revolt. Kennedy and Secretary of State Dean Rusk did not want Latin America to see the United States flagrantly assisting aggression against a sovereign country, and withheld air and naval support. Cuban forces rapidly killed or captured the invaders. The administration then launched "Operation Mongoose," a program to foment an insurrection that might give a pretext for a U.S. invasion. CIA efforts begun under Eisenhower to kill Castro continued.[73] But the "perfect failure" at the Bay of Pigs cast doubts on Kennedy's leadership. A disheartened president was eager for a meeting with Khrushchev (his brother, Attorney General Robert Kennedy, opened a "back-channel" through the military intelligence agent Georgi N. Bolshakov) that would produce progress toward a nuclear test-ban treaty, defuse the conflict between pro-Western and Communist forces in Laos, and allow him to show resolve.[74]

In retrospect, Kennedy's position looks enviable compared to Khrushchev's. The Soviet leader had instinctively taken to the 32-year-old Castro and his band of bearded revolutionaries. In a January 6, 1961 speech Khrushchev proclaimed that history was on Communism's side and the USSR would back "wars of national liberation."[75] While Moscow had had nothing to do with events in Cuba before 1959, allowing the Americans to remove Castro would seriously damage its credibility. Khrushchev was engaged in a competition with Mao for world Communist leadership. Soviet prestige was even more tied to the fate of someone for whom Khrushchev felt no affection: the Stalinist martinet Ulbricht. During the first six months of 1961, 100,000 East Germans left the country. The regime desperately needed control over the sectoral boundary in Berlin and/or the routes from West Berlin to the FRG.[76]

These threats developed against the background of a deteriorating strategic balance. In February 1961 the Americans tested their solid-fueled "Minuteman" ICBM (1,000 would be deployed in hardened silos between 1962 and 1965) and Kennedy's Defense Secretary Robert McNamara revealed his view that there was no "missile gap." By September 1961 the Corona spy satellite had confirmed America's overwhelming superiority. In an October 21 speech, a Pentagon official would warn Moscow that, with 600 intercontinental bombers, 6 Polaris missile-carrying submarines, and dozens of ground-based ICBMs, the United States had "a second strike capability which is at least as extensive as what the Soviets [could] deliver by striking first."[77] NATO also had medium-range Jupiter missiles in Italy and Turkey. For Soviet leaders stalked by the memory of June 22, 1941, the situation raised the prospect of a devastating surprise attack. Indeed (and as Soviet military intelligence would report in March 1962), the Kennedy administration discussed a possible preemptive strike in the context of Berlin tensions in summer–fall 1961.[78]

Khrushchev's "congenital impatience" gnawed at him.[79] Messianic pronouncements notwithstanding, time was not on his side. His mood recalls Stalin's after Hiroshima. He feared U.S. power but would not be cheated. Bitterly disappointed by his failure to conciliate Eisenhower, he decided to try to bluff and bully the novice Kennedy. At a Presidium meeting before their summit in Vienna, he spoke of concluding the treaty giving the GDR control of the air corridors, and if necessary shooting down Western aircraft. The Americans might want to start a nuclear war but the British, French, and Germans would stop them.

Mikoyan cautioned against cornering Kennedy and the possibility that, despite the Red Army's local superiority, the West might decide to fight without early resort to nuclear weapons. Khrushchev dismissed this and forged ahead.[80]

Vienna (June 1961) witnessed the rawest exchanges between U.S. and Soviet leaders on record. Khrushchev demanded recognition that "Communism exists and has won its right to develop." He reiterated Moscow's intention to sign the treaty with the GDR. Kennedy appealed to Khrushchev to understand that "if we were to accept the Soviet proposal US commitments would be regarded as a mere scrap of paper." Khrushchev warned that if the GDR's borders were violated after the treaty, "force would be met with force." It was "up to the US to decide whether there will be war or peace." He left open the possibility of an interim arrangement but otherwise the Soviet Union would sign the treaty by December 31. If so, Kennedy concluded, "it would be a cold winter."[81]

Kennedy left Vienna shaken but quickly recovered his composure. After an intensive debate, he announced his answer to Khrushchev on July 25, 1961: "We cannot and will not permit the Communists to drive us out of Berlin, either gradually or by force." Washington would raise defense spending by $3.45 billion (for a total increase of $6 billion since January) to fund more ground forces and public nuclear fall-out shelters. Kennedy and McNamara had rejected Dean Acheson's advice to declare a national emergency, and left the door open for negotiation. But the essential message, confirming Mikoyan's intuition, was that the United States would plan to fight initially with armor and infantry rather than nuclear weapons. In doing so it challenged Khrushchev's premise that the Americans would be afraid to begin hostilities. As Kennedy put it: "We need the capability of placing in any critical area at the appropriate time a force which, combined with those of our allies, is large enough to make clear our determination and our ability to defend our rights... We intend to have a wider choice than humiliation or all-out nuclear action."[82] The crisis was the impetus for the move to a strategy of "flexible response," or having a wide range of options: a counter-insurgency capability, conventional forces, tactical nuclear weapons, accurate "counter-force" weapons (aimed at Soviet military targets), and a secure second strike capability consisting of submarine-based missiles.[83]

Kennedy's speech angered and troubled Khrushchev. He knew the risk of war was real and that his bluff had been called. The GDR's survival was now an urgent problem. Under intense pressure from Ulbricht, Khrushchev authorized the closing of the sectoral border in August. The resulting barbed wire and concrete barrier caused revulsion in the West. Washington answered by reinforcing its Berlin garrison and dispatching General Lucius Clay of 1948 airlift fame. In October tensions escalated into the memorable show-down at the "Checkpoint Charlie" crossing where U.S. and Soviet tanks faced off at a distance of one hundred meters.[84] But the Berlin wall was a tourniquet on the East German economy and eased pressure to resolve the broader question. Khrushchev noted that the Allies did not try to destroy the wall or challenge GDR control of East Berlin. Indeed, Kennedy quickly grasped that the wall was defensive. While deplorable, it offered propaganda advantages and did not threaten West Berlin.[85] Moscow answered Western saber-rattling by reversing conventional force cuts and resuming atmospheric testing of nuclear weapons. War games in September–October practiced a major attack and marked the Warsaw Pact's adoption of an offensive strategy. But Khrushchev signaled he wanted a solution that would safeguard Western prestige.[86] In October he dropped the December 31 deadline. Discussions on Berlin resumed.

Khrushchev's Final Hand, 1962–1963

The Kremlin's motives in placing missiles on America's doorstep, inadvertently provoking the gravest crisis of the Cold War, contain an element of mystery. Soviet justifications were sketchy or self-serving. American explanations were subject to a kind of political solipsism, the inability to fathom the impact of one's own actions on others. At the heart of the May 1962 decision probably lay Khrushchev's smoldering resentment over what he saw as the "position-of-strength" policy being pursued against him. He had failed twice to settle the Berlin question, and his authority and credibility were in question. "Besieged by troubles," his instinct was to shore up his defenses but also to raise the stakes.[87] Eloquent of his thinking are remarks to his colleagues on January 8, 1962:

We should increase the pressure, we must not doze off and, while growing, we should let the opponent feel this growth. But don't pour the last
drop to make the cup overflow; be just like a meniscus, which, according
to the laws of surface tension in liquid, is generated in order that the liquid
doesn't pour out past the rim. If we don't have a meniscus, we let the
enemy live peacefully.[88]

Cuba looked increasingly vulnerable. The United States had become
host to a myriad of anti-Castro organizations and the Republicans were
sure to make Cuba an issue in 1964. In a private interview with Khrushchev's son-in-law, the journalist Aleksei Adzhubei, on January 30, 1962,
Kennedy denied that he would invade but drew an analogy between
Cuba and the Hungary problem the Soviets had liquidated in 1956.[89]
The Americans tightened the economic embargo in March and conducted landing exercises in the Caribbean in April 1962. Khrushchev's
decision to deploy 36 medium (2,000 kilometer) range SS-4 and a lesser
number of intermediate (4,000 kilometer) range SS-5 missiles, as well as
to increase military aid to Cuba, was intended in part to deter a U.S.
invasion that would make a mockery of Moscow's claims.[90]

A connected motive was to address the strategic imbalance. In 1961 the
ICBM gap in America's favor stood at approximately 190 to 25. Soviet
MRBMs and IRBMs in Cuba were a short-cut to a more credible second
strike capability, and provided more leverage in a showdown. There was
also undoubtedly an element of sheer anger and defiance. According to
Fursenko and Naftali, Khrushchev made the missile decision just after
hearing Washington planned to deploy marines to Thailand to counter a
North Vietnamese-backed Laotian Communist offensive. This may be
so, although the two sides subsequently (July 1962) agreed to a neutral
and independent Laos. Certainly, Khrushchev found it hard to stomach
U.S. bases lining the Soviet periphery: "now they would learn just what
it feels like to have enemy missiles pointing at you."[91]

At the heart of the missile mystery are its connection, if any, to
Moscow's German agenda and the meaning of Khrushchev's words
"Deliver it [the missiles] secretly. Declare afterwards. . . . This will be an
offensive policy."[92] At no point did the Russians link the missiles to
Berlin. There are indications that, although Khrushchev would continue

to threaten to sign the treaty, he was resigned to the post-wall situation, and even preferred it to the concessions necessary for an agreement.[93] In February 1962, he told Ulbricht, "The main question is not the peace treaty, but a consolidation of the [GDR] economic situation."[94] But there is also plenty of evidence that Khrushchev intended to bring the Berlin issue—for what he must have seen as the last time—to a head. Between July and October 1962, he told anyone who cared to listen that he would raise the treaty question after the U.S. mid-term elections in November and might come to the United Nations to settle it personally.[95]

It may be that Khrushchev was not thinking of Berlin in May 1962 when he proposed the deployment and spoke of an "offensive policy." Later denials of a Berlin connection are understandable in light of the fact that nothing was achieved. But it is likely that Khrushchev intended to unveil the Cuba-based missiles after the elections as part of his German strategy.[96] The missiles would serve both to deter an attack on Cuba and pressure Washington into accepting his demands. It is conceivable that he planned to offer to trade them for an Allied exit from West Berlin. This is the sense in which the missiles would serve an "offensive policy." He assuredly did not mean they were to be used in a suicidal first strike.

Crucial to Khrushchev's plan was that the missiles remain secret until he was ready to put his cards on the table. But the Soviets carelessly tipped their hand in August. When U-2 overflights revealed construction of anti-aircraft missile installations, John McCone, the shrewd CIA head, deduced that their purpose was to protect longer-range missiles that could pose a threat to America's second strike capability.[97] In theory, rather than raising the stakes by issuing a public challenge, Kennedy might have pursued the question privately with Khrushchev. But this was not really an option. Cuban exile and U.S. intelligence sources had passed reports of missiles to Republicans eager to embarrass Kennedy. On September 4 Kennedy replied to Republican charges, stating that rumors of Soviet combat forces or offensive weapons in Cuba were unconfirmed. "Were it to be otherwise," he said, "the gravest issues would arise."[98]

With some reason, the Soviets denied that they were installing offensive weapons, while proceeding with sites for the SS-4s and SS-5s.[99] By

October 16, 1962, the Americans had evidence of the longer-range missiles. An "Excom" composed of Kennedy and his advisers convened to discuss the options.[100] These included an ultimatum, air-strikes of various dimensions, and a full-scale invasion. Kennedy leaned initially toward strikes but opted, following the July 1961 Berlin precedent, for a middle course. In an October 22 speech, after learning that some eight of the SS-4s were operational, he announced a naval "quarantine" of Cuba to prevent more weapons from arriving, and demanded that those there be dismantled.[101] U.S. forces prepared a five-division invasion of Cuba. A chill descended over much of the world as Moscow considered whether to defy what was, in effect, an illegal blockade on the high seas.

Khrushchev's reaction was also true to form. Although he wrote to Kennedy that Soviet mariners would not retreat "one step," the Presidium decided that ships carrying weapons would halt or turn back.[102] On October 25 the Presidium approved Khrushchev's proposal that the missiles be traded for a U.S. pledge not to invade Cuba. A private letter to this effect was transmitted on October 26.[103] Kennedy, at some level, may have recognized that U.S. aggressiveness had helped to provoke the crisis. Khrushchev's offer, in any case, was one the Americans could accept. But to the Excom's consternation a second (this time public) message arrived on October 27, adding that Jupiter missiles in Turkey should also be dismantled. Soviet expert Llewellyn Thompson thought hard-liners had overruled Khrushchev. In fact, Khrushchev was either taking up a suggestion from Ambassador Anatoly Dobrynin in Washington, and/or had been inspired by a Lippmann column suggesting such a deal.[104]

Kennedy's advisers fretted over the consequences for U.S credibility. But Kennedy, revealing his basic prudence and pragmatism, was ready to remove the Jupiters and believed the public would see the transaction as eminently reasonable.[105] The president also knew that the day before Khrushchev's latest message, Bobby Kennedy and Dobrynin had privately discussed just such a trade.[106] On October 27 the president answered Khrushchev, accepting the no invasion-no missiles deal proposed in the latter's October 26 letter.[107] The same evening, however, Bobby summoned Dobrynin to say that, while there could be no quid pro quo, and insisting on "strict secrecy," the Jupiters issue could be "satisfactorily resolved" in a few months. According to his own account, Bobby added: if Moscow said no, there would be "drastic consequences." Khrushchev immediately endorsed the deal that he (at Dobrynin's and/ or Lippmann's prompting) had proposed the day before.[108]

Catastrophe had been avoided above all because Khrushchev had been willing to drop the broader strategy connected to the missiles and accept the loss of face involved in their removal.[109] But without timely American concessions, the crisis might well have ended differently. Evidence emerging years later indicated, moreover, that Kennedy had been ready to accept a public trade of the Jupiters, if necessary. Several of his advisers admitted that the invasion allegedly threatened by Bobby Kennedy would not necessarily have happened. Although the world judged John Kennedy the master brinksman and clear winner of the confrontation, it was thanks to compromise that the Cuba time-bomb had been defused.[110]

Conclusion: The Cold War Transformed

On several occasions in the 1950s and early 1960s, Soviet leaders stated their desire to bring the Cold War to an end.[111] There is little reason to doubt their sincerity. But if Western leaders were overly rigid in rejecting Moscow's terms to resolve the Berlin conflict, they could be forgiven for reacting as they did to Soviet methods, frequently amounting to a pointed pistol. Even if the USSR and the West had sealed a bargain on Berlin, and agreed to compete peacefully, neither was prepared to renounce involvement in the third world. By 1960, moreover, the Cold War had become a multi-part drama with a radical, ambitious China following its own script.

Nonetheless, between 1953 and 1963, the East–West contest in its original, central theater was transformed and stabilized.[112] De-Stalinization, doctrinal revision, and preoccupation with economic conditions in the USSR, combined with prosperity in Western Europe to soften the ideological conflict.[113] After the crises of 1956–62, Moscow and Washington viewed a divided Europe as preferable to any likely alternative. France might try to dismantle the "Yalta system" but with the Berlin wall, the division was literally set in concrete. The USSR had no intention of relinquishing its satellites. In theory, the Kennedy administration favored a united Western Europe, but the U.S. build-up there in the early sixties marked the end of the policy whereby the Americans would foster European self-reliance in order to go home. By the same token, although Adenauer doubted U.S. staying-power, his party rejected de Gaulle's project of an exclusive Franco-German partnership and reaffirmed the FRG's ties to the United States.[114]

The de facto European settlement was ultimately the result of nuclear weapons. Reflecting their untold destructiveness, they had proved useful in defending but useless in changing borders. Coming to the edge reminded Washington and Moscow that an imperfect status quo was preferable to a war to have one's way. The age of brinkmanship led to an explicit recognition of the superpowers' common interest in avoiding disaster.[115] Khrushchev's hopes for a durable détente after Cuba were disappointed, but the two sides agreed to the installation of an instantaneous "hot-line" communications system, and a treaty banning atmospheric testing of nuclear weapons.[116]

The decision to live and let live provoked bitterness, and was not without its consequences. If for Kennedy a wall was "a hell of a lot better than a war," for West Berlin Mayor Willy Brandt, accepting it signaled the emptiness of Western policy. Although Kennedy gave a narrow interpretation to the "promise" not to invade Cuba, his JCS saw the crisis-ending deal as a U.S. capitulation. The perception that Kennedy had sold out the anti-Castro cause may have been a factor in his assassination in November 1963.[117] Demanding to know when the often-announced treaty would be delivered, Ulbricht was unsatisfied with Khrushchev's answer: "On August 13 [1961] we achieved the maximum of what was possible." Castro was incensed when weapons to defend Cuba were traded away and his conditions for removing them forgotten. China and its ally Albania compared Khrushchev's concessions to Kennedy to Chamberlain's appeasement of Hitler. The Kremlin had shown patience with the Chinese, but now switched its support to India in its border dispute with Beijing.[118]

In October 1964 a coterie led by president Leonid Brezhnev voted to send the Presidium chairman into early retirement. For the most part, the new leaders were self-interested, parochial characters with dogmatic views. They were fed up with Khrushchev's economic experiments and high-handed treatment of the *nomenklatura* class.[119] But they also took him to task for nearly provoking World War III, and then folding. The lesson was that never again would the USSR have to retreat from a position of inferiority. The Soviets accelerated their drive to match the Americans in strategic weaponry. A second source of renewed tension was the course of events in a part of the world where Moscow would happily have avoided problems. Despite his enthusiasm for national liberation movements, Khrushchev had agreed to the neutralization of Laos and discouraged the Vietnamese Communists from challenging Diem. He did not want U.S. power to threaten North Vietnam and feared that war would interfere with détente. But (and as many were to discover) the Vietnamese Communists had ideas of their own. The Americans, in turn, opted for escalation, brazenly bombing Hanoi during Soviet Premier Aleksei Kosygin's visit in February 1965. That year marked a turning point. The USSR joined China as an indispensable backer of North Vietnam and the bloody campaign in the south.

CHAPTER 6
THE STRUGGLE IN THE THIRD WORLD, 1950–1968

After 1945 a combination of defensive expansionism and belief in a mission to uplift humanity drove the superpowers to consolidate their spheres of influence in Europe. The obvious contradiction between a sometimes brutal control and an ideology promising liberation and material improvement bedeviled Moscow's Eastern empire from the beginning. Frustrated nationalism and relative economic backwardness there were an Achilles' heel that the West would eventually turn to its advantage. America's protectorate over Western Europe's capitalist democracies, although spurned by left-wing, neutralist, and nationalist forces, was based on a far greater degree of local support or acquiescence. It was strengthened and legitimized by a massive inflow of U.S. dollars, products, and consumer culture, as well as high levels of economic growth.[1]

In much of the rest of the world, this situation was reversed. The age of the European economic "miracles" and the emergence of a thriving European Economic Community (EEC) coincided with the culmination of the "revolt against the West."[2] Marxist–Leninist ideology, synonymous with oppression and stagnation in Warsaw and Budapest, signified liberation and economic development to indigenous intellectuals and aspiring leaders in colonial and post-colonial areas. U.S. policy was bedeviled by the contradiction between the necessity of retaining control of regions considered vital to the West, and the need to be true to the American mission and win converts in the struggle against Moscow and Beijing.

World War II fatally undermined the French, Dutch, and British empires. Between 1945 and 1960, some forty countries with a combined population of 800 million defied their European rulers and achieved independence. India made its debut in 1947; Indonesia, in 1949. With indispensable Chinese backing, the Viet Minh defeated France in 1954. Inspired by this example, Algerian rebels formed a *Front de Libération Nationale* (FLN) in November 1954. The FLN raised a guerrilla force and placed bombs in Algiers and Paris cafés to try to drive out the French. In April 1955 President Sukarno hosted a conference at Bandung, Indonesia, of twenty-nine Asian and African states, designed to foster closer cultural and economic co-operation. The gathering was a platform for the third world's most outspoken and charismatic leaders: Nasser, premier Jawaharlal Nehru of India, and Sukarno himself. Also present were delegates from anti-colonial movements and premier Zhou Enlai, who called on participants to unite in support of those still under the yoke of imperialism.[3] A year later, Nasser, who made no bones about his aim to unite the Arab world against the West, defied Britain and France in the Suez crisis, ending London's career as a maker and breaker of regimes in the Middle East.

The Bandung communiqué's call for "abstention from the use of arrangements of collective defense to serve the particular interests of any of the big powers" troubled the Eisenhower administration. For Nehru, "If all the world were to be divided up between these two blocs...the inevitable result would be war." This was an attack on Dulles's policy of lining the Sino-Soviet periphery with the NATO, CENTO, and SEATO pacts.[4] Even more disturbing to Washington than the example of non-aligned, "nativist" nationalists like Nasser, Nehru, and Sukarno was the Soviet precedent's appeal.[5] Lenin had showed that a disciplined elite could infuse the masses with revolutionary consciousness and mobilize them against their exploiters. According to Lenin, moreover, it was not to be assumed that "the capitalist stage of development" was "inevitable for the backward nationalities."[6] The collectivization of agriculture and dramatic increase in industrial production in the USSR in the 1930s showed that nations eager to develop need not wait decades as suggested by the classic Marxist view.

Under Soviet Communism, millions of illiterate peasants had become technicians, teachers, doctors, and engineers, working to build a society based (in theory) on the ideals of equality and fraternity. Stalin's achievements had enabled the USSR to defeat history's most formidable war machine and extend the boundaries of socialism. During the 1950s the cultivation of vast tracts of virgin land in Kazakhstan and Siberia, and technological advances like Sputnik, suggested Communism was still a dynamic and innovative system. Although Stalin had been Kremlin-bound, and rather pessimistic in his attitude toward Asia, Khrushchev visited India, Burma, Afghanistan, and Indonesia, exuding faith in the future. The USSR was prepared to assist its brethren in China and the third world, as well as progressive, "Jacobin" governments in Jakarta, New Delhi, and Cairo, where Soviet credits provided for arms as well as the Aswan irrigation project. If third world activists turned a blind eye to the frightful losses of lives and freedom involved in the Soviet and Chinese experiments, it was because the potential rewards seemed to justify the sacrifices. And what freedoms had they enjoyed under imperialism? As Marx and Engels had written, they had nothing to lose but their chains.

Dulles summed up Washington's dilemma at the time of the Suez crisis: "For many years now the United States has been walking a tightrope between the effort to maintain our old and valued relations with our British and French allies on the one hand, and on the other trying to assure ourselves of the friendship and understanding of the newly independent countries... Unless we now assert and maintain this leadership, all of these newly independent countries will turn from us to the USSR."[7] Just as the United States was determined to avoid Soviet control of Europe's war-making potential, it was intent on preventing the oil of the Middle East, and the tin, rubber, oil, iron ore, and agricultural bounty of Southeast Asia from falling into hostile hands. The United States initially depended on Britain to fill gaps in the line in the Middle East and Malaya, and on France in Indochina. For Dulles, Indochina was not of "great significance" per se, but its loss would send a message of weakness and give the Communists "staging grounds for further forward thrusts." This was Eisenhower's message in propounding what became known as the "domino theory" in April 1954.[8]

The Americans were exasperated by what they saw as British myopia and stubbornness in dealing with Iranian and Egyptian grievances, and by French lethargy and obtuseness in combatting the Viet Minh.[9] Paris had granted Laos, Cambodia, and Vietnam merely limited autonomy within the French Union (or commonwealth) in 1950, and full sovereignty only in April 1954, on the eve of defeat at Dien Bien Phu. The French, Eisenhower bitterly remarked, had used "weasel words in promising independence and through this reason as much as anything else have suffered reverses that have been inexcusable."[10] As these and Dulles's November 1956 words suggested, European behavior created two problems for Washington. Frustrating independence and development would push the third world into the arms of the Communists. Dulles admitted the Soviet experiment had "won for itself a considerable popular prestige." Secondly, the United States risked guilt by association and betrayal of its principles. As Dulles put it, "This Nation was conceived with a sense of mission and dedicated to the extension of freedom throughout the world."[11]

Washington's near-automatic response was to supplant the Europeans while using aid and (where possible covert) intervention to try to defeat enemies and build up competent anti-Communist regimes. Having largely replaced British influence in Iran after the 1953 coup, Washington declared the so-called "Eisenhower doctrine" in the aftermath of Suez. It said the United States would assume chief responsibility for defending the region against Soviet penetration. Although the Eisenhower administration was deeply annoyed by Israel's role in the Suez affair, Washington gradually joined Paris in supporting Tel Aviv, one of the few Western outposts in the Middle East.[12]

After the 1954 Geneva agreements had partitioned Vietnam at the seventeenth parallel, the Americans largely replaced French influence in the south. According to Geneva, the division was temporary: elections would create a government for a united, neutral Vietnam in July 1956. Determined to hold the line against Communism and realizing the Viet Minh would probably win, Washington sponsored a Republic of Vietnam (RVN) and encouraged its Saigon-based government not to feel bound by the elections provision. Although initially divided, the Eisenhower administration decided it had found an effective anti-Communist nationalist in Ngo Dinh Diem (born 1901). Diem was a cultivated former minister of the interior who had clashed in the 1930s with the French, and lived in the early 1950s in Roman Catholic monasteries in

New Jersey and Belgium. Thanks in part to generous U.S. aid, Diem had some success in consolidating his position and stabilizing the economy in 1955–8. A 692-man U.S. Military Assistance and Advisory Group (MAAG) supervised creation of a 150,000-strong Army of the Republic of Vietnam (ARVN).[13]

Unfortunately for the Americans, Diem proved a stubborn, clannish, and autocratic ruler, lacking the common touch of his rival, Ho Chi Minh (born 1890). Ho, a former Comintern operative, had declared an independent Democratic Republic of Vietnam (DRV) in 1945, and led the Viet Minh campaigns against the Japanese and the French. In the name of "Personalism," a supposed third way between capitalism and communism, Diem concentrated power in the hands of his family, starting with his brother Ngo Dinh Nhu, who oversaw the secret police, army Special Forces, and a clandestine political network (Can Lao). The Ngo family's Christianity, like Chiang Kai-shek's and Syngman Rhee's, was an asset in gaining U.S. support but a liability at home where only 10 percent of the population professed the religion of the ex-colonial power.[14] The Ngos' relations with the army were tense after a group of officers tried to overthrow them in 1960. The search for reliable anti-Communist leadership was to be an elusive one in Vietnam.

In Latin America Washington faced a similar dilemma, but of its own making. In a 1954 National Security Council meeting, Treasury Secretary Humphrey recommended that "the United States should make it absolutely clear that we will not tolerate Communism anywhere in the Western Hemisphere. We should stop talking so much about democracy, and make it clear that we are quite willing to support dictatorships of the right if their policies are pro-American." Eisenhower interrupted, half-facetiously: "you mean they're OK if they' re *our* s.o.b.'s."[15] No one endorsed Humphrey's suggestion, but the administration made no secret of its preference for dependable tyrants over popular governments (e.g. Arbenz's in Guatemala) that might offer a foothold to the Soviets. In line with its economizing approach, the administration rejected large-scale economic aid, but purchased fealty by arming Latin America's militaries. By the mid-fifties, trouble was brewing. Washington and its friends were ill-equipped to deal with a continent-wide crisis resulting from falling commodity prices, and spreading discontent over corruption and the

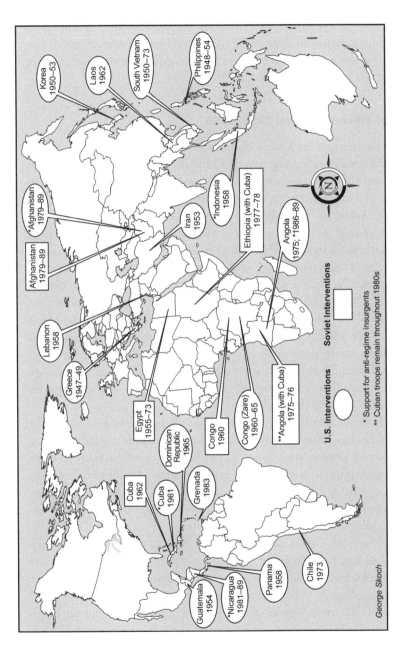

Map 3. U.S. and Soviet Interventions during the Cold War.

Korea
1950–53

Laos
1962

South Vietnam
1950–73

Philippines
1948–54

*Indonesia
1958

Ethiopia (with Cuba)
1977–78

Angola
1975; *1986–89

Iran
1953

*Afghanistan
1979–89

Afghanistan
1979–89

Lebanon
1958

Greece
1947–49

Egypt
1955–73

Dominican
Republic
1965

Congo (Zaire)
1960–65

Congo
1960

**Angola (with Cuba)
1975–76

Cuba
1962

*Cuba
1961

Grenada
1983

Guatemala
1954

*Nicaragua
1981–89

Panama
1958

Chile
1973

U.S. Interventions

Soviet Interventions

* Support for anti-regime insurgents

** Cuban troops remain throughout 1980s

George Skoch

repression of dissent. Unable to deliver economic stability and progress, ten Latin American dictatorships lost power between 1956 and 1960. The United States would have to re-examine its policy toward Latin America and the rest of the third world.[16]

The Wind of Change: 1958–1965

In January 1961 the United Nations proclaimed the 1960s the Decade of Development. The same month, Khrushchev pledged Soviet support for national liberation movements and Kennedy delivered his stirring inaugural. "To those new states whom we welcome to the ranks of the free," he gave America's "word that one form of colonial control shall not have passed away merely to be replaced by a far more iron tyranny." "To our sister republics south of the border," there was a "special pledge: to convert our good words into good deeds, in a new alliance for progress, to assist free men and free governments in casting off the chains of poverty." Six months later at Vienna, Khrushchev bluntly told Kennedy that Communism was a fact and had "won its right to develop." The Americans should not interfere with liberation movements or "seek any special rights." Kennedy was equally frank, warning that, with the global power balance in rough equilibrium, Communist victories outside Europe would create "strategic problems." The "New Frontier" of endeavor invoked by Kennedy and his advisers began in the third world.[17]

In reality, the East–West struggle outside Europe had entered a new and deadlier phase in 1958. Nasser, although no Communist, had moved closer to Moscow after Suez. The pro-Western regime in Iraq had fallen in 1958, prompting Eisenhower to send marines to Lebanon. The same year, fanatically pro-*Algérie française* elements of the French army, supported by the 900,000-strong *colon* community of Algeria, had precipitated the fall of the Fourth Republic, and the return of de Gaulle. Although de Gaulle intended to leave Algeria, some 500,000 French troops had been deployed in a vicious war against the Egyptian- and Yugoslav-backed FLN. The Suez fiasco prompted Britain to accelerate the granting of independence to its African colonies. Prime Minister Harold Macmillan spoke of "the wind of change" sweeping the continent. Twenty-five new states emerged there between 1957 and 1962.

Some were marginal strategically but others became important piece the global chessboard. The latter included the Congo, whose birth in 1960 was accompanied by the break-away of mineral-rich Katanga province and a power struggle to control the country. Around the time it decided to kill Castro, Washington ordered the assassination of Congo's premier Patrice Lumumba, considered an unstable rabble-rouser who might deliver the ex-Belgian colony's copper, uranium, and diamonds to the USSR.[18]

In East Asia 1958 was marked not only by the unnerving Quemoy crisis, but ominous developments in Indonesia and Vietnam. In 1957 Sukarno had received a $100 million Soviet credit to buy weapons and announced his aim to create a paternalistic "guided democracy," including a cabinet role for the Indonesian Communist Party (PKI). The Eisenhower administration's reflexive reaction was an elaborate covert operation to support dissident officers and Muslim-separatists on the island of Sumatra. After the capture of an American pilot revealed CIA involvement in a campaign to oust his regime and/or break up his country, Sukarno, supported by his nationalist generals, further distanced himself from the West.[19]

In 1957-8, Viet Minh elements who had gone underground in southern Vietnam launched an armed struggle against the RVN. Hounded by government forces and hoping to prevent the Diem regime from consolidating itself, the Viet Minh (called "Viet Cong"—Vietnamese Communists—by the South Vietnamese) assassinated village officials and conducted hit-and-run attacks. With the possible exception of the contemporaneous campaign of the Cuban 26th of July Movement, there is no better example of how local actors' decisions affected the big powers, and through them the Cold War's course. Having decided to renew the fight more or less on their own, the southern-based Communists lobbied for northern help. Many in Hanoi were reluctant to risk a major conflict. With reason, however, they felt cheated by the results of Geneva. Fearing Diem would grow stronger, Hanoi approved a "people's war" in January 1959. In 1960 it infiltrated a 10,000-strong cadre into the south and sponsored a multi-party (although Communist-controlled) organization committed to reunification, the National Liberation Front (NLF). Moscow and Beijing were even more skeptical of the chances of winning and warned Hanoi in May 1960 against an "insurrectionist" strategy. But as the anti-RVN campaign gained momentum, first Beijing, and later Moscow, threw its weight behind the struggle. Saigon's response, including the forced transfer of peasants and brutal suppression of non-Communist opposition groups, incurred hatred and won support for the NLF. [20]

It was 1958 events closer to home that truly alarmed Washington and forced it to recalibrate its general third world approach. The year that ended with Castro's victory included Vice President Nixon's May trip to Uruguay, Peru, and Venezuela. Nixon was booed and stoned by students protesting over U.S. support for dictatorships and denial of economic assistance. In Caracas, an angry crowd smashed the windows of his car. Dulles and Nixon himself blamed Communists, but the CIA and Latin American experts pointed to the region's stark inequality and economic stagnation. The administration accepted the need to add a second arm to a policy based almost solely on military aid and covert meddling. The "wind of change" in the hemisphere received new impetus from the advent of Pope John XXIII in October 1958. The new pontiff was more sympathetic to reform than his austere predecessor, Pius XII, and his arrival encouraged elements of the Latin American church to back democratization. A more open, generous U.S. policy gained momentum with Dulles's resignation in 1959, and the appointment of the Wall Street banker C. Douglas Dillon as under secretary of state. Dillon and Assistant Secretary for Latin American Affairs Thomas Mann oversaw the launching of an Inter-American Development Bank, and a Social Progress Trust Fund to finance health, education, and housing projects, and land reform. The emerging conventional wisdom, reinforced by progressive leaders like Auturo Frondizi of Argentina, Juscelino Kubitschek of Brazil, and Romulo Betancourt of Venezuela, was that state-sponsored programs, supported by U.S. aid, were essential ingredients of a strategy to defeat the left.[21]

Third world turmoil was grist for the mill of "modernization" theorists. In the autumn of 1958 Professor Walt Rostow (born 1916) gave a series of lectures at Cambridge University. They were published in 1960 as *The Stages of Economic Growth*, a seminal work furnishing an intellectual justification for large-scale aid programs. For Rostow, all economies went through a series of stages. Stage one, the "traditional society," was "pre-Newtonian" in science and technology, and locked in a hierarchical social structure. The primary feature of stage two, "the preconditions for take-off," was the building of an effective state by progressive forces, often in opposition to landed interests or the colonial power. The third or "take-off" stage was the "great watershed" where old blocks to steady growth were overcome. Liberal forces expanded and dominated society. The rural sector was commercialized and labor released for more productive employment elsewhere. In stage four, "the drive to maturity," an economy "demonstrated the capacity to move beyond the original industries which powered its take-off. . . ." Finally, in "the Age of High Mass-Consumption," the leading sectors shifted to durable consumer goods and services. The idea of the sovereign consumer emerged. The cheap mass automobile had been the decisive element in this stage.[22]

In its self-serving notion of a single path along which all humanity traveled, and with America as vanguard and arrival-point, Rostow's theory was a precursor of "the end of history" popularized after 1989. More importantly, it contained a message perfectly timed to affect policy in the early 1960s. An urgent problem for Washington was that key countries were presumably in or close to "take-off" but moving too slowly of their own volition. What seemed required was outside help to push them forward and allow them to avoid the Stalinist short-cut. Hence the need for new aid programs, as well as tools like the Peace Corps and Army Special Forces. The first sent idealistic American youths to remote villages as teachers and technicians; the second as trainers and practitioners of "civic action" and "counter-insurgency warfare."

The early-sixties White House, nicknamed "Camelot," was known for its brainpower, glamor, and élan. As Special Assistant for National Security Affairs, Kennedy chose McGeorge Bundy (born 1919), an urbane former dean of Harvard College. Rostow became Bundy's deputy and later Counselor, and Chairman of the Policy Planning Council, of the State Department. Rostow's research suggested India was the best candidate for a big aid program. But, given the emergency created by the Cuban revolution, and the foundation laid by the previous administration, attention focused on the Western Hemisphere. Argentina and Mexico were thought to be in take-off, but others lagged behind.

Along with Rostow, the administration's "mandarins of the future" included historian Arthur M. Schlesinger, Jr., a friend of social democrats like Betancourt, and Adolf M. Berle, Jr., a Latin America hand from the days of FDR.[23] Kennedy also kept on board Eisenhower's innovators, Dillon (now Treasury Secretary) and Mann. The centerpiece of their policy, unveiled at the Punta del Este, Uruguay, conference in August 1961, was the "Alliance for Progress," a kind of Marshall Plan for the South. Its objective was to transfer $20 billion in U.S. public and private capital to Latin America over ten years to promote growth and reform. According to the program's charter, tax and land-tenure systems perpetuating gross inequality and inefficiency would have to change.[24] Privileged positions had to be broken up and new energies released. According to Schlesinger, what was needed was "a middle class revolution where the processes of economic modernization carry the new urban middle-class into power and produce, along with it, such necessities of modern technical society as constitutional government, honest public administration, a responsible party system, a rational land system, and an efficient system of taxation."[25]

Inevitably, the administration's self-confidence and exuberance met recalcitrant reality. Abetting change risked opening a Pandora's box in places of strategic and economic importance, and triggering a conservative backlash in the United States. The Brazilian case was emblematic. President João Goulart was not a Communist but former protégé of the nationalist Getulio Vargas. The Americans noted that Castro had made a similar claim. Goulart's government recognized Cuba, restricted remittances by foreign corporations, and pursued a controversial land reform in the poor northeast. Although such a reform was in the Alliance's spirit, U.S. officials in Brazil adopted the position of the regional elites that it might deliver the area to the Communists.[26] The new Johnson administration, facing an election and in no mood to take chances, encouraged the military and land-owning class to get rid of Goulart. When messianism failed, Washington resorted to proven Hobbesian methods. Shortly before the anti-Goulart coup (April 1964), Mann had convoked U.S ambassadors to Latin America and laid down what became known as the "Mann Doctrine": promote economic growth but not democratization, protect U.S. private investment, and fight Communism. (In 1960, there was some $8.6 billion in U.S. private direct investment in Latin America, mainly in oil, copper, and public utilities; in 1970 the figure was $ 12.3 billion.[27]) In 1965 Washington launched a full-scale invasion of the tiny Dominican Republic to prevent the remote possibility of a Communist take-over. The CIA began a campaign of disinformation and sabotage against socialist premier Cheddi Jagan in Guiana.[28] The Brazilian coup (during the decade, dictatorships replaced thirteen constitutional governments in the region) marked the end of the Latin American wind of change that had risen in 1956–8.

For Moscow, the Alliance for Progress's failure was neither surprising nor reassuring. Washington's reformist rhetoric had been merely a cover for the subordination of exploited countries to the international capitalist division of labor. Although Castro survived, the Khrushchev era's promise was fading, and not only in Latin America. In the Congo, the Americans consolidated their relationship to Joseph-Désiré Mobutu, the army chief-of-staff who had helped to finish off Lumumba. Mobutu seized power in a CIA-supported coup in November 1965. The same year General Houari Boumédienne ousted Mohamed Ahmed Ben Bella, the FLN leader and Soviet favorite who had become Algeria's first president after independence in 1962.

Worse was to come. Under Kennedy and Johnson the CIA resumed covert activity against the pro-Chinese PKI, along with the army, nationalists, and Islamists, a pillar of Sukarno's "guided democracy." Angered by British and U.S. support of an independent Federation of Malaysia on the Malay penninsula, Sukarno moved further to the left. In September 1965, with the economy in crisis, a group of radical junior officers tried to overthrow their commanders who, they claimed, were plotting against Sukarno. The head of the army's Strategic Reserve, General Suharto, blamed the PKI for supporting the coup. With the connivance of Muslim and nationalist forces (and using lists of Communists provided by the U.S. embassy), he unleashed a nation-wide purge of the left. An estimated 500,000 Indonesians were butchered, and the PKI destroyed. Sukarno remained nominally in power until 1967, when he was replaced by Suharto. For the Americans, who had not been directly involved, Indonesian events were "almost too good to be true."[29] For the Soviets, although on bad terms with the PKI, these events formed a disturbing pattern. Ugly but reliably pro-U.S. military regimes were now firmly entrenched in Brazil, Congo, and Indonesia. The reason, fundamentally, was that local vested interests had chosen to crush enemies and ally with Washington for their own reasons, and with a minimum of U.S. prompting. The USSR had been unable seriously to contest any of these large, rich, and strategically located countries. American liberal idealism and "modernization theory" had been discredited. Rostow (as of 1966, Johnson's National Security Adviser) and his colleagues were fixated on Vietnam. But even if the Americans had trouble seeing the forest for the trees in the third world, half the battle there had been won.

The first half of the 1960s also marked the height of China's challenge to Soviet influence in the developing countries. Zhou and Liu Shaoqi traveled frequently to the third world, and China financed a showcase railway from Zambia to the Tanzanian coast. Khrushchev's perceived defeat in Cuba undermined Soviet prestige, and Beijing excoriated the USSR's "revisionism" and "capitalist restoration." Mao had blamed the failure of his Great Leap Forward partly on Moscow's withdrawal of experts from China. In 1964, in preparation for another internal mobilization, he introduced the "three-worlds theory" according to which the United States and USSR constituted an imperialist first world, the industrialized states a subordinate second world, and the PRC and other developing countries, the third. He raised the Sino-Soviet border issue, suggesting China would eventually present a bill for Russian occupation of territories in the Far East.[30] As of October 1964, the PRC had a nuclear weapon to back up its talk. Over the course of the decade, the USSR and PRC came to view the other as the number one threat to its security. Only on one issue, the escalating war in Southeast Asia, did they seem to have common interests, but even there they did not see eye-to-eye.[31]

"Waist-Deep in the Big Muddy": America in Vietnam[32]

A strong case can be made that America's war in Vietnam was the logical result of basic trends since 1947, and few events had a larger impact on subsequent U.S. foreign policy. The cost of the United States's twenty-five-year involvement (from the decision to aid the French-controlled Bao Dai government in May 1950 to Saigon's fall in April 1975) was, to say the least, stunning: some $550 billion (in 2010 dollars), 58,000 U.S. dead, 153,000 wounded, as well as domestic strife and serious splits in the Democratic Party. An estimated 3 million Vietnamese died in the Cold War's bloodiest conflict, although exact figures do not exist.

Analysts have advanced various arguments to explain a quarter-century of tragically self-defeating conduct. For left-wing critics, policy was driven mainly by the military-industrial complex, and, indeed, armaments firms profited from the war. But the study of U.S. decision-making indicates that considerations of private profit were irrelevant, and by the late 1960s policymakers and private-sector observers were increasingly disturbed by the war's inflationary effects. Another set of arguments focuses on U.S. strategy. According to the military and its apologists, the war could have been won if winning decisively had been the politicians' real objective, if the military had been able to do as it pleased (including ground operations against North Vietnam and the use of tactical nuclear weapons), and if civilians at home had not withdrawn their support. It is true that political and military leaders were sometimes at cross purposes, that the military was subject to restrictions, and that domestic opinion was vital. But the military did receive much of what it wanted, including 550,000 personnel in Vietnam by 1968. Those who take this line fail to explain what they mean by "win" and why the war was worth fighting in the first place, or else offer unconvincing arguments as to how the United States might have won.[33]

A variant on the military argument is that Vietnam represented the failure of U.S. doctrine with its reliance on overwhelming firepower, tendency to measure progress on the crude basis of the enemy "body count," and inability to conduct counter-insurgency operations. Despite U.S. insistence to the contrary, the conflict was not a clear-cut case of inter-state aggression.[34] While the United States viewed the 17th parallel as a legitimate border, North Vietnam convincingly argued that it was artificial and in violation of the Geneva agreements. And unlike Korea, there was no clear front line, rather a leopard-skin pattern. The NLF had local support and held areas (especially in the Mekong delta, south and west of Saigon) with limited northern help. A flaw in this argument, however, is that to win the war, it *was* necessary to mount the kind of conventional offensive the Americans were equipped to deal with. Although the Chinese generally recommended a gradual, "protracted war," Mao told the North Vietnamese in 1964, "ineffective and indecisive skirmishes will not solve problems, and only large and decisive battles can solve problems."[35] Two such offensives (in 1968 and 1972) were halted with heavy Communist losses. A third (in 1975) succeeded partly because the Americans had departed and Congress prevented any last-minute attempt to intervene.

A third line of argument emphasizes the decision-making process: high officials were cut off from reality and waded into the quagmire on the basis of the delusion that success required only another incremental investment. Officers in Vietnam misled their superiors because of subtle pressure to paint a rosy picture and their own wish to believe in progress. A domineering president suppressed dissent and demanded, in effect, that subordinates craft their advice to suit his political requirements. Indeed, the U.S. military was strongly committed to success and sometimes unrealistically upbeat in its assessments.[36] But the argument that the war's civilian managers were systematically misled, or self-deluded, does not bear serious scrutiny. Reports brought back after visits to the field were rarely favorable, and often pessimistic.[37] In late 1962 Senator Mike Mansfield (Democrat of Montana), a respected authority on Asia, gave Kennedy a skeptical and downbeat assessment. Vice President Hubert Humphrey delivered a similar message to Johnson. De Gaulle, Lippmann, and the *New York Times* warned that the game was not worth the candle and called for a negotiated settlement. Johnson's confidant Senator Richard Russell (Democrat of Georgia) told him: "It's a tragic situation. It's just one of those places where you can't win."[38] In February 1965 National Security Adviser Bundy wrote Johnson: "The situation is deteriorating, and without new action defeat appears inevitable—probably not in a matter of weeks or even months, but within the next year or so. There is time to turn it around but not much."[39]

Officials like Bundy and McNamara were overly optimistic about the possibility of "turning it around." They habitually lied to the public and concealed U.S. provocations of the North.[40] But they did not sugarcoat the situation for the president. On July 21, 1965, on the eve of the crucial decision to "Americanize" the war (raising U.S. troop strength from 75,000 to 125,000, with another 100,000 to follow in early 1966), Under Secretary of State George Ball told Johnson: "We cannot win, Mr. President . . . The least harmful way to cut losses in SVN is to let the government decide it doesn't want us to stay there . . . [But] I have no illusions that after we were asked to leave South Vietnam, that country would soon come under Hanoi control." The Truman protégé and Democratic insider Clark Clifford echoed this assessment: "I don't believe we can win in South Vietnam . . . I cannot see anything but catastrophe for our nation in this area."[41] It is hard not to be struck by the vigor with which some of Johnson's advisers implored him not to throw good money after bad.

Why did Washington persist? And why was the war un-winnable? The answer to the first question begins with policymakers' own explanations. Nitze traced involvement to the way U.S. responsibilities had been defined in NSC 68.[42] According to NSC 124–2 (June 25, 1952), Indochina was "essential to the security of the Free World, not only in the Far East, but in the Middle East and Europe as well." Eisenhower's domino theory reflected the same reasoning. According to Johnson's ambassador to Saigon (September 1964): "If we leave Vietnam with our tail between our legs, the consequences of this defeat in the rest of Asia, Africa and Latin America would be disastrous." A final, compelling, example is Secretary of State Henry Kissinger's statement in 1975: "We must understand that peace is indivisible . . . We cannot abandon friends in one part of the world without jeopardizing the security of friends everywhere. Abandoning Vietnam will produce a fundamental threat over a period of time to the security of the United States."[43]

The underlying assumption dated back to Wilsonian collective security, reinforced by the 1930s: aggression must not be allowed to succeed lest the Free World's integrity be undermined. The loss of marginal areas would embolden the enemy to thrust forward. It was better to draw the line in a place like Vietnam than have to fight closer to home and for bigger stakes. Some supporters eventually saw that the original commitment had been mistaken. As early as January 1966, McNamara privately confessed his aim was "withdrawal with honor." Although the Americans were correct to think that China wished to spread the revolution in domino fashion, following 1965 events in Indonesia, Vietnam's geopolitical significance was trivial. But it was still considered essential to avoid humiliation. As Pericles had warned the Athenians, "Your empire is now like a tyranny: It may have been wrong to take it. It is certainly dangerous to let it go."[44]

While much can be learned from the policymakers' statements, it is necessary to delve into their emotions and (at times) unspoken assumptions. Especially in the 1954–61 phase, when Eisenhower and Dulles ran roughshod over the Geneva agreement and flooded South Vietnam with dollars and advisers, U.S. policy was animated by a self-confident messianism later described as "the arrogance of power."[45] The Americans had few doubts about their capacity to conduct a successful experiment in "nation building." As for the military contest, it was inconceivable to most Americans that they could be beaten. France's message that no military solution was possible was dismissed as flat wrong (how could a colonial war be compared to a crusade for freedom?) and poisonous to South Vietnamese morale.

As conditions grew problematic in 1961–2, U.S. officials generally retained their faith in ultimate victory, pointing to the success in parts of South Vietnam of a system of fortified villages, or "strategic hamlets," administered by Ngo Dinh Nhu. But NLF strength continued to grow, and the political situation precipitated in May 1963 with the start of Buddhist and student protests (including highly publicized self-immolations) against the Ngos' authoritarian behavior. In August 1963 Nhu's Special Forces carried out brutal punitive raids against the pagodas, provoking international outrage. Nhu and his razor-tongued wife made no secret of their animus toward America's invasive presence and interest in a negotiated settlement with the Communists. In August 1963 de Gaulle called for a solution based on reunification, neutralization, and withdrawal of foreign troops. (Later, he privately remarked: "If the Americans are not too stupid they will put an end to this absurd Vietnam war.")[46] Hanoi was keenly interested in such an arrangement (even if it meant a separate neutral RVN for the time being) as a way of removing the Americans and avoiding all-out war.

Washington now faced the possibility of military failure and/or a government that might invite it to leave as part of a deal with the North. As the situation deteriorated, U.S. officialdom divided on whether to encourage a take-over by disgruntled ARVN generals, or sink or swim with Diem. They were united, however, by a now-dominant emotion: fear of defeat. While sincerely subscribing to the notion of the indivisibility of peace, they also saw the administration's domestic fortunes as indivisible from the war's outcome. Despite a bout of anguish (if the coup failed, he said, "We could lose our entire position in Southeast Asia overnight"), Kennedy backed a military takeover.[47] Diem and Nhu were overthrown and shot on November 2, 1963. Kennedy himself was assassinated in Dallas on November 22, 1963.

Vietnam is the best illustration of how the U.S. two-party competition biased the executive toward military activism. Johnson (born 1908) was a former Democratic leader of the Senate who had coveted the presidency. Once he had it, he felt with particular acuteness the iron law of U.S. politics: the opposition will make you pay if you look weak. In May 1964 Rusk, McNamara, and Bundy recommended that if North Vietnam ignored warnings to end the war, the United States should "use selected and carefully graduated military force" against it. The formidable Texas politician had an expensive, ambitious domestic agenda. His doubts were evident in his reply to Bundy, "It's damned easy to get in a war but it's gonna be awfully hard to ever extricate yourself". But he did not seriously consider withdrawing. Johnson had opposed the coup, and while under few illusions about exporting reform, felt an obligation to Saigon. Above all, the memory of McCarthyism was ever-present. As he put it: "The loss of China is chicken-shit compared to what might happen if we lost Vietnam."[48] He followed his advisers' suggestion, relaying secret warnings to Hanoi and taking advantage of an attack on a U.S. destroyer in the Gulf of Tonkin in August 1964 to bomb North Vietnam and obtain a sweeping Congressional mandate (the "Tonkin Gulf Resolution") authorizing him to take whatever steps he considered necessary to protect U.S. lives in Southeast Asia. While assuring the electorate that "we still seek no wider war," Johnson shielded himself against his right-wing opponent, Senator Barry Goldwater, and won a landslide victory in November 1964.[49]

After crushing Goldwater, Johnson might have felt freer to leave Vietnam. But, having raised the stakes partly to cover himself politically, it was (just as he had predicted) more difficult to pull out. Johnson had his eye on the 1968 elections and had no intention of being the first president to lose a war. Fredrik Logevall's verdict is harsh but convincing: Johnson and his advisers "chose the war option . . . because of the threat of embarrassment—to the United States, to the Democratic Party, and, most of all, to themselves personally."[50]

Would Kennedy have done differently? He was a more seasoned foreign policy operator and had proved himself in Cuba and Berlin. Although he had increased the number of U.S. personnel in Vietnam from about 900 to almost 17,000, he approved a plan in October 1963 to remove 1,000 at the end of the year, and which foresaw the winding down of the U.S. role by the end of 1965.[51] Bobby Kennedy later claimed that under no circumstances would his brother have committed combat units. Some scholars contend that he planned to withdraw even if the situation worsened. But there is evidence to suggest otherwise.[52] The October 1963 decision had been intended partly to pressure Saigon, and even before Kennedy's death McNamara was expressing doubts about a pull-out.[53] The Ngos's demise did nothing to stem war-weariness and pro-neutralist sentiment in Saigon and was followed by NLF gains in the field. The anxious Americans welcomed a second coup in January 1964 by hard-line ARVN generals because it removed officers reportedly leaning toward a deal with the Communists. It is hard to believe Kennedy would have been less determined than Johnson to avoid such an outcome before the 1964 elections. If reelected, Kennedy would have been freer of the "iron law." Still, it requires a considerable leap of faith to believe that he would have withdrawn regardless of conditions on the ground and/or pursued neutralization as proposed by de Gaulle.[54]

Why was victory elusive, even defining the term as a Korea-like stalemate allowing a pro-U.S. southern regime to survive? There are two, interrelated, reasons, either of which would suffice to answer the question. The first is that because of a series of objective factors, or "givens," the war was virtually impossible to win. The first factor was the war's geopolitical setting. In contrast to Korea, America's opponent had adjacent areas in Laos and Cambodia providing sanctuaries and transport routes (the famous Ho Chi Minh trail) for supplies and manpower from the north. Even more important was North Vietnam's Chinese hinterland and the possibility of PRC intervention. In the final analysis, the only way to win the war was probably to invade and secure North Vietnam. According to Mark Moyar, the United States missed an opportunity to do so without provoking a serious Chinese reaction in late 1964. But occupying all or part of the DRV not only would have dramatically expanded the insurgency faced by U.S. and RVN forces, it would almost certainly have brought China into the conflict. Although Beijing neither expected nor welcomed a big U.S. intervention, in January and June 1964 meetings with the North Vietnamese, Mao pledged his support: "the Chinese had legs." If the Americans invaded North Vietnam, the Chinese would come in. After the Gulf of Tonkin incident, the PRC began moving coastal industrial facilities inland in preparation for war. In December 1964 the PRC and DRV signed an agreement providing for major assistance to North Vietnam.[55]

In January 1965 Mao gave a conciliatory interview to the American journalist Edgar Snow, suggesting Chinese forces would remain in China.[56] But when Washington signaled a major escalation in March–April 1965, Beijing laid down three principles:

First, if the Americans went beyond the bombing of the North and used land forces to invade North Vietnam, China would have to send military [i.e. combat] forces. Second, China would give clear warning to the Americans so that they would not feel free to expand military operations into the North, let alone bring the war into China. Third, China would avoid a direct military face-off with the United States as long as possible, but it would not shrink from a confrontation.[57]

The near-certainty of a second war with China deterred the Americans from taking the ground war beyond the 17th parallel. Between 1964 and 1968, moreover, China provided indispensable material and logistical support. At the height of Chinese involvement, in 1967, there were 170,000 Chinese engineering and anti-aircraft personnel in North Vietnam. This allowed the DRV to cover its rear and operate on a far greater scale in the South.[58]

In 1965 the USSR also began to provide significant aid. Moscow and Beijing, in effect, competed to be "big brother" to North Vietnam.[59] For the Chinese, the Russians could do no right. At first they suspected Moscow was trying to lure North Vietnam into the "revisionist" camp and would eventually sell it out for the sake of better relations with the Americans. In 1967 Zhou Enlai warned North Vietnamese leaders Pham Van Dong and Vo Nguyen Giap that, just as Stalin (cowed by the atomic bomb) had told the Chinese Communists to co-operate with the Nationalists, Moscow wanted Hanoi "to stop halfway" in the war. In June 1968, however, Zhou blamed the Soviets for inspiring the recent, costly offensive, a mistaken departure from "protracted war"! But, although telling the North Vietnamese to refuse the USSR's aid, the Chinese agreed to allow Soviet-bloc air-defense equipment, tanks, and other supplies to transit their territory to the DRV. Beijing criticized Hanoi in April 1968 for agreeing to negotiate with Washington, and had withdrawn its personnel from North Vietnam by the end of 1970. For its part, Hanoi was no one's "little brother" and determined to avoid another Geneva, where it had been persuaded to compromise by Beijing and Moscow. But despite growing PRC–DRV tensions, and Hanoi's increasing closeness to Moscow, China never abandoned support for the complete victory of the North.[60]

A second objective factor was the nature of America's enemy. The fighting skill and resilience of the NLF and DRV regular forces amazed the world. They also proved more adept, persistent, and ruthless than the Americans and the Saigon regime in fighting for political control of the countryside, where both sides used intimidation, incarceration, and assassination to "win hearts and minds."[61] The Communists held the decisive nationalist card, and naturally saw their stake in the outcome as higher than the Americans. The NLF and North Vietnamese were committed to total victory and willing to fight for decades. They pursued negotiations to divide and divert the enemy (as in late 1967), buy time and/or lick their wounds when on the defensive (as in 1965 and mid-to-late 1968), or to win international sympathy and bring about a U.S. withdrawal in order to deal with South Vietnam one-on-one (as in 1969–72).

The third, and probably most important, factor was the Saigon regime. The Ngo family, while genuine nationalists, lacked support from much of the rural population. Their ruthless suppression of dissent was not an invention of American journalists, and played into the hands of the NLF.[62] The ARVN had brave soldiers and effective units, but its top leaders often lacked energy and ability, and in many cases were corrupt. It was operationally timid and dependent on U.S. support. The Americans repeated that only the South Vietnamese could win the war and occasionally sought to link aid to more determined action. But the politically ambitious officers who ruled the RVN after Diem knew that threats to withhold help lacked credibility because the Americans feared defeat. By late 1964 Bundy and McNamara argued that a bigger U.S. effort might raise morale and stop the rot. By February 1965 their thesis was that without a sustained bombing campaign against the North, South Vietnam's collapse was inevitable.[63] Using a Communist attack on the U.S. base at Pleiku as a pretext, and essentially out of desperation, Washington launched "Operation Rolling Thunder" in March 1965. Some believed the war's Americanization might breathe new life into Saigon's efforts, but it did not require great psychological insight to see this was unlikely. In theory, the United States could have sent a million men and occupied every hamlet in the country for an indefinite period. But this would hardly have accomplished the aim of creating a viable, independent RVN.

The second basic reason why victory remained elusive is simply that America did not fight to win. Kennedy and Johnson were deeply ambivalent toward the commitment. Growing doubts about the war's cost, rationality, and morality afflicted many, including McNamara, who used his influence to block a further sharp escalation desired by the military in 1967, and resigned in early 1968.[64] Johnson feared that conservatives would crucify him if he lost. But he also feared the political and financial costs of all-out escalation. Liberal Democrats would turn against him and the country would be unable to afford his "Great Society" and "War on Poverty." He rejected the JCS's advice to declare a national emergency and mobilize reserve forces, and avoided raising taxes to finance the war before 1967. Johnson saw the troop increases of 1965-7 not as a way of winning decisively, but of stabilizing the situation and avoiding defeat. In effect, Johnson adopted a middle course.[65]

Ambivalence, and outright opposition, naturally grew along with the level of violence. The 1966–8 "search and destroy," or war-of-attrition, phase meant major sweeps by U.S. combat forces. It produced no decisive encounters but rising numbers of U.S. killed and wounded.[66] In pursuit of "territorial denial," the Americans declared vast "free fire zones" that were obliterated by B-52s and sprayed with defoliants. U.S. aircraft continued to pound the North but with limited effects on the DRV's will or capacity to fight. During 1965–8, Washington followed a policy of gradual escalation—doing what seemed necessary to meet the present situation. The North Vietnamese saw that such an approach betrayed political and moral reservations. As early as May 1965, Zhou observed that gradual escalation was "the worst taboo in a military sense," and that the Americans lacked a long-term strategy. Hanoi saw it was in a test of wills and that sooner or later America's morale would crack, just as France's had. As Ho had told the French in 1946, "You will kill ten of us and we will kill one of you, but you will be the ones who grow tired."[67]

A crucial moment in this test was February–March 1968. Under the cover of the lunar new year celebration, NLF and DRV regular forces began a series of audacious, coordinated assaults on South Vietnam's main population centers. The "Tet offensive" was a serious military setback (the Communists lost 40,000 people, about half the manpower committed, and the NLF did not recover as an independent military force) and failed to provoke the intended "general uprising." But it was an important political and psychological victory. The U.S. commander in Vietnam, General William Westmoreland, had given an optimistic assessment in November 1967, and (in contrast to the CIA) underestimated NLF strength. In a misguided attempt to sustain support, the administration had conveyed the message that the situation was improving.[68] Hence (and to a degree the North Vietnamese probably had not anticipated) Tet delivered a major shock to American public opinion. There had been nothing like it since MacArthur's rout in 1950. This time Americans were not only reading the news but watching it in "living color" on television. Having been told "there was light at the end of the tunnel," they saw NLF fighters inside the U.S. embassy compound in Saigon, one of the sprawling city's most heavily fortified structures. They saw the Saigon police chief summarily execute a Viet Cong soldier with a pistol shot to the temple. They heard an American major explaining to a journalist why his men had put a village to the torch: "It became necessary to destroy the village in order to save it." To many, these remarkable words summarized what the United States was doing on a vast scale in Vietnam, and to capture the absurdity of the war.

Tet triggered a world-wide sell-off of the dollar, forcing Washington to confront the war's inflationary effects and end its policy of trying to have "guns and butter." It also led Johnson to order his new defense secretary, Clark Clifford, to reassess U.S. strategy. After a review lasting several weeks, Clifford recommended that the president reject the military's request for over 200,000 more troops and an expanded war, including amphibious landings in southern North Vietnam.[69] The request, leaked to the *New York Times* and published on March 10, prompted disbelief. Finally, Tet galvanized the "doves" in Congress (Senators Mansfield, Fulbright, Eugene McCarthy, Frank Church, Wayne Morse, and George McGovern, among others) and on the campuses, and a Democratic Party revolt. First McCarthy and then Bobby Kennedy (a New York senator) challenged Johnson for the presidential nomination. On March 22 Johnson formally accepted Clifford's advice, although partly, he avowed, because the U.S.–ARVN counter-offensive after Tet had rendered the increase unnecessary.[70] With some reluctance and bitterness, he also accepted Clifford's recommendation (endorsed by a group of "Wise Men" including Acheson, Ball, Bundy, Lodge, and generals Taylor, Ridgway, and Bradley), that Washington begin to de-escalate and seriously pursue a negotiated settlement.[71] Johnson, backed by Rusk and Rostow, never abandoned his belief in the goal of an independent, non-Communist RVN. But he recognized political and economic realities. Worn-down and deeply unpopular, he decided that his own role in the drama was over. On March 31 he announced a halt in bombing north of the 20th parallel and nominated Averell Harriman as his personal representative to possible peace talks. He then stunned the nation, stating he would neither seek nor accept the nomination to run for another term.[72]

The precise impact of the anti-war and broader "counter-cultural" movements is hard to assess. Kissinger later observed: "The internationalist establishment, which had been responsible for the great achievements of our foreign policy, collapsed before the onslaught of its own children, who questioned all its values." This exaggeration contained an element of truth. As Clifford discovered, influential businessmen, professionals, and journalists across the country who had backed the war had changed their minds. In addition to the economic damage, Vietnam was beginning to tear apart the social fabric of the United States. Evidence for this were the sit-ins, draft-card burnings, and boisterous demonstrations spearheaded by the long-haired, restless children of the affluent. The anti-war movement was self-interested ("hell no, we won't go!" was one of its slogans). It was outraged by the war's apparent senselessness and human costs ("hey, hey, LBJ, how many kids did you kill today?" was another). It romanticized the defiers of U.S. power—Che, Mao, and Ho—and turned their faces into icons. In 1967, in the context of rising racial tensions and riots in America's ghettos, Martin Luther King, the leader of the non-violent civil rights movement, had denounced the waste of lives and resources in Southeast Asia. His courage cost him the support of the White House. But the anti-war movement was mainly white and privileged. Therein lay its capacity to gain the attention of the powerful and (as Kissinger suggested) its basic strength.[73]

Tet-inspired turmoil in the United States reached a crescendo in violent clashes between police and demonstrators outside the Democratic Party convention in Chicago in August 1968, and had two longer-term consequences. The Democrats split into several foreign policy currents. The anti-war left under McGovern would lead the party to defeat in the 1972 elections. Centrists who had turned against the war but not U.S. world leadership would later regroup around Governor Jimmy Carter of Georgia. Democrats identifying with Truman's policies, some eventually known as "neoconservatives," kept alive the notion that the war had been necessary and winnable. A second important consequence of 1968 events was Richard Nixon's narrow victory. Johnson's announcement just before the elections of a total bombing halt failed to stave off defeat for Hubert Humphrey. Simultaneously, Nixon countered the Democrats' bid to present themselves as the peace party by secretly encouraging RVN President Nugyen Van Thieu not to send a delegation to talks underway in Paris.[74] Nixon won thanks to a platform of "law and order," an appeal to middle-class loathing of the disorder associated with the civil rights and anti-war movements, as well as his plan for an "honorable peace" in Southeast Asia. But things were not to be so simple. Johnson's war was now Nixon's war.

CHAPTER 7
THE RISE AND DECLINE OF DÉTENTE, 1969-1977

The scene greeting the White House's new occupants appeared much changed from the simpler days of the 1950s. But Nixon and his adviser Henry Kissinger were not modest about their capacity to manage the country's uncertain fortunes. Nixon, a former congressman, senator, and vice president, had traveled and written widely during his political exile (1960–8). Kissinger had advised the Kennedy administration and was a leading international affairs expert. What struck both was the degree to which the world, although bipolar militarily, was evolving toward political multi-polarity. This trend could be coped with, even exploited, but probably not reversed.

Western Europe was now an economic power-house, and de Gaulle had removed France from NATO's integrated military command in 1966. His attempt to undermine the "Yalta system" suffered a severe reverse when Warsaw pact members invaded Czechoslovakia to crush Alexander Dubcek's reformist Communist experiment in August 1968. Moscow brutally reaffirmed the logic of the blocs, while Washington, beset by its own troubles, barely lifted a finger. But the German Social Democrats, reacting to the Berlin wall and bankruptcy of Adenauer's "policy of strength," had earlier set in motion a more durable détente policy, *Ostpolitik*. SPD leader Willy Brandt and his adviser Egon Bahr based their strategy on the notion of "change through rapprochement." Closer ties to the East would improve life there and lessen mutual hostility. NATO, reacting to de Gaulle and budding *Ostpolitik*, had proclaimed détente and the overcoming of Germany's division to be official alliance objectives. After becoming chancellor in 1969, Brandt

Figure 5. Willy Brandt at the 1944 Warsaw uprising monument, December 7, 1970.

pursued friendlier relations with the USSR, Poland, and East Germany. Nixon and Kissinger distrusted Brandt but knew it would be counter-productive to try to stop a policy as popular as *Ostpolitik*. They aimed to harness it and prevent Germany from weakening NATO by becoming too cozy with the East.[1]

In Asia, Japan was on its way to economic superpower status. The PRC was now a major rival of the USSR as well as the United States. Nixon and Kissinger saw advantages in developing a new relationship with China, although they were at a loss as to how to proceed.[2] Rising Soviet power, Washington believed, was irreversible. The liquidation of the "Prague Spring," while not destroying the hopes of Soviet reformers, bolstered Brezhnev's position atop a conservative oligarchy.[3] Around 1970, the USSR and United States reached rough strategic nuclear parity. In Moscow this was believed to mark the end of an era of free-wheeling U.S. interventionism and underpin a dawning period of superpower equality.[4]

As for the United States, Kissinger had written, "Political multipolarity makes it impossible to impose an American design."[5] This was an understatement. There were clear signs of a "Vietnam syndrome," or public allergy to the use of force. Not the least of America's problems was the economy. The annual inflation rate in 1970 was around 5 percent, compared to 1 percent in 1960. Reflecting declining competitiveness, a long-standing trade surplus would disappear in 1971. Plausible culprits included the Bretton Woods monetary system perpetuating an over-valued dollar, EEC and Japanese protectionism, and the Johnson admin-istration's inflationary macroeconomic policies. Whatever the cause, relative economic decline strengthend the case for a new Cold War approach.[6]

The Nixon–Kissinger collaboration was frequently marked by petty jealousy and mistrust. But it lasted until Nixon's resignation in August 1974, under threat of impeachment for covering up the June 1972 break-in at Democratic National Committee headquarters in the Watergate building. (National Security Adviser Kissinger also became Secretary of State in September 1973.) Both were conservatives in two senses: the aim to conserve U.S. power, and a "realist" outlook. They were inclined to minimize the role of ideology, as opposed to the quest for geopolitical advantage, in state behavior. Nixon would tell Mao, "what is important is not a nation's internal political philosophy. What is important is its policy toward the rest of the world and toward us."[7] Each considered himself an iconoclast with respect to a mainly Eastern, Anglo-Saxon Protestant "Establishment" long in charge of foreign policy. Nixon, son of a struggling California lemon farmer, was a product of the Republican far right. Some saw a mellower "new Nixon," but he was still a hard-fisted, unforgiving figure who viewed human affairs through Hobbesian lenses. Kissinger was a German Jew whose family had fled Nazism. Steeped in the Old World's tragic experience, he was at odds with the belief in progress typical of the New. Both saw bureaucracy as the enemy of policy. True statesmanship was the realm of the heroic and lonely individual. Kissinger's first book had romanticized early nineteenth-century European diplomacy. In an account of his early political battles, Nixon had romanticized himself.[8]

Erecting a "New Structure"

Nixon was troubled to the point of obsession by the question: did the United States have the "guts" and "stamina" to defend its position? He was sure its enemies would capitalize on a policy of retreat. When opportunities arose, he tried to signal a willingness to use massive force.[9] But Nixon was a hobbled Hobbesian. America was unable to pursue a policy relying on raw power, and messianism had lost credibility. Ways had to be found to reduce pressures and (to use Nixon's own expression) to "live and let live" with adversaries.[10] His answer was *gattopardesco* (leopard-like), a neologism taken from a famous line in Giuseppe Tomasi di Lampedusa's novel *Il Gattopardo* (*The Leopard*) about Sicilian aristocrats during Garibaldi's invasion: "Everything must change so that nothing changes." Nixon and Kissinger aimed to create a "new structure of global relationships" to preserve existing power.[11] The structure can be compared to a building: the ground floor represented the domestic base; one supporting pillar was détente, or new relationships with the USSR and PRC; the second pillar was "devolution," new relationships with friendly states. The pillars supported a roof representing America's world position.

At the domestic level, the approach was marked by an extreme concentration of power. The White House established a "back-channel" to Moscow through Soviet ambassador Dobrynin. Kissinger's maiden trip to China (July 9–11, 1971) was a cloak-and-dagger affair in which pains were taken to deceive most of the U.S. government. In pursuit of détente, Nixon and Kissinger laid down three principles: concreteness, agreements on the basis of strict reciprocity rather than mere atmospheric changes; mutual restraint, especially in the third world; and linkage, meaning outstanding issues (arms control, regional conflicts, economic ties) were interconnected. Soviet concessions in one area might lead to U.S. concessions in another, and vice versa. Washington would use the carrot and the stick.[12]

Nixon's main innovation was to lean on Moscow (and through Moscow, he hoped, Hanoi) by going first to Beijing. A premise of the "opening to China" was the waning of the Cultural Revolution. Mao was no follower of Jesus Christ, but his late-1960s motto might have been "the first shall be last and the last shall be first." Determined to destroy supposed enemies and stamp out privilege, Mao had purged the CCP and unleashed youthful zealots known as Red Guards against the established order in the universities and ministries. Millions of state and party bureaucrats were killed, imprisoned, or sent to the countryside to do "corrective labor." The result was social and economic chaos. By 1969, Mao's mania with purification was giving way to greater sobriety. The context of the "opening" also included bloody border clashes between Soviet and Chinese troops (March and August 1969) and Moscow's consideration of preemptive strikes on China's nuclear facilities. By the late 1960s, the USSR had nearly a million men on its frontier with the PRC. Washington sought, in effect, to use China's fear of the USSR to develop a U.S.–Chinese relationship that would both counter-balance Soviet power and push Moscow toward better relations with America. In classic balance-of-power fashion, Nixon and Kissinger rejected combining with the stronger of the Communist giants, in favor of a quasi-alliance with the lesser of the two.

Publicly, the Americans denied playing the "China card."[13] Privately, Nixon told British Prime Minister Edward Heath, "As for China, when you have two enemies, we want to tilt towards the weaker, not towards the stronger--though not in a way that we can be caught at it." They were not simply trying to change Soviet behavior toward America. From their basically Mackinderian perspective, they were genuinely worried that an expansionist USSR might control the PRC. Kissinger told the Chinese: "it is against our interests to permit the establishment of an hegemony in Eurasia dominated from Moscow." Aside from geopolitical affinities, Kissinger tended to idealize the Chinese as the custodians of a superior civilization while seeing the Russians, by comparison, as boorish and insecure.[14]

Just as the United States viewed China as the weaker Communist power, China saw the United States as the less lethal of its adversaries. A venerable tradition called for "borrowing the strength of barbarians to check barbarians." But Chinese-American rapprochement developed fitfully. Signals were misread or ignored.[15] The Chinese did not want to be seen as rushing to embrace the imperialists. Premier Zhou Enlai (who had tried to contain the excesses of the Cultural Revolution) favored the opening. But a powerful figure, vice-premier, defense minister, and (as of 1969) Mao's designated "heir and successor," Marshal Lin Biao, opposed it. Lin had helped to create the Maoist cult of personality and was a leader of the Cultural Revolution. The serendipitous meetings of U.S. and Chinese ping-pong players in Japan in April 1971 (prompting Mao to invite the U.S. team to China) helped to break the ice. But it was the failure of the apparent coup and assassination attempt against Mao by Lin Biao's son, air force officer Lin Liguo, and the Lin family's flight and death in a plane crash in Outer Mongolia in September 1971, that finally cleared the path.[16]

During Nixon's public visit (February 21–8, 1972), the China lobby's former champion toasted Communism's Great Helmsman and signed the Shanghai communiqué. Although the Chinese insisted on spelling out their differences, the two sides noted a common opposition to (Soviet) "hegemony" in the Asia-Pacific region. The Americans accepted the PRC's position that there was only one China, and pledged gradually to end their military presence on Taiwan.[17] During an October 1971 preparatory visit, Kissinger had shown the Chinese satellite photos and other data on Soviet military activity, presumably to underline the threat and suggest the rewards of closer relations. Nixon now offered the Chinese an informal alliance, telling them: "In December, when the situation was getting very sensitive in the subcontinent . . . I was prepared to warn the Soviet Union against undertaking an attack on China . . . I can also give assurances that the U.S. would oppose any attempt by the Soviet Union to engage in an aggressive action against China." This was a reference to the December 1971 war in which India, a Soviet client, had defeated Pakistan, a friend of China and the United States.[18]

But while eager to reap concessions on Taiwan, the Chinese were chary of dependency and less concerned about a Soviet attack on China than the Americans. Although the situation remained tense, shortly after the August 1969 clash, Zhou and Premier Alexei Kosygin had met at Beijing airport. The two sides pledged to settle their border dispute through peaceful negotiations, and talks resumed after a five-year hiatus.[19] Kissinger habitually repeated the Russians' hostile or provocative remarks about the PRC, but the Chinese never seemed to be too impressed. Mao, echoed by Zhou Enlai's successor Deng Xiaoping, made light of the Mackinderian argument:

They [the Russians] have to deal with so many adversaries. They have to deal with the Pacific. They have to deal with Japan. They have to deal with China. They have to deal with South Asia which also consists of quite a number of countries. And they have only a million troops here—not enough even for the defense of themselves and still less for attack forces. But they can't attack unless you let them in first, and you first give them the Middle East and Europe so they are able to deploy troops eastward. And that would take over a million troops.[20]

Another limit to "triangular diplomacy" was Beijing's suspicion of U.S.–Soviet détente. To the Chinese, Kissinger characterized U.S.–Soviet agreements as a kind of shadow-boxing designed to disarm or "paralyze" left-wing opinion in Europe and America, and way to create political obstacles to the extension of Soviet power. But the Chinese, who preferred bad U.S.–Soviet relations, suspected the Americans of double-dealing.[21] They insisted, as Zhou told Kissinger's assistant Alexander Haig, even before Nixon's visit, that "no country should depend upon a foreign power in maintaining its own independence and viability." In October 1975 Deng told Kissinger: "We have always believed that we should rely on our independent strength to deal with the Soviet Union, and we have never cherished any illusions about this." The Chinese had no intention of provoking Moscow by embracing Washington, or of becoming beholden to the United States.[22]

The opening's undeniable payoff for Washington was that it provided leverage in dealing with the USSR. After his first visit to China became known, Kissinger recalled, "Other [U.S.–Soviet] negotiations deadlocked for months began magically to unfreeze."[23] This was an exaggeration but Moscow eventually decided to proceed with U.S.–Soviet détente. Strategic Arms Limitation Talks (SALT) had begun in Helsinki in 1969, as well as negotiations on the still-nagging question of West Berlin. Each side had tried to extract concessions in return for agreeing to a summit. In October 1969 Nixon attempted to tie an improvement in relations to Soviet help in pressuring North Vietnam for a settlement.[24] But Moscow was not able (even if it had wanted to) to dictate terms to Hanoi.

Another problem was discord and jockeying for position in Moscow. Foreign Minister Gromyko and KGB Chairman Andropov supported détente, first with the FRG, then with the United States. Ambassador Dobrynin, a fellow supporter, explained their reasoning:

First, a nuclear war was utterly unacceptable, as the Cuban crisis had clearly demonstrated. Second, there was the enormous burden of military expenditures... Third, the process of improving relations between the Soviet Union and Western Europe, especially with the Federal Republic of Germany through the so-called Berlin Agreements, would become extremely complicated if the United States were to try to impede it, and the American position was largely determined by the prospects for strategic arms limitation talks. Fourth... it was essential to avert or neutralize any collusion between Washington and Beijing.

He added that although "dogmatic domestic ideology remained unchanged... the realities of the rest of the world and the strains on our economy prompted the Soviet leadership to improve relations with the nations of Europe and the United States." Soviet economic problems were of a different nature than America's but no less alarming. Growth rates had declined after the late 1950s. To feed its people and develop its resources, the supposed beacon of Communism needed Western grain and technology. Détente appeared to promise benefits that would allow Khrushchev's successors to *avoid* structural reforms of the kind tried before 1964, while continuing high levels of military spending.[25] Even so, Politburo stalwarts like President Nikolai Podgorny, Defense Minister Andrei Grechko, and the armed forces chief-of-staff Dmitry Ustinov opposed arms agreements and cozying up to the Americans. Grechko and Ustinov, hard-bitten soldiers in charge of the Soviet military-industrial complex, and cronies of Brezhnev, were "worthy counterparts of American hawks."[26] Premier Kosygin wanted better relations with China and was unenthusiastic about détente.

Dobrynin mentions a final factor in the Kremlin's move toward détente: it would "consolidate the prestige of Brezhnev's leadership."[27] The jovial collector of luxury cars relished the popularity and status that his role as negotiating partner of the German chancellor and U.S. president brought him. A former divisional commissar, he was deeply committed to avoiding war. As a perceptive historian observes, "It was Brezhnev's personal and increasingly emotional involvement and his talents as a domestic consensus builder that proved to be the most important factor in securing the policy of détente in the period from 1968 to 1972."[28] At the 24th CPSU Congress (March–April 1971), Brezhnev's position became the party line. Following Kissinger's July China trip, Nixon wrote him a personal letter and Brezhnev replied that he was ready for a summit. In 1970 Moscow and Bonn had concluded a largely symbolic friendship treaty, but the Germans made Bundestag ratification conditional on a Quadripartite Agreement on West Berlin. This historic step was taken in September 1971.[29] Moscow and Washington announced a date for their Moscow summit (May 1972) in October 1971.

At this point a pair of unforeseen events on the "periphery" suggested the pitfalls of U.S.–Soviet détente. Washington's "tilt" toward Pakistan in the December war, including a gratuitous warning to Moscow not to intervene, angered the Kremlin. More seriously, on March 30, 1972, without consulting Moscow, Hanoi launched a major offensive across the demilitarized zone separating North and South Vietnam. Nixon was eager for another election-year summit, but could not afford to be drinking toasts in Moscow as Soviet-supplied tanks attacked South Vietnam. Infuriated with Hanoi, he ordered B-52 strikes and sent Kissinger to Moscow. Kissinger was to threaten to cancel the summit to extract Soviet help. Realizing Moscow could or would do little to stop the offensive, Kissinger was conciliatory. He accepted, for example, the Soviet position on the text of "basic principles of relations" to be signed by Nixon and Brezhnev.[30] By disregarding his instructions, Kissinger raised Brezhnev's expectations for a successful meeting and helped shelter the summit from the unprecedented steps, including the mining of Haiphong harbor, Nixon announced on May 8, 1972. Nixon told Kissinger, "I intend to stop at nothing to bring the enemy to his knees."[31]

With Hanoi under a hail of bombs, the summit "hung in the balance." Podgorny and Grechko spoke against it but Brezhnev pulled out the stops to convince the Politburo and a secret plenary session of the Central Committee. Cancelling the meeting, he argued, would give ammunition to conservative opponents of the FRG-Soviet treaty due to be ratified on the eve of Nixon's arrival in Moscow. Hanoi should not have a veto over Soviet policy, and cancellation would not help its cause. Above all, the agreements to be concluded were too important to be put in jeopardy. With the Central Committee Plenum's last-minute endorsement in hand, the way was finally clear.[32]

*   *   *

As they groped their way toward détente, the Americans tried to raise the second pillar of their structure. Kissinger had written, "Regional groupings supported by the United States will have to take over major responsibility for their immediate areas, with the United States being concerned with the overall framework of order." Commentators dubbed this the "devolution" of responsibility to "surrogates" of U.S. power.[33] Nixon broached the policy during a July 1969 trip to Asia: the United States would honor existing commitments, maintain its nuclear shield, and supply aid, but expect local forces to do the fighting.[34] An area of concern was the Persian Gulf, where Britain's late-1960s pull-out left a vacuum. America's designated surrogate would be the Shah of Iran, eager to play the local policeman. But the initial, urgent application of the "Nixon Doctrine" was in South Vietnam.

Nixon and Kissinger lacked a clear plan to end the war and they did not always see eye-to-eye. Despite denials, Kissinger was probably readier to settle for what on one occasion he called a "decent interval," a face-saving arrangement guaranteeing South Vietnam's temporary survival after America's withdrawal, before its probable surrender. Although pessimistic about Saigon, Nixon was no less a believer in the domino theory, and no less in thrall to the political "iron law," than his predecessors.[35] If the war's outcome were interpreted, he said, "as the failure of the United States . . . to achieve a minimum goal, not victory over North Vietnam, but simply the right of the South Vietnamese to choose their own way without having it imposed, the impact would be enormous and I think devastating."[36] "[I]f we were to lose," Nixon told Kissinger, "our foreign policy would be in shambles. And domestically, it would kill us." He did not intend to be the "first American President to lose a war."[37]

The administration settled on a four-part approach. "Vietnamization" turned the ground war over to the locals. The ARVN was armed to the teeth, becoming the world's fifth-largest army. Second, the phased withdrawal of U.S. troops by the end of 1972 drastically reduced American casualties. Third, although Nixon rejected a big offensive in 1969, he oversaw a truly staggering escalation of the air war (including the secret bombing of supposed Cambodian sanctuaries in 1969–70, and of North Vietnam in May–October and December 1972), and broke taboos on ground operations. U.S. troops conducted a major incursion into Cambodia in May 1970. ARVN forces invaded southern Laos in February 1971. Along with disrupting supply-lines and boosting the ARVN, these actions were supposed to show Hanoi that it could not defeat or wait out the Americans. U.S. ground forces were leaving but U.S. air power remained. Fourth, Kissinger and his DRV counterpart Le Duc Tho began negotiations in Paris. Initially secret, the talks were disclosed to the world in January 1972.[38]

Nixon's approach encountered serious problems. The most significant result of the Cambodia operation was an outburst of indignation in Congress and on the campuses. Nixon and Vice President Spiro Agnew dismissed war opponents as "nattering nabobs of negativism," and appealed for backing to the "great silent majority."[39] But although a majority trusted Nixon to end the conflict more than they did the Democrats, Americans were war-weary. Nixon himself was intent on removing the Vietnam millstone from his neck by the start of his second mandate. Even with U.S. air-support, the ARVN's best units limped out of Laos with heavy losses. The Russians and Chinese, even if not wanting to prolong the war, were of little use, and Hanoi felt strong enough to make a major gamble in 1972. Although Washington initially sought an agreement removing both U.S. and DRV troops from South Vietnam, by October 1970 it was ready for a major concession: a cease-fire in place rather than the evacuation of enemy forces.[40] By late 1972 there were some 150,000 North Vietnamese troops south of the 17th parallel. Fortunately for Washington, Hanoi, after months of aerial punishment, was also flexibile. In October 1972 it dropped insistence on an immediate coalition including the NLF, and agreed that the Thieu government could remain after a cease-fire. Southern Communists were furious with Hanoi, but the North needed a respite and was confident of the final outcome. On October 31, 1972, Kissinger famously proclaimed to reporters: "peace is at hand."[41]

Euphoric, and evidently wanting to take credit for a break-through, Kissinger had jumped the gun. Thieu refused to accept a deal leaving enemy forces on his doorstep. Nixon, vexed with his over-eager envoy, and strengthened by his landslide victory over McGovern, sent Kissinger back to Paris to strike a better deal. Now it was the North Vietnamese's turn to be angry. They refused to reopen the question of their forces in the south, and Nixon suspended negotiations. What followed was the most savage and concentrated display of air power of the war. In twelve days in December, B-52s and tactical aircraft dropped over 36,000 tons of bombs on Hanoi and Haiphong. Nixon was determined to take advantage of a final opportunity to cripple the north and buy additional time for the ARVN, as well as to secure marginal improvements in the settlement. To Saigon, the bombing was meant to show U.S. support, and accompanied by a pledge to "respond with full force" in case of North Vietnamese violations of the cease-fire. To Nixon's domestic supporters, the message was: we have gone the extra mile to help our friends and to reach an honorable agreement.[42]

The devastating "Christmas bombing" persuaded Hanoi to resume talks and accept cosmetic changes, but not to concede the crucial point of its soldiers in the south. Saigon, although deeply skeptical, had little choice but to go along lest Washington make a separate deal (as it threatened to) with Hanoi to secure its prisoners of war, and leave. Americans were shocked by the spectacle of the world's biggest power trying to bomb one of the smallest "back to the stone age," and the loss to anti-aircraft fire of at least twelve behemoth B-52s. According to the agreement concluded in January (close to the one Kissinger had announced in October), the last U.S. troops would depart within two months, an International Control Commission would supervise a cease-fire, and a "National Council of Reconciliation and National Concord" would oversee a political dialogue and organize free, democratic elections. Few had illusions about these arrangements, but Nixon intended to keep his promise to help Saigon if necessary. The January 1973 agreement was a gamble, but one he did not intend to lose.

1972: Mackinder Meets FDR

Détente's meaning gave rise to debate and confusion. Was it merely a new kind of containment while the United States recharged its batteries? Or was it an attempt to change the international system and move beyond the Cold War? The parallels between Nixon's policy and turn-of-the-century "proto-containment" (including the "Open Door" notes supporting Chinese sovereignty) are striking. At the height of détente, Nixon remarked that Soviet leaders were "no more interested in peace as an end in itself than the Fascists were." But he also believed that "as a result of what we have done [at the Moscow summit], the chances of having a more peaceful world 50 years from now are substantially increased." Washington agreed to a regular series of summits. Brezhnev visited America in 1973, and Nixon (although beset by Watergate) returned to the USSR in 1974. Détente had an optimistic element, harking back to the tendency in Anglo-American policy that sought to to co-opt Russia into a co-operative relationship with the West.[43]

The Soviet understanding of détente (or *razryadka*) contained its own ambiguities. For Moscow, détente was connected to the older notion of peaceful coexistence which it was meant to reinforce. It was also supposed to ensure that neither side would seek superiority or use the threat of force. A premise of this shift, Moscow told itself, was the inexorable build-up of Soviet power *obliging* America to accept the USSR as an equal, and moderate its behavior.[44] Like peaceful coexistence, however, détente did not mean freezing the status quo and renouncing messianism. History's march toward socialism continued. Raymond Garthoff, paraphrasing Wilson, observes that for the Soviets détente was a way to "'make the world safe for historical change.'" Military parity, and U.S.–Soviet agreements, would supposedly de-fang the United States and allow change to occur peacefully. Like the Americans, the Soviets saw détente as a way of enjoying the benefits of better relations without abandoning long-standing goals.[45]

Détente's promise and fragility become clearer by looking at the Moscow summit (May 22–9, 1972), and subsequent agreements. The strategic arms accords rested on two principles: "strategic sufficiency," as opposed to the search for a fleeting superiority, and "mutual assured destruction," meaning war was prevented by the capacity of each side to inflict unacceptable damage on the other even after absorbing a nuclear attack.[46] Central to MAD's logic was that if one or both sides were able to destroy incoming missiles, mutual destruction would no longer be assured. The SALT I, or the Interim Agreement on Strategic Offensive Arms, attempted to codify the rough parity in the two arsenals. It was valid for five years, during which negotiations would continue. It froze the number of permissible ICBMs (1,054 for the U.S., 1,618 for the USSR) and set numbers for submarines (710 missiles on 44 subs for the U.S., 950 on 62 subs for the USSR). Moscow was allowed higher numbers to compensate for U.S. B-52s and "forward-based systems" (nuclear weapons deployed on the USSR's periphery). The Anti-Ballistic Missile (ABM) Treaty banned the development, testing, or deployment of defensive missiles, other than the limited systems in place on each side.[47]

SALT I evidenced a mutual will to tame the arms race, but contained serious shortcomings. The most glaring was that it did not cover multiple, independently targetable re-entry vehicles (MIRVs), that is, ICBMs fitted with several warheads. At the October 1974 Vladivostok summit, the two sides adopted a framework allowing each up to 2,400 delivery vehicles, 1,320 of which could be "MIRVed." But this did not limit the total number or the size of the warheads permitted. The Americans might have seriously tried to negotiate a ban on MIRVs in 1969–72. The Pentagon preferred to proceed with U.S MIRVing, wrongly assuming the Soviets were far behind.[48]

This decision would haunt the supporters of détente. SALT's critics fixed on "throw-weight," the amount of destructive power carried by each missile. Since Soviet SS-18s were bigger than U.S. missiles, they carried more and bigger warheads. The Soviets ultimately deployed more than 300 SS-18s, some carrying ten warheads apiece. This was perfectly legal under SALT. In 1976 Eugene Rostow (brother of Walt), Paul Nitze, and other disgruntled ex-officials revived a Truman-era lobby called the Committee on the Present Danger (CPD). Nitze, chief Pentagon negotiator for SALT, had resigned in disgust in May 1974.[49] The CPD claimed the USSR was deploying heavy missiles that would give it a "theoretical war-winning [first-strike] capability" against U.S. land-based missiles and thus the ability to commit aggression with impunity and/or extract political concessions. The same year, prominent weapons scientists and military officers persuaded the White House and CIA to create ad hoc "team Bs" to dispute official intelligence assessments. The team evaluating Soviet strategic objectives detected a liberal bias in official estimates and concluded that within ten years, "*the Soviets may well expect to achieve a degree of military superiority which would permit a dramatically more aggressive pursuit of their hegemonial objectives,* including direct military challenges to Western vital interests."[50] Kissinger rightly dismissed the CPD thesis as preposterous. As he explained to the Chinese, Moscow "would have to be insane to attack 1,000 [U.S. land-based] missiles when we would have 1,500 and more left over". The Soviets were making "all their improvements in the most vulnerable forces, namely in the land-based forces. We are making ours in the sea-based and air-based forces—which are not vulnerable or much less vulnerable." But the CPD bombarded the public with its doomsday scenarios after 1976.[51]

At Moscow, the two sides also signed the "Declaration of Basic Principles" desired by the Russians. According to the first of twelve points, the two sides would "proceed from the common determination that in the nuclear age there is no alternative to conducting their mutual relations on the basis of peaceful coexistence. Differences in ideology... are not obstacles to the bilateral development of normal relations based on the principles of sovereignty, equality, non-interference in internal affairs and mutual advantage." The second pledged both sides to "do their utmost to avoid military confrontations and to prevent the outbreak of nuclear war. They will always exercise restraint in their mutual relations." According to the third: "The USA and the USSR have a special responsibility... to do everything in their power so that conflicts or situations will not arise which would serve to increase international tensions." The eleventh stated: "The USA and the USSR make no claim for themselves... to any special rights or advantages in world affairs."[52]

Although the Russians considered it "essentially a treaty," it was wishful thinking to believe the Americans would abide by the declaration.[53] Nixon took scant notice and Kissinger had agreed partly to humor the Kremlin. "At this point," he told senators, the principles reflected "an aspiration and an attitude" rather than a code of conduct. The two sides also gave different weights to an agreement to hold a Conference on Security and Cooperation in Europe (CSCE), including all of Europe, the United States, and Canada. The Soviets had pushed this as a way to gain recognition of the territorial status quo (something sought since the 1950s). The Americans tended to dismiss it as window dressing for Moscow and pablum for left-wing opinion in Western Europe. They agreed in exchange for Mutual Balanced Force Reduction (MBFR) talks, which they hoped would lead to Soviet conventional cuts.[54]

Still, Kissinger's description of the Declaration as an "aspiration" was revealing. Although a historian has pointed to similarities with Kennan's "asymmetrical" containment, the Nixon-Kissinger approach was a hybrid of Mackinder and Franklin Roosevelt.[55] Kissinger had written, "The greatest need of the contemporary international system is an agreed concept of order."[56] An NSC study, approved by Kissinger, provided grounds for cautious optimism: "in so far as the U.S. is engaged in a contest with the USSR and Communist China . . . it is a limited competition for influence in which the threat of communist take-over by peaceful or violent means is considerably less than was generally supposed to be the case in the early 1960s." Kissinger told Gromyko in 1975: "it is important for our two countries to keep a long term perspective in mind. I am convinced that by the 1980s the identity of interest will become self-evident. Now it is self-evident with respect to nuclear weapons; by the 1980s it will be true of many political issues."[57]

The Rooseveltian element is clear in the case of economic agreements signed later in 1972: major grain sales and the granting (pending Congressional approval) of Most Favored Nation (MFN) trading status and Export-Import Bank credits to Moscow. The aim was "to create vested interests for peace within the Soviet structure which would help encourage restraint on their actions."[58] The Nixon and Kissinger approach to Europe also recalls FDR. In contrast to those who deplored the "Yalta system," they worked to stabilize the status quo.[59] Although belittling (and deliberating delaying) agreements to be signed at the July 1975 session of the CSCE, Kissinger basically agreed with Moscow on the "basket one" component of the "Helsinki Final Act," *inter alia* endorsing existing European borders. Like the Kremlin, he dismissed the conference's humanitarian agenda (promoting freer movement of ideas and people), known as "basket-three."[60] Kissinger's associate, State Department Counselor Helmut Sonnenfeldt, told U.S. diplomats: "it must be our policy to strive for an evolution that makes the relationship between the Eastern Europeans and the Soviet Union an organic one." Sonnenfeldt meant a relationship closer to Finlandization than to liberation of the sort that might destabilize Europe and provoke a violent Soviet reaction. A kind of Finlandization is what FDR and the State Department had aspired to for Eastern Europe in 1944–6.[61]

The New Structure under Stress

The brick and mortar of the Nixon–Kissinger "structure of relationships" had hardly set before it came under converging pressures. Cracks opened up on the periphery, where neither Washington nor Moscow could control events but felt obliged to defend their positions. Simultaneously, the devolution of responsibility to America's friends in Asia and Africa was tested. The utter failure of this approach fed domestic discontent.

The October 1973 Arab–Israeli war, an indirect result of closer U.S.–Soviet relations, raised basic doubts about détente. Moscow had supported the Egyptian president Anwar Sadat's war of attrition to regain the Sinai peninsula, occupied by Israel in the June 1967 war. Sadat was furious when, in the interest of Soviet–U.S. comity, the Kremlin failed to press his case during the Moscow summit. He ordered 17,000 Soviet advisers to pack their bags, and launched a surprise attack against Israeli positions on the Suez canal (coordinated with a Syrian attack on the Golan heights) on October 6, 1973. Although the war took the Americans by surprise, the Russians appeared to have known without trying to stop it.[62] The superpowers attempted to sustain their beleaguered clients with airlifts of supplies, but also worked together to pass a cease-fire resolution in the Security Council on October 22. When the cease-fire broke down, and with Ariel Sharon's forces poised to crush the Egyptian army, the Politburo proposed a U.S.–Soviet intervention to enforce the resolution. Imprudently, and rather desperately, Brezhnev added that otherwise Moscow would have to consider intervening on its own. Although thinking Moscow was probably bluffing, an unnerved Kissinger and other administration officials decided on drastic action. With Nixon preoccupied by Watergate (and literally drunk), they ordered U.S. forces to Defense Condition-3 (DEFCON-1 was the routine level; DEFCON-5 was war). Brezhnev reacted with sangfroid, declining to match the nuclear alert and dropping the idea of intervention. Kissinger restrained Israel, allowing Sadat to save face.[63]

Kissinger, not unreasonably, assumed that joint action would have smacked of condominium, whereas a unilateral Soviet move would have discredited détente. But nuclear saber-rattling was hardly in the spirit of the new relationship. More damaging to détente, and eloquent of its limitations, was Kissinger's frenetic "shuttle diplomacy" to broker cease-fire agreements and solidify U.S.–Egyptian ties. For Brezhnev, a lesson of the crisis was that *more*, not less, détente was needed but U.S. policy left him fuming. The morning after the nuclear alert Kissinger confessed to China's UN Ambassador Huang Hua: "My honest view is that the Soviet Union has suffered a major strategic defeat . . . So we now have a very good position to reduce the Soviet political influence."[64] It would have been hard to resist the temptation to woo Moscow's main client in the area (Sadat had sent encouraging signals before the war). But in systematically excluding the Soviets from the region Washington treated the Declaration of Principles like a scrap of paper. Its broader strategy would pay a price.[65]

Events elsewhere further undermined the fragile structure. Nixon's Vietnam gamble proved a losing one for two reasons. The first was Nixon's own decline after early 1973. As Congressional and criminal investigations homed in on his Watergate cover-up role, Nixon became morose and distracted. Angered by continued bombing of Cambodia, and sensing Nixon's weakness, Congress voted to cut off funds for U.S. military activity in Southeast Asia, effective August 15, 1973. Nixon's successor, Congressman Gerald R. Ford, lacked the authority to prevent aid-cuts or mount a last-minute rescue of Saigon. The second reason was more predictable: the 1973 armistice broke down and fighting resumed. Even so, the ARVN's Caporetto-like collapse during North Vietnam's early 1975 offensive surprised Hanoi and shocked Saigon's supporters.

Only in their worst dreams had they pictured an end game where fleeing South Vietnamese scrambled to board helicopters on the roof of the U.S. embassy and enemy tanks crashed through the gates of the RVN presidential palace: a debacle. The North's offensive sealed the fate of the pro-U.S. Lon Nol regime in Cambodia. The Chinese-backed Khmer Rouge captured Phnom Penh in April 1975.[66]

The European allies, meanwhile, had declined to co-operate with Washington's pro-Israel airlift or attempt to organize a "consumer cartel" to roll back the fourfold increase in oil prices adopted by the Organization of Petroleum Exporting Countries (OPEC) in early 1974.[67] Although the Americans were quick to cut bilateral deals with Saudi Arabia and Iran, Kissinger considered Europe's conduct stupid and craven. The overthrow of the pro-U.S. dictatorship in Lisbon in April 1974 by left-wing officers raised the specter of a Communist take-over. Economic stagnation and political deadlock in Italy, seemingly benefiting the PCI under its charismatic Euro-Communist (democratic and independent) leader Enrico Berlinguer added to Washington's despondency. The Soviets did not like Euro-Communism but the Americans believed Berlinguer, like Togliatti, was playing a double-game.

The new Portuguese government granted independence to Guinea-Bissau and signed the Alvor agreement with local liberation movements, promising to withdraw from Angola by November 11, 1975. The initial phase of the subsequent civil war pitted the Cuban and Soviet-backed Popular Movement for the Liberation of Angola (MPLA) led by the Marxist poet and physician Agostinho Neto, against the U.S.- and Zairian-supported National Front for the Liberation of Angola (FNLA), under the anti-communist nationalist Holden Roberto (Mobutu's brother-in-law) based in northeast Angola near Zaire.[68] The FNLA's de facto ally was the U.S.- and South African-backed National Union for the Total Liberation of Angola (UNITA), led by a resourceful war lord from southeastern Angola, Jonas Savimbi. In January 1975 the Ford administration increased aid to the FNLA, prompting it to attack the MPLA. After the fall of Saigon, Washington approved a major CIA operation to arm the FNLA and UNITA. The MPLA posed no threat to U.S. oil companies operating in the Cabinda region of Angola; rather, to the administration's credibility.[69] Havana's ties to

Neto's faction of the MPLA (as well as liberation movements in Algeria, Zaire, Congo-Brazzaville, and Guinea-Bissau) dated from the 1960s. Almost alone among major Communist leaders, Castro had retained a strong commitment to revolution. His relations with Moscow had been cool since 1962, and he opposed a détente that might sacrifice the interests of Cuba and its friends.[70]

In early November 1975 a small Cuban contingent, acting autonomously of Moscow, rescued the MPLA by helping to defeat FNLA fighters and CIA-hired mercenaries just north of the capital, Luanda.[71] The Republic of South Africa (RSA), meanwhile, although initially hesitant, had penetrated deep into Angola with a 2,500-man force in October. The Afrikaner regime feared a Soviet client-state bordering on South African-occupied Namibia (where the SWAPO insurgency operated), and was probably encouraged by the CIA and Kissinger to act. By performing as America's surrogate, Pretoria also hoped for a generous political pay-off.[72] At this point (early November 1975), Moscow responded to Castro's mid-August request by conducting an airlift of Soviet weapons and tens of thousands of Cuban troops into Angola.[73] The Cubans and MPLA halted the RSA-UNITA offensive, obliging the South African Defense Forces to withdraw. (They left Angola at the end of March 1976.) Castro observed that the myth of white invincibility in southern Africa had been exposed. To add insult to injury for Washington, after leaks of the CIA operation and a public controversy, Congress voted (December 1975 and January 1976) to prohibit further funding for covert activities on behalf of the FNLA and UNITA.[74]

The Nixon–Kissinger structure's weakest element proved to be its domestic base. The problem was less détente's "over-selling" than the administration's high-handed methods, and the fact that support was superficial on both sides of the political spectrum.[75] The center, such as it was, could not hold. Liberals supported arms control but bemoaned the administration's indifference to international law and human rights. After Nixon unveiled a unilateralist "New Economic Policy" in August 1971, they charged that he treated friends as adversaries and adversaries as friends.[76] The liberal camp, including the *Washington Post*, had long despised "tricky Dick" and relished the chance to help to drive him from office. After taking over Congress in 1974, the Democrats stepped up efforts to rein in the "imperial presidency," including investigations publicizing the CIA's "family jewels."[77] Nixon's abuse of power and Kissinger's "amoral realism" gave rise to calls for a return to idealism. The stage was set for Georgia Governor Carter, in 1976.

The White House's more serious problem was on the right. Many Republicans came to loathe "Henry," saw détente as appeasement, and deplored the "abandonment" of Taiwan. Skeptics included President Ford's chief of staff, the former fighter pilot and congressman Donald Rumsfeld. In November 1975, following his political counselors' advice, Ford dropped Vice President Nelson Rockefeller, a liberal Republican, from the 1976 ticket, and obliged Kissinger to cede the position of national security adviser. The firing of James Schlesinger, a hard-line, abrasive defense secretary, appeared to help Kissinger but his replacement, Rumsfeld, was another thorn in Kissinger's side.[78] By March 1976 the centrist Ford faced a serious challenge for the nomination from California Governor Ronald Reagan. A talented and genial demagogue, Reagan charged that the administration had sold out Eastern Europe at Helsinki, snubbed the exiled novelist Alekandr Solzhenitsyn, and allowed the Communists to seize Angola. In the grips of the "iron law," Ford suspended SALT II treaty negotiations and use of the word "détente."

An important component of the anti-détente camp were conservative Democrats, including soon-to-be Republican "neoconservatives." At the core of the neo-conservative movement were Jewish commentators, staffers, and academics (Irving Kristol, Norman Podhoretz, Richard Perle, Richard Pipes, among others) angered by Moscow's treatment of their co-religionists, including imposition in August 1972 of an "exit tax" on Jewish emigrants to pay back the cost of their educations. U.S.–Soviet co-operation in the Security Council and Kissinger's halting of Sharon's offensive during the October war indicated to them that détente limited Israel's freedom of action.[79] The neo-conservatives shared Nitze's view that the Soviets were seeking strategic superiority. Several were members of Team "B".[80] At heart, the neoconservatives were messianists who rejected the premise of indefinite coexistence with the USSR and detested the premise of the two systems' "moral equivalence" on which (so they claimed) détente was based.[81]

The conservative Democrats' champion was Senator Henry "Scoop" Jackson of Washington. Jackson was close to organized labor but also known as the "senator from Boeing" for services to the big defense contractor in his state. With support from the AFL–CIO union confederation, opposed to trade with the Soviet bloc, Jackson and Democratic Congressman Charles Vanik sponsored an amendment to a trade bill that tied the granting of MFN status to the end of emigration restrictions. The Kremlin (which had allowed increased Jewish emigration to Israel after 1969) was prepared to waive the tax but not to kowtow to Jackson. Passage (with bipartisan support) of the Jackson–Vanik amendment (and separate measures cutting credits) in December 1974 eviscerated economic détente. Moscow responded by deepening commercial ties to Western Europe (for example, to expand oil and natural gas production), something U.S. policy had aimed to prevent. Jackson had advanced his presidential campaign, but had done little or nothing for Jews in the USSR.[82]

Kissinger had told his staff in March 1974: "What bothers me...is that the Soviets are getting nothing out of détente...Given their system they have tried to be fairly reasonable all across the board...Even in the Middle East where our political strategy put them in an awful bind, they haven't really tried to screw us."[83] As Kissinger feared, détente at a certain point began to look like a "one-way street" favoring the Americans. His later accusation that Moscow had violated the 1972 Basic Principles in Angola sounded like the pot calling the kettle black.[84] The Russians distrusted U.S.–Chinese contacts, probably suspecting that Washington sought military co-operation with Beijing. Nixon's August 1974 resignation was baffling, but they assumed it must be the work of their common enemies. In late 1974 the much-anticipated economic benefits of détente went up in smoke.

Brezhnev remained doughtily committed, but his health began to fail in 1974, and other influences operated.[85] Odd Arne Westad discerns "two parallel tracks of Soviet foreign policy" in the mid-1970s. One, associated with Brezhnev, Gromyko, and the foreign ministry, led toward détente. The other, associated with the KGB, the MO (International Department of the CPSU Central Committee), and the military, led toward greater entanglement in the third world. KGB operatives and

MO intellectuals were eager to match Chinese and American efforts, and not to be shamed by the ubiquitous Cubans. In the MO, headed by the Gromyko rival Boris Ponomarev, the Khrushchev spirit of solidarity with the developing world, and belief in the Leninist model's relevance, were alive and well. When opportunities to act arose, together with urgent calls for aid against the imperialists, the temptation was irresistible. Moscow believed it was a "'moral internationalist duty'" to help Angola.[86] Brezhnev was aware of the risks to détente and had turned down Castro's initial request for help in August 1975. But once the South Africans had violated the border, the Politburo endorsed the airlift, although with operations to begin only after the MPLA had declared itself the government of an independent Angola on November 11, 1975.[87]

Vietnam and Angola generated a heady sensation in Moscow. Supporters of better relations with Washington rationalized activism on the grounds that the United States was behaving as it pleased and détente had never meant the end of systemic competition. Together with America's internal troubles and generalized "stagflation" (simultaneous recession and inflation induced by the oil shock), third world events suggested to some a "structural crisis of US hegemony and the international capitalist system."[88] The steady economic growth that had stabilized and enriched Western societies seemed to be ebbing. Simultaneously, increased revenues thanks to higher energy prices were available to pay for a more adventurous Soviet foreign policy. In fact, Soviet leaders were living in a fool's paradise. Growth rates turned sharply downward after the mid-1970s, as did rates for industrial production and labor productivity. But for a fleeting moment, the USSR seemed to be riding high.[89]

The same developments that discredited détente in America and breathed life into Soviet messianism contributed to a cooling of U.S.–Chinese relations. Starting in 1973, Beijing became more insistent that the United States must follow the "Japan model" to full normalization: breaking relations with Taiwan, ending the defense treaty, and removing all U.S. troops from the island. Kissinger's main interlocutor, the courtly Zhou, was mortally ill in 1973, and died in January 1976. His protégé and heir apparent, first vice premier Deng Xiaoping, was a more acerbic character.[90] A modernizer and "capitalist roader" exiled during the Cultural Revolution, Deng was also under continuing threat from the

"Gang of Four" led by Mao's wife, the viperish Jiang Qing. The Gang were the Shanghai-based, ultra-left faction Mao had used as attack-dogs during the recent purges and campaign against bourgeois and ancient Chinese culture. In the midst of a power struggle, Deng was in no position to be flexibile on Taiwan.[91] But with Vietnam lost and the Republican primaries approaching, neither was Washington. Normalization (originally scheduled for 1976) would have to wait.

Since they wanted a strong America, at loggerheads with Russia, the Chinese disliked SALT, the Helsinki Final Act, and the failure to stop the Soviets in Angola. They suspected Washington of making deals allowing Moscow to turn its attention to the East. In a striking display of cheek and Realpolitik, the Chinese leadership who had accused the Soviets of appeasing America over Cuba now warned the Americans against behaving like Chamberlain and Edouard Daladier in their dealings with the Soviets over Europe. Kissinger had been too optimistic when telling Nixon, "With conscientious attention to both capitals, we should be able to continue to have our mai tai and drink our vodka too."[92]

Conclusion

In the end, the Nixon-Kissinger "structure" proved an intellectual conceit rather than a geopolitical reality. Devolution of responsibility was a clamorous failure. Defeats in Southeast Asia and Africa sent a message of American weakness to the world. Détente was partly undone by its internal contradictions: it was hard to convert the USSR to "an agreed concept of order" while simultaneously trying to reduce its global clout. Events beyond the superpowers' control (the India-Pakistan and Arab-Israeli wars; the Portuguese revolution) caused them to react in ways damaging to détente. America's hoped-for quasi-alliance with China was incompatible with fruitful U.S.–Soviet relations. Beijing distrusted Washington's ties with Moscow; Moscow, Washington's with Beijing. The Soviet concept of *razryadka* was equally wishful and contradictory. It assumed the USSR could wage the international class struggle while improving relations with the United States.

If the Nixon administration's approach was essentially a *gattopardesco* holding action, would a fundamentally different strategy have been possible? The answer is probably not. There was limited domestic backing, even in light of Vietnam, for a genuine U.S. retrenchment. Nor was there much for an expensive bid to restore U.S. power of the kind Reagan would later try. Nixon and Kissinger, moreover, deserved credit for the rapprochement with China, removing American troops from Vietnam, and concluding important arms agreements. But this does not mean (as Kissinger later suggested) that the scandal that compromised the administration's authority and credibility was a kind of bolt from the blue.[93]

On the contrary, the Watergate break-in was part of a pattern including the bugging by Nixon and Kissinger of their staffs' telephones, and the burglary at Daniel Ellsberg's psychoanalyst's office in Los Angeles.[94] (Ellsberg, a Pentagon employee-turned anti-war activist, had illegally copied and distributed a secret Defense Department study of the war known as *The Pentagon Papers*.) The White House "plumber's unit" responsible for the break-ins had been set up to plug leaks in the realm of national security. The Watergate scandal and Nixon's demise were consequences of the administration's obsession with secrecy and the concentration of power. A conservative commentator speculated that Nixon's fall had been engineered by CIA personnel who had assisted the *Washington Post* in exposing the White House.[95] The theory was wrong (the world learned in 2005 that the paper's "Deep Throat" source had been a high FBI official) but plausible. Nixon held the CIA in contempt and had excluded it from high policy. It was one of several agencies with a motive for revenge.

The same commentator had earlier identified an emerging Republican party majority.[96] Urban workers who had voted Democratic were moving to the suburbs and joining the middle class. The South, a Democratic Party bastion, was turning Republican in reaction to 1960s Civil Rights legislation. Nixon's 1972 landslide appeared to confirm the theory. But the Republicans lost Congress in 1974, and the Presidency in 1976. What seemed an irreversible swing of the pendulum had been interrupted, just as in 1948. Once again, the right reacted angrily after the defeat of a centrist Republican candidate. Among their main culprits were Nixon and Kissinger, guilty of squandering their party's advantages and the misguided pursuit of détente.

CHAPTER 8
TO THE PANIC OF '79

Despite détente's setbacks in 1973–6, Kissinger, for one, had not abandoned hope. Had he been left in charge, he later suggested, the Cold War might have been ultimately transcended. Defusing the East-West confrontation, albeit in a way allowing humanity to progress toward socialism, had long been Moscow's aim. In a January 18, 1977 speech, Brezhnev laid out a doctrine of strategic sufficiency: "the allegations that the Soviet Union is going beyond what is sufficient for defense, that it is striving for superiority in arms, with the aim of delivering a 'first strike', are absurd and utterly unfounded." Détente, he added, "is above all an overcoming of the Cold War, a transition to normal, equal relations between states." In a letter to President Jimmy Carter, he repeated that the USSR did "not strive for superiority" and was ready for "a new major shift."[1] He meant prompt agreement on a SALT II treaty based on the Vladivostok framework, followed by a more radical SALT III.

Brezhnev's aspirations were to be disappointed. Did his post-1976 nostalgia for the previous administration have a rational foundation? The Soviets had yet to grasp the extent of the attempt to deceive them through triangular diplomacy, but Kissinger would always have a saving grace in Moscow: his utter lack of messianism.[2] A second Ford administration would have been beset by rivalries and the thin-skinned Kissinger might well have been the loser.[3] But it would not have suffered (or not to the same degree) from the problems afflicting Carter's: unbridgeable internal divisions, an obsession with differentiating itself from its predecessor, and a lack of experience at the top.

189

The National Security Adviser Zbigniew Brzezinski was a center-right Democrat with a dogmatic Mackinderian outlook: Russia must be prevented from expanding over the rimlands of Eurasia. Unlike Kissinger, he did not wish to minimize ideological differences. Quite the opposite: championing human rights was a way to pump up U.S. morale and prestige after Vietnam and Watergate and "focus global attention on the glaring weaknesses" of the Soviet system. The "comprehensive and reciprocal détente" the Columbia political scientist professed to support was not about live and let live, but turning the tables and undermining Communism. Messianism was back in style.[4]

Brzezinski (born 1928; son of a Polish diplomat) saw himself as part of a new elite replacing the WASP establishment he believed had met its Waterloo in the 1960s. Carter's secretary of state Cyrus Vance (born 1917, a Yale-educated former Pentagon official) came from that establishment, and the Democratic Party center-left. He strongly supported SALT, favored improved relations with Vietnam, Cuba, and North Korea, and helped inspire Carter's statement that America must go beyond its "inordinate fear of Communism." The sharp-elbowed Brzezinski considered his genteel colleague a nice man, but burned by Vietnam.[5]

Carter himself was steeped in evangelical Christianity and the vision of his fellow Georgian, Woodrow Wilson. He believed the country had been "strongest and most effective when morality and a commitment to freedom and democracy [had] been most clearly emphasized." He, too, "hoped and believed that the expansion of human rights might be the wave of the future throughout the world" and wanted America "on the crest of this movement."[6] Less often mentioned was that human rights was a way to cover the administration's flank and mend fences with Jackson's wing of the party. The policy was both a tonic and a tool. Having supported the Jackson–Vanik amendment, Carter lost no time in rebuking Moscow for cracking down on "Helsinki Watch groups" who monitored violations of "basket three" provisions. He wrote dissident physicist Andrei Sakharov pledging to promote human rights, and invited a prominent exile and former political prisoner, Vladimir Bukovsky, to the White House, something Ford had declined to do.

But Carter appeared to have few fixed views beyond upholding moral standards and behaving differently than Ford and Nixon. His conflicting instincts, along with intra-party divisions, led him to zigzag in a way not seen since the elevation of another principled amateur, Harry Truman. As he berated the USSR, Carter denied any intention to interfere in its internal matters. In March 1977, despite Vance's reservations, he advanced a new SALT II proposal. It reflected Carter's wish to disassociate himself from Kissinger and move toward nuclear abolition, while appealing to critics like Jackson and Nitze. The proposal lowered the Vladivostok ceilings for total delivery vehicles from 2,400 to 1,800 or 2,000, and of MIRVed missiles from 1,320 to 1,100 or 1,200. New types of ICBMs, and subsonic, highly accurate "cruise missiles" above the 2,500 kilometer range, would be banned. The proposal called on Moscow to reduce its heavy MIRVed missiles from 308 to 150, with no analogous U.S. cut.[7] When Moscow rejected this out of hand, Washington returned to the Vladivostok framework. Meanwhile SALT II was delayed and Jackson unappeased.[8]

A similar pattern played out in the Middle East. Kissinger had excluded the Soviets. Carter brought them back. On October 1, 1977, Vance and Gromyko issued a joint statement calling for an international conference to negotiate a comprehensive settlement, implying one that addressed Palestinian grievances. Then, when Israel and American pro-Israeli groups protested, Carter returned to Kissinger's approach. It must be said that Carter, second only to Sadat (whose dramatic November 1977 trip to Israel broke a deadlock), deserved credit for the September 1978 "Camp David agreements." But the Egyptian–Israeli separate peace, underwritten by huge aid programs to Cairo and Tel Aviv, was another nail in the coffin of U.S.–Soviet relations.

Bilateral affairs went downhill despite an occasional "zag" (e.g. the signing of the SALT II treaty in Vienna in June 1979) toward détente. The Kremlin saw U.S. criticism as a violation of the "Basic Principles" stricture against internal meddling. In reality, and although they were not prepared to admit it, Soviet leaders had dug a large hole for themselves on human rights. In their eagerness for the Helsinki territorial-political agreements, they had decided to run the risk that basket three would empower Soviet and Eastern European dissidents and had overlooked the possibility of a changed U.S. approach. Eventually it would become clear that the Soviets had made an even more basic miscalculation when embarking on détente. The normalization of relations between Bonn and Moscow and its satellites (Chancellor Helmut Schmidt continued *Ostpolitik* after Brandt's resignation in 1974) generated West German–American strains, but also altered Germany's image in Eastern Europe as a revanchist power, and undercut the rationale for Soviet "protection." Something changed the day in December 1970 when Brandt knelt with hands clasped before the monument to those killed in the 1944 Warsaw uprising, an unforgettable gesture of contrition for German sins.[9]

As for Carter's arms proposal, Politburo grandees Gromyko, Andropov, and Ustinov thought it smacked of "political demagoguery and propaganda." Brezhnev himself was incensed by what looked like dilettantish toying with the Vladivostok agreement. The general secretary had pushed himself to the point of physical collapse in negotiating the framework and had had to browbeat his World War II comrade, then-defense minister Grechko, to get his agreement.[10] The new proposal gutted the basic Vladivostok bargain: Soviet tolerance of U.S. forward-based systems (resisted by Grechko) in return for U.S. acceptance of the Soviets' prized heavy ICBMs. Brezhnev wrote to Carter: "There is no dealing with the Soviet Union in this way."[11]

Moscow politics featured its own conflict. Ultimately, it arose from the contradiction in Soviet policy since Lenin: one must avoid a disastrous war and reap the benefits of normal relations with the capitalists, while not renouncing the international class struggle. Gromyko, his assistant Georgi Kornienko, and Dobrynin tried to keep U.S.–Soviet relations on an even keel. Lower in the bureaucracy self-styled *zapadniki* ("Westernizers") promoted adherence to Helsinki basket three.[12] They contended with the messianists, MO head Ponomarev, his deputy, the Africa expert Karen Brutents, and ideologist Mikhail Suslov, who imagined a historic shift toward socialism. The military brass, Dobrynin recalled, were "emotionally pleased by the defiance of America implied by our showing the flag in remote areas."[13] The more provocatively Washington behaved, the less Moscow heeded warnings against third world activism. Brezhnev clung to the illusion that he could eat the détente cake and spread socialism too.

The focus was now the Horn of Africa, adjacent to the strategic Persian Gulf. In 1974, radical officers calling themselves the *Derg*

(Coordinating Committee) overthrew the aging Emperor Haile Selassie. Ethiopia, a multi-ethnic empire and U.S. aid recipient, lurched to the left. Moscow was initially skeptical, and hesitant to antagonize neighboring Somalia. In 1974, the Soviets had done a deal with the Somali autocrat (and self-declared Marxist) General Mohammad Siad Barre, providing arms in return for use of local ports. Nervous about tensions between Somalia and Ethiopia over the southeastern Ethiopian province of Ogaden, but encouraged when the *Derg* adopted a Soviet-style program, Moscow agreed to an assistance package in December 1976. The "real turning point" came two months later.[14] Colonel Mengistu Haile Mariam (born 1937, son of a former slave) moved to end turmoil in the *Derg* by wiping out most of his rivals. Ponomarev and the Soviet ambassador in Addis Ababa decided they had a promising interlocutor. Castro, too, was impressed. After trying to mediate the Ogaden conflict during an African tour in March 1977, he had concluded that Siad Barre was "above all a chauvinist." But Mengistu was "a quiet, serious, and sincere leader." Ethiopia could be "a great counterweight to Egypt's betrayal."[15] Carter inherited a situation in which the ruthless and (as Eritrean independence fighters learned) chauvinist Mengistu held power, and his Soviet ties were a fact.

Nevertheless, Washington's reaction complicated matters. In June 1977 Carter indicated to the Somali ambassador that, while the United States would not aid Somalia directly, it was ready to do so covertly and would ask France, Britain, Egypt, and Saudi Arabia to help. Carter handed over satellite pictures of the Horn. Siad Barre appears to have decided in July 1977 to invade the Ogaden assuming substantial aid would be forthcoming.[16] This proved to be mistaken (Washington would not abet clear-cut aggression), but the operation went well nonetheless. The Cubans and Soviets, until autumn 1977 reluctant to intervene, now acceded to Mengistu's pleas for assistance. Starting in late November, they repeated their 1975 exploit, air-lifting Cubans and Soviet weapons to Ethiopia. By March 1978 the Somalis had been expelled from the Ogaden and heavy fighting was over. Compared to Angola, fewer (about 12,000) Cuban troops were involved, but the intervention was more closely coordinated with Moscow, and a Soviet general, Vasilii I. Petrov, oversaw the counter-offensive, accompanied by

1,000 Red Army personnel. Gromyko later damaged his credibility with Carter by denying Petrov's presence, but he may have been left in the dark.[17]

Having encouraged the Somalis, Washington rejected Moscow's suggestion of U.S.–Soviet mediation of the Ogaden issue. The Americans remained allergic to anything resembling a "condominium." At the same time, Vance and Defense Secretary Harold Brown scotched Brzezinski's proposal to send an aircraft carrier task force to the area to show resolve. (Brzezinski's reaction was that they had been "badly bitten by the Vietnam bug.")[18] The State Department realized that the Soviet–Cuban defense of an existing border was welcome to much of Africa. But Brzezinski's warnings about growing right-wing opposition at home (also fed by Carter's controversial Panama canal treaties) were neither baseless nor without effect.[19] They contributed to an eventual merging of the administration's positions with those of its severest critics. The national security adviser used the crisis to convince Carter that the Soviets were employing Cuban "proxies" to endanger access to Middle East oil and that a clear signal was required. In fact, Moscow did not order, or hire, Havana. If anything, the Cubans had egged on the Russians, and Castro had become a kind of enemy-brother of American conservatives. Their common objective was to bury what was left of détente.[20]

After January–March 1977, a milestone on the road to renewed confrontation was May 1978. NATO members agreed to modernize their forces and increase military spending by 3 percent per year through the mid-1980s. The same month, Brzezinski traveled to Beijing. After soliciting an invitation, he had badgered Carter to let him accept it, isolated Vance (who was opposed) by lining up Brown's and Vice President Walter Mondale's support, and penned his own instructions. Brzezinski's message was that "the United States ha[d] made up its mind" and was ready to accept China's conditions for normalization: breaking relations with Taiwan, abrogating the treaty, and removing U.S. forces from the island.[21] To Deng Xiaoping, Brzezinski outlined a Soviet design "involving an attempt to achieve strategic superiority, to gain political preponderance in Western Europe, to radicalize the Middle East, to destabilize southern Asia, to penetrate the Indian Ocean region, and to encircle China."[22] The visit paved the way for deepening intelligence co-operation, the sale to China of dual-use technology, and the restoration of full diplomatic relations, announced (after intensive secret negotiations) in December 1978.

The humorously inclined noted that Brzezinski's trip extended Polish encirclement of Russia. The Kremlin would soon have to contend with Archbishop Karol Wojtyla of Krakow, as of October 1978, Pope John Paul II. Brzezinski's geopolitical analysis, reflecting a fertile Mackinderian imagination, was music to Chinese ears. They welcomed his visit at a time of rising Sino-Soviet tensions, and were happy to see (and if possible to sow) discord between the USSR and the United States. The Soviets had begun to deploy mobile SS-20 intermediate-range missiles in the Lake Baikal area, and medium-range "Backfire" bombers in the Far East. In early March 1978 Beijing opted to reject a secret Soviet offer to renew high-level talks, demanding first a partial military withdrawal along the frontier. In late March Brezhnev and Ustinov made a highly publicized inspection tour of Soviet forces on the Chinese border.[23] Chinese–Vietnamese relations also worsened. Hanoi had been on a collision course with the pro-PRC Cambodian regime of Pol Pot since 1975, while its socialization of the economy provoked mass flight by the ethnic-Chinese commercial class of Vietnam. In October 1978, in the context of negotiations with China, Carter decided to postpone U.S.–Vietnamese normalization. In November Vietnam and the USSR signed a treaty of friendship and assistance. In December, shortly before a state visit by Deng Xiaoping to Washington, Vietnam invaded Cambodia and ousted Pol Pot. China answered with a punitive expedition into Vietnam which appeared to Moscow to have been coordinated with the Americans.[24] The Cold War battle-lines emerging since Kissinger's first trips to China were now clearly drawn.

It is uncertain whether Deng's decision to play the U.S. and Japanese cards in 1978 was a cause or effect of deteriorating Sino-Soviet relations. It may well have been both, and it clearly served his internal consolidation of power. After Mao's death in September 1976 and the Gang of Four's arrest, Zhou's protégé had been reappointed (July 1977) to the positions held before the Gang's attack and his second purge by Mao (April 1976). Although nominally subordinate to Mao's chosen successor, the party chairman and premier Hua Guofeng, Deng's portfolios included education, foreign and military policy, and science and technology. He aimed to modernize the economy using free market reforms and imported technology. Thus there were compelling economic as well as strategic reasons for normalizing relations with Japan and the United States. In August 1978 Beijing and Tokyo signed a Treaty of Peace and Friendship, including language about common opposition to "hegemony" (e.g. Soviet policy). Hua retained his posts until the end of 1980. But Deng's visit with great fanfare to the United States in January 1979 left no doubt about who was in charge.[25]

A Trio of Controversies

When Carter eventually adopted a clear policy it was with a vengeance few had imagined possible. In retrospect, his 1979–80 measures make Reagan's look, if not tame, less novel than they may appear. The package included withdrawal of the SALT II treaty from the Senate and raising defense spending by 5 percent in 1980–1. According to NATO's "two-track" decision (December 12, 1979), the alliance would try to negotiate removal of Soviet SS-20s by the end of 1983, but failing that deploy 572 intermediate-range weapons (464 ground-launched cruise, and 108 Pershing II ballistic, missiles, plus secret replacement stocks). The highly accurate Pershings, with a flying time of six to ten minutes to the western USSR, were dangerous first-strike weapons from the Soviet standpoint. In July 1980 Carter signed Presidential Directive 59, refining doctrine in ways indicating the United States was preparing to fight (should deterrence fail) a sustained nuclear war, including the decapitation of the Soviet leadership.[26] Soon after Moscow's December 1979 intervention in Afghanistan, he proclaimed the "Carter Doctrine."[27] The United States would defend Saudi Arabia and the Persian Gulf. Around the same time, the administration re-instituted draft registration for 18-year-old males, and embargoed grain sales to the USSR. In a final slap, it declared the United States would boycott the 1980 Moscow Olympics and pressured others to do the same.

Carter's radical turn was connected to three interrelated controversies. The first concerned the "window of vulnerability" allegedly arriving in the early 1980s when the Soviets had deployed their SS-18s and SS-19s. According to SALT II opponents, Moscow would then be able to destroy America's 1,054 land-based missiles, while deliberately sparing the civilian population. The president would have either to retaliate against Soviet cities using less-accurate B-52s and sub-based missiles—launching all-out nuclear war—or (supposedly his more likely choice) surrender. Critics worried about "crisis stability," namely, that in an emotionally charged showdown Moscow would be tempted to carry out such a preemptive attack. The mere theoretical capacity to do so allegedly gave it a decisive political advantage, demoralizing America's allies and allowing Moscow to blackmail Washington into accepting its demands.[28]

To believe the Kremlin would launch such an attack was not only to doubt the sincerity of its statements that nuclear war represented "a danger to all mankind." As Kissinger had argued, it was to question its sanity.[29] As far as Moscow knew, U.S. Minutemen would be automatically launched on warning of incoming missiles. Moreover, a single warhead (as the 1983 ABC Television docu-drama, *The Day After*, demonstrated) on a military target (SAC headquarters in Nebraska) *would* kill hundreds of thousands of civilians. The Soviets could only assume the United States would strike back. The SALT II treaty signed in Vienna in June 1979 was hardly an arms reduction agreement. But it capped warhead totals. It also allowed each side to deploy a new ICBM. Just before Vienna, Carter announced the United States would build the "MX" missile. This showed unnecessary deference to SALT II's critics, but silenced their basic argument. The MX would sit in super-hardened silos or else be constantly moved and therefore invulnerable to surprise attack.

The SALT II brouhaha raised basic questions. Why *were* the Soviets so attached to their giant missiles? One reason was they hoped to compensate for inferior quality with quantity. Thanks to superior technology, the Americans had more reliable and accurate ICBMs, and were constantly improving what they had. A Soviet official later admitted that the heavy missiles "were one of the few things we could build well."[30] The Russians, moreover, had not only U.S., but British, French, and Chinese nuclear weapons to counter. Brezhnev undoubtedly saw the

ICBM build-up as part of the price to be paid the defense ministry and military for their support of détente. For reasons of background (he had headed the military-industrial complex) and temperament (he was collegial-minded), Brezhnev disliked challenging the military. But neither did he see the need to in order to appease American critics. After all, to think the USSR was planning to commit suicide was absurd.

Why *was* SALT II attacked so ferociously? There were at least three reasons. The anti-treaty camp was an ingrown community of serial alarmists and super-patriots—military officers, former officials, weapons scientists, defense experts associated with the RAND Corporation—periodically obsessed with "window of vulnerability" scenarios. Nitze was a dogged Cassandra whose view of the USSR (rooted in an analogy with Nazi Germany dismissed by Kennan) had not changed since NSC 68: Moscow sought a position of military superiority from which to leverage world conquest and/or attack the United States.[31] A second reason, not shared by Nitze and the CPD, was the belief that deterrence based on assured destruction *was* mad because if it failed hundreds of millions would die. If anti-missile systems were technically feasible, as some argued, they should be developed. The third reason was old-fashioned politics. Just as the Democrats had used the "missile gap," conservatives flayed Carter with SALT II. After taking power, the Republicans buried the "window of vulnerability." In a farcical ending, only fifty of one hundred planned MX missiles were deployed and in the same silos supposedly vulnerable to attack.

A second, related, controversy concerned the USSR's alleged attempt to Finlandize Western Europe. According to the 1976 "team B" report, a primer of anti-détente thinking, Moscow intended to "drive a wedge" between America and its allies:

> The separation of Europe can be attempted by a variety of means: establishing on Europe's eastern frontier a military force of such overwhelming preponderance that resistance to it will appear futile and the continuation of NATO not only pointless but dangerous; making Western Europe increasingly dependent economically on the USSR by incurring heavy debts there; entering with it into all sorts of co-operative arrangements, and supplying an increasing share of Western Europe's energy needs;

insisting on the participation of Communist parties in national governments; arousing doubts in Western Europe about the U.S. commitments to its defense; and so forth. This objective undoubtedly enjoys very high priority in Russia's strategic thinking. Severance of Western Europe from the U.S. would reduce any military threat or opposition from that area as well as deprive the U.S. of its European forward bases, eventually bringing Europe's immense productive capacities within the Soviet orbit.[32]

The mobile and accurate SS-20 missile (deployed 1977–82) confirmed to some this disturbing scenario.[33] Since NATO had no equivalent, and the SS-20s could strike Europe but not the United States, the Americans might not respond. Europe would be "decoupled" (a synonym for "Finlandized") and open to blackmail. Here was a reprise of the earlier debate about Washington's reliability, but in the context of strategic parity. According to Chancellor Helmut Schmidt, SALT neutralized the superpowers' strategic nuclear capabilities. In Europe this allegedly magnified "the significance of the disparities between East and West in nuclear tactical and conventional weapons."[34] The controversy played out in the context of concern about Eurocommunism. With SPD financial support, the Portuguese Social Democrats had won the elections of April 1976. But the PCI got 34 percent of the vote in June 1976 Italian elections. With Italy on the verge of insolvency and Christian Democratic Premier Giulio Andreotti's government dependent on PCI support, the supposed Communist menace to a key ally remained.

To its credit, Washington did not initially see why NATO needed an equivalent to the SS-20. There were plenty of U.S. nuclear weapons in Europe earmarked for Soviet targets, and the Americans significantly reinforced their conventional forces and nuclear forward-based systems in 1977–8.[35] But the TNF (theater nuclear force) question became caught up in a crisis of confidence in Carter's leadership. The administration had made a damaging zigzag on the "neutron bomb."[36] Schmidt was angered by U.S. human rights policy (tilting at windmills in his view) and held Carter in contempt. He and the French president Valéry Giscard d'Estaing were also antagonized by American economic behavior. Washington appeared to be driving the dollar's value down to favor American exports. Despite lip-service to conservation, rising U.S.

consumption of imported oil kept energy prices high for everyone. With growing trade and current account deficits, Schmidt warned, the United States was living beyond its means.[37]

The Carter administration eventually persuaded itself that TNF modernization was necessary to reassure Europe and dispel the impression of U.S. weakness. Typically, it acted in ways that left critics unappeased and inadvertently worsened the situation. The NATO two-track decision stimulated the growth of anti-nuclear movements where governments had agreed to host cruise missiles or Pershing IIs (the FRG, Britain, Italy, Belgium, the Netherlands), and aggravated tensions with Moscow. The USSR insisted it was merely replacing older missiles and denied any intention to intimidate Europe. Despite mountains of polemics, there is little evidence to contradict this. Nor did the Russians (pace "team B") encourage PCI participation in the Italian government. They took a dim view of Italian Communism, an independent brand that might contaminate Eastern Europe. In NATO's new weapons, which it considered unjustified by its own actions, Moscow saw a violation of SALT II limits and evidence that the West was seeking a first-strike capability against the USSR.[38]

Here Moscow's blindness and bungling matched NATO's. The Russians had failed to anticipate the West's reaction to a missile that was significantly more powerful than the one it replaced. Moscow was too quick to dismiss NATO's objections as a mere pretext to seek superiority by installing its own weapons. Attributing SS-20 deployment to military pressure (the generals were "mesmerized" by its performance), Dobrynin called it a "gross miscalculation." He added, however, that on frequent trips home he detected no trace of political designs connected to the missiles.[39] Washington could not ignore the fact that some Europeans feared them. But the view that Moscow intended to use the SS-20s to Finlandize America's allies was a fantasy. And even if it had, as Kennan, an observer of these events, argued: "it takes two to make a successful act of intimidation; and the very improbability of the actual use of these weapons means that no one in Western Europe needs to be greatly intimidated by them unless he wishes to be."[40]

A third, overlapping, controversy concerned Soviet conventional military power and activism in developing regions. Some contended that, even as the SS-20s cowed Europe, control of the Horn of Africa (and then Afghanistan) would allow Moscow to threaten its oil supply.[41] Indeed, there was a significant Soviet conventional build-up, and influential actors promoted power projection in the third world. Meanwhile, Soviet intelligence agencies inflated the size of U.S. forces and production capabilities in case of war.[42] Yet the picture was not as simple as those who spoke of a relentless Soviet build-up and "drastic decline in American power" suggested.[43] In 1970–5, Soviet military expenditures rose 4–5 percent per year in real terms. Between 1976 and 1983, however, the annual increase was around 2 percent. The U.S. intelligence community erroneously claimed that the 4–5 percent annual rises continued until 1983. While Castro and some Soviet leaders were eager to compete in the third world, they were usually responding to local requests for assistance. The Angola and Ethiopia operations were successful and popular because the Soviets and Cubans had defended their allies from attack.[44]

A detached view of the 1970s competition showed that the outcome was, at best, a draw from the Soviet point of view. Moscow acquired friends in Iraq, Angola, Ethiopia, South Yemen, Afghanistan, and temporarily in Somalia and Chile. It lost Egypt, the Sudan, and Somalia. In 1979 leftist governments were overthrown in a number of smaller African states: the Central African Empire, Uganda, Equatorial Guinea, Guinea-Bissau, and Ghana. Washington consolidated relationships with Egypt, Kenya, Somalia, Oman, not to mention China. It lost Ethiopia, South Vietnam, Cambodia, Nicaragua, and Iran. The loss of the Gulf's policeman was particularly shocking. But the Russians, already beginning to rue the financial costs of their African clients, had little reason to welcome the rise of Islamic fundamentalism. The Shia cleric Ayatollah Ruhollah Khomeini, the new strongman after the Shah's departure in January 1979, proclaimed: "We have turned our backs on the East and the West, on the Soviet Union and America, in order to run the country ourselves."[45]

Exhibit A in the case that the USSR was inexorably expanding toward Eurasia's "inner crescent" was Afghanistan. If the Soviets dominated that country, Brzezinski warned, they could "promote a separate Baluchistan, which would give them access to the Indian Ocean while dismembering

Pakistan and Iran." (He also briefed Carter "on Molotov's proposal to Hitler in late 1940 that the Nazis recognize the Soviet claim to preeminence in the region south of Batum and Baku." In reality Berlin had proposed this to Moscow.) A Pentagon official recalled that much time was spent in 1979 planning how to stop a hypothetical Soviet offensive southward across Iran's rugged Zagros mountains. After the invasion of Afghanistan, many in Washington believed Russia's objective was the Persian Gulf.[46]

The hawks were misled by their schematic conceptions. Few Cold War episodes are better documented than Afghanistan.[47] It was a classic case of Hobbesian fatalism, or defensive expansion, with a reinforcing element of Leninist messianism. The Russians invaded once they were convinced that, without decisive action, Afghanistan would probably be lost to their enemies. Strictly from the standpoint of geography, Brzezinski was right that occupying Afghanistan put the Soviets in a better position to march southward.[48] But to consider such a move plausible meant assuming Moscow believed it could overcome the combined resistance of Afghanistan, Pakistan, and Iran. Once again it required doubting not only the Russians' declarations but their sanity as well.

Afghanistan was a kind of primitive Central Asian Switzerland, officially neutral, with marked ethnic divisions, and presenting forbidding obstacles to anyone who hoped to subdue it. The chain of events leading to the invasion began in April 1978 when the government of Mohammed Daoud was overthrown by officers close to the Khalq ("the Masses") faction of the Afghan Communist Party (PDPA). Daoud, a modernizer and republican, had been in power since 1973, when he had ousted his brother-in-law, King Zahir. Encouraged by Tehran, Daoud had moved away from an initially pro-Soviet policy and imprisoned the Khalq leaders Nur Mohammad Taraki and Hafizallah Amin. Moscow had not known about Khalq's coup plans and supported a less radical PDPA faction called Parcham ("the Banner"). But, according to an established pattern, the Kremlin saw no choice but to tutor the Khalq comrades, who eagerly sought its aid. With the prospect of a hostile Iran, Afghanistan also took on more importance as a buffer to the bacillus of religious fanaticism, and base for watching and trying to influence events in Tehran.[49]

The Russians were quickly exasperated by their pupils. President Taraki proved incompetent; Prime Minister Amin, a sort of Afghan Cesare Borgia: energetic, brutal, and addicted to intrigue. The government zealously pushed social reforms on recalcitrant rural areas. Resourceful tribal and Islamist resistance groups soon appeared. A March 1979 revolt in the western city of Herat (in which Afghan army units turned against the government and 5,000 died, including fifty Soviet citizens) began a civil war and brought the Politburo into emergency session. Speaking on March 17, Gromyko saw the hands of Pakistan, Iran, the United States, and China behind the rebels. In the case of Pakistan, he was correct; concerning the Americans, premature. Carter would authorize non-lethal (for the time being) aid to Pakistan-based Afghan insurgents on July 3, 1979.[50]

Gromyko emphasized: "one thing is clear: we cannot surrender Afghanistan to the enemy." The others agreed, but Andropov spoke forcefully *against* intervention. The KGB chairman was a well-informed realist with a propensity for worst-case scenarios. Rebuking MO fantasies, he denied that a revolutionary situation existed in backward, Muslim Afghanistan. "To deploy our troops would mean to wage war against the people, to crush the people, to shoot at the people." Gromyko added that it would sink upcoming meetings with Carter and Giscard d'Estaing, and be a gift to China. The Politburo decided to send more food aid, weaponry, and advisers. Taraki was summoned to Moscow where a frail Brezhnev told him to broaden his base of support.[51]

If Andropov's analysis remained valid, why did the Politburo change its mind? By fall 1979 the Vienna summit had come and gone and SALT II was in dire straits in the Senate. In August–September, a bizarre controversy erupted in Washington over a 2,000–3,000–man Soviet "combat brigade" in Cuba since 1962. Instead of dismissing this political red herring, the White House solemnly declared the status quo unacceptable, suggesting to the Kremlin that it was looking for any excuse to quarrel.[52] By late 1979, in sum, Moscow saw less to lose in terms of U.S.–Soviet relations. Kabul, meanwhile, was starting to look like late 1963 Saigon. An unpopular, faction-ridden government was struggling to cope with an unpromising military situation. Added to this was fear that it might make a deal with the enemy. In September, Brezhnev and

Gromyko urged Taraki to replace the thuggish Amin and co-opt the Parcham faction. After a botched attempt by presidential guards to kill him, Amin had Taraki arrested and strangled, despite Soviet pleas to spare him. Taraki's murder shocked Brezhnev and was a turning point for the general secretary.[53] He had personally given his support to Taraki, and may have felt partly responsible for his death.

With his ties to Moscow compromised, Amin (in an odd twist, he had studied at Brzezinski's university, Columbia) opened contacts with the local U.S. embassy. Although Amin's intentions were unclear, this move seems to have shaken Andropov. A fresh nightmare scenario trumped the previous one. U.S–Iranian relations had gone from bad to worst when radical students attacked the U.S. embassy in Tehran, taking its staff hostage, on November 4. The Soviets suspected that without Iran the Americans would be seeking new bases and electronic spying facilities. It is unlikely Washington would have accepted an invitation to set up shop in Afghanistan. But Soviet leaders were victims of their own schematic thinking. Avoiding a repetition of Sadat's "betrayal" was a fixation. In a December 1 letter to Brezhnev, Andropov spoke of "alarming information" about "Amin's secret activities, forewarning of a possible political shift to the West." He outlined an operation to install the Parcham leader Babrak Karmal.[54] On December 8 the "troika" of Andropov, Gromyko, and Ustinov made the case for Amin's removal to Brezhnev. News had just arrived of Germany's agreement to NATO's "two-track" decision and Ustinov and Andropov argued that if Amin switched sides, the Americans could use Afghanistan to aim additional missiles at the Motherland. Brezhnev assented. Four days later, a broader Politburo group went along.[55]

Andropov, with his well-founded fear of blood-letting, had favored a small KGB operation. Fatally, he seems to have allowed Ustinov to persuade him that a 75,000-man force was necessary, and that Soviet operations would be over in several weeks. Ustinov, in turn, shouted down Chief of Staff Marshal Nikolai Ogarkov, who expressed reservations. On December 24 the Red Army entered Afghanistan. On the 27th, KGB special forces stormed Amin's residence in the Dar-ul-Aman Palace. Amin and his close aides were executed on the spot. Soviet leaders had their new man, Karmal. They, and the Afghans, would pay a high price for another major miscalculation, this time made in a state of nervous agitation. But positioning themselves to threaten the West's oil supplies was probably the last thing on their minds.

* * *

For its part, the Carter administration's 1979–80 measures incorporated the assumptions of its diehard opponents. But the latter did not win on the merits of their arguments. There were two immediate reasons behind Washington's "panic of '79." The first was a series of events: the Shah's fall in January, the overthrow of the Somoza dictatorship in Nicaragua by the left-wing Sandinistas in July, the humiliating Tehran hostage crisis beginning in November, a radical Sunni attack on Mecca's Grand Mosque, raising questions about Saudi Arabia's stability, in December, and the invasion of Afghanistan to end the year. Contemporaneously, an overheated economy stimulated inflation and triggered a flight from the dollar. Consumer prices rose by 11.2 percent in 1979 and 13.6 percent in 1980, a post-war record. Reacting to the dollar's decline, OPEC raised oil prices by 120 percent in December 1979.[56]

Most of these events had nothing to do with (and did not help) the Soviet Union. Moreover, they tended to obscure a historic turn benefiting America and Europe: China's embrace of market liberalization. Simultaneously, the Soviet growth rate continued to decline.[57] The most significant development of 1979 for the West, representing a strategic and ideological sea change in the Middle East, was the Iranian revolution. Basic prudence called for a policy to defend the Gulf's oil-producing states against a hostile Iran, but this would have been true if the USSR had not existed. (By the same token, American inflation called for the appointment of a new Federal Reserve chairman, Paul Volcker, who began to defend the dollar by tightening monetary policy.) But coming in quick succession, 1979 events appeared to be part of single, chain-reaction crisis, and to signal a kind of general collapse of a U.S. world position under threat since 1968.

The second reason why it was nearly impossible to view events with equanimity was the upcoming U.S. election. Indeed, no post-war president succumbed more abjectly to the "iron law" than Carter. Reflecting on events in March 1980, Brzezinski believed that American "underreaction" to the 1978 Ethiopia crisis had "then bred overreaction." He referred to the administration's panicky handling of the Soviet brigade affair which had further poisoned the atmosphere in which the Senate considered the SALT II treaty. He could have added Carter's description of the Afghanistan invasion as "the greatest threat to peace since the Second World War," and consequent U.S. measures.[58] But it is more accurate to say that Carter's perception that he had under-reacted, together with the deluge of criticism he faced in 1978–80, bred over-reaction. Ford's pre-election capitulation to his opponents had been partial. Carter's was total. He was politically "born again."

The Republican camp in 1979–80 was a marriage of convenience of moderates aiming for a return to the Nixon–Kissinger approach, neo-conservatives supporting an anti-Soviet crusade, and right-wingers favoring dialogue with Moscow from a position of strength, if at all. For reasons having as much to do with domestic as external developments, the right had recovered steadily after its crushing defeat in 1964, and 1980 appeared to mark the beginning of a new political era.[59] Ronald Reagan, like Margaret Thatcher, was the paladin of a reaction to what some saw as oppressive state interference in the economy and society. But Reagan's victory was more the product of immediate circumstances than it was a mandate for a conservative revolution. Carter's conversion did not dispel the view that he was a feckless vacillator. Bombarded by bad news, millions of Democrats voted for a right-wing Republican with a simple message: the restoration of U.S. power.

CHAPTER 9
STIRRINGS OF CHANGE, 1980–1985

The now-standard account of the new U.S. administration features the themes of paradox and reversal. An influential study underlines the contrast between its "declaratory" and "operational" policies, in plain English, between bark and bite.[1] Beginning with his first press conference when he observed that "[T]he only morality they [the Russians] recognize is what will further their cause: meaning they reserve unto themselves the right to commit any crime, to lie to cheat . . . ," and most famously in his description of the USSR as "an evil empire," Reagan took the verbal offensive.[2] His crude vocabulary provoked indignation in Moscow and Western progressive circles. But despite the charged atmosphere, there were no major superpower confrontations. Despite talk of exorcising the "Vietnam syndrome," the administration limited itself to operations like the seizure of tiny Marxist-controlled Grenada. It relied instead on the "Reagan Doctrine": funding indigenous resistance movements like Savimbi's UNITA in Angola, the anti-Sandinista "contras" in Nicaragua, above all the Islamist Mujahedin in Afghanistan.

Reagan raised defense spending by 43 percent between 1981 and 1984, but as a percentage of GDP it remained well below 1950s levels.[3] His administration funded new weapons (e.g. "stealth" aircraft and the D-5 Trident missile) and unveiled new conventional war plans (the "Lehman doctrine" to defeat the Soviet navy and an offensive "air–land battle" for Europe). But its most radical undertaking, the Strategic Defense Initiative (SDI) to develop a space-based anti-missile system, remained unfulfilled. In January 1983 the administration defined its goals as reversing Soviet expansionism and promoting "within the narrow limits available" greater pluralism in the USSR. But notwithstanding Reagan's rhetoric and apologists' claims, it did not plan to end the Cold War. According to an influential NSC staffer, it excluded from its policy "challenging the legitimacy" of the Soviet system or forcing the USSR's collapse.[4]

A second paradox involves Reagan's outlook and behavior. His public views, consisting of conservative banquet circuit clichés, were repeated in his diaries and presumably firmly held.[5] But he ran anything but a tight ship and tolerated bitter feuding between anti-Soviet militants and moderates. This created the impression that he was either waiting for the real decision-makers to agree on the script, or that his opinions were less fixed than it appeared. A person who knew him predicted that, although stubborn, Reagan was someone with whom the Soviets could eventually establish good relations.[6] It became clear that, while shunning confrontations and despising details, Reagan set the basic direction. After the resignation of his first secretary of state, Alexander Haig, in June 1982, Reagan remarked that their lone disagreement had been "over whether I made policy or the Sec. of State did."[7] As his principal aim, Reagan eventually seized on humanity's liberation not from Communism but the curse of nuclear weapons, something that self-evidently required Soviet collaboration. Although anti-Communist stereotypes had been his stock-in-trade, he proved more open to persuasion by centrists, chief among them Haig's replacement George Shultz, than many had believed possible. Progressives who had excoriated Reagan would later praise him as a visionary who helped to end the Cold War.[8]

The problem with focusing retrospectively on the gap between words and deeds is that one may lose sight of the early 1980s reality. It was the most dangerous moment of the Cold War since 1958–62. There were few inklings of Reagan's redeeming flexibility. A combustible mixture of U.S. zealotry and Soviet paranoia threatened disaster.[9] Dwelling on the eventual U.S. shift also distracts attention from a Soviet reassessment that began before Reagan's. The key figure was Andropov, even before he replaced Brezhnev on the latter's death in November 1982. The whisky-drinking, English-speaking KGB chairman was no closet Westernizer or bold reformer.[10] But he understood that the USSR faced a multi-layered crisis and that as Mikhail Gorbachev and the "new thinkers" would put it, *tak zhit' nel'zia—"We can't go on living like this."*[11]

The Soviet Impasse

Brezhnev's USSR was "a mighty world power."[12] By 1980, it had accumulated nearly seventy satellites and dependencies with claims on its largesse. As early as 1971, however, Soviet observers had raised doubts about aiding "revolutionary" elites in Asia and Africa. By the late 1970s, government and MO experts were questioning the cost and feasibility of teaching socialism to petty tyrants like Mengistu.[13] Andropov's fatal weakness was his reluctance to challenge Defense Minister Ustinov. But he recognized the outer layer of the crisis, observing in 1982, "It is one thing to proclaim socialism . . . and quite another to build it." In Afghanistan the army had become engaged in a war against the people, just as Andropov had predicted. As general secretary (November 1982– February 1984), he gave freer rein to the press and specialized journals to criticize policy. In November 1983 a think-tank analyst would warn of the danger "when messianism becomes the official ideology of a superpower."[14]

A more important catalyst for change was the growing crisis in the "near-empire." In July–August 1980, a wave of strikes hit aviation works in Lublin and the Lenin shipyards in Gdańsk on the Baltic coast. Ironically, the Polish strikes were the consequence of austerity measures (the raising of subsidized prices and dismissing of workers) of the kind urged by Western banks on heavily indebted countries like Poland, and favored by Thatcher in Britain, to improve productivity and cut labor costs. But the Polish government, remembering bloody disturbances in 1956 and 1970, opted for conciliation. In an unprecedented step, it recognized workers' right to strike and permitted a non-Communist union, *Solidarność* (Solidarity), composed of diverse regional unions and led by a charismatic electrician, Lech Wałęsa. Solidarity rapidly became a broad movement calling for the democratization of Polish life. In early 1981, John Paul II gave Wałęsa his blessing during a pilgrimage to Rome. The Pope had quite intentionally stirred the nationalist, as well as religious, sentiments of his compatriots during a 1979 visit to Poland. (He would do the same when returning in 1983 and 1987.) After thugs beat up Solidarity activists in Bydgoszcz in March 1981, the union showed its clout by calling a "warning strike" that brought Poland to a halt.[15]

The Soviet Politburo set up a special commission to prepare a response and exerted intense pressure on PZPR head Stanyslaw Kania and defense minister General Wojciech Jaruzelski to eliminate the Solidarity threat. Major Warsaw Pact maneuvers in December 1980 were designed to force the Poles to act and to assist them, if necessary, in implementing a crackdown. But Soviet leaders decided early on that, barring a total breakdown, another Budapest, Prague, or Kabul was not in the cards. The costs to the Soviet economy and relations with Western Europe would be too high. Andropov told a close associate in the autumn of 1980: "The quota of interventions abroad has been exhausted."[16] In December 1980 when Kania warned of a bloodbath if the Warsaw Pact intervened, Brezhnev endorsed a local solution to "rout" the opposition. Kania's cold feet reinforced and justified Soviet reservations. The Kremlin reached its wits' end with Kania (voted out by a PZPR central committee plenum in October 1981 and replaced by Jaruzelski) and wondered if the Hamlet of Warsaw, tortured by doubt, would ever move. Jaruzelski's nerves held and the Polish military imposed martial law, arresting 6,000 opposition activists, on December 12–13, 1981.[17]

Although Solidarity had been crushed (for the time being), and the world did not know (for now), something fundamental had happened: the so-called Brezhnev doctrine, if not abolished, had been seriously questioned. Awaiting Jaruzelski's crackdown, Andropov told the Politburo that Soviet intervention was not an option:

> We can't risk such a step. We do not intend to introduce troops into Poland. That is the proper position and we must adhere to it until the end. I don't know how things will turn out in Poland, but even if Poland falls under the control of Solidarity, that's the way it will be. And if the capitalist countries pounce on the Soviet Union, and you know they have already reached an agreement on a variety of economic and political sanctions that will be very burdensome for us. *We must be concerned above all with our own country and about the strengthening of the Soviet Union. That is our main line.*[18]

Andropov's core concern was the crisis's inner layer: the state of the economy, society, and the political regime itself.

The Soviet economy's problems had been evident since the late 1950s. The centralized system of planning allocated resources inefficiently and offered few rewards for innovation and hard work. Growth had continued to be more "extensive" (based on developing new resources, as in Khrushchev's "Virgin Lands" program) than "intensive" (derived from the rising productivity of existing factors of production).[19] After the mid-1970s decline, annual GDP growth rates were a mere 1–2 percent, and labor productivity was around 40 percent of the U.S. level.[20] Living standards were not falling and the economy was not in danger of collapsing. Still, the external context was changing in ways that would aggravate existing weaknesses. Staying up-to-date in technology sectors essential to military strength increasingly meant allying with international firms and attracting foreign investment.[21] But, despite signs of stagnation and appeals by experts for greater openness, the economy remained largely autarkic. Indeed, there were no easy or obvious recipes for its revitalization. The defense budget was a "Moloch" representing 40 percent of state spending and 20 percent of GDP, but seriously tackling the problem was taboo until the late 1980s.[22] China was liberalizing, but it was unburdened by a "ten-time zone rust belt" of aging factories and infrastructure, and could call on an overseas Chinese community with hoards of capital to invest.[23]

Early 1980s observers noted "mass dissatisfaction" with chronic shortages and pervasive corruption. Worker discipline was lax and alcoholism rife.[24] Dissatisfaction translated into apathy or resignation and posed no threat to the regime. But ordinary people, not to mention diplomats and scholars who traveled abroad, realized that promises of a bright future were empty. Meanwhile the *nomenklatura* class enjoyed access to Western goods, dachas, and special clinics denied the majority. Atop the structure sat a senescent (and literally sedated) general secretary. Compared to his predecessors, Brezhnev had been a tolerant despot who guaranteed his colleagues job security and the perquisites of power. The result was an entrenched, consensus-based oligarchy, devoid of energy and new ideas.

Biology had begun to correct what to some had become an embarrassing and intolerable situation. Nearly all the major figures of the Brezhnev era died between December 1980 and March 1985. Andropov's main contribution was to call in no uncertain terms for scientific–technological innovation and give responsibility to dynamic younger men like his protégé, Gorbachev.[25] In contrast to the Brezhnev generation, Gorbachev (born 1931) and the "new thinkers" (Yevgeny Velikhov, Anatoly Chernyaev, Vadim Medvedev, Alexander Yakovlev, Eduard Shevardnadze, among others) who would advise him were "children of the 20th Party Congress." They had come of age in the post-1956 "thaw," seen Eastern Europe and the West, and grown to deplore their country's backwardness and isolation. After visiting Czechoslovakia in 1969, Gorbachev had reached "the distressing conclusion that something was really wrong with us." Chernyaev, a cosmopolitan MO official, noted three features in Gorbachev's pre-1980s outlook: an openness to foreigners, an interest in social democracy and attraction to parties like the PCI, and disgust with Soviet–East European relations, as if (as he later put it) the USSR were "running a kindergarten." Called to Moscow in 1978 as Central Committee secretary for agriculture and candidate Politburo member, the ambitious party boss from Stavropol established ties with the leading reformists of the day.[26]

Andropov, Reagan, and the War Scare of 1983

Andropov emerged as a proto-reformer when the West began to ratchet up pressure on Moscow, raising the question of a cause-effect relationship. Indeed, if Andropov worried about anything it was that internal stagnation coincided with a growing external threat. His December 1979 analysis of Afghanistan and December 1981 remark about the capitalists' "pouncing" indicated his awareness that the Americans would try to exploit Soviet vulnerabilities. The USSR needed to modernize to compete with and defend itself against the United States, as well as to deliver the goods to a disillusioned population. Andropov knew Soviet problems were to a degree self-inflicted. But he and the Politburo had no intention of being *coerced* by the United States. The principal effect of Reagan's words and deeds intended to extract concessions was to convince Soviet leaders that Reagan was "a dangerous individual" whose actions might trigger war.[27]

In the context of the U.S. build-up and rhetorical offensive, Moscow discounted occasional conciliatory gestures (like Reagan's hand–written letter to Brezhnev composed as he recuperated from an assassination attempt in March 1981) as public relations gimmicks.[28] In May 1981 the Politburo authorized a special alert and KGB-GRU information-gathering program to furnish early warning of a preemptive nuclear attack. "VRYaN," (the acronym for "Surprise Nuclear Missile Attack") became the biggest peacetime intelligence operation in Soviet history. Such was the fear of a decapitating blow that the Kremlin authorized development and deployment of "Perimeter," a system designed to guarantee the launch of Soviet missiles even after the leadership had been wiped out.[29] Moscow interpreted Reagan's March 1983 speech announcing SDI to mean the Americans were seeking a breakthrough allowing them to cripple the USSR's nuclear arsenal. Although Soviet scientists dismissed the feasibility of space-based defenses, top leaders dreaded a new arms race. Indeed, "Star Wars" supporters like deputy National Security Adviser Robert McFarlane counted on such fears to produce an eventual "grand compromise" whereby Moscow would radically cut its ICBMs in return for the scrapping of SDI.[30]

In a June 1983 speech, Andropov warned of an "unprecedented sharpening" of the East–West confrontation and expressed dissatisfaction with the "pace in shifting the economy onto the rails of intensive development."[31] In September, when nervous air defenses mistook a Korean Airlines 747 (far off-course in Soviet airspace) for a U.S. spy plane and shot it down, Reagan accused the Russians of deliberately massacring 269 civilians. Andropov, although passing up the opportunity to apologize for a tragic error, considered Washington's reaction to the KAL007 disaster "hysterical." A Soviet statement (September 29, 1983) declared: "if anybody ever had any illusions about the possibility of an evolution to the better in the policy of the present American administration, these illusions are completely dispelled now."[32] On November 7 the conservative Politiburo member Grigory Romanov publicly described the international situation as "white hot, thoroughly white hot."[33]

Controversy surrounds the link between Moscow's mood and a NATO exercise known as "Able Archer 83," and this intriguing episode's impact on the Cold War. The exercise (held November 2–11, 1983), testing nuclear weapons release procedures in case of war, and involving Thatcher and German Chancellor Helmut Kohl (although not Reagan), could not have been scheduled at a less opportune moment. KGB sources mistakenly reported a heightened alert at U.S. bases in Europe. Some Soviet forces in the GDR and Baltic area, including nuclear-capable tactical aircraft, were put alert. On November 8 or 9, KGB Center in Moscow sent flash telegrams to Western European residencies requesting information and warning that NATO might launch a surprise nuclear attack in the guise of a drill. The deputy resident in London, Oleg Gordievsky, who was spying for Britain's MI6, had earlier told his handlers about VRYaN and now warned that Able Archer had his superiors in a state of near-panic. McFarlane (he had become full National Security Adviser) recalled that the situation had been "very grave."[34]

At the same time, there is little evidence the Politburo itself was alarmed by Able Archer or even received reports about it.[35] Although McFarlane was aware of Soviet jitters (and had advised Reagan not to participate in the exercise), neither he, Defense Secretary Caspar Weinberger, nor Shultz could convince themselves that Moscow *really* believed NATO would attack without provocation. Shultz took the line (advanced in a later CIA analysis) that the Kremlin had orchestrated a "war scare" to panic European opinion and pressure the Italian and German parliaments into voting against deploying cruise missiles (in Italy) and Pershing II's (in Germany). Despite large demonstrations and emotionally charged debates, the late-November votes approved deployment. Moscow responded by walking out of the Intermediate-range Nuclear Forces (INF) negotiations in Geneva and refusing to set a date for the resumption of talks (dubbed "START" by Washington) on strategic arms.[36]

Had Shultz known of VRYaN and the Kremlin's mood, he might have been less sure. More consequently, Reagan took a different view. The president's concern about war had been stimulated by a private showing of *The Day After*. He recorded that the docu-drama, depicting the catastrophic effects of a limited nuclear attack, left him "greatly depressed."[37] Unlike his secular advisers, Reagan took the notion of Armageddon seriously. According to McFarlane, the president mentioned the Biblical prophecy to his advisers and showed "genuine anxiety" on hearing Gordievsky's reports of the KGB's reaction to Able

Archer.[38] Although Reagan appears to have misread the effect of the exercise itself, he proved more attuned than his advisers to Moscow's frame of mind: "Three years had taught me something surprising about the Russians. Many people at the top of the Soviet hierarchy were genuinely afraid of America and Americans. Perhaps this shouldn't have surprised me, but it did."[39] In effect, Reagan had unnerved the Soviets to the point that Reagan *himself* became alarmed. His quirky faith (if thus it can be described) in scripture interacted with Soviet dread of an attack in ways that began to change the course of events. On November 11 he spoke publicly of his dream of banishing nuclear weapons. A week later he recorded in his diary: "I feel the Soviets are so defensive minded, so paranoid about being attacked that without being in any way soft on them we ought to tell them no one here has any intention of anything like that." ("What the h—l have they got," he added, "that anyone would want.") *Time* and *Newsweek* interviews conveyed a message: he would no longer use the expression "focus of evil" to describe the USSR.[40]

Reagan's awareness that his administration had nearly over-played its hand with the Kremlin coincided with an equally crucial realization: it risked over-playing its hand at home. Reagan's March 1983 "evil empire" speech had aimed to engage evangelical pastors in a campaign against the growing "nuclear freeze" movement.[41] But public fear of nuclear war and dismay over administration policies continued to rise in the United States as well as Europe. Reagan's gloom after *The Day After* probably had partly to do with its anti-administration propaganda value.[42] The political adviser Stuart Spencer warned Nancy Reagan that many voters were disturbed by Reagan's confrontational stance, and the pollster Richard Wirthlin confirmed the point. Joining Shultz, McFarlane, NSC staffer Jack Matlock, and White House deputy chief-of-staff Michael Deaver, Mrs. Reagan threw her considerable influence behind a policy of dialogue.[43] On January 3, 1984, Reagan's probable Democratic opponent in November, former Vice President Mondale, charged that "the risk of nuclear war" had increased under the present administration. A Gallup poll conducted in mid-January indicated that 38 percent of the public approved of Reagan's handling of foreign policy while 49 percent disapproved.[44]

Reinforcing Reagan's novel open-mindedness were political self-interest and personal vanity. Thanks to the climate the administration had helped to create, the 1984 elections were emerging as the one such contest during the Cold War when fear of war would prove a more exploitable issue than fear of weakness. Keen to counter the view that he was a warmonger (and against the advice of hard-liners like Weinberger and the CIA head William Casey), Reagan was inclined to follow the public mood, which increasingly favored lowered tensions. His carefully-crafted speech given on January 16, 1984, was a collective effort. (Nancy, who sought to micromanage her husband's schedule using astrology, chose the date.[45]) It began with a barrage of boilerplate that undermined its basic purpose.[46] Referring to America's "rebuilt" defenses, Reagan noted the Soviets had "been saying for years that our demise was inevitable ... I think they can see now they were wrong." Still, the speech spoke of "common interests" and called for "genuine co-operation." Along with Achesonian saws such as "strength is essential to negotiate," the speech (at Matlock's urging) alluded to Kennedy's conciliatory American University address in June 1963. Reagan himself inserted a homely yarn about Ivan and Anya and Jim and Sally, ordinary couples with a capacity for friendship. He concluded: "Together we can strengthen peace, reduce the level of arms, and know in doing so that we have helped fulfill the hopes and dreams of those we represent and, indeed, of people everywhere. Let us begin now." Predictably, Soviet observers saw the speech as an election-year event.[47] But it was a victory for administration moderates and (like the Politburo's suspension of the Brezhnev doctrine) a little-noticed milestone on the road to the end of the Cold War.

"As you Say, Live and Let Live..."

In September 1984 the White House staged a "photo-opportunity" in the form of a lunch for Gromyko during which Reagan referred again to his dream of a nuclear-free world. Moscow was not displeased, but viewed the meeting as more domestic propaganda.[48] The pro-dialogue camp's effort to steer the president proceeded (to paraphrase Lenin) two steps forward, one step back. Following his re-election, Reagan and other officials routinely used harsh anti-Soviet rhetoric. An internal dispute over whether to keep SDI development within the strict limits of the ABM treaty intensified before the Soviet–American summit meeting agreed upon for November 1985.[49] For their part, the Americans could be forgiven for thinking they had no one to talk to in Moscow. Andropov, in failing health for months, died in February 1984. His successor, Brezhnev's trusted aide Konstantin Chernenko, suffered from severe emphysema—an apt metaphor for the state of the Soviet system. For Chernyaev, an already embarrassing situation "became a shameful farce."[50] Only with Chernenko's death in March 1985 did the USSR acquire a leader with the vigor that circumstances required.

Once in power, Gorbachev and fellow Andropov legatees Nikolai Ryzhkov and Yegor Ligachev quickly retired rivals like Romanov, Vladimir Tikhonov, and Victor Grishin. But 1984–5 events were hardly a foregone conclusion. Chernenko's election reflected a deadlock between renovators and the "old guard." The siege mentality ran deepest among those (Ustinov, Chief of the General Staff Ogarkov, and Andropov) who remembered June 22, 1941. But the war scare left few unaffected and strengthened the conservatives. Gorbachev recalled: "Things were near a boiling point... Wherever you went you encountered the same question. When will the war come?"[51] Neo-Stalinists favored a crackdown on dissent and sharp increase in defense spending, while other conservatives preferred a continuation of Andropov's approach, emphasizing discipline and vigilance against the imperialists. Stalin enjoyed a brief revival in film and books, and the Politburo decided to re-admit Molotov (banished by Khrushchev) to the CPSU.

The old guard distrusted and resented Gorbachev, seen as a rising star and known not to suffer fools. He owed his unanimous election partly to the fact that opponents had no real alternative and wishfully assumed he would follow in Andropov's footsteps. Luck may have had a role. Gorbachev believed Ustinov's death in late 1984 had hurt his chances, but others argue the defense minister might have opposed him. The Ukraine party boss Vladimir Schcherbitsky, a hard-liner, found himself (of all places) on a visit to Washington, and did not vote.[52] Gromyko played a key part by making the official nomination. The foreign minister believed Gorbachev stood head-and-shoulders above the competition but he too may have had illusions, hoping to remain in the younger man's good graces. Gromyko had let slip that Mikhail Sergeyevich was a publicity seeker during the latter's trip to England in December 1984.[53] The Western press had seized on Gorbachev's statement that Europe was the USSR's "common home," and Thatcher had called him "a man we can do business with." But even if Gorbachev had not learned of Gromyko's remark, he planned "a sharp change of direction." He chose the Georgia party head Shevardnazde (born 1928), a close friend, to replace Gromyko in July 1985.[54]

To some degree Gorbachev had concealed his hand to secure power. But to a degree, it was unclear even to himself. Chernyaev, his personal foreign policy adviser after early 1986, depicts him as a hybrid: "an intelligent and honest person, conscientious and passionate, at the same time well-versed in the art of apparat games...He had some ideas about how to 'live better,' but they didn't go beyond the limits of the existing order." It would "take years of tortuous struggle for him to realize that it was impossible [merely] to renovate our society."[55] Gorbachev's March 1985 acceptance speech echoed Andropov's call to shift the economy "onto the path of intensive development." After much discussion, the choice was to renew the "outdated technological base" (with emphasis on machine-building), thus raising productivity and supposedly creating conditions for radical reform in the early 1990s.[56] The flaws in this "acceleration" strategy, preceded by a campaign to cut alcohol production and consumption, would shortly be evident. To avoid an immediate showdown with vested interests, the system of centrally allocated resources and party control of enterprises remained intact. The sacred cow of military spending was not only left untouched, but was to be fattened as a percentage of GDP. The anti-alcohol effort met with resistance and ridicule. It brought declining tax revenues and (combined with lower earnings owing to falling world prices of oil and gas) serious budget deficits after 1986.[57]

Although destined to fail, this initial approach coincided with the launching of a more flexible foreign policy, raising the question of a link. In the minds of Gorbachev and his advisers, the connection was intimate. *Perestroika* (the term given domestic restructuring or modernization) required "propitious international conditions." This meant closer ties to Western Europe. Before his November 1985 Geneva meeting with Reagan, Gorbachev went to Paris, where he tried (with limited success) to woo President François Mitterrand with the notion of a "common European home." It also meant alleviating "the pressure that had borne down on us due to our involvement in conflicts all over the world and in the debilitating arms race."[58] Slowing the arms race and leaving Afghanistan would eventually allow more investment in health, housing, and consumer-oriented industries. In the meantime, those steps were necessary for "accelerated development." Otherwise the West would continue to widen its technological lead over a USSR still stuck in the starting blocks. In October 1986, several months after the approval of "acceleration," Gorbachev told the Politburo: "Our main goal now is to prevent the arms race from entering a new stage . . . We will lose because right now we are already at the end of our tether."[59] How then did SDI affect Soviet policy? In line with scientists' doubts, Chernyaev and Dobrynin deplored the SDI fixation and making its limitation a condition of agreements. But this was a minority opinion. Before Geneva, Moscow offered a 50 percent cut in strategic arms in return for a pledge not to develop, test, or deploy "space strike weapons."[60] What Gorbachev called the "notorious" SDI was a key factor driving his foreign policy in its initial phase.[61]

In a way more conventional politicians would never have imagined, Reagan believed he could free the superpowers (anti-missile know-how was to be shared with Moscow) from their surprise attack syndromes. Like many Westerners, Soviet leaders did not take Reagan's professed beliefs at face value and sought ulterior motives. Perhaps, they reasoned, SDI was ultimately intended as a bargaining chip, but in the meantime it was a $70 billion R&D program in computers, lasers, robotics, and fiber optics, areas where the West was already far ahead.[62] Gorbachev's pointed remarks in Geneva suggest he saw SDI as the U.S. military-industrial complex's attempt to cripple a Soviet strategy of technological catch-up.[63] Moreover, since a total shield against a first strike was a fantasy, SDI's real purpose must be offensive. A partial shield might neutralize the USSR's diminished second-strike capability following an American first strike. The United States might also place arms in space that could destroy targets on Earth. Gorbachev assured Reagan that the

USSR could counter SDI, if necessary.[64] But Soviet willingness to make unprecedented concessions to curb SDI and space weaponry was a measure of Moscow's preoccupation. As late as 1988, Gorbachev insisted that SDI was not purely defensive.[65] The tendency to assume the worst about U.S. leaders was not a monopoly of the Brezhnev generation. Yakovlev, the most Westernized of Gorbachev's advisers, wrote in June 1985 that the Americans did not exclude "unleashing an attack on the USSR."[66]

To American journalists, Gorbachev expressed frustration that a Soviet nuclear test moratorium and proposal to prevent a space arms race were treated as propaganda, and bellicose talk continued to emanate from Washington. The principal question was whether "we are prepared to switch our mentality and our mode of acting from a warlike to a peaceful track. As you say, live and let live. We call it peaceful coexistence."[67] In the event, the Geneva meeting was not without results. A joint communiqué affirmed that "nuclear war cannot be won and must never be fought." Fireside chats and lakeside walks marked the start of a rapport. Reagan, who had developed a curiosity about Russia, was intrigued by Gorbachev's occasional references to God, and found the general secretary likable as well as tough. Although angered by lectures on SDI, Afghanistan, and human rights, Gorbachev sensed Reagan might be someone he "could do business with."[68] They agreed to follow-up summits. Born performers, Reagan and Gorbachev were now in a kind of international popularity contest. It did not escape Reagan that his approval rating for the ice-breaking summit was 81 percent.[69]

Still, the Americans had rejected Gorbachev's proposed deal and Geneva brought the USSR no closer to the conditions needed for domestic progress. The pressure of time and a determination to prove its good faith pushed Moscow toward new initiatives and a reexamination of basic concepts. After all, previous leaders had talked of peaceful coexistence and ending the Cold War. Paradoxically, securing the international agreements necessary to salvage socialism would require showing that the USSR was not simply seeking breathing room, while continuing to wage the international class struggle. With Western hostility persisting and internal problems festering, there was no turning back.

CHAPTER 10
PUTTING AN END TO THE COLD WAR, 1986–1990

When, and if, Soviet "new thinking" took a decisive turn making the end of the East–West conflict inevitable, are questions that (like its origins) historians will long debate. It is hard to say at what point Gorbachev ceased to be an optimistic Leninist who believed "that *perestroika* could give the socialist world a second wind."[1] For much of his tenure, he seemed to be an elusive hybrid who put a brave face on the unforeseen consequences of his actions. A close collaborator eventually despaired that he had "no concept of where we are going."[2] Another controversy surrounds the link between domestic and foreign policy. According to the same observer, Gorbachev's foreign policy, originally meant to create favorable external conditions for reform, became *perestroika*'s "locomotive." To make foreign policy work, "we had to demolish the myths and dogmas of a confrontational ideology."[3]

Similarly, according to one analyst, ending the USSR's isolation eventually became a goal independent of internal needs, and "a determinant of domestic policy." This is because, although reforms failed and Gorbachev's stock fell, he became the "darling of the West." The Soviet leader embraced "romantic schemes" like the renunciation of force and "a common European home" that ensured his international popularity. Gorbachev, as the Polish dissident Adam Michnik put it, became "the prisoner of his foreign policy successes."[4] But whether he threw out the baby of national interests with the bathwater of Hobbesian fatalism, and surrendered the Soviet empire in a fit of narcissism, are more questions on which historians will disagree. What seems clear is that early 1986 represented a point of no return for Gorbachev's foreign policy.

Although "new thinking" acquired its own momentum, it continued to be driven partly by internal requirements. But U.S. policy, too, reflected domestic imperatives, especially after late 1986.

Chernyaev pinpointed "the exact time when Gorbachev placed his stake on a direct dialogue with the Americans." On January 15, 1986, Moscow answered the Geneva failure by proposing to eliminate all nuclear weapons by 2000, including an agreement reducing intermediate-range (INF) weapons in Europe to zero.[5] An "intellectual turn" occurred during preparations for the February–March CPSU Congress. The new party program excluded the notion that peaceful coexistence was a form of the class struggle. Gorbachev's report spoke of "global problems affecting all of humanity," and of the "contradictory, but *interdependent and in many ways integral world that is taking shape.*" A "comprehensive system of international security" was required. The general secretary's evolution was encouraged by Mitterrand, who advised him to go beyond the view of Reagan as mere spokesman for military-industrial interests, and the Spanish prime minister Felipe Gonzales, who stimulated a nascent social democratic tendency in Gorbachev's views.[6]

If Soviet leaders expected conciliatory gestures from Washington, they were disappointed. Nitze, Shultz's arms control adviser, opined that there was "nothing new" on foreign policy in Gorbachev's report. The CIA and Pentagon, Shultz recalled, continued to portray the USSR as "a mighty nation confronting us everywhere."[7] In a muscle-flexing display to sustain Congressional support for defense spending, U.S. ships violated Soviet waters off the Crimea in March 1986. With Reagan's avid support, the CIA increased aid to insurgencies in Nicaragua, Angola, and Afghanistan. McFarlane and Casey promoted weapons sales to Iran to counter Moscow's alleged plans to expand influence in Tehran. Espionage cases, and tit-for-tat expulsions, ratcheted up tensions.[8] Gorbachev assured the French ambassador: "What the Soviet Union is undertaking in foreign policy is not a political game or tactical move." Moscow, he admitted, should overcome its "obsession" with SDI. But, he added: "We will not beg for peace. We've always responded to any challenge, and we can respond to this one too."[9]

Soon after, according to Vladislav Zubok, an event occurred which "was much more responsible for the drastic changes in Soviet official mentality than the previous years of American pressure."[10] The April 26, 1986, explosion at the Chernobyl (Ukraine) nuclear reactor delivered a dose of electroshock to the Soviet system. Local and Moscow-based officials tried to conceal the disaster's size but reports from the West gave the lie to their efforts. Gorbachev was dismayed by the revelation of a cover-up, and infuriated with the military-industrial bureaucracy (a "state within the state") responsible for the nuclear program. The incident was an important fillip to his policy of *glasnost*, or open discussion, and shattered lingering illusions about Soviet technological prowess and the survivability of a nuclear conflict.[11]

Chernobyl also became a black hole swallowing billions of rubles. In an impassioned speech, Gorbachev told foreign ministry officials that policy must "do anything in its capabilities to loosen the vise of defense expenditures." He called for a "radical restructuring" of the Soviet approach, including policy toward Eastern Europe, China, and on human rights.[12] Delegates to the Stockholm Conference on Disarmament in Europe (CDE) were ordered to endorse on-site inspection measures, permitting agreement on conventional arms cuts. In August 1986 Gorbachev and Chernyaev conceived of an informal summit at Reykjavik (a city half-way between the two countries). Gorbachev rejected a proposal from the foreign ministry and Chief of the General Staff Marshal Sergei Akhromeyev in favor of Chernyaev's more radical suggestions. (Akhromeyev almost resigned but was brought to Reykjavik to defend what he had opposed.) Gorbachev aimed to get the Americans to a meeting "necessary for one vital goal of *perestroika*—the easing of the military burden," and once there, "to sweep Reagan off his feet."[13]

Although the face of U.S. policy wore a snarl in 1986, Moscow's gamble was rational. Gorbachev correctly sensed Reagan also wanted a breakthrough. One key official, moreover, considered 1986 America's "year of maximum leverage." Shultz saw the chickens returning to roost after the enormous arms build-up. "With our budget deficit," he said in January 1986, "we are going to be strapped financially as never before in the Cold War." The president, meanwhile, would lose clout when the electoral campaign began in 1987–8. (Reagan, widely credited with restoring American strength, would reach a 68 percent public approval rating in July 1986.) For Shultz, the administration "had twelve months or so in which to break the Soviet shell" on arms control.[14]

The meetings (October 11–12, 1986) in the cramped quarters of "Hofdi House," a seaside structure provided by Iceland, brought Gorbachev and Reagan tantalizingly close to a historic agreement. The Soviets opened with an unprecedented offer: a 50-percent reduction in both sides' "strategic offensive arms" (ICBMs and heavy bombers) and elimination of INF missiles in Europe. The cuts were contingent on a ten-year commitment to the ABM treaty, to be followed by negotiations on defensive systems. Testing in space of "missile-defense space elements" was prohibited, but laboratory work could go forward. The Americans quickly agreed to the INF and strategic cuts (the latter to be completed in five years) and upped the ante with a second five-year phase in which "offensive ballistic missiles" would be abolished. But SDI testing in space, and after ten years deployment of defensive systems, would be allowed.[15]

In a pair of tense final conversations, the two sides tried to bridge their differences. As Gorbachev and Shultz discussed the distinction between "strategic offensive arms" and "offensive ballistic missiles," Reagan interjected: "it would be fine with me if we eliminated all nuclear weapons." Gorbachev and Shultz concurred.[16] But due partly to their prior fixations on SDI, both sides had backed themselves into a corner. In insisting on space testing and the deployment option, Reagan appeared most concerned with not betraying his conservative constituency. He admitted that SDI might prove too expensive and never be implemented. For his part, Gorbachev could hardly allow the Americans to perfect space-based weapons and ready deployment while the USSR dismantled its nuclear arsenal. If he agreed to that, he said, he would be seen as a "fool." Space weaponry was a question of "principle" but also a test of his domestic credibility. On the U.S. side, Matlock believed Shultz had been "obtuse" not to advise Reagan to accept Soviet terms on testing once Gorbachev had agreed to eliminate ballistic missiles—the sort of "grand bargain" some had imagined. But Shultz knew that Weinberger (who had been left home but was still influential) would fiercely oppose limits, and that SDI was not a bargaining chip for Reagan. In any case, it had acquired a domestic significance few had anticipated. U.S. conservatives had warned of an "SDI sellout." The opportunity for a major break-through was lost because Reagan, too, had become a prisoner of SDI.[17] European leaders, Pentagon officials, and right-wing commentators were appalled that Reagan and Shultz had been prepared to abolish nuclear weapons, the sinews of post-war security. Observers pointed out that an INF "zero-option" would magnify the USSR's conventional superiority. Former National Security Adviser Brent Scowcroft wrote in 1987: "We have for some 40 years relied on the threat of nuclear weapons to keep the Soviet hordes at bay."[18] Such objections would have created problems for a Reykjavik agreement, especially if there had been little progress on human rights and regional conflicts. Sensing this, Gorbachev ordered Andrei Sakharov's release from internal exile. On taking power, he had given the army "a year or two" to win in Afghanistan, while deciding to reduce Soviet forces. In a Politiburo meeting after Reykjavik, he said his goal was to "work toward establishment of a friendly and neutral government and then get out." Unfortunately, as Akhromeyev said, the army "had lost the battle for the people." The war was deeply unpopular domestically. Nevertheless, Gorbachev was reluctant to with-draw under U.S. pressure, leaving chaos behind, and with the USSR's tail between its legs.[19]

Reykjavik left Reagan angry and disappointed. Gorbachev, character-istically, refused to call it a failure. The world, he believed, had seen agreement was possible and that SDI was the "main obstacle."[20] Gorba-chev was not only optimistic by nature, but forced by circumstances to cast his throw-of-the-dice in a positive light, and redouble his efforts. Contrary to one argument, Reagan had done little thus far to help Gorbachev.[21] But as luck would have it, and in a manner resembling late 1983, circumstances in America came to Moscow's assistance. More reasons to deal with Gorbachev were added to those Shultz had adum-brated in early 1986.

"Doomed to it": 1987–1988

Reagan, for his admirers the "Great Communicator," was riding for a fall in late 1986. In November, his party lost control of the Senate and news from Beirut and Tehran precipitated the "Iran–Contra" affair. Intent on sustaining Republican, and his personal, popularity by freeing American hostages (and uncritically accepting the McFarlane–Casey geopolitical argument), Reagan had authorized secret arms sales to Iran.[22] The revelation that the United States had, in effect, paid ransoms to Lebanese kidnappers triggered outrage and disbelief. The administration's problems worsened after clumsy efforts to mislead the media and news that profits from sales had helped to fund another Reagan pet project: the war of anti-Sandinista "contras" in Nicaraugua. Shultz, who had opposed the policy, publicly attacked it. After Casey's failed attempt to have him fired, and the CIA director's fatal illness, Shultz emerged stronger. In the meantime, Congress launched an inquiry and the justice department named a special prosecutor. Reagan's answers to investigators were contradictory. His approval rating plunged to around 40 percent in March 1987. Televised hearings absorbed the country's attention for many months.[23]

Reagan was spared Nixon's fate thanks to the widespread view that he was inattentive rather than deceitful. But his reputation was damaged, and losing the Senate undermined his conservative domestic agenda. As his biographer observes, "[l]ike other presidents dogged by domestic scandal, [Reagan] sought solace by playing the role of statesman."[24] By early 1987 he was eager for the summits decided on at Geneva. Shultz, while agreeing, could feel Reagan's impatience. When the new National Security Adviser Frank Carlucci reported that the Reagans were determined to host the Gorbachevs at their California ranch for Thanksgiving, Shultz had to tell him to "quit pressing."[25] Betting on Gorbachev was controversial not only with Reagan's rightwing constituency but sophisticated pessimists like Nixon and Kissinger who doubted that *perestroika* was meant to do more than strengthen the USSR, and feared Europe's decoupling.[26] Their interpretation was mistaken but not implausible. Out of pride, conviction, and political necessity, Gorbachev continued to send mixed signals, for example, by arming Cuba and Ethiopia until 1989. But Reagan, an optimist and sentimentalist, stuck to his intuition that Gorbachev was a new kind of Soviet leader.[27] He also understood that dialogue with Moscow had become his main source of popularity, and claim to achievement, in his second term.

In 1987-8, Gorbachev and Reagan locked arms on the road leading to the end of the Cold War because their political needs fortuitously coincided. As Iran–Contra enveloped Reagan, Gorbachev vented his own deep frustration. "We are plagued," he said in December 1986, "by conservatism, complacency, inertia, an unwillingness to live in new ways." "Acceleration" had failed to take hold and the budget was hit by falling oil prices and tax revenues. Although the Politburo continued to temporize on cutting military spending, reform took a more radical turn with a law giving greater freedom to enterprises.[28] In January 1987 Gorbachev broached the necessity of democratizing the CPSU. In October the Moscow party chief Boris Yeltsin lashed out at "foot-draggers" led by Yegor Ligachev. Gorbachev supported Yeltsin's demotion, but then resumed a leftward course, rehabilitating Nikolai Bukharin and pointing to "blank [Stalinist] pages" in history. According to Chernyaev, reevaluation of the NEP's patron "opened the sluice gates" to ideological revision.[29] In 1988, although (or rather because) *persetroika* was not working, *glasnost*, in the form of withering criticism of the system by intellectuals, journalists, and ordinary people, began to work all too well.

The implications for foreign policy, meanwhile, had never been clearer. On February 26, 1987, Gorbachev told the Politburo that "as difficult as it is to conduct business with the United States, we are doomed to it." The previous day, Suzanne Massie, the popular historian used by Reagan as an occasional go-between, had delivered a message from the Kremlin: *"He [Gorbachev] has nothing to show. Needs something to show."*[30] On February 28, before hearing Reagan's answer that he wished to welcome Gorbachev in America, Moscow made a key concession. Following Yakovlev's advice, Gorbachev decided to accept the INF accord discussed at Reykjavik without prior agreement on SDI or strategic weapons. In April Gorbachev offered a "double zero" deal, eliminating shorter range (SRINF) missiles in Europe as well as INF.[31] Gorbachev was "doomed to it" to divert resources to productive uses, but also because he had little to show for his frenetic efforts. The relationship between domestic and foreign policy was changing in that achievements in the latter arena were beginning to look to Gorbachev like a partial substitute, as well as a prerequisite, for change at home.

A year after Chernobyl, another unforeseen event stunned the hierarchy. On May 28, 1987, a German teenager boarded a single-engine Cessna and flew it unmolested from Finland to central Moscow. Gorbachev may have believed the military had staged the flight to humiliate him.[32] The theory was implausible because the military itself now became the object of unprecedented scorn.[33] But the impact of Mathias Rust's stunt can be compared to that of the Bay of Pigs on Kennedy. A furious general secretary lost trust in the armed forces. He seized the opportunity to replace the defense minister with a more pliant figure and began a purge of the military's senior ranks. The incident happened to coincide with an important shift in Warsaw Pact doctrine (announced May 30, 1987) influenced by West German Social Democratic notions of "defensive defense," or structuring forces to be unable to launch a sudden offensive. Gorbachev had been impressed by Thatcher's recent warning that the West still feared the USSR.[34]

During a brief visit to Berlin on June 12, 1987, Reagan delivered a speech on a platform erected near the wall. Referring to *perestroika*, he asked: "Are these the beginnings of profound changes in the Soviet state? Or are they token gestures...?" "There is one sign," he continued, "the Soviets can make that would be unmistakable...Mr. Gorbachev, tear down this wall!" Shultz and his subordinates had considered the line too provocative and tried to excise it. But at some level, Gorbachev may have taken the message to heart, and satisfaction from the consternation it caused Erich Honecker. The GDR leader had refused to emulate *perestroika* and was deeply suspicious of Moscow's opening to the West.[35]

Shultz undoubtedly saw that Reagan's speech served to reply to domestic charges that the administration had "gone soft."[36] Weinberger, unable to prevent an INF treaty, tried to strangle it with conditions.[37] In a now-established pattern, Gorbachev cut through the latest obstacles by proposing a "global double-zero" agreement eliminating INF and SRINF in Asia and America as well as Europe. Worn down by endless battles, Weinberger announced his retirement in October 1987. Gorbachev may have seen Reagan as vulnerable to pressure and/or open to a change of heart with the defense secretary's imminent departure. He abruptly tried to link the holding of the summit to a strategic arms accord and an interpretation of the ABM treaty preventing space-based

Figure 6. Shultz and Gorbachev in Moscow, April 1987.

"strategic offensive arms." Shultz and Reagan refused, obliging Gorbachev to settle for the INF agreement.[38] Moscow could take solace from a Senate Foreign Relations Committee report calling the administration's reading of the treaty "the most flagrant abuse" of the Constitution's treaty power in history, and a Congressional vote mandating a strict interpretation.[39] But Weinberger's influence persisted. He had proved more royalist than the king in helping to make SDI a touchstone of conservative principle. Although the program had prompted Moscow to make major concessions, its sponsors were unwilling and unable to use it to deliver the major prize.

With or without START, the Washington summit (December 7–10, 1987) was a historic occasion and boosted the prestige of both leaders. By signing the INF treaty, the United States and USSR agreed for the first time to destroy entire classes of weapons, including 2,611 SS-20s and Pershing IIs in Europe. The Soviet leader was treated to a display of "Gorbymania," as crowds pressed to greet him in downtown Washington. Shortly after his return to Moscow, Gorbachev announced a plan to remove Soviet troops from Afghanistan. UN-sponsored agreements between Afghanistan and Pakistan, and the United States and the

USSR (April 14, 1988), called for the withdrawal (although they did not ban arms aid to the local parties) to be completed by early 1989. The Senate approved the INF treaty on May 27, 1988, in time for Reagan's return visit to the USSR. Reagan's Moscow trip (May 29–June 2, 1988) was the end of a personal political odyssey. When asked there if the USSR were still the "evil empire," he replied: "No. I was talking about another time, another era." But the summit produced little of substance, and marked the end of Reagan's sporadic and self-serving efforts to assist Gorbachev in his Herculean undertaking. The INF treaty had finally provided "something to show," but the Afghanistan agreements were little more than a face-saving cover, and START and SDI were unresolved. Overruling Reagan, his advisers blocked inclusion of the words "peaceful coexistence" in a joint statement. The Americans had not received the message that the term had a new meaning.[40] After the summit, with the electoral campaign in full swing, U.S.–Soviet relations entered a "limbo" from which they would not emerge for months.[41]

Early to mid-1988 marked the point-of-no return for Gorbachev's domestic program. He supported a counter-offensive after the so-called Nina Andreyeva letter, a neo-Stalinist attack on reform published in a Leningrad newspaper. At a special party conference in July, Gorbachev rammed through a plan to elect local councils and a national Congress of People's Deputies.[42] This was a bid to foster a pro-reform power base but, according to his later account, Thatcher had also convinced him of the connection between democracy and Western trust.[43] He pressed on amid signs that *glasnost* had opened the Pandora's box of ethnic nationalism. There was unrest in Nagornyi-Karabakh, the Armenian enclave in Azerbaijan, and demonstrations against Soviet dominion in the Baltics. Gorbachev further consolidated his position by replacing Gromyko as head of state, transferring Ligachev to a marginal post, and starting to dismantle party supervision of the economy, unfortunately before market mechanisms were in place.[44]

Gorbachev also stepped up his effort to create "a common European home," a kind of *Ostpolitik* in reverse. The home would be built on "a disarmament policy based on the principle of equal security, on economic links between countries, in particular between the EEC and the Council for Mutual Economic Assistance (CMEA), on cultural exchanges, on the solution to ecological problems." Reinforced CSCE institutions would house transformed military alliances.[45] In October–November 1988 he established a relationship with Kohl, and discussed pan-European co-operation with Mitterrand.[46] Having strengthened his hand at home and altered Warsaw Pact doctrine, Gorbachev was finally ready to make drastic cuts in the military. He told the Politburo, "this will make a huge impression" in the West. Moreover, "without reductions in the army and the military-industrial complex we won't be able to deal with *perestroika*'s tasks."[47]

Notes for another meeting shed light on what the anonymous author called the "dialectical" relation between internal and external policy, and the remarkable state of "new thinking" by late 1988. Under Stalin and his successors, the USSR's "spiritual autarchy" had become a "comfortable cradle in which self-adoration and communist arrogance on a national scale, dogmatism, scholasticism and stagnation enjoyed themselves." Just as individuals acquired self-knowledge and confidence in interaction with others, a country discovered its "national self-respect—and we are lacking this acutely—[and] a sense of national dignity . . . only through interactions with others in the world arena." Overcoming isolation was a form of collective therapy as well a precondition for material betterment. But the point was not to renounce messianism. Rather, the prophet of *perestroika* and his disciples would give a purified and humanized "socialism back to the world."[48]

In December 1988 Gorbachev prepared a major pronouncement conceived of as "Fulton in reverse."[49] Fulton, Missouri, was the site of Churchill's celebrated "Iron Curtain" speech. Gorbachev's mood was also reminiscent of Kennan's in early 1946. His listeners had discounted his words: "Now, by God, they would have it."[50] On December 7, 1988, Gorbachev told the UN General Assembly, "Further world progress is now possible only through the search for a consensus of all mankind, in movement toward a new world order." A basic requirement was that "force and the threat of force can no longer be, and should not be instruments of foreign policy." Another was that *Freedom of choice is a universal principle to which there should be no exceptions.* Although no country should have to renounce its "convictions, philosophy, or traditions," a third was "de-ideologization of interstate relations." He announced a 500,000-man reduction in the Soviet military. Forces in the GDR, Hungary, and Czechoslovakia would be cut by 50,000, including 5,000 tanks. There was a message to president-elect George H. W. Bush (who had told Gorbachev to discount hard-line talk heard in the campaign, but whose entourage included conservative skeptics): "to continue the dialogue in a spirit of realism, openness, and goodwill."[51] Gorbachev was taking unprecedented steps to end the Cold War. But this was true in ways he probably did not intend or realize. A more Machiavellian statesman would have been less absolute in proclaiming freedom of choice, and avoided extending an invitation not only to Eastern Europe, but the peoples of the USSR itself, to decide to stay or go.

The "Velvet Revolutions," 1989

"In Poland it took ten years, in Hungary it took ten months, in East Germany it took ten weeks, in Czechoslovakia it took ten days, in Romania it took ten hours!" Timothy Garton Ash's quip was not far off the mark. After violent clashes between students and and riot-police, and renewed strikes in 1988, the Polish authorities agreed to church-sponsored "round-table" talks with Solidarity to reach an "anti-crisis pact." Legalized in April 1989, Solidarity stunned the PZPR by winning semi-free elections for a bi-cameral legislature in June. After initial hesitation, Solidarity leader Wałęsa engineered a parliamentary majority, and a government with the Communists in the minority was formed under the Catholic intellectual Tadeusz Mazowiecki in September 1989.

Hungary, in the hands of radical reform Communists, opened its border with Austria in September, precipitating the flight of tens of thousands of GDR "tourists." In October the Communists transformed themselves into a social democratic party and Hungary adopted a multi-party system. The same month, thousands of East Germans marched against the regime in Leipzig, provoking Honecker's ouster by SED colleagues and (after more protests in Leipzig and the capital) the decision on November 9 to open the GDR's borders, including the Berlin wall.[52] The GDR announced multi-party elections, scheduled for May 1990. On November 20 throngs of key-shaking demonstrators returned to Prague's Wenceslas Square (where they had battled riot police in January and October), chanting "[Vaclav] Havel to the Castle [the seat of power]!" Their wish was granted when the dashing dramatist and dissident was elected president of the Federal Assembly on December 29. A brief, violent uprising overthrew the most tyrannical of the Eastern regimes in Bucharest. Nicolae Ceaușescu was tried by a drumhead court and shot on Christmas Day.[53]

Historians disagree on when the Brezhnev doctrine expired, but it had clearly lapsed into disuse long before foreign ministry spokesman Gennadi Gerasimov announced the "Sinatra doctrine"—the Eastern Europeans could "do it their way"—on October 25, 1989.[54] By October 1985 Gorbachev had told leaders of the "socialist commonwealth" that ties would be based on equality and national sovereignty. In October 1986 he told the Politburo that the methods used in Hungary and Czechoslovakia "will not work!" In March 1988, he said that in relations with Eastern Europe "we have to take care of our own people first of all." A public statement the same month called for unconditional respect for "the independence of parties and socialist countries to define, for themselves, the path of their own development."[55] More important than exactly when the doctrine died is what has been called "the enigma of 1989": *why* the USSR not only did not intervene but at times facilitated the "velvet revolutions," or negotiated, largely peaceful, transfers of power. This contrasted not only with the bloody upheavals of the past but the contemporaneous choice of Beijing.[56]

Deng and his colleagues were scions of a self-confident and insular civilization. They were also hardened survivors of civil war and cultural revolution. This rendered them more resistant than Gorbachev to the siren call of the West. The Chinese *nomenklatura* might enrich itself but the genies of political democracy and regional separatism were to be kept tightly in the bottle. Observing Eastern Europe, and their own youths' enthusiasm for Gorbachev during a May 1989 visit, the leadership decided on martial law to deal with pro-democracy protests. The army used tanks to clear Beijing's Tiananmen Square, killing hundreds, in early June. The explanation for Moscow's choice begins with the fact that the stagnant, debt-ridden Eastern European economies, like the arms race with the West, had become a burden *perestroika* could ill afford.

Eastern Europe's salvation lay in reform and greater integration into the world economy.[57] Moreover, with war unthinkable and military doctrine changing, the area had lost importance as a glacis and staging area. Remarkably for a Soviet leader, Gorbachev strongly opposed violence in principle.[58] He also knew that intervention would destroy his credibility. And on whose behalf would he act? The leaderships who might have welcomed Soviet tanks were the ones hostile to reform. A motto of the velvet revolutions was "the return to Europe."[59] Gorbachev aimed to live and let live with the West. Intervention would have been illogical, as well as "insane, ineffective, and suicidal" in 1989.[60]

According to one account, by late 1988, Soviet leaders had seen the Eastern European crisis coming, and tried to avoid "the Khrushchev Dilemma": uprisings that would have hurt Gorbachev regardless of his response.[61] In September 1988, seeing Solidarity's help was essential to deal with Polish economic woes, Moscow signaled it would accept the union's re-emergence. Gorbachev stood by the election results and telephoned the PZPR head Mieczyslaw Rakowski to convince him to facilitate the new government's formation.[62] In East Berlin for the GDR's 40th anniversary, Gorbachev warned Honecker (privately calling him an "asshole") that parties which did not adapt "to the demands of reality" were doomed. On November 1, Gorbachev urged Honecker's replacement Egon Krenz to allow the people to travel freely, and to pursue reform.[63]

But Moscow was not an active and willing liberator. It was absorbed by internal affairs and mostly reacting (albeit with striking equanimity) to a chain reaction beyond its control. The USSR held its own semi-free elections in March 1989. The 2,250 members of the new Congress of People's Deputies included hundreds of liberals, including Yeltsin, who had campaigned for a multi-party system. Twelve days of its raucous, televised debates in late May–early June helped to complete *glasnost*'s work of "desacralizing" the system.[64] A campaign for republic sovereignty, soon to include Russia itself, was underway. Although looking increasingly like a sorcerer's apprentice, Gorbachev continued to hope for democratized Communism in Eastern Europe.[65] He told Krenz that it was "necessary to revive creative Marxism," while admitting there were those at home who "wanted to go much further."[66] Gorbachev clung to his Lenin-inspired optimism, but the new leaders of Poland, Hungary, and Czechoslovakia had their own ideas. Poland led the way with its "big bang" transition to a market economy, and drastic reorientation of trade, on January 1, 1990. Chernyaev later commented: "these countries brutally turned their back on us."[67]

An illusion with a somewhat solider basis was that, although domestic systems changed, a Moscow-led alliance might survive. The Cold War could end on the basis of the kind of "open" sphere the State Department had favored in 1945-6. A February 1989 analysis observed hopefully that the Polish Communists might lose but "the geopolitical situation of the country is such that even in the opposition there is an understanding of the necessity of preserving some form of alliance with our country." Moscow feared that the Warsaw Pact's collapse, without some kind of new pan-European structure, would leave it without influence in Europe. Before giving its approval to the new Polish government, Moscow had requested and received Solidarity's assurances that it would honor Poland's alliance commitments.[68] The least of Moscow's problems, it seemed, was the West's attitude. In June, when Gorbachev visited Bonn, the two sides signed a declaration affirming self-determination. But when Gorbachev told Kohl, "I think you would agree with me that you should not stick a pole into an anthill," the chancellor did not demur. Thatcher told Gorbachev that the West was "not interested in the destabilization of Eastern Europe or the dissolution of the Warsaw Treaty."[69]

To Moscow's frustration, the new U.S. administration was agonizingly slow to put its cards on the table. Bush had distanced himself in the campaign from what many Republicans considered Reagan's hasty embrace of "new thinking." His administration included skeptics like Defense Secretary Richard Cheney and the National Security Adviser, Scowcroft. After an internal debate, it rejected Kissinger's proposal of an agreement (the press dubbed it "Yalta II") whereby Moscow would allow liberalization in Eastern Europe in return for Washington's pledge to respect Soviet security interests.[70] Yet there was never a serious possibility that Bush and his pragmatic Secretary of State James Baker would reverse Reagan's "reversal." Bush had privately said as much to Gorbachev.[71] Moreover, although State Department officials rejected the

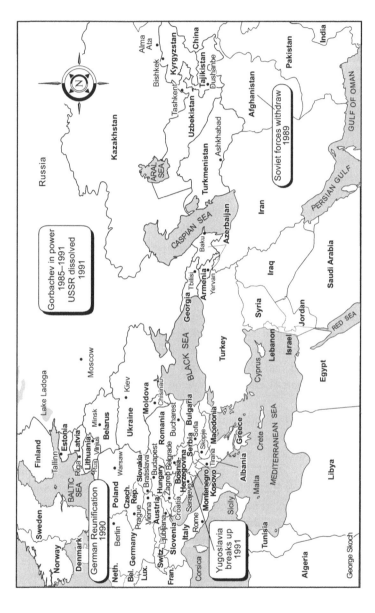

Map 4. Territorial Changes at the end of the Cold War.

proposed deal on the grounds that the United States need not pay a price for change that was occurring anyway (and Baker had no intention of letting Kissinger decide policy), Bush authorized the former secretary of state to discuss the idea with Gorbachev, and was prepared to be guided by the spirit of "Yalta II."[72]

In May–June 1989 Washington settled on a policy of going "beyond containment" and promoting a Europe "whole and free."[73] It insisted on more evidence of Moscow's seriousness, for example in the conventional arms (CFE, or Conventional Forces in Europe) negotiations underway in Vienna. But it did not demand the end of the Warsaw Pact. During a visit to Poland, Bush persuaded Jaruzelski to run for the new post of president. In Hungary, he told Communist leaders he did not want to force them "to choose between East and West." Saddled with enormous budget deficits, Washington was notably stingy regarding aid. When Thatcher told Gorbachev that the West wanted changes to remain "strictly internal," she added that this was the U.S. position. Bush had asked her to say that "the United States would not do anything that could threaten the security interests of the Soviet Union."[74] In deference to a warning from Gorbachev that chaos might develop, Bush reacted cautiously to the extraordinary events of November 9.[75] U.S. interests dictated helping Gorbachev, since further progress in relations depended on his survival. But Bush, too, was concerned about the strategic implications of the end of the GDR.

End Game, 1989–1990

The Cold War's last episode had many protagonists. These included the 130,000 East Germans who "voted with their feet" by departing in November 1989, and their compatriots who proclaimed "We are one people" in the streets. Of the high-level players, one stands above the rest: Adenauer's pupil Helmut Kohl. Early on, Kohl saw a historic opportunity for his country, his party, and himself, and took the bit between his teeth. His policy was to make virtue, and political capital, of necessity. The necessity had to do with the GDR economy which, as in 1961, might collapse unless East Germans could be persuaded to stay at home. Even before the wall's fall, Kohl remarked that the exodus would be "catastrophic" for the GDR. Yet Kohl himself had abetted it, secretly providing DM 1 billion to Budapest in return for the opening of the Hungarian–Austrian border.[76] The post-wall flow was grist for Kohl's mill because it allowed him to argue that reunification would remove the incentive for East Germans to emigrate. Before GDR parliamentary elections in 1990, moreover, Bonn would offer what amounted to a gigantic bribe on behalf of pro-reunification candidates: monetary union on the basis of a one-to-one exchange of the worthless east mark for the DM, the strongest currency in the world.

Kohl's initial task was to counter the effort of a new GDR government under Hans Modrow, supported by the SPD, to advance an alternative to reunification in the form of a "treaty community." Gorbachev had warned Kohl not to undermine the GDR and force events.[77] But a curious episode seems to have reassured Bonn. The MO head Valentin Falin, an expert on Germany, made it known to Kohl's foreign policy adviser Horst Teltschik that Moscow might be open to a confederation of East and West Germany. Falin was hoping the Germans would then try to convince Gorbachev. But Bonn, misunderstanding the message, or wishfully believing Gorbachev was on board, took it as a green light for a bold démarche.[78] Kohl's Ten Point Plan, announced on November 28, 1989, linked aid to the dismantling of the GDR's Communist system and called for free elections, development of "confederative structures," and an eventual federation.[79] Kohl was thinking in terms of several years, not ten months, but the speech succeeded to a degree he had not anticipated. Reunification opponents never recovered the initiative after November 28.[80]

This was hardly a foregone result. Changes in Germany's status required four-power approval. Washington was happy to live with arrangements short of reunification. Thatcher had assured Gorbachev that, regardless of the words in a recent NATO communiqué, Britain and Western Europe "were not interested in the unification of Germany." Gorbachev himself had told the USSR's ambassador to East Berlin, "The Soviet people will never forgive us if we lose the GDR."[81] After Kohl's speech, the Russians berated foreign minister Hans Dietrich Genscher. "Even Hitler," said Shevardnadze, had not interfered so brazenly in the affairs of another state! Gorbachev asked: "What does a confederation mean?...And what would NATO mean without the FRG?" What, he was probably wondering, would the Warsaw Pact mean without the GDR?[82] Yet meeting Bush for the first time at Malta (December 2–3, 1989), Gorbachev had indicated a certain flexibility in return for American promises of restraint. Two months later Gorbachev accepted reunification in principle and informed a delighted Kohl in Moscow in February. Why?

The decision arose from several considerations. With grass-roots support for reunification growing and elections scheduled for March 18, Moscow essentially gave up on Modrow. Indeed the CDU–CSU, running on a platform of reunification using Article 23 of the West German Basic Law, won 48 percent. (The SPD took 22, and the former SED, 16 percent.)[83] Washington, moreover, had decided to back Kohl, while insisting that a united Germany remain in NATO and Bundeswehr units be allowed on former-GDR territory. The Americans had long supported reunification on Western terms on the assumption that to do otherwise would lose the Germans' loyalty. By the same token, they had been prepared to keep troops in Europe only so long as the Germans participated in their own defense. The U.S. decision further weakened Gorbachev. But while conceding reunification, and endorsing a "Two plus Four" negotiating framework, the Soviet leader insisted on a neutralized Germany or one belonging to both NATO and the Warsaw Pact.[84]

For months Moscow said NATO membership was "inadmissable." In early May, Gorbachev told the Politburo, "We will not let Germany into NATO, and that is the end of it. I will even risk the collapse of the [Conventional Forces in Europe] negotiations in Vienna and START."[85] But a few weeks later, during a summit in Washington (May 30–June 3, 1990), in answer to Bush's question whether a united Germany, in accordance with the Helsinki Final Act, would not have the right to decide on alliance membership, he stunned those present by answering in the affirmative.[86] At meetings with Kohl in Moscow and the North Caucasus resort of Arkhyz (July 14–16, 1990), Gorbachev agreed that four-power rights would end upon reunification and Germany could be a full NATO member (although the alliance's jurisdiction would not extend to the former GDR until Soviet troops were gone, a delay of three to four years).[87]

Again, why? The Russians obviously lacked leverage and were beset by internal troubles. In 1990, the spillover from Eastern European events hit home with a vengeance.[88] There were bloody nationalist riots in Azerbaijan in January. Lithuania's Supreme Soviet declared sovereignty in March, and Russia's followed in June. But much of the Soviet establishment, and not only the embittered KGB and military officers who would try to remove him from power in August 1991, believed Gorbachev had played a poor hand badly. For Dobrynin, Gorbachev consistently brushed aside expert advice and had unaccountably settled at Malta for Bush's soothing promises regarding *perestroika* rather than fighting for an all-European security system based on a reinforced CSCE.[89] East Germany was sold for a bowl of porridge and the West later outwitted Moscow by expanding NATO eastward. Falin called the agreement an "act of political masochism." During a Congress of People's Deputies debate, he compared it to Beria's attempt to betray the GDR in 1953.[90]

One reason is that Gorbachev got little help from his "friends." While Mitterrand was hoping to slow reunification, his priority was to ensure it went hand-in-hand with deepened European integration, and he did not make an issue of NATO membership. On the contrary, just before the Gorbachev–Bush meeting in May 1990, Mitterrand convinced the Soviet leader not to insist on French NATO-status for Germany because Bonn would not agree.[91] Thatcher feared German power and had no close relationship with Bonn to protect, but was unwilling to jeopardize ties to Washington. A second reason is that Gorbachev and Shevardnadze were apparently persuaded by the argument Baker had made to them in February 1990: a united Germany in NATO, with U.S. troops continuing, in effect, to contain it, was preferable to one pursuing an independent course, and perhaps acquiring nuclear weapons.[92] Washington wisely sweetened the deal with "nine-assurances" before the May summit, and NATO's "London Declaration" in July. The latter, in conjunction with an imminent Conventional Forces in Europe (CFE) agreement, was more than symbolic. NATO would adopt a new strategy, including a reduced forward presence and making the use of nuclear weapons a last resort.[93] Interestingly, in March 1990 the Polish and Czechoslovak governments had announced opposition to German neutrality. Gorbachev probably made his May 1990 concession assuming that, with a united Germany in NATO, Warsaw and Prague would want to continue some sort of alliance with Moscow. A June 1990 Warsaw treaty summit called for transforming the pact into a political organization and ending the Soviet-dominated command structure. This came to nothing because Eastern Europe decided to sever political as well as economic connections.[94] The Warsaw Pact was dissolved in July 1991.

A third reason explaining Gorbachev's decision was Bonn's greasing of the wheels. Before the May 1990 summit, the FRG offered the USSR a desperately needed DM 5 billion credit. As part of the final deal, Bonn assumed East Germany's foreign debt of around DM 40 billion, promised to buy Soviet exports earmarked for the GDR, and pay DM 12 billion to re-house Red Army soldiers in the Soviet Union. At the Kohl-Gorbachev summit, Bonn also agreed to a 370,000 limit on the Bundeswehr, the exclusion of nuclear weapons and non-German forces from former GDR territory, and to treaties of friendship and economic co-operation. The treaty ending four-power control and reunifying Germany was signed by the "two plus four" parties in Moscow on September 12, 1990. Germany became fully sovereign and united on October 3. The Soviet–German bilateral treaties were signed in Bonn on November 9.[95]

Gorbachev thus received concessions allowing him to say that he, too, had made virtue of necessity, although few Russians believed it. He was perhaps fortunate that, by September 1990, attention at home was focused not on Germany but the imminent breakdown of the economy and of the USSR itself. As for who should take credit for reunification, Kohl was gracious and honest enough to share the stage at October 3 ceremonies with Brandt, whose policies had begun to unfreeze the division. Six week later, NATO and Warsaw Pact members formalized an agreement creating equal ceilings for conventional weaponry between the two groups of states in the area from the Atlantic to the Urals.[96] If one is looking for an official end to the Cold War, the signature of the CFE Treaty in Paris on November 17, 1990, is a worthy choice.

The final, perhaps decisive, reason for Gorbachev's acquiescence to Eastern European and German self-determination was that to do otherwise would have been to violate what he had eloquently declared on December 7, 1988. It is easy to see him as a naïve and inadvertent "grave digger of Soviet power" who allowed himself to be hoist by the petard of abstract principle.[97] Among its other effects on the USSR, the sudden rupture with Eastern Europe would soon contribute to an economic collapse without precedent in modern times. But it is fairer to say that Gorbachev had correctly understood that it was necessary to break the age-old, self-defeating habit of seeking security at one's neighbors' expense, that a multi-national empire based on domination was an untenable anachronism, and that military power was counter-productive in the circumstances. It was not his responsibility that by the 1980s the USSR had no other strings in its bow. Although a prophet without honor in his own country, he was the indispensable architect of the Cold War's peaceful conclusion, something few had imagined possible. Millions had reason to be grateful for Gorbachev's "naïveté."

CONCLUSION

Arguments over the beginning, development, and end of the Cold War will probably never be settled. If the "history of history" teaches anything, it is that new evidence will come to light and novel perspectives will emerge. But let us conclude this attempt to tell the story with a decalogue of observations. They summarize, if not exactly what the world now knows about the Cold War, what the book has tried to show.

The Cold War began partly because the superpowers had ingrained tendencies to prepare for the worst and see their security requirements in expansive terms—a frame of mind referred to here as Hobbesian fatalism. Recent events strongly reinforced this habit. Although their war experiences were profoundly different, the ways in which both entered the conflict in 1941 produced a "surprise attack syndrome." Each tended to confuse the other with its recent World War II adversaries, and feared unprovoked aggression as well as internal subversion. For George Kennan, the Soviet Union, unlike Nazi Germany, was neither inherently adventuristic nor inclined to fulfill its aims militarily. But other influential voices insisted that the USSR might well see advantages in striking first.[1] For its part, the United States considered but rejected preventive war. No U.S. president believed a nuclear conflict could be won. But Soviet leaders feared that the Americans, like the Germans, might see the USSR as "a colossus with feet of clay" and act accordingly. The two sides armed to the teeth, wasting enormous resources, in preparation for a war neither intended to begin.

The Cold War continued partly because preparedness against attack and exaggeration of the threat were effective weapons in domestic politics. According to what this book has called the "iron law" of the U.S. two-party system, politicians were afraid to look soft and competed to be "tough on Communism" at home and abroad. Although the Soviet system was no democracy, "[i]t was widely argued that the people would forgive the leadership anything but a repetition of the tragedy at the beginning of World War II, and that this was the primary political priority." In the cut-throat competition for power, the appearance of weakness was a serious liability. Beria, Malenkov, and Khrushchev discovered this to their chagrin. Satisfying the military-industrial complex's appetite for weapons was a prerequisite for Brezhnev's pursuit of détente. National defense remained "the holy of the holies" well into the 1980s.[2] Gorbachev did not seriously try to cut defense spending until 1988–9.

The Cold War was a competition between social-economic systems that regarded each other as natural enemies. Each side's ideology, or secular religion, conditioned its choice of friends and determined its basic objectives: safeguarding and advancing capitalism and democracy, on one hand; protecting and expanding Communism, on the other. Each side espoused a directional and messianic view of history, believing its cause would prevail. At the same time, since Lenin, Communist ideology had allowed for considerable flexibility in dealing with the capitalists, and there were always progressive and/or pragmatic Western forces which discounted the Mackinderian view and sought a modus vivendi with the East. After Stalin, Moscow abandoned the idea that world war was inevitable. Throughout the Cold War, the United States and the USSR were part of the same "Westphalian" system. They maintained diplomatic relations, carried on some trade, concluded agreements, and sat together at the UN. The ideological-religious conflict made normal relations impossible, and the Cold War could not end until Gorbachev had revised the Soviet world-view beyond recognition. But ideology did not condemn the two sides to war.

The U.S.–Soviet contest remained cold partly because, thanks to Hiroshima, the world knew what the next general war would be like. Nuclear weapons were a basic reason for the revision of Soviet ideology in the 1950s and reinforced both sides' tendency to live and let live with the other. Nuclear weapons proved to be essentially useless as tools for changing the situation on the ground in one's favor. As Aron noted, "It was during the years 1945–49, when the United States enjoyed an atomic monopoly, that the Soviet Union won its greatest successes (the consolidation of the Communist regimes in Eastern Europe, the conquest of power by the Chinese Communist party). It was also during these years that Moscow's diplomacy was most aggressive—in Czechoslovakia, in Berlin, at international conferences, and in its propaganda."[3] This was when Stalin, although fearing attack, sought to show he would not be intimidated. By the same token, nuclear weapons proved useful in deterring attack, defending what one possessed, and inducing the superpowers to compromise. Khrushchev failed in his attempts to use the prospect of nuclear war to pressure the Western powers out of West Berlin. At the same time (and however qualified Kennedy's promise), he used nuclear weapons in Cuba to obtain a U.S. pledge not to invade. Despite hysteria in some circles, there was no evidence that Moscow intended (or would have been able) to use its SS-18s or SS-20s to obtain political concessions. The Cold War provides strong evidence, in effect, that "nuclear blackmail" does not work.

In its central theater, the conflict was a total mismatch. Thanks to the way World War II ended, most of the rich, industrially advanced regions of Europe fell into the Western sphere. The EEC's founding members were the main beneficiaries of the U.S.–Soviet confrontation as well as important protagonists of the eventual Western victory. Thanks partly to U.S. aid and protection, they recovered quickly, developed generous welfare systems, and pursued a successful strategy of integration. The Berlin wall gave a new lease on life to the GDR economy but became a monument to Eastern shabbiness and inferiority. In the 1970s, Western growth gave way to stagflation. But this was more than offset by *Ostpolitik* and the Helsinki Final Act which took away the image of the German enemy, allowed greater access to Western media, and drove home the difference in living standards. Poland's contemporaneous attempt to modernize industry and subsidize consumption using Western loans precipitated a crisis fatal to the Eastern bloc. In the 1980s Western Europe restructured industry and embarked on a new round of integration. Central and Eastern Europe's per capita GDP was 51 percent (on average) of Western Europe's in 1950; 47 percent in 1973; a mere 40 percent in 1989. By then, countless Eastern Europeans, including once-loyal Communists, were ready to reinvent themselves as capitalists and join the West.[4]

In the developing world, the Soviet model had wide appeal, and the struggle there seemed at times to be a close-run thing. But the turning point came in 1964–5, when three large, rich, and strategically important countries went solidly into the Western camp. Brazil, Indonesia, and the Congo were not pawns but rooks on the Cold War chessboard, and the West's position was now impregnable. The fall of Haile Selassie and of Portugal's African empire appeared to reopen the contest, but this was an illusion. The USSR's new wards proved more of a burden than a bonus. Billions of rubles were squandered. During the same period another high-value piece, Sadat's Egypt, fell out with the Kremlin and switched allegiances. Partly to avoid "another Egypt," the Soviet Union made the serious error of occupying Afghanistan (making Sadat one of the Cold War's unsung heroes from the Western point of view.) The 1980s phase of the match, featuring the "Reagan doctrine," made for good political theater, but was not decisive.[5] Moscow was looking for ways to extricate itself from Afghanistan almost as soon as it became involved.

Once the tide had turned in the third world in 1964–5, ensuring South Vietnam's survival was of even more marginal significance to the West than it had been before that date. In the over-all scheme of things, Vietnam was a tragic side-show. The expenditure of 58,000 American lives and some 550 billion (in 2010) dollars there was an act of folly and masochism without parallel in the Cold War. Given the trivial geopolitical stakes, and that most of America's allies did not believe good money should be thrown after bad for the sake of U.S. credibility, it is hard to avoid the conclusion that the escalation was above all the result of internal political considerations. Having embarked on a fool's errand, the United States could not escape certain consequences of defeat. Those who wished to challenge it did so accurately assuming that America was on the defensive in the 1970s. A "Vietnam syndrome" and Congressional assault on presidential powers tied Washington's hands. But, given America's residual strength, losing did not entail dire long-term effects and even had a kind of silver lining. Saigon's fall contributed to Soviet over-confidence and (as war opponents like de Gaulle had suggested) soon pitted Hanoi against Beijing. By the same token, it stimulated a conservative hunger for resurgence in the United States that contributed to Reagan's rise.

If the West owed victory in World War II to a considerable degree to Stalin, someone Djilas called the greatest criminal in history, it owed success in the Cold War to some degree to Mao, perhaps the greatest (and certainly the most capricious) mass murderer of his day.[6] Driven by ideological fanaticism and personal megalomania, Mao turned against the Soviet Union. Although Chinese backing of the north was a key factor in the Vietnam war, the PRC and the United States recognized their common interests. In accordance with the oldest tenet in statecraft, "my enemy's enemy is my friend," China became the biggest and most valuable chess piece to change sides in the Cold War. Its move facilitated America's task of dealing with the USSR at a time of U.S. weakness, and led the USSR to tie down huge forces in Asia. After 1989 Americans liked to think they had won the Cold War and that Western ideas had triumphed. But China, whose government used tanks to dispatch demonstrators in May 1989, was also a winner. It survived and thrived not only because it partially liberalized its economy, but because it remained true to its centralizing traditions. More than two decades later (and in light of the country's internal chaos during much of the twentieth century), there were few signs that China intended to embrace democracy Western-style.

In 1994 the Council on Foreign Relations held a dinner marking Kennan's ninetieth birthday. In his remarks, the guest of honor took no credit for recent events. Instead, he rebuked the triumphalism of those who thought the West had been right to pursue a policy amounting to seeking the USSR's "unconditional surrender" in Europe. Following containment's initial success, Kennan argued, Washington should have entered into serious negotiations with Moscow. Echoing a point made years earlier in his memoirs, he suggested the contest might have been called off, or rendered far less costly and risky, early on. "We will never know who was right and who was wrong. One course was tried . . . The other remained hypothetical. Its results will never be known." What we *do* know is that Kennan had been right all along that the USSR was "by far the weaker party" and bore "within it the seeds of its own decay."[7]

Three seeds, in particular, helped to account for the Cold War's outcome. Economic achievements under Stalin had been based on methods his successors were no longer prepared to use, or the population to accept. The post-1953 Soviet economy, largely closed to the world and administered from the center, was inefficient and sclerotic. Its backwardness became increasingly visible and disillusioning when the capitalist economies began a new phase of growth propelled by market liberalization and new technologies. Increasing concern about the Soviet economy (in size a mere 50 percent of the U.S.'s in the 1980s[8]) coincided with a biologically driven renewal of the *nomenklatura*. Perception of economic decline prompted Gorbachev to attempt in earnest what Khrushchev had tried and failed to do: defuse the East-West conflict in order to liberate resources and buy time for Communism to catch up.

The second seed was identified early on by Kennan and his fellow Cold War optimist, de Gaulle. "Communism," said de Gaulle in 1954, "subsists to the extent that it is nationalism."[9] By the same token, where synonymous with imperialism, it would fail. Nationalism, itself a potent secular religion, inspired the USSR's extraordinary wartime sacrifices. In China, Vietnam, and Cuba, the Communists were patriots who opposed foreign domination or meddling. Not by coincidence, those regimes retained their legitimacy and survived after 1989. Kennan and de Gaulle believed Soviet control over Eastern Europe was doomed because it was in conflict with nationalism. For various reasons (they would have cited prolonged U.S. hegemony over Western Europe, providing Moscow a much-needed crutch), the Soviet presence lasted longer than they had predicted. But it ended as they had foreseen. The Soviet Union, "the last and greatest colonial power of the times," said de Gaulle in 1964, would be challenged by China and "little by little part company with its European satellites."[10] A similar principle applied to the USSR itself. When Gorbachev deliberately weakened the CPSU and unleashed criticism of the system, suppressed nationalism in the constituent republics reemerged and took its revenge.

Kennan, a devotee of pre-1917 Russia, especially of the liberal humanist Anton Chekov, observed in 1950: "I am sure that the organic development of moral feeling, so closely linked with the great figures of Russia's cultural past, must some day take its place in the creation of new political forms."[11] On another occasion he stressed the importance of leaving the way open for "that renewed evolution of the Russian state

in the direction of liberalism which I believe to be entirely possible . . .
but which must be a spontaneous Russian process organically connected
with those deep strange groundswells of Russian development that are so
hard for the Western mind to fathom."[12] The third seed, if not of the
USSR's decay, of the transformation of its relationship to the West, was
the one Khrushchev inadvertently nourished when he denounced Stalin
and allowed a cultural thaw. In a "groundswell" unobserved by most
Westerners (who focused instead on high-profile dissidents), children of
the 20th party congress quietly and gradually adopted the liberal and
social democratic views that influenced policy after 1985. Their eventual
champion had no clear plan, and misplaced hopes, for Communism's
revitalization. But he understood that a foreign policy driven by Hobbesian fatalism and the assumption of a two-camp world condemned his
country to an endless labor of Sisyphus. With the help of European and
U.S. leaders, he proceeded to bring the Cold War to an end.

Lastly, the way the Cold War concluded confirmed the West's initial
advantages and vindicated Kennan's original notion: firm containment
combined with a willingness to talk. The obvious beneficiaries of 1989
were the former Warsaw Pact countries who were permitted self-determination, democracy, and the long-denied fruits of European integration. The world as a whole was freed from the threat of nuclear
catastrophe. But victory was not without costs for the winners, and
sowed the seeds of future tensions. The staggering sums spent on
"defense" by the United States, especially in 1980–6, far exceeded what
would have been required to impress the USSR. The Cold War left
behind a mountain of debt to be paid off, not to mention a vast
infrastructure of empire (U.S. bases, commitments, and vested interests)
that assumed a life of its own. Although Bush, Kohl, and other Western
statesmen conscientiously tried to avoid humiliating Gorbachev, they
could not resist the temptation to dictate their terms to the loser. Rather
than a new security system based on the CSCE, the West insisted on the
supremacy of (an albeit refashioned) NATO. The basic rationale for
NATO's expansion in the 1990s differed little from Mackinder's 1919
argument: take advantage of Russia's weakness to create a "cordon
sanitaire." There was no guarantee a different approach would have
meant a friendly, benign Russia, but no course was better designed to

perpetuate Russian Hobbesian fatalism, subsequently on display in Moscow's relations with its "near-abroad."

Victory also encouraged the view that 1989–90 marked the imminent breasting of "those great heights" described by Wilson where humanity would adopt liberal democracy and capitalism.[13] Messianic thinking inspired the 1990s exaltation of economic globalization as a panacea supposed to alleviate world poverty, civilize China and Russia, and open new markets to U.S. exports and investment. It reinforced the dubious assumption that the United States would "keep military strengths beyond challenge, thereby making the destabilizing arms races of other eras pointless."[14] It informed a U.S. strategy according to which there "is a single, sustainable model of national success: freedom, democracy and free enterprise," and America's mission was to transplant it to recalcitrant regions of the globe.[15] In reality, after a transitional moment of unchallenged American hegemony, the post-Cold War world found itself on a probably irreversible course in the direction of political multi-polarity. It was idle to proclaim that U.S. power was destined to remain supreme and the Western model to prevail.

Among its other benefits, studying the Cold War provides an antidote to delusions of omnipotence. One need only recall Mao's mad schemes to mobilize his people and Moscow's claims to be the vanguard of mankind. By the same token, the ruthless, dictatorial nature of the West's best friends in the third world belied the conceits of a "Free World," and of a single, liberal path to modernization. America's two-party political system, with its inherent bias toward bellicosity, was a questionable model for export. Its extraordinarily successful economic formula, based on natural wealth, entrepreneurial prowess, and cultural allure, but also the capacity to borrow practically unlimited sums from abroad, was unique. Finally, the West won the contest partly because the playing field was always tilted in its favor, and the United States shared the laurels not only with Europe, but the world's largest one-party system. A degree of Western triumphalism was understandable in 1989–90. But a clear look back on the Cold War's battlegrounds, along with a sense of relief that the world survived forty-five years of confrontation, evokes feelings of humility and regret.

ENDNOTES

Introduction

1. See John Lewis Gaddis, *The Long Peace: Inquiries into the History of the Cold War* (Oxford: Oxford University Press, 1987).

2. George Orwell, Herbert Bayard Swope, and Walter Lippmann were the first to use the term "cold war" in English, shortly after World War II.

3. See Odd Arne Westad, *The Global Cold War: Third World Interventions and the Making of our Times* (Cambridge: Cambridge University Press, 2005), 4. "Ideology" is used here to mean a secular religion: a set of beliefs purporting to explain reality and indicating the path to temporal redemption. But such beliefs, by definition, represent a *limited* perspective, reflecting the experience and interests of a particular class or nation, rather than objective truth.

4. Louis J. Halle, *The Cold War as History* (New York: Harper and Row, 1967).

5. Raymond Aron, *Le Grand Schisme* (Paris: Gallimard, 1948), 13. The term "superpower" was first used by Nicholas Spykman in *The Geography of the Peace* (New York: Harcourt Brace, 1944).

6. See Geoffrey Barraclough, *An Introduction to Contemporary History* (London: Penguin, 1990), ch. 6.

7. The term "tiers monde," evoking the notion of a disenfranchised "third estate," was coined in the early 1950s. It came to designate the areas not part of the capitalist (first) and Communist (second) worlds.

8. The expression is George F. Kennan's in an article authored as Mr. "X". See "The Sources of Soviet Conduct," *Foreign Affairs*, 25/4 (July 1947), 582.

9. Raymond Aron, *On War* (New York: Norton, 1968), 120.

10. Churchill to FDR, Nov. 28, 1944, in Warren F. Kimball, ed., *Churchill and Roosevelt: Their Complete Correspondence* (Princeton: Princeton University Press, 1984), 3: 419–21.

11. Some 70,000 Soviet cites, towns and villages were destroyed, as well as 98,000 farms and 32,000 factories. See Geoffrey Roberts, *Stalin's Wars: From World War to Cold War, 1939–1953* (New Haven: Yale University Press, 2006), 5.

12. Quoted in Melvin Leffler, *A Preponderance of Power: National Security, the Truman Administration, and the Cold War* (Stanford, CA: Stanford University Press, 1992), 99.

13. Karl Marx, *The Eighteenth Brumaire of Louis Napoleon*, (New York: International Publishers, 1964), 15.

14. Berlin quoted in Ramin Jahanbegloo, "Philosophy and Life: An Interview," *New York Review of Books*, 39/10 (May 28, 1992), 51.

15. R. G. Collingwood, *The Idea of History* (Oxford: Oxford University Press, 1956), 215.

16. Ibid. 242.

Documentary Traces

1. The exception is Greece, where the Communists tried to take power by force.

2. "The Tasks of Economic Executives" (Feb. 4, 1931), in J. V. Stalin, *Problems of Leninism* (Beijing: Foreign Languages Press, 1976), 527.

3. Huerta was responsible for the murder of president Francisco Madero, who had forced the long-time dictator Porfirio Dìaz from power. Wilson's steps included allowing arms to reach Huerta's enemies, and the U.S. Navy's seizure of Vera Cruz in April 1914. Huerta fled Mexico in July 1914.

4. Address to the Southern Commercial Congress, Mobile AL, Oct. 27, 1913.

5. Huerta's flight was followed by a prolonged power struggle.

6. V. I. Lenin, *Collected Works*, Vol. 28 (Moscow: Progress Publishers, 1965), 62–75.

7. Stimson memo to Truman, Sept. 11, 1945, *FRUS*, 1945, 2: 40–44.

8. Truman pursued plans for international control in the UN, where the United States had allied support.

9. "We Will Never Step Aside," G. Malenkov speech to the Supreme Soviet, Aug. 8, 1953, *Vital Speeches of the Day*, 19/22 (Sept. 1, 1953), 688–9.

Chapter 1—Russia and the West: Destined to Collide?

1. Alexis de Tocqueville, *Democracy in America*, I (New York: Modern Library, 1981), 559.

2. See Stalin's speech quoted in Documentary Traces.

3. See Lothar Ruehl, "The historical background of Russian security concepts and requirements," in Vladimir Baranovsky, ed., *Russia and Europe* (Oxford: Oxford University Press, 1997), 40.

4. Politburo member Vadim Medvedev, in Michael Ellman and Vladimir Kontorovich, eds., *The Destruction of the Soviet Economic System: An Insiders' History* (London: M. E. Sharpe, 1998), 96. Andropov was CPSU general secretary 1982–4; Gorbachev, 1985–91. On the program, in flagrant violation of the 1972 Biological Weapons Convention, see David E. Hoffman, *The Dead Hand* (New York: Doubleday, 2009), chs. 15, 20.

5. Hamilton, in *The Federalist* (New York: Bantam, 1982), No. 6, 22; ibid., No. 8, 32; ibid., No. 7, 27–32.

6. See Russell F. Weigley, *The American Way of War: A History of United States Military Strategy and Policy* (New York: Macmillan, 1973).

7. Brooks Adams, *America's Economic Supremacy* (New York: Harper Bros., 1947; first published in 1900), 147, 167–70.

8. Halford Mackinder, *Democratic Ideals and Reality: With Additional Papers* (1919) (New York: Norton, 1962), 244.

9. Ibid., 70, 150, 160.

10. See Norman E. Saul, *War and Revolution: The United States and Russia, 1914–1921* (Lawrence: University Press of Kansas, 2001), 340.

11. See Clifford Kinvig, *Churchill's Crusade: The British Invasion of Russia, 1918–1920* (London: Hambledon Continuum, 2006).

12. Carl Schurz, "Manifest Destiny," *Harper's New Monthly Magazine*, 87/521 (July 1893), 737.

13. Leffler, *A Preponderance of Power*, 17.

14. Foreign Minister V. Molotov, speaking in 1946. Quoted in Roberts, *Stalin's Wars*, 305.

15. See Fred Halliday, *The Making of the Second Cold War* (London: Verso, 1983), 122–6.

16. See John L. Harper, "Anatomy of a Habit: America's Unnecessary Wars," *Survival*, Summer 2005.

17. Ernest Lee Tuveson, *Redeemer Nation: The Idea of America's Millennial Role* (Chicago: University of Chicago Press, 1968), 42–3.

18. Reinhold Niebuhr, *The Irony of American History* (New York: Scribner, 1952), 24.

19. Thomas Paine, *Common Sense, and Other Political Writings* (New York: Liberal Arts Press, 1953), 3.

20. O'Sullivan, quoted in Albert K. Weinberg, *Manifest Destiny: A Study of Nationalist Expansionism in American History* (Gloucester, MA: Peter Smith, 1958), 145.
21. Beveridge quoted in ibid., 308.
22. Wilson's Fourteen Points message, Jan. 8, 1918; speech at Cheyenne, WO, Sept. 24, 1919 in Woodrow Wilson, *Addresses of President Wilson* (Washington: Government Printing Office, 1919), 336.
23. Lenin, Decree on Peace, Nov. 8, 1917.
24. Wilson's Fourteen Points message, Jan. 8, 1918.
25. Berdiaev quoted in Peter J. S. Duncan, *Russian Messianism: Third Rome, Revolution, Communism and After* (London: Routledge, 2000), 55. See also Robert D. English, *Russia and the Idea of the West: Gorbachev, Intellectuals and the End of the Cold War* (New York: Columbia University Press, 2000), 19–25.
26. Duncan, *Russian Messianism*, 21, 31, 40, 57; Milovan Djilas, *Conversations with Stalin* (New York: Harcourt Brace, 1962), 114.
27. See Duncan, *Russian Messianism*, 53; English, *Russia and the Idea of the West*, 28–9.
28. In reality these supplies had mostly been removed by the Bolsheviks when U.S. and British troops arrived in Sept. 1918.
29. On May 9, 1919, Wilson stated that "the proper policy of the Allied and Associated Powers was to clear out of Russia." *FRUS, Siberia* (Washington: U.S. Government Printing Office, 1919), 346.
30. George F. Kennan, *Russia and the West under Lenin and Stalin* (London: Hutchinson, 1961), 132.
31. This was Kennan's view. Ibid., 132.
32. The expression "prairie-fire" was Palmer's. Quoted in Jussi Hanhimäki and Odd Arne Westad, eds., *The Cold War: A History in Documents and Eyewitness Accounts* (Oxford: Oxford University Press, 2003), 5. On non-recognition, see Bainbridge Colby to Wilson, Aug 1920, ibid., 10.
33. Kennan, *Russia and the West*, 224.
34. Lenin quoted in Arthur M. Schlesinger's (untitled) contribution to Lloyd C. Gardner, Arthur M. Schlesinger, Jr., and Hans Morgenthau, *The Origins of the Cold War* (Lexington MA: Xerox Books, 1970), 70. See also Wilson's war message, Apr. 2, 1917.
35. Ruehl, "The historical background (n. 3 above)," 27. "Common European home" was an expression used by Mikhail Gorbachev.
36. Kennan, *Russia and the West*, 188–9.

37. Ibid., 55, 124.
38. See Documentary Traces.
39. See Lenin, *Imperialism, the Highest Stage of Capitalism* (New York: International Publishers, 1939); Erik Van Ree, *The Political Thought of Joseph Stalin* (London: Routledge, 2002), ch. 15.
40. Josef Stalin, "The Growing Crisis of World Capitalism and the External Situation of the USSR," Political Report to the Central Committee given during the 15th Congress of the CPSU, Dec. 2–19, 1927, in J. S., *Works*, vol. 10. available at www.marx2mao.com
41. See Gabriel Gorodetsky, *Grand Delusion: Stalin and the German Invasion of Russia* (New Haven: Yale University Press, 1999), 5.
42. Robert C. Tucker *Stalin in Power: The Revolution from Above, 1928–1941* (New York: Norton, 1990); Gerhard Weinberg, *The Foreign Policy of Hitler's Germany: Starting World War II, 1937–1939* (Atlantic Highlands, NJ: Humanities Press, 1994).
43. See Orlando Figes, "The Making of a Gangster," *New York Review of Books*, 64/17 (Nov. 8, 2007), 36–8.
44. Djilas, *Conversations with Stalin*, 132.
45. Kennan, *Russia and the West*, 317, 305; Adam Ulam, *Stalin: The Man and his Era* (New York: Viking, 1973), 399; Van Ree, *Political Thought*, 116, 117; Feliks Ivanovich Chuev, *Molotov Remembers: Inside Kremlin Politics. Conversations with Feliks Chuev* (London: Ivan Dee, 1991), 254.
46. Churchill BBC radio speech, "The Russian Enigma", Oct. 1, 1939. http://www.churchill-society-london.org.uk/RusnEnig.html.
47. Djilas, *Conversations with Stalin*, 162.
48. TR to Cecil Spring-Rice, June 16, 1905, in S. Gwynn, ed., *The Letters and Friendships of Cecil Spring-Rice: A Record* (London: Constable, 1929), I. 472.
49. Walter Lippmann, *U.S. Foreign Policy: Shield of the Republic* (Boston: Little, Brown, 1943), 142. Lippmann is quoting the views of the U.S. diplomat DeWitt Clinton Poole.
50. Ibid., 143. Lippmann is quoting Poole.
51. See John Lamberton Harper, *American Visions of Europe: Franklin D. Roosevelt, George F. Kennan, and Dean G. Acheson* (Cambridge: Cambridge University Press, 1994), 267.
52. Convergence was the hope later held out by the physicist Andrei Sakharov. See his *Progress, Co-existence and Intellectual Freedom* (London: Penguin, 1968).
53. Quoted in Kennan, *Russia and the West*, 172.

54. FDR's plans will be discussed in Ch. 2.

55. Kennan, *Russia and the West*, 386.

Chapter 2—The End of Illusions, 1945–1946

1. For FDR's juggler remark, see John Morton Blum, ed. *From the Morgenthau Diaries* (Boston: Houghton Mifflin, 1959–1987), III., 197. See also Harper, *American Visions*, ch. 3.

2. Moscow and Tokyo had remained at peace after December 1941.

3. See Robert Gannon, *The Cardinal Spellman Story* (Garden City, NY: Doubleday, 1962), 222–4. See also, A. Harriman, "Memorandum of Conversations with the President during Trip to Washington, October 21–November 19, 1944," Averell Harriman Papers, Public Service, World War II, Moscow Files, chronological file, Nov. 19–24, 1944, box 175, Library of Congress.

4. See Bohlen to State Dept., Dec. 15, 1943, *FRUS: Conferences at Cairo and Tehran*, 846.

5. See *Molotov Remembers* (Ch. 1 n. 45 above), 8, 53; Roberts, *Stalin's Wars*, 22.

6. In return Stalin agreed to recognize the government of Chiang Kai-shek, and enter the Pacific War three months after Germany's defeat.

7. On this question, see Vladimir O. Pechatnov, "'The Allies are Pressing on you to Break your Will.' Foreign Policy Correspondence between Stalin and Molotov and other Politburo Members, September 1945–December 1946," CWIHP Working Paper no. 26, Sept. 1999.

8. *Molotov Remembers*, 63.

9. Litvinov quoted in Geoffrey Roberts, "Litvinov's Lost Peace, 1941–1946," *Journal of Cold War Studies* 4/2 (spring 2002) (23–54), 32. See also Djilas, *Conversations with Stalin*, 73.

10. See Vladislav M. Zubok and Constantine Pleshakov, *Inside the Kremlin's Cold War: From Stalin to Khrushchev* (Cambridge, MA: Harvard University Press, 1996), 7.

11. For Soviet documentation of the May 1942 discussions, see Oleg A. Rzheshevsky, ed., *War and Diplomacy: The Making of the Grand Alliance. Documents from Stalin's Archives edited with a commentary* (Amsterdam: Harwood, 1996), 179–227. See also *Molotov Remembers*, 45–7; W. Averell Harriman and Elie Abel, *Special Envoy to Churchill and Stalin, 1941–1946* (New York: Random House, 1975), 314.

12. See Eduard Mark, "Revolution by Degrees: Stalin's National Front Strategy for Europe, 1941–1947," CWIHP Working Paper no. 31, Feb. 2001, 14.

13. Stalin speech quoted in Vladimir O. Pechatnov, "The Big Three after World War II: New Documents on Soviet Thinking about Post War Relations with the United States and Great Britain," CWIHP Working Paper no. 13, May 1995, 21; Stalin to Molotov, June 1, 1942, in Rzheshevsky, ed., *War and Diplomacy*, 204.

14. See Harper, *American Visions of Europe*, 98, 119.

15. At Tehran FDR insisted, over British objections, on confirming the second front for 1944. At Yalta he distanced himself from the more demanding British position on Poland.

16. That is to say, Stalin aimed mainly to recover territories lost in 1905 and after 1918, and to participate as an equal in the European power game.

17. See Zubok and Pleshakov, *Kremlin's Cold War*, 7; Van Ree, *Political Thought*, 142–7.

18. Mark, "Revolution by Degrees," 15–33.

19. Ibid., 37–8; Van Ree, *Political Thought*, 245, 246, and ch. 16.

20. On Hopkins's remark, see Lord Halifax to Churchill, Apr. 6, 1945, FO 945/30, PRO.

21. Martin Gilbert, *Winston S. Churchill, vii. Road to Victory 1941–1945* (Boston, MA: Houghton Mifflin, 1986), 1232.

22. This was the "percentages deal" of October 1944 whereby Stalin nominally accepted a division of influence between the USSR and Britain along the following lines: Romania: 90% Russia, 10% Britain; Greece: 10% Russia, 90% Britain; Yugoslavia: 50% Russia, 50% Britain; Hungary: 50% Russia, 50% Britain; Bulgaria: 75% Russia, 25% Britain.

23. See Churchill speech, Feb. 27, 1945, quoted in Harriman and Abel Special *Envoy*, 418–19. See also Churchill to Roosevelt, Apr. 1, 1945, in Warren Kimball, ed., *Churchill and Roosevelt*, iii. 603–6; Churchill to Eisenhower, Apr. 2, 1945, quoted in Gilbert, *Road to Victory*, 276. Churchill to Truman, quoted in Wilson D. Miscamble, *From Roosevelt to Truman: Potsdam, Hiroshima and the Cold War* (Cambridge: Cambridge University Press, 2007), 159.

24. Arthur M. Schlesinger, Jr., essay in Gardner et al., *The Origins of the Cold War*, 47.

25. FDR's report to Congress on Yalta, Mar. 1, 1945. FDR took the former senator and Supreme Court Justice Byrnes to Yalta. See Robert Messer, *The End of an Alliance: James Byrnes, Roosevelt, Truman and the Origins of the Cold War* (Chapel Hill: University of North Carolina Press, 1982), 10, chs. 3 and 4.

26. The quoted phrase is from a speech announcing conditional support of the UN by the former isolationist senator on Jan. 10, 1945. See Arthur

H. Vandenberg, Jr., *The Private Papers of Senator Vandenberg* (Boston: Houghton Mifflin, 1952), 136–8.

27. John L. Gaddis, quoted in Miscamble, *Roosevelt to Truman*, 9. On Truman's background and preparation see ibid., ch. 1.

28. Truman was from Independence, Missouri.

29. See Messer, *The End of an Alliance*.

30. See Harry S. Truman, *Year of Decisions 1945* (London: Hodder and Stoughton, 1955), 85; Geoffrey Roberts, "Sexing Up the Cold War: New Evidence on the Molotov-Truman Talks of April 1945," *Cold War History*, 4/3 (April 2004), 105–25; Charles E. Bohlen, *Witness to History, 1929–1969* (New York: Norton, 1973), 213; Miscamble *Roosevelt to Truman*, ch. 3.

31. May 23, 1945 memo by Truman cited in ibid., 145. The politicians mentioned were thought to routinely fix elections.

32. "Provisional," because it was to be confirmed by the final peace settlement. On Potsdam see ibid., ch. 5. Vladimir O. Pechatnov and C. Earl Edmondson, "The Russian Perspective," in Ralph B. Levering et al., *Debating the Origins of the Cold War: American and Russian Perspectives* (London: Rowman and Littlefield, 2002), 103–6; Charles Mee, *Meeting at Potsdam* (New York: M. Evans, 1975).

33. See Eduard Mark, "The War Scare of 1946 and Its Consequences," *Diplomatic History*, 21/3 (summer 1997), 383–415.

34. See Eduard Mark, "American Policy toward Eastern Europe and the Origins of the Cold War, 1941–1946: An Alternative Interpretation," *Journal of American History*, 68/2 (Sept. 1981), 313–36.

35. Eduard Mark contribution to the H-Diplo Roundtable on Miscamble, *From Truman to Roosevelt*, Sept. 10, 2007, 31–2.

36. See Miscamble, *Roosevelt to Truman*, ch. 6, John L. Harper, "Henry Stimson and the Origin of America's Attachment to Atomic Weapons," *SAIS Review*, 5/2 (summer–fall 1985), 17–28; Tsuyoshi Hasegawa, *Racing the Enemy: Stalin, Truman and the Surrender of Japan* (Cambridge, MA: Harvard University Press, 2005).

37. Churchill quoted in Lord Moran, *Churchill: Taken from the Diaries of Lord Moran* (Boston: Houghton Mifflin, 1965), 301; Stimson quoted in Harper, "Henry Stimson," 20, 24.

38. Martin Sherwin, *A World Destroyed: The Atomic Bomb and the Grand Alliance* (New York: Random House, 1977), 290; Barton Bernstein, "Roosevelt, Truman and the Atomic Bomb: A Reinterpretation," *Political Science Quarterly*, 90/1 (spring 1973), 23–40, 31 n. 23.

39. Byrnes and Molotov quoted in Miscamble, *Roosevelt to Truman* 252–3.
40. Zubok and Pleshakov, *Kremlin's Cold War* 39.
41. Molotov quoted in Pechatnov, "The Big Three after World War II," 23. On the Berne affair, and Stalin's reaction to FDR's death, see, Harper, *American Visions*, 128.
42. Pechatnov and Edmondson, "The Russian Perspective," 105–7.
43. See Vojtech Mastny, *Russia's Road to the Cold War: Diplomacy, Warfare and the Politics of Communism* (New York: Columbia University Press, 1979), 138.
44. Eduard Mark, "Revolution by Degrees," 39, 42.
45. See Gregg Herken, *The Winning Weapon: The Atomic Bomb in the Cold War, 1945–1950* (New York: Vintage 1981), ch. 3.
46. See Pechatnov, "'The Allies are Pressing on You to Break Your Will...'", 5, 6, 18; Roberts, "Litvinov's Lost Peace," 45–50.
47. Melvin P. Leffler, *For the Soul of Mankind: The United States, the Soviet Union, and the Cold War* (New York: Hill and Wang, 2007), 46.
48. Stalin quoted in Pechatnov, "'The Allies are Pressing on You to Break Your Will...'", 14.
49. See "Answers to the Questions Posed by A. Werth," Sept. 17, 1946, in Werth, *Russia: The Post-War Years* (London: Hale, 1971), 142–147. Werth was correspondent for the London *Sunday Times*.
50. Odd Arne Westad, for example, quoted in Leffler *Soul of Mankind* (p. 52), as well as Leffler himself.
51. "Speech delivered by JV Stalin," Feb. 9, 1946.
52. See Pechatnov, "The Allies are Pressing on You to Break Your Will...", 10, 24. Morgenthau quoted in Gardner et al., *Origins of the Cold War*, 22.
53. See Documentary Traces.
54. Mark, "War Scare of 1946" 392–3.
55. See Acheson, *Present at the Creation: My Years at the State Department* (New York: Norton, 1969).
56. The nature of a Dec. 29 Truman-Byrnes confrontation, and whether, as Truman claimed, he read the Jan. 5 letter to Byrnes, are in dispute. See Miscamble, *Roosevelt to Truman*, 272–6, and Messer (n. 25 above), 159–66.
57. Pechatnov, "The Allies are Pressing on You", 14.
58. After commerce secretary Wallace gave a speech in Sept. 1946 attacking Byrnes's policy as anti-Soviet, Byrnes essentially demanded that Truman

choose between them. Truman, whose views were closer to Byrnes's, fired Wallace, leading to his departure from the party.

59. Truman to Byrnes, Jan. 5, 1946, in Truman, *Year of Decisions*, 604–5.

60. See Leffler, *A Preponderance of Power*, 78. Mar. 17, 1946 U.S. JCS paper quoted in Mark, "War Scare of 1946," 392. On war plan, see ibid.

61. See the Long Telegram, Part 5, *FRUS*, 1946, 6:696–709.

62. See "The Sources of Soviet Conduct," *Foreign Affairs*, 25/4 (July 1947).

63. The Long Telegram, Part 5.

64. See Harper, *American Visions*, ch. 5.

65. Winston Churchill, *The Sinews of Peace: Post-War Speeches* (Boston: Houghton Mifflin, 1949), 93. See also David McCullough, *Truman* (New York: Simon and Schuster, 1992), 490.

66. See Mark, "The War Scare of 1946," 401–15; Harper, *American Visions*, ch. 6; Robert Beisner, *Dean Acheson: A Life in the Cold War* (Oxford: Oxford University Press, 2006), ch. 3.

67. See the so-called Novikov Telegram, Sept. 27, 1946, in *Diplomatic History*, 15/4 (Oct. 1991), 527–37.

68. See Pechatnov and Edmondson "The Russian Prespective," 114–20.

69. *Molotov Remembers*, 73.

Chapter 3—The Consolidation of the Blocs, 1947–1949

1. See Thanasis D. Sfikas, "War and Peace in the Strategy of the Communist Party of Greece, 1945–1949," *Journal of Cold War Studies*, 3/3 (fall 2001), (5–30), 13.

2. On Stalin's motives, see Zubok and Pleshakov, *Kremlin's Cold War*, 128, who stress Greek and Yugoslav pressure. See also, John O. Iatrides, "Revolution or Self-Defense? Communist Goals, Strategy, and Tactics in the Greek Civil War," *Journal of Cold War Studies*, 7/3 (summer 2005), (3–33). The expression "faint green light" is Iatrides's.

3. Harry S. Truman, Address before a Joint Session of Congress, March 12, 1947.

4. Walter Lippmann, *The Cold War: A Study in U.S. Foreign Policy* (containing 12 New York *Herald-Tribune* columns) (New York: Harper and Bros., 1947), 18, 60.

5. Acheson, *Present at the Creation*, 375.

6. Ibid., 219.

7. Acheson, "Random Harvest," a talk given at the State Department, June 4, 1946, State Dept. *Bulletin*, June 16, 1946, 1045.
8. A. J. P. Taylor, writing in Nov. 1945, quoted in Leffler, *Soul of Mankind*, 59.
9. Unnamed official quoted in Alexander Werth, *France, 1945–1955* (Boston: Beacon Press, 1966), 394.
10. See Silvio Pons, "Stalin, Togliatti, and the Origins of the Cold War in Europe," *Journal of Cold War Studies*, 3/2 (spring 2001), (3–27), 19–20. The words in quotes are Pons's.
11. About 85% of plant capacity survived in Italy and Germany.
12. "Policy of the UK and the Empire toward the US" (unsigned Foreign Office draft statement), Mar. 16, 1944, FOI 371/38522, Public Record Office, Kew.
13. Anecdote recounted to the author by the diplomat Egidio Ortona.
14. Acheson, *Present at the Creation*, 212. Clayton quoted in Leffler, *Soul of Mankind*, 62.
15. See Alan Milward, *The Reconstruction of Western Europe, 1945–1951* (London: Methuen, Routledge, 1984), 8.
16. John Lamberton Harper, *America and the Reconstruction of Italy, 1945–1948* (Cambridge: Cambridge University Press, 1986), ch. 8.
17. On this point see, Vladislav M. Zubok, *A Failed Empire: The Soviet Union in the Cold War from Stalin to Gorbachev* (Chapel Hill: University of North Carolina Press, 2007), 71–2.
18. Marshall speech on Germany, Apr. 28, 1947 in State Dept. *Bulletin*, May 11, 1947, 919–24; June 5, 1947 speech in *FRUS*, 1947, 3: 238–9. See also Douglas T. Stuart, *Creating the National Security State: A History of the Law that Transformed America* (Princeton: Princeton University Press, 2008), chs. 3–5.
19. On the ERP, Michael Hogan, *The Marshall Plan* (Cambridge: Cambridge University Press, 1987).
20. Britain received $3,297,000,000; France, 2,296,000,000; Germany, 1,448,000,000; Italy, 1,204,000,000.
21. Kennan, *Memoirs*, i. 343.
22. See Harper, *American Visions*, ch. 7.
23. Marshall speech at Berkeley CA, Mar. 19, 1948. James E. Miller, "Taking the Gloves Off: The United States and the Italian Elections of 1948," *Diplomatic History*, 7 (1983), 35–55. The Christian Democrats won an absolute majority in the chamber of deputies.
24. Strings would include the dismantling of trade barriers and subjection of internal policy to U.S. supervision.

25. Kennan, PPS/38, later designated NSC 20/1, Aug. 18, 1948, in Thomas H. Etzold and John Lewis Gaddis, eds., *Containment: Documents on American Policy and Strategy, 1945–1950* (New York: Columbia University Press, 1978), 50. See also Wilson D. Miscamble, *George F. Kennan and the Making of American Foreign Policy, 1947–50* (Princeton: Princeton University Press, 1992), 198.

26. Kennan, PPS/38, cited previous note, 44, 49.

27. NSC 20/4, Nov. 23, 1948, *FRUS* 1948, 1: 663–9; Gregory Mitrovich, *Undermining the Kremlin* (Ithaca, NY: Cornell University Press, 2000), 34–36.

28. Roberts, *Stalin's Wars*, 317.

29. Pechatnov and Edmondson, "The Russian Perspective," (Ch. 2 n. 32 above) 129–30.

30. See Vojtech Mastny, *The Cold War and Soviet Insecurity: the Stalin Years* (Oxford: Oxford University Press, 1996), ch. 2: Van Ree, *Political Thought*, 248–51.

31. Pechatnov and Edmondson, "The Russian Perspective," 131, 133; Zubok, *A Failed Empire*, 73.

32. Pechatnov and Edmondson, "The Russian Persective," 144.

33. See Mastny, *The Cold War*, 24; Zubok, *A Failed Empive*, 73–5. See also Wilfred Loth, *Stalin's Unwanted Child: The Soviet Union, the German Question, and the Founding of the GDR* (New York: St. Martin's Press, 1998).

34. Charles S. Maier, "The Marshall Plan and the Division of Europe," *Journal of Cold War Studies*, (winter 2005), 168–89.

35. Kennan, PPS/23, Feb. 1948, *FRUS*, 1948, 1: 510–29.

36. Lippmann, *The Cold War*, 18, 60.

37. See Pechatnov and Edmondson, "The Russion Perspective," 135; Kennan, "Résumé of World Situation," Nov. 6, 1947, *FRUS*, 1947, 1: 770–1.

38. Geir Lundestad, "Empire by Invitation? The United States and Western Europe, 1945–1952," *Journal of Peace Research*, 23 (Sept. 1986), 263–77.

39. The remark is associated with Lord Ismay, first secretary general of NATO.

40. The expresion is Louis J. Halle's. See *The Cold War as History* (Intro. n. 4 above), 133.

41. See Norman Naimark, "Stalin and Europe in the Postwar Period, 1945–53: Issues and Problems," *Journal of Modern European History*, 2 (Mar. 2004), (28–56), 41–4.

42. Halle, *The Cold War as History*, 166.

43. PPS/59, quoted in Miscamble, *Kennan*, 206.

44. See ibid., 106–11, 199–205; Mitrovich, *Undermining the Kremlin*, 18–23.

45. For Kennan's 1949 statement on Tito, see Miscamble, *Kennan*, 195–6.
46. Kennan, "The Gorbachev Prospect," *New York Review of Books*, Jan. 21, 1988. Kennan, in fact, called sponsorship of the OPC his "greatest mistake." Miscamble, *Kennan*, 109.
47. *FRUS*, 1948, 2: 1324–38.
48. Kennan, PPS/23, Feb. 24, 1948, *FRUS*, 1948, 1: 516.
49. An exception was the new Secretary of State, Acheson, who reserved judgment in early 1949.
50. Kennan, *Memoirs*, i. 444.
51. On this point, see Zubok, *A Failed Empire*, 76–7.

The Cold War as History

1. See Thomas A. Bailey, *America Faces Russia* (Ithaca, NY: Cornell University Press, 1950) and Herbert Feis's trilogy, *Churchill–Roosevelt–Stalin: The War they Waged and the Peace they Sought* (Princeton: Princeton University Press, 1957), *Between War and Peace: The Potsdam Conference* (Princeton: Princeton University Press, 1960), and *The Atomic Bomb and the End of World War II* (Princeton: Princeton University Press, 1966). Churchill's *The Second World War* (6 vols) (Boston: Houghton Mifflin, 1948–53), in particular, the final volume, is a pillar of the traditionalist account. Memoirs by U.S. protagonists include Harry S. Truman, *Memoirs* (2 vols., Garden City, NY: Doubleday, 1955), and James Byrnes, *Speaking Frankly* (New York: Harper, 1947). Prominent members of the school include Arthur M. Schlesinger, Jr., author of the influential *The Vital Center* (Boston: Houghton Mifflin, 1949), and Robert H. Ferrell, whose works include *America in a Divided World, 1945–1972* (Columbia: University of South Carolina Press, 1975). Britain's steadfast role is a theme of Alan Bullock, *Ernest Bevin: Foreign Secretary, 1945–1951* (New York: Norton, 1983).
2. See Denna Frank Fleming, *The Cold War and its Origins, 1917–1960* (2 vols.) (Garden City, NY: Doubleday, 1961); C. Wright Mills, *The Power Elite* (Oxford: Oxford University Press, 1956), and William Appleman Williams, *The Tragedy of American Diplomacy* (Cleveland: World Publishing, 1959). Williams, Professor of History at the University of Wisconsin during the 1960s, trained or inspired a group of younger revisionists, including Walter LaFeber, author of *America in the Cold War: Twenty Years of Revolution and Response, 1947–1967* (New York: Wiley, 1969), and Lloyd C. Gardner, author of *The Architects of Illusion: Men and Ideas in American Foreign Policy,*

1941–1949 (Chicago: Quadrangle, 1970), and other works. Gar Alperowitz, *Atomic Diplomacy: Hiroshima and Potsdam* (New York: Simon and Schuster, 1965), arguing that the Truman administration had used the atomic bomb to try to intimidate the Russians, became a *cause célèbre*. See also David Horowitz, *Free World Colossus* (New York: Hill and Wang, 1965), Gabriel Kolko, *The Roots of American Foreign Policy: An Analysis of Power and Purpose* (Boston: Beacon, 1969) and Gabriel Kolko and Joyce Kolko, *The Limits of Power: The World and United States Foreign Policy, 1945–1954* (New York: Praeger, 1972).

3. See George F. Kennan, *Memoirs, i. 1925–1950*, Dean Acheson, *Present at the Creation*, Charles E. Bohlen, *Witness to History*, W. Averell Harriman and Elie Abel, *Special Envoy*, Arthur M. Schlesinger, Jr.'s essay in Gardner et al., *The Origins of the Cold War*, and John Lewis Gaddis, *The United States and the Origins of the Cold War, 1941–1947* (New York: Columbia University Press, 1972).

4. George F. Kennan, *American Diplomacy: 1900–1950* (Chicago: University of Chicago Press, 1951), 73.

5. See Lippmann, *The Cold War: A Study in U.S. Foreign Policy*. Kennan, *American Diplomacy*; Hans J. Morgenthau, *Politics among Nations: The Struggle for Power and Peace* (New York: Knopf, 1954), and his contribution to Gardner et al., *The Origins of the Cold War*; Niebuhr, *The Irony of American History*; Halle, *The Cold War as History*.

6. See Schlesinger's essay in Gardner et al., *The Origins of the Cold War*, 69, 70.

7. John Lewis Gaddis, "The Emerging Post-Revisionist Synthesis on the Origins of the Cold War," *Diplomatic History*, 2/1 (summer 1983) (171–204), 181.

8. Ibid for Gaddis's assessment. See also, J. Samuel Walker, "Historians and the Cold War's Origins: The New Consensus," in Gerald K. Haines and J. Samuel Walker, eds., *American Foreign Relations: A Historiographical Review* (Westport, CN: 1981), 207–36. Studies developing "post-revisionist" themes include Daniel Yergin, *Shattered Peace: The Origins of the Cold War and the National Security State* (Boston: Houghton Mifflin, 1977); Mastny, *Russia's Road to the Cold War*, Bruce R. Kuniholm, *The Origins of the Cold War in the Near East: Great Power Conflict and Diplomacy in Iran, Turkey, and Greece* (Princeton: Princeton University Press, 1979); Messer, *The End of an Alliance: James F. Byrnes, Roosevelt, Truman, and the Origins of the Cold War*, Terry H. Anderson, *The United States, Britain, and the Cold War, 1944–1947* (Columbia: University of Missouri Press, 1981); Fraser J. Harbutt,

The Iron Curtain: Churchill, America, and the Origins of the Cold War (Oxford: Oxford University Press, 1986); Geir Lundestad, *America, Scandinavia, and the Cold War, 1941–1949* (New York: Columbia University Press, 1980), and (by the same author), "Empire by Invitation? The United States and Western Europe, 1945–1952."

9. See, Gaddis, "Post-Revisionist Synthesis," especially the responses of Gardner and Kimball.

10. Zubok and Pleshakov, *Kremlin's Cold War*. See also David Holloway, *Stalin and the Bomb: The Soviet Union and Atomic Energy, 1939–1956* (New Haven: Yale University Press, 1994), and Vojtech Mastny, *The Cold War and Soviet Insecurity:The Stalin Years*. The first major post-Cold War biography of Stalin was Dimitri Volkogonov's *Stalin: Triumph and Tragedy* (New York: Grove Weidenfeld, 1991).

11. See John Lewis Gaddis, *We Now Know: Rethinking Cold War History* (Oxford: Oxford University Press, 1997), and *The Cold War: A New History* (New York: Penguin, 2005).

12. See Melvyn Leffler, "The Cold War: What do we Now Know," *American Historical Review*, April 1999. This critique drew on his study of early postwar U.S. policy, *A Preponderance of Power: National Security, the Truman Administration, and the Cold War*. By the same author see, *For the Soul of Mankind: The United States, the Soviet Union, and the Cold War*.

13. Mark's opus included "Charles E. Bohlen and the Acceptable Limits of Soviet Hegemony in Eastern Europe: A memorandum of 18 October 1945," *Diplomatic History* 3 (spring 1979), 201–13; "American Policy Towards Eastern Europe and the Origins of the Cold War, 1941–1946"; "The War Scare of 1946 and its Consequences,"; "Revolution by Degrees: Stalin's National Front Strategy for Europe, 1941–1947," CWIHP Working Paper No. 31 (Feb, 2001). See also Pechatnov and Edmondson, "The Russian Perspective" Sergei Goncharov, John Lewis, and Xue Litai, *Uncertain Partners: Stalin, Mao, and the Korean War* (Stanford, CA: Stanford University Press, 1993); Chen Jian, *Mao's China and the Cold War* (Chapel Hill: University of North Carolina Press, 2001); Lorenz M. Lüthi, *The Sino-Soviet Split: Cold War in the Communist World* (Princeton: Princeton University Press, 2008).

14. See Wilson D. Miscamble, *From Roosevelt to Truman: Potsdam, Hiroshima, and the Cold War* (Cambridge: Cambridge University Press, 2007); Beisner, *Dean Acheson: A Life in the Cold War*, 646. Allen Weinstein and Alexander Vassiliev, *The Haunted Wood: Soviet Espionage in America in the Stalin Era*

(New York: Random House, 1999); Gregory Mitrovich, *Undermining the Kremlin*, NY; Campbell Craig and Fredrik Logevall, *America's Cold War: The Politics of Insecurity* (Cambridge, MA: Harvard University Press, 2009); Roberts, *Stalin's Wars: From World War to Cold War, 1939–1953*. See also Isaac Deutscher, *Stalin: A Political Biography* (Oxford: Oxford University Press, 1966); Vladimir Zubok, *A Failed Empire: The Soviet Union and the Cold War from Stalin to Gorbachev*.

Chapter 4—The Globalization and Militarization of the Contest, 1949–1953

1. Kennan, "Foreign Service Dispatch 116, Sept. 8, 1952: The Soviet Union and the Atlantic Pact," in *Memoirs*, vol. ii (Boston: Little, Brown, 1972), 333, 335, 336, 342, 350.

2. See Eduard Mark's intervention on H-Diplo (H-Diplo@h-net.msu.edu), Apr. 12, 2008; Vojtech Mastny, "NATO in the Beholder's Eye," CWIHP Working Paper no. 35, Mar. 2002, 26–7; Yoram Gorlitzki and Oleg Khlevniuk, *Cold Peace: Stalin and the Soviet Ruling Circle, 1945–1953* (Oxford: Oxford University Press, 2004), 98–9.

3. "Report by L. P. Beria and I. V. Kurchatov to I. V. Stalin," Aug. 30, 1949. Document reproduced in Levering et al. *Debating*, 176–8.

4. See his March 1950 *Reader's Digest* article, quoted in Mitrovich, *Undermining the Kremlin*, 55.

5. Stalin quoted in Pechatnov and Edmondson, "The Russian Perspective," 145–6.

6. See Harper, *American Visions*, 222–6.

7. NSC 68, Apr. 14, 1950, in *FRUS* 1950, 1: 251, 264; Mitrovich, *Undermining the Kremlin*, 48–59; Paul H. Nitze, *From Hiroshima to Glasnost: At the Center of Decision* (New York: Grove Weidenfeld, 1989), 93–100.

8. NSC 68, *FRUS* 1950, 1: 253, 282, 284, 285.

9. Kennan, *Memoirs* i: 408.

10. Bohlen, *Witness to History*, 290; Acheson, *Present*, 378.

11. See Matthew A. Evangelista, "Stalin's Postwar Army Reappraised," *International Security*, 7/3 (winter 1982/83), 7, 110–29.

12. For the distinction between "symmetrical" and "asymmetrical" containment, see John Lewis Gaddis, *Strategies of Containment* (Oxford: Oxford University Press, 2005).

13. NSC 68, *FRUS* 1950, 1: 240–1.

14. These included German reunification under a freely elected government; Soviet withdrawal from Austria; reunification of Korea through free elections; and Soviet military withdrawal from Eastern Europe. See Beisner, *Dean Acheson*, 249.

15. Nancy Tucker, *Patterns in the Dust: Chinese–American Relations and the Recognition Controversy, 1949–1950* (New York: Columbia University Press, 1983), 81.

16. Ibid., ch. 5. See also Robert M. Blum, *Drawing the Line: The Origin of the American Containment Policy in East Asia* (New York: Norton, 1982), 18–23, and Ross Y. Koen, *The China Lobby in American Politics* (New York: Macmillan, 1960).

17. Truman was challenged by the anti-civil rights "Dixiecrat" candidate, Strom Thurmond, and former commerce secretary Wallace.

18. Truman's Executive Order 9835 (March 1947) established the Federal Employee Loyalty Program. FBI investigations led to some 5,000 voluntary resignations and 378 dismissals.

19. See Shen Zhihua, "Sino-Soviet Relations and the Origins of the Korean War: Stalin's Strategic Goals in the Far East," *Journal of Cold War Studies*, 2/2, (spring 2000), 55.

20. Tucker, *Patterns in the the Dust*, 9.

21. See Barbara W. Tuchman, *Stilwell and the American Experience in China, 1911–1945*, (New York: Macmillan, 1970), 460.

22. U.S. Department of State, *United States Relations with China with Special Reference to the Period 1944–1949*, Department of State Publication 3573, Far Eastern Series 30. (Stanford, CA: Stanford University Press, 1967).

23. Blum, *Drawing the Line*, 164–5, 176–7. NSC 48/2: The Position of the United States with Respect to Asia, Dec. 30, 1949 in *FRUS*, 1949, 7 (part 2): 1215.

24. U.S. Department of State *Bulletin*, 22/550, Jan. 16, 1950, 79. Acheson's speech, ibid. 22/551, Jan. 23, 1950, 111–18.

25. This was because of Communist spy Elizabeth Bentley's defection to the FBI in Nov. 1945.

26. See Acheson, *Present*, 360; Beisner, *Dean Acheson*, 297–8.

27. The move also prevented Chiang from attacking the mainland, thus limiting fighting to Korea.

28. Acheson, *Present*, 369.

29. Chen Jian, *Mao's China*, chs. 1–2.

30. Ibid., 50. For memos of conversations of Mikoyan with top Chinese officials (Jan. 31–Feb. 6, 1949), and between Mao and Stalin (Dec. 1949–Jan. 1950), see CWIHP Virtual Archive, Sino-Soviet Relations Collection. See also Chen Jian, "The Sino-Soviet Alliance and China's Entry into the Korean War, CWIHP Working Paper no. 1, June 1992; Blum, *Drawing the Line*, 63.

31. Chen Jian, "Mao's China," 46–8.

32. Pechatnov and Edmondson, "The Russian Perspective," 146.

33. As late as early 1949, Stalin favored Communist–Nationalist negotiations and his ambassador followed Chiang's government as it retreated before the advancing Communists. On Stalin's fear of Chinese Titoism, Mao later commented: "This lack of belief remained in Stalin even during the first stages of the formation of the PRC." Record of Pavel Iudin–Mao conversation, Mar. 31, 1956," quoted in David Wolff, "'One Finger's Worth of Historical Events': New Russian and Chinese Evidence on the Sino-Soviet Alliance and Split, 1948–1959," CWIHP Working Paper no. 30, Aug. 2000, 5.

34. See Odd Arne Westad, "The Sino-Soviet Alliance and the United States: War, Politics, and Perceptions, 1950–1961," paper presented to the CWIHP conference, "The Cold War and Asia," Jan. 1996; Shen Zhihua, "Sino-Soviet Relations," 44–68.

35. See Kathryn Weathersby, "Soviet Aims in Korea and the origins of the Korean War: New Evidence from Russian Archives," CWIHP Working Paper no. 8, Nov. 1993, 10.

36. The plan, agreed by Moscow and Washington in Dec. 1945, was vigorously opposed by most Koreans. Washington did not press it but it remained Moscow's official position. Soviet forces withdrew in late 1948; U.S. forces in 1949.

37. The U.S. and the USSR had agreed to this line, dividing their occupation zones in August 1945.

38. Shen Zhihua, "Sino-Soviet Relations," 50–3; Kathryn Weathersby, "'Should We Fear This?' Stalin and the Danger of War with America," CWIHP Working Paper no. 39, July 2002, 7–8, 11. See also Goncharov, Lewis, and Xue Litai, *Uncertain Partners: Stalin, Mao and the Korean War*.

39. Shen Zhihua, "Sino-Soviet Relations," 63; Weathersby, "'Should We Fear This?'", quoting a Soviet report on the Kim–Stalin conversations in Apr. 1950, 9

40. Foreign Minister Vyshinski tel. to Chinese leaders, May 14, 1950, quoted in Shen Zhihua, "Sino-Soviet Relations," 67.

41. The USSR's absence from the Security Council (protesting the PRC's exclusion) allowed for passage of a resolution.
42. Stalin telegram to Gottwald, Aug. 27, 1950, quoted in Zubok, *A Failed Empire*, 80.
43. Chen Jian, *Mao's China*, 55–6.
44. Roschin (Soviet ambassador in Beijing) telegram to Stalin, Oct. 3, 1950. CWIHP Virtual Archive, Sino-Soviet Relations Collection.
45. Stalin telegram to Shtykov (Soviet ambassador to N. Korea) for Kim Il Sung, Oct. 7, 1950, quoting at length Stalin's reply to Mao's message. CWIHP Virtual Archive, Sino-Soviet Relations Collection.
46. In a draft of the message, although not in the telegram itself, Stalin called the contingency of a big war with the United States "not very likely." See Wolff, "'One Finger's Worth of Historical Events'", 27.
47. On Oct. 13, Stalin cabled Kim: "continuation of resistance is hopeless. Chinese comrades refuse to get involved militarily." Message quoted in Weathersby, "'Should We Fear This?'", 19. See also, Chen Jian, *Mao's China*, 58; Mao telegram to Stalin, Oct. 14, 1950. CWIHP Virtual Archive, Sino-Soviet Relations Collection.
48. Marshall was defense secretary, Sept. 1950 to Sept. 1951. See William Stueck, *The Korean War: An International History* (Princeton: Princeton University Press, 1995), 89, 94.
49. See Rosemary Foot, *The Wrong War: American Policy and the Dimensions of the Korean Conflict, 1950–1953* (Ithaca, NY: Cornell University Press, 1985), 81–2.
50. On MacArthur's reaction, see Steuck, *Korean War*, 95; Foot, *Wrong War*, 89.
51. U.S. statement quoted in Steuck, *Korean War,* 61; Matthews quoted ibid., 69.
52. See Irving L. Janis, *GroupThink* (Boston: Houghton Mifflin, 1982), 67.
53. Foot, *Wrong War*, 101–2, 123.
54. See Beisner, *Dean Achesen*, 428; Stueck, *Korean War*, 178–81.
55. According to Steuck (p. 361), nearly three million Koreans were killed, wounded or missing.
56. Chen Jian, *Mao's China*, 97–117; Stueck, *Korean War*, ch. 8; 330.
57. NSC 124/2, June 25, 1952, *FRUS*, 1952–1954, 2: 129; Beisner, *Dean Acheson*, 485.
58. Lisbon called for increasing NATO's effective divisions from 34 to 55 by 1953. See Harper, *American Visions*, ch. 7.
59. This included propaganda, disinformation, economic pressure, sabotage, and support for resistance groups.

60. Between 1949 and 1952 OPC personnel increased from 302 to 2,812 with 3,142 more under contract. Overseas stations increased from 7 to 47 and the budget from $4.7 to $82 million. See Mitrovich, *Undermining the Kremlin*, 182, and ch. 2, in general.

61. Other UN forces suffered around 15, 000 killed; ROK losses were over 800,000. Beisner, *Dean Acheson*, 446.

62. Congress refused to comply in full with requested tax increases, leading to budget deficits of $4 billion in 1952 and $5 billion in 1953. Rearmament generated severe commodity shortages and inflationary pressures, leading to wage, price and rent controls. See Michael Hogan, *A Cross of Iron: Harry S. Truman and the Origins of the National Security State, 1945–1954* (Cambridge: Cambridge University Press, 1998), ch. 8.

63. Quoted in Robert Bowie and Richard Immerman, *Waging Peace: How Eisenhower Shaped an Enduring Cold War Strategy* (Oxford: Oxford University Press, 1998), 31 NSC 135/3, "Reappraisal of U.S. Objectives and Strategy for National Security," Sept. 25, 1952, *FRUS*, 1952–54, 2: 142–50; Mitrovich, *Undermining the Kremlin*, ch. 3.

64. Bohlen, *Witness to History*, 176.

65. Quoted in Ronald Steel, *Walter Lippmann and the American Century* (New Brunswick: Transaction, 1999), 455.

66. See, for example Eisenhower's Oct. 25, 1950, campaign speech blaming Truman and Acheson for inviting the Korean war.

67. Gorlitzki and Khlevniuk, *Cold Peace*, 98–101.

68. The U.S., Britain and France were due to sign "contractual agreements" and the EDC Treaty with Bonn. For Stalin's statements, see memos of conversations of Apr. 1 and 7, 1952, CWIHP Virtual Archive, Germany in the Cold War. See also Zubok, *Failed Empire*, 78–85; Ralf Steininger, *The German Question and the Stalin Note of 1952* (New York: Columbia University Press, 1992); Geoffrey Roberts, "A Chance for Peace? The Soviet Campaign to end the Cold War, 1953–1955", CWIHP Working Paper no. 57, Dec. 2008.

69. Beisner, *Dean Acheson*, 446; Chen Jian, *Mao's China*, 116–17.

Chapter 5—The Age of Brinkmanship, 1953–1963

1. Aron, *Le Grand Schisme*, 13.

2. See Leffler, *Soul of Mankind*, ch. 2; K. Larres and K. Osgood, eds., *The Cold War after Stalin's Death: A Missed Opportunity for Peace?* (Lanham MD: Rowman and Littlefield, 2006).

3. Eisenhower Inaugural address, Jan. 20, 1953, Dulles, "A Policy of Boldness," *Life*, May 19, 1952, 146.

4. See Leffler, *Soul of Mankind*, 101–03.

5. Mitrovich, *Undermining the Kremlin*, 108, 130; Eisenhower speech, "A Chance for Peace", Apr. 16, 1953.

6. The Presidium, formerly (and later) called the Politburo, of the Communist Party central committee became the seat of power.

7. Quoted in Leffler, *Soul of Mankind*, 91–2.

8. The SED program "drastically increased investments allotted to heavy industry, strangled small private enterprises with increased taxation, accelerated the collectivization of agriculture, restricted travel between East and West Germany, and launched a concerted campaign against religious activity." See James Richter, "Reexamining Soviet Policy towards Germany during the Beria Interregnum", CWIHP Working Paper no. 3, June 1992, 13.

9. Malenkov statement, June 2, 1953, quoted in Roberts, "A Chance for Peace?", 11–12.

10. Ibid. 13–14.

11. NSC 158, "United States Objectives and Actions to Exploit the Unrest in the Satellite States", June 29, 1953, in Etzold and Gaddis, eds., *Containment*, 332–4.

12. C. Wright Mills, *The Causes of World War Three* (New York: Simon and Schuster, 1958), 1.

13. Khrushchev quoted in Norman Cousins, *Improbable Triumvirate: John F. Kennedy, Pope John, Nikita Khruschev* (New York: Norton, 1972), 54–5.

14. See Technological Capabilities Panel of the Scientific Advisory Committee of the Office of Defense Mobilization, "Meeting the Threat of Surprise Attack" (The Killian Report) (Feb. 1955); Albert Wohlstetter et al., "Protecting U.S. Power to Strike Back in the 1950s and 1960s" (R-290, Sept. 1956); Security Resources Panel of the President's Science Advisory Committee, "Deterrence and Survival in the Nuclear Age" (the Gaither Report, Nov. 1957); NIE 11–5–58 (Aug. 19, 1958); NIE 11–5–58 (Nov. 25, 1958).

15. Malenkov speech, "We Will Never Step Aside," Aug. 8, 1953, in *Vital Speeches of the Day*, 19/22, Sept. 1, 1953, 679–91. Mar. 1954 speech quoted in O. P. Chaney, *Zhukov* (Norman: University of Oklahoma Press, 1996), 391.

16. See Leffler *Soul of Mankind*, 106; Klaus Larres, *Churchill's Cold War: The Politics of Personal Diplomacy* (New Haven: Yale University Press, 2002).

17. Apr. 16 speech, "A Chance for Peace." Remarks to Republicans, Editorial Note, *FRUS*, 1952-4, 2: 317.

18. See ibid., 360-5, 388-412; Kennan, *Memoirs*, ii. 181-2.

19. *FRUS*, 1952-1954, 2: 416-31; Mitrovich, *Undermining the Kremlin*, 140-3.

20. See memo of discussion at NSC meeting, Aug. 27, 1953, *FRUS*, 1952-1954, 2: 443-55; Cutler to Dulles, quoting Eisenhower, Sept. 3, 1953, ibid., 455-57.

21. Dulles to Eisenhower, Sept. 6, 1953, ibid., 457-60. See also Mitrovich, *Undermining the Kremlin*, 136.

22. For text of NSC 162/2, see *FRUS*, 1952-1954, 2:578-96. See also minutes of the Oct. 7, 1953, NSC meeting, ibid., 514-34.

23. For Dulles's characterization, see his "Policy for Security and Peace," *Foreign Affairs*, 3/3, Apr. 1954, 354-5.

24. For Eisenhower's 1955 remark, see *FRUS*, 1955-57, 4: 349.

25. Dulles speech, "Maximum Deterrent at Bearable Cost," Jan. 12, 1954, *Vital Speeches of the Day*, 20/8, Feb. 1, 1954, 232-5. See also "Policy for Security and Peace" (cited n. 23 above), 359-60.

26. For Dulles's view, see ibid., 232; Richard H. Immerman, ed., *John Foster Dulles and the Diplomacy of the Cold War* (Princeton: Princeton University Press, 1990).

27. *FRUS*, 1952-1954, 2: 580, 595.

28. NSC 5412/2 (Dec. 28, 1955), an up-dated directive stated that covert action should aim "to create and exploit troublesome problems for International Communism" but no longer spoke of the retraction and reduction of Soviet power. See Mitrovich, *Undermining the Kremlin*, 163-6; 171-2. For Dulles's comments, see Memo of Discussion of NSC meeting, Dec. 21, 1954, *FRUS*, 1952-1954, 2: 832-3.

29. See David Kaiser, *The Road to Dallas: The Assassination of John F. Kennedy* (Cambridge MA: Harvard University Press, 2008), ch. 3; Stephen G. Rabe, *Eisenhower and Latin America: The Foreign Policy of Anti-Communism* (Chapel Hill: University of North Carolina Press, 1988), chs. 8-9.

30. Eisenhower's Apr. 7, 1954 press conference quoted in Mark Atwood Lawrence and Fredrik Logevall, eds., *The First Vietnam War: Colonial Conflict and Cold War Crisis* (Cambridge MA: Harvard University Press, 2007), 228.

31. See Roberts, "A Chance for Peace?"

32. James Shepley, "How Dulles Averted War", *Life*, Jan. 16, 1956.

33. See Ralph A. Thaxton, Jr., *Catastrophe and Contention in Rural China: Mao's Great Leap Forward Famine and the Origins of Righteous Resistance in Da Fo Village* (Cambridge: Cambridge University Press, 2009).

34. Chen Jian, *Mao's China*, 71, 189–90, and ch. 7 in general.
35. See *Khrushchev Remembers* (Boston: Little, Brown, 1970), 393.
36. See Oleg Grinevsky, *Tysyacha I Odin den' Nikity Sergeyevicha* [*A Thousand and One Days of Nikita Khrushchev*] (Moscow: Vagrius, 1998), 54.
37. Khrushchev told Mao that "we also are not without sin. It was we who drew the Americans to South Korea." Memo of conversation, Oct. 3, 1959, CWIHP Virtual Archive, Sino-Soviet Relations Collection.
38. "Secret Speech delivered by First Party Secretary at the 20th Party Congress of the CPSU, Feb. 25, 1956," *Congressional Record* (May 22, 1956–June 11, 1956), CII, Part 7 (June 4, 1956), 9389–403.
39. These included, IMEMO, the Institute of World Economy and International Relations; MGIMO, the Moscow State Institute of International Relations; and IEMSS, the Institute of the Economy of the World Socialist System. ISKAN, the USA–Canada Institute, was launched in the sixties. The expression "oases" is ISKAN-head Georgi Arbatov's, quoted in English, *Russia and the Idea of the West*, 71.
40. Gomulka quoted in Charles Gati, *Failed Illusions: Moscow, Washington, Budapest, and the 1956 Hungarian Revolt* (Washington: Wilson Center Press, 2006), 142.
41. Ibid., ch. 5. See also "Working Notes from the Session of the CPSU CC Presidium on 30 Oct. 1956," CWIHP Virtual Archive; "Declaration by the Government of the USSR," *Pravda*, Oct. 31, 1956.
42. See, for example, Zubok, *Failed Empire*, 117.
43. Khrushchev quoted in Minutes no. 49 of Presidium Session of 31 Oct. 1956 (V. Malin notes), Kremlin Decision-Making Project, Miller Center of Public Affairs, University of Virginia (UVA).
44. Gati, *Failed Illusions*, chap 6.
45. Memo of discussion of NSC meeting, Dec. 21, 1954, *FRUS*, 1952–54, 2: 841.
46. Remark quoted in William Taubman, *Khrushchev: The Man and his Era* (New York: Norton, 2003), 427.
47. De Gaulle press conference, Jan. 14, 1963, in Charles de Gaulle, *Discours et messages: pour l'effort, août 1962–décembre 1965* (Paris: Plon, 1970–1), 73.
48. See memo of Khrushchev–Sen. Hubert Humphrey conversation, Dec. 3, 1958, *FRUS*, 1958–60, 8: 151.
49. On the "seventy–thirty ratio" and the October 1959 visit, see Chen Jian, *Mao's China*, 65, 80–1. Eisenhower had asked Khrushchev to raise the issue of five American prisoners. Khrushchev took the Chinese to task for a recent border skirmish with India. Memo of conversation, Oct. 3, 1959,

CWIHP Virtual Archive, Sino-Soviet Relations. See also Lüthi, *The Sino-Soviet Split*, chs. 2–3.

50. See A. Fursenko and T. Naftali, *Khrushchev's Cold War: The Inside Story of an American Adversary* (New York: Norton, 2006), 188–91. 188–91; Marc Trachtenberg, *A Constructed Peace: The Making of the European Settlement, 1945–1963* (Princeton: Princeton University Press, 1999).

51. See Hope Harrison, *Driving the Soviets up the Wall: Soviet–East German Relations, 1953–1961* (Princeton: Princeton University Press, 2003), 220.

52. See, for example, U.S. ambassador to Moscow Llewellyn Thompson to State Dept., Nov. 11, 1958, *FRUS*, 1958–60, 8: 48.

53. See memo of Khrushchev–Mao conversation, July 31, 1958, CWIHP Virtual Archive, Sino-Soviet Relations; Thompson to State Dept., Dec. 3, 1958, reporting Senator Humphrey's Dec. 1 conversation with NK. *FRUS*, 1958–60, 8: 150; Fursenko and Naftali, *Khrushchev's Cold War*, 248.

54. Liquid-fueled rockets took longer to prepare for launch than the solid-fueled missiles under development, and were vulnerable to preemptive strikes.

55. In their July 31, 1958 conversation (cited n. 53) Khrushchev told Mao, "When we wrote letters to Eden and Guy Mollet . . . they immediately stopped the aggression."

56. See Keith Kyle, *Suez* (London: Tauris, 2003), 492–5.

57. The pact (formed in 1955 and later called the Central Treaty Organization, or CENTO) also included Britain, Turkey, Iran, and Pakistan.

58. See Fursenko and Naftali, *Khrushchev's Cold War*, 134–7; 194, 208.

59. Khrushchev used this expression with Humphrey in Dec. 1958, in conversation cited in n. 53.

60. Fursenko and Naftali, *Khrushchev's Cold War*, 201–5.

61. See memo of Mikoyan-Eisenhower conversation, Jan. 17, 1959, *FRUS*, 1958–60, 8: 276–81; tel. from U.S. delegation at Geneva to State Dept., May 16, 1959, summarizing Gromyko's presentation, ibid. 8: 708–11.

62. See U.S. Moscow Embassy to State Dept., June 25, 1959, ibid. 8: 941.

63. Memo of Eisenhower-Khrushchev conversation, Sept. 26, 1959, ibid., 9: 36.

64. Ibid. 9: 350.

65. Khrushchev was particularly suspicious of Herter, Allen Dulles, and Nixon.

66. Memo of Eisenhower–Khrushchev conversation, Sept. 26, 1959, *FRUS*, 1958–60; ibid., 9: 36. See also Macmillan to Eisenhower, (undated, but June 1959), ibid., 8: 939–40.

67. In 1960, Soviet GDP was around 40 percent of the United States's; per capita GDP, about 35 percent. A seven-year plan launched in 1958, aiming

to raise agricultural output by 70 percent, would produce a 14 percent increase by 1965. Steven Rosefielde, *The Russian Economy: From Lenin to Putin* (Oxford: Blackwell, 2007), 157–9; Alec Nove, *An Economic History of the USSR, 1917–1991* (London: Penguin, 1992), 372.

68. Sergei Khrushchev, quoted in Taubman, *Khrushchev*, 440. Khrushchev quoted in Fursenko and Naftali, *Khrushchev's Cold War*, 241.

69. On this point, see Fursenko and Naftali, *Khrushchev's Cold War*, 246–47. See also Minutes of Dec. 14, 1959 Presidium meeting (Malin notes), Kremlin Decision-Making Project, Miller Center, UVA.

70. See Taubman, *Khrushchev*, ch. 16; Fursenko and Naftali, *Khrushchev's Cold War*, ch. 11; minutes of meeting, May 16, 1959, *FRUS*, 1958–60, 9: 441–8.

71. Sporadic flights began in July 1956. Eisenhower had discontinued them for seven months after Khrushchev's 1959 visit. Under CIA pressure, he authorized one for April 9, 1960, and another to occur no later than April 24. Due to unfavorable weather, he extended the deadline to May 1. He was torn over the decision, wanting up-to-date information but fearing an incident. See Taubman, *Khrushchev*, 443–4.

72. On Mar. 17, 1960, Eisenhower approved a covert action program against Castro and his regime. Although Castro had begun to socialize the economy, he did not declare his Marxism–Leninism until Dec. 1961. See Rabe, *Eisenhower and Latin America*, 128.

73. On Mongoose, see Kaiser, *The Road to Dallas*, ch. 5; Lawrence Freedman, *Kennedy's Wars* (Oxford: Oxford University Press, 2000), ch. 17.

74. See Trumbull Higgins, *A Perfect Failure: Kennedy, Eisenhower, and the CIA at the Bay of Pigs* (New York: Norton, 1987).

75. The Jan. 6, 1961 speech was published in the CPSU journal *Kommunist*, Jan. 17, 1961.

76. See Soviet ambassador in Berlin, Pervukhin, to Gromyko, May 19, 1961, CWIHP Virtual Archive, Germany in the Cold War Collection.

77. Roswell Gilpatric, quoted in Freedman, *Kennedy's Wars*, 83.

78. Fursenko and Naftali, *Khrushchev's Cold War*, 424. See also Freedman, 97–100. In an Oct. 10 meeting, Asst. Sec. of Defense Nitze argued for a preemptive strategic strike on the USSR, should the Berlin situation precipitate. McNamara and Rusk disagreed. See Fred Kaplan, "JFK's First-Strike Plan," *Atlantic Monthly*, Oct. 2001, 81–6.

79. Taubman, *Khrushchev*, 486.

80. Minutes of Presidium meeting, May 26, 1961 (Malin notes), Kremlin Decision-Making Project, Miller Center, UVA. See also Fursenko and Naftali, *Khrushchev's Cold War*, 355–59.

81. This draws statements from three different conversations at Vienna on June 4, 1961. See *FRUS*, 1961–63, 5:174; ibid., 14: 67–98. The interim arrangement would allow Western troops to remain temporarily, accompanied by Soviet troops in West Berlin.

82. "Radio and Television Report to the American People on the Berlin Crisis," July 25, 1961. JFK Presidential Library and Museum, On-line Archives.

83. See McNamara's June 1962 speech, "Defense Arrangements of the North Atlantic Community." State Dept. *Bulletin*, 47 (July 9, 1962), 67–8; Lawrence Freedman, *The Evolution of Nuclear Strategy* (New York: Palgrave, 2003), ch. 15.

84. The showdown arose out of a GDR challenge of U.S. diplomats' right to travel in East Berlin without showing identification. At Clay's urging Washington authorized probes by diplomats with an armed escort. U.S. tanks were deployed at the checkpoint to enforce the point. The Soviets deployed their own tanks, lest the Americans (as Clay had recommended) try to tear down parts of the wall. But neither side wanted war as the result of rash actions by local representatives. Contacts between Khrushchev and Kennedy led to a defusing of the crisis.

85. See Robert Dallek, *An Unfinished Life: John F. Kennedy, 1917–1963* (Boston: Little, Brown, 2003), 425.

86. See Vojtech Mastny, Sven G. Holtsmark, and Andreas Wenger, eds., *War Plans and Alliances in the Cold War* (New York: Routledge, 2006), 46–71; Khruschev's interview with Cyrus L. Sulzberger in early Sept. 1961, *FRUS*, 1961–3, 14: 401; Khrushchev to Kennedy, Sept. 29, 1961, ibid., 444–55.

87. For one of Khrushchev's frequent references to the "policy of strength," see Fursenko and Naftali, *Khrushchev's Cold War* 433.

88. Ibid., 414.

89. Memo of conversation, Jan. 30, 1962, *FRUS* 1961–3, 5: 356–60. See also Aleksandr Fursenko and Timothy Naftali, *"One Hell of a Gamble": Khrushchev, Castro, and Kennedy, 1958–1964* (New York: Norton, 1997).

90. Khrushchev later said protecting Cuba had been his sole motive. See J. Schechter and V. Luchkov, *Khrushchev Remembers: The Glasnost Tapes*, (Boston: Little, Brown, 1990), 170–2.

91. Fursenko and Naftali, *Khrushchev's Cold War*, 433–44.

92. Minutes of Presidium meeting, May 21, 1962, approving the decision (Malin Notes), Kremlin Decision-Making Project, Miller Center, UVA.

93. See Minutes of Presidium meeting of Jan. 8, 1962 (Malin notes), Kremlin Decision-Making project, Miller Center UVA. Khrushchev observed: "The peace agreement and the neutralization of West Berlin are now unattainable... Conduct a pressure policy. Do not give them any reason [to think] that we will not sign a peace agreement, but to retain the initiative... It's better to have Berlin and aggravation with the West rather than making concessions at the expense of the GDR's sovereignty."

94. See "Note on the Discussion between Khrushchev and Ulbricht," Feb. 26, 1962, CWIHP Virtual Archive, Germany in the Cold War Collection.

95. See Khrushchev to Kennedy (undated but probably July 5, 1962), *FRUS*, 1961–63, 6: 137–40; memo of Khrushchev–U Thant conversation, Aug. 28, 1962, CWIHP Virtual Archive, Germany in the Cold War Collection; Khrushchev to Kennedy (undated but probably Sept. 28, 1962), *FRUS*, 1961–63, 15: 337–8; memo of Khrushchev–Stuart Udall conversation, Sept. 6, 1962, ibid., 308–10; Khrushchev conversation with new U.S. amb. Floyd Kohler, ibid., 359–62; Khrushchev's mid-Sept. conversation with departing German ambassador Hans Kroll, summarized in ibid., 324, n. 1.

96. On Soviet denials, see Bruce J. Allyn, James G. Blight, and David A. Welch, "Essence of Revision: Moscow, Havana, and the Cuban Missile Crisis," *International Security*, 14/4 (winter 1989/90), 139. For an account advancing Berlin's importance, see Fursenko and Naftali, *Khrushchev's Cold War*, ch. 18.

97. As Rusk later put it: "IRBM's in Cuba would be free of radar detection and with zero alert time both ICBM sites and SAC bases could come under attack without warning and with greater accuracy due to short range." Rusk to U.S. NATO Mission, Oct. 28, 1962, *FRUS*, 1961–2, 15: 405.

98. Kennedy quoted in Dallek, *An Unfinished Life*, 539.

99. The Soviets considered the missiles in Cuba defensive just as NATO considered the Jupiters in Turkey and Italy defensive. See Khrushchev to Kennedy, Oct. 26, 1962, *FRUS*, 1961–3, 6: 173.

100. "Excom" meant Executive Committee of the NSC.

101. Kennedy speech, Oct. 22, 1962, JFK Library & Museum, On-Line Archives.

102. See Khrushchev to Kennedy, Oct. 24, 1962, *FRUS*, 1961–3, 6: 169–70; Fursenko and Naftali, *Khrushchev's Cold War*, 468–82.

103. See Minutes of Presidium meeting of Oct. 25, 1962, (Malin notes). Kremlin Decision-Making Project, Miller Center, UVA; Khrushchev to Kennedy, Oct. 26, 1962, *FRUS*, 1961–3, 6: 172–7.

104. Khrushchev to Kennedy, Oct. 27, 1962, ibid., 178–81. On Dobrynin as the idea's source, see Allyn et al., "Essence of Revision," 158–9. Mikoyan told the Cubans that Lippmann had inspired Khrushchev. Fursenko and Naftali, *Khrushchev's Cold War*, 488.
105. See transcript of Excom's Oct. 27, 1962 discussions, in Ernest R. May and Philip D. Zelikow, eds., *The Kennedy Tapes: Inside the White House During the Cuban Missile Crisis* (Cambridge, MA: Harvard University Press, 1997), 498–9, 513.
106. Bobby and Dobrynin met secretly at least seven times between Oct. 22 and 27. On their Oct. 26 meeting, see Allyn et al., "Essence of Revision", 158–9.
107. Kennedy to Khrushchev, Oct. 27, 1962, *FRUS*, 1961–3, 6: 181–2.
108. According to Fursenko and Naftali, *Khrushchev's Cold War* (490), Khrushchev had decided on Oct. 28 to publicly accept Kennedy's Oct. 27 proposal *before* hearing that the Americans had conceded on the Jupiters. See Khrushchev to Kennedy, Oct. 28, 1962, *FRUS*, 1961–63, 6: 183–7. This is possible but Khrushchev may have acted assuming there would be a side-deal on the Jupiters. On the Bobby Kennedy–Dobrynin Oct. 27 conversation, see Khrushchev to Kennedy, Oct. 28, 1962, ibid., 189–90. The words "strict secrecy" (attributed to Bobby) appear in Dobrynin to Soviet Ministry, Oct. 28, 1962, CWIHP Virtual Archive, Cuban Missile Crisis Collection. For Bobby's account of the Oct. 27 meeting (using the words "drastic consequences") see his memo to Rusk, in May and Zelikow, eds., *The Kennedy Tapes* 607–9. Bobby's account, playing down the notion of a trade, has been challenged by Dobrynin and Theodore Sorenson, editor of Bobby's memoir, *Thirteen Days*. Dobrynin disputed Bobby's claim that the Americans had given an ultimatum. See Allyn et al., "Essence of Revision," 163–4. For Dobrynin's view, see his *In Confidence: Moscow's Ambassador to America's Six Cold War Presidents (1962–1986)* (New York: Times Books, 1995), ch. 2.
109. The Americans also insisted that Soviet Il 22 bombers in Cuba be removed and did not end the blockade until this had happened in late November 1962.
110. Kennedy had secretly arranged for UN Secretary General U Thant to call for removal of the missiles in Turkey and Cuba. On the invasion, see James G. Blight and David A. Welch, eds. *On the Brink: Americans and Soviets Reexamine the Cuban Missile Crisis* (New York: Hill and Wang, 1989).
111. On Jan. 17, 1959, Mikoyan suggested to Eisenhower that "we should end the cold war." *FRUS*, 1958–60, 8: 280. In his Sept. 29, 1961, letter to Kennedy, Khrushchev said a German treaty would make possible the "elimination of the state of 'cold war.' Ibid., 1961–3, 6: 25–38.

112. See Trachtenberg, *A Constructed Peace.*
113. See, Daniel Bell, *The End of Ideology: On the Exhaustion of Political Ideas in the Fifties* (Glencoe, IL: Free Press, 1960). The Third Party Program of the CPSU, adopted in 1961, defined peaceful coexistence as "a specific form of the international class struggle," but the assumption of inevitable war was abandoned.
114. The Jan. 1963 Franco-German treaty laid the foundations for a privileged partnership, but (at U.S. urging) the CDU's "Atlanticist" wing attached a preamble underlining the FRG's NATO ties.
115. In a June 10, 1963 speech at American University in Washington, Kennedy asked Americans to re-examine their attitude toward the Cold War, paid tribute to Soviet sacrifices in World War II, and called for the two sides to direct their attention to their "common interests." Khrushchev called the speech the greatest by a U.S. president since FDR.
116. Soviet objections to inspections made a total test ban impossible. See Jennifer W. See, "An Uneasy Truce: John F. Kennedy and Soviet–American Détente, 1963", *Cold War History*, 2/2 (Jan. 2002), 161–4.
117. Kennedy's remark to Kenneth O'Donnell, quoted in Dallek, *An Unfinished Life*, 426. See also Kennedy to Brandt, Aug. 18, 1961, *FRUS* 1961–3, 14: 352. On the JCS, see ibid., 570–1. See also Kaiser, *The Road to Dallas*, chs. 13–17.
118. Aug. 13, 1961 was the day the wall's construction began. Memo of Khrushchev–Ulbricht conversation, Feb. 26, 1962, CWIHP Virtual Archive, Germany in the Cold War Collection. On Castro's reaction, see Allyn et al., "Essence of Revision," 168–9; Fursenko and Naftali, *Khrushchev's Cold War*, ch. 20.
119. Khrushchev had cut ministerial salaries, sent personnel from the economics ministries to the provinces, and required the elites' children to acquire vocational experience. On this, and the notion of a "nomenclature class," see Robert C. Tucker, *Political Culture and Leadership in Soviet Russia: From Lenin to Gorbachev* (New York: Norton, 1988), 108–26. Along with Brezhnev, who became CPSU general secretary, the group included Nikolai Podgorny, Aleksandr Shelepin, Vladimir Semichastny, Aleksei Kosygin, and Mikhail Suslov.

Chapter 6—The Struggle for the Third World

1. On growth rates, see Angus Maddison, *Contours of the World Economy 1–2030 AD* (Oxford: Oxford University Press, 2007), 380. On U.S. cultural influence see Richard Kuisel, *Seducing the French: the Dilemma of Americanization* (Berkeley: University of California Press, 1996); David W. Ellwood

and Rob Kroes, eds., *Hollywood in Europe: Experiences of a Cultural Hegemony* (Amsterdam: VU University Press, 1994).

2. Barraclough, *An Introduction to Contemporary History*, ch. 6. The EEC, consisting of Germany, France, Italy, Belgium, the Netherlands, and Luxembourg, was launched in 1957.

3. See Westad, *The Global Cold War*, 98–103.

4. Communiqué and Nehru speech quoted ibid., 101–2. SEATO, the South-East Asia Treaty Organization, was created after the 1954 Geneva conference at American prompting and included Australia, the Philippines, New Zealand, Pakistan, Thailand, France, the UK. and USA.

5. Westad uses "nativist" to describe the non-Marxist progressive-nationalist outlook of Sukarno and Nehru.

6. Quoted in Barraclough, *An Introduction to Contemporary History*, 215–16.

7. Dulles (Nov. 1, 1956) quoted in Immerman, ed., *John Foster Dulles and the Diplomacy of the Cold War*, 153.

8. On "domino theory," see previous chapter. See also Dulles speech, "Indo-China and the Chinese Communist Regime," Mar. 29, 1954, *Vital Speeches of the Day*, 20/13, Apr. 15, 1954, 386–7. See also George C. Herring, *America's Longest War: The United States and Vietnam, 1950–1975* (New York: John Wiley, 1979), 12.

9. See Acheson, *Present at the Creation*, chs. 52, 58, 71; W. R. Louis, "American Anti-Colonialism and the Dissolution of the British Empire," *International Affairs*, 61/3 (summer 1985), 395–420.

10. Eisenhower quoted in Herring, *America's Longest War*, 35.

11. Dulles speech, "Freedoms New Task" Feb. 26, 1956, *Vital Speeches of the Day*, 22/11, Mar. 1, 1956, 329–31.

12. The Eisenhower doctrine was used to justify the 1958 Lebanon intervention.

13. In Oct. 1955, Diem organized a referendum to oust Bao Dai and create a republic. See Herring, *America's Longest War*, 51–6. On the transition from French to U.S. influence see also, Mark A. Lawrence, *Assuming the Burden: Europe and the American Commitment to War in Vietnam* (Berkeley: University of California Press, 2005); Kathryn C. Statler, *Replacing France: The Origins of American Intervention in Vietnam* (Lexington: University Press of Kentucky, 2007), Jessica M. Chapman, "Staging Democracy: South Vietnam's 1955 Referendum to Depose Bao Dai," *Diplomatic History*, 30/4, (Sept. 2006), 671–703.

14. "Personalism" derived from the thought of Emmanuel Mounier, studied by Nhu in France. See Edward Miller, "Vision, Power and Agency: The Ascent

of Ngo Dinh Diem; 1945–54," *Journal of Southeast Asian Studies*, 35/3 (Oct. 2004) 433–58.

15. Minutes of NSC meeting, Dec. 21, 1954, *FRUS*, 1952–4, 2: 838.

16. See Rabe, *Eisenhower and Latin America*, 104–8.

17. JFK inaugural address. http://www.jfklibrary.org. On the June 1961 Vienna conversations, see *FRUS*, 1961–3, 5: 174, 194, 208.

18. Before a CIA-hired assassin could act, Lumumba was overthrown in a Dec. 1960 coup by General Joseph Mobutu. Mobutu delivered Lumumba to his enemies in Katanga province, who killed him.

19. On Indonesia, see Westad, *The Global Cold War*, 129–30; Bradley Simpson, *Economists with Guns: Authoritarian Development and U.S.–Indonesian Relations, 1960–1968* (Stanford, CA: Stanford University Press, 2008).

20. On Vietnam events, see Herring, *America's Longest War*, 66–7.

21. On policy shift, see Rabe, *Eisenhower and Latin America*, chs. 6–8.

22. W. W. Rostow, *The Stages of Economic Growth: A Non-Communist Manifesto* (Cambridge: Cambridge University Press, 1960), introdution and ch. 1.

23. See Nils Gilman, *Mandarins of the Future: Modernization Theory in Cold War America* (Baltimore: Johns Hopkins University Press, 2003); Michael E. Latham, *Modernization as Ideology: American Social Science and Nation-Building in the Kennedy Era* (Chapel Hill: University of North Carolina Press, 2000).

24. See Stephen G. Rabe, *The Most Dangerous Area in the World: John F. Kennedy Confronts Communist Revolution in Latin America* (Chapel Hill: University of North Carolina Press, 1999), 169.

25. Schlesinger quoted in Latham, *Modernization as Ideology*, 81.

26. Rabe, *The Most Dangerous Area*, 170–1.

27. Ibid., 166, 177.

28. See Piero Gleijeses "A Sordid Affair: The Alliance for Progress and British Guiana" in *Diplomatic History*, 31/4 (Sept. 2007), 793–6.

29. Westad, *The Global Cold War*, 188.

30. Ibid., 160–5; Chen Jian, *Mao's China*, 82–4.

31. See Yang Kuisong, "Changes in Mao Zedong's Attitude toward the Indochina War, 1949–1973," CWIHP Working paper no. 34, Feb. 2002, 31–2.

32. "Waist-deep in the big muddy" was an anti-war song by Pete Seeger.

33. See H. R. McMaster, *Dereliction of Duty: Lyndon Johnson, Robert McNamara, the Joint Chiefs of Staff, and the Lies that Led to Vietnam* (New York: HarperPerennial, 1997); Mark Moyar, *Triumph Forsaken: The Vietnam War, 1954–1965* (Cambridge: Cambridge University Press, 2006).

34. See the Taylor–Rostow report (Nov. 3, 1961) which speaks of "external aggression" against the RVN. *FRUS*, 1961–3, 1: Part 210.

35. Mao's talk with DRV delegation, Jan. 30, 1964, quoted in "Changes in Mao Zedong's Attitude toward the Indochina War, 1949–1973", Working Paper no. 34, CWIHP, Feb. 2002, 28.

36. See Janis, *Group-Think* (Ch. 4 n. 52 above), ch. 5; Daniel Ellsberg, "The Quagmire Myth and the Stalemate Machine," *Public Policy*, 19/2 (spring 1971) 217–74.

37. After visiting Vietnam in Nov. 1961, Gen. Maxwell Taylor and Walt Rostow reported that a "radical increase" in U.S. support was required. See *FRUS*, 1961–3, 1: Part 9. The McNamara–Taylor report (Oct. 2, 1963), following a similar visit, was rather more hopeful, but its authors were well aware of the obstacle represented by the Diem regime. See ibid., doc. 167.

38. Mansfield to Kennedy, Dec. 18, 1962, *FRUS*, 1961–3, 2: Part 330. See Fredrik Logevall, *Choosing War: The Lost Chance for Peace and the Escalation of War in Vietnam* (Berkeley: University of California Press, 1999), 328, on de Gaulle, Lippmann, and the *New York Times*. Transcript of Russell–LBJ tel. conversation (May 27, 1964), in Michael R. Beschloss, ed., *Taking Charge: The Johnson White House Tapes, 1963–64* (New York: Simon and Schuster, 1997), 367.

39. Bundy to LBJ, Feb. 7, 1965, *FRUS*, 1964–8, 2: Doc. 84.

40. For example, U.S.-supported and monitored OPLAN 34-A raids by RVN and mercenary commandoes against North Vietnam.

41. Quoted in George McT. Kahin, *Intervention: How America Became Involved in Vietnam* (New York: Knopf, 1986), 374–80.

42. W. Scott Thompson and Donaldson D. Frizzell, *The Lessons of Vietnam* (New York: Crane, Russak, 1992), 2–3.

43. For NSC 124/2 see *FRUS*, 1952–4, 2: 129. Maxwell Taylor quoted in Marilyn Young, *The Vietnam Wars* (New York: HarperCollins, 1991), 134. Kissinger press conference, March 26, 1975.

44. McNamara quoted in Arthur M. Schlesinger, Jr., *Journals, 1952–2000* (New York: Penguin, 2007), entry for Jan. 21, 1966. See also Stein Tonnesson, "Tracking Multi-Directional Dominoes," in Odd Arne Westad, Chen Jian, Stein Tonnesson, Nguyen Vu Tungand, and James G. Hershberg, eds., "77 Conversations Between Chinese and Foreign Leaders on the Wars in Indochina, 1964–1977," CWIHP Working Paper no. 22, May 1998; Thucydides, *History of the Peloponnesian War* (Harmondsworth: Penguin, 1972), 161.

45. J. William Fulbright, *The Arrogance of Power* (London: J. Cape, 1967).

46. See Herring, *America's Longest War* ch. 3. On de Gaulle's statements, see Logevall, *Choosing War*, 1–16, 95–107.

47. The anti-Diem faction included State Department officials Averell Harriman and Roger Hilsman, NSC staffer Michael Forrestal, and ambassador to Saigon Henry Cabot Lodge. Opposed were the CIA station chief, John Richardson, (recalled in Oct. at Lodge's request) and the head of the U.S. military mission, Gen. Paul Harkins. McNamara and JCS chief Taylor took the position that a coup should not be thwarted. For Kennedy's Oct. 29, 1963, statement, see *FRUS*, 1961–3, 4: doc. 235.

48. After a Nov 24, 1963 meeting, McCone wrote that LBJ was "anxious to get along, win the war—he didn't want as much effort placed on so-called social reforms." Ibid., doc. 33. May 24, 1964, recommendation quoted in Beschloss, ed., *Taking Charge*, 362. See also transcript of LBJ-Bundy conversation, May 27, 1964. China comparison quoted in Barbara Tuchman, *The March of Folly: From Troy to Vietnam* (London: Abacus, 1997).

49. An attack by a North Vietnamese patrol boat occurred on Aug. 2, 1964 in DRV territorial waters. A reported attack on another destroyer on Aug. 4, much further from the coast, probably never occurred. Nonetheless, it was the alleged second attack that triggered Washington's response. See Daniel Ellsberg, *Secrets: A Memoir of Vietnam and the Pentagon Papers* (New York: Penguin, 2002), ch. 1; Edward Moïse, *Tonkin Gulf and the Escalation of the Vietnam War* (Chapel Hill: University of North Carolina Press, 1996). Acting through Canadian diplomat Blair Seaborn, Washington had warned Hanoi in June that its patience with "aggression" was "growing extremely thin," and that if the conflict escalated North Vietnam would suffer the "greatest devastation." See Ellsberg, *Secrets*, 17.

50. Logevall, *Choosing War*, 411–12.

51. The decision was based on Taylor's and McNamara's report following their recent trip to Vietnam. According to the Oct. 2, 1963, report, "It should be possible to withdraw the bulk of U.S. personnel" by the end of 1965. *FRUS*, 1961–3, 4: doc. 167.

52. See Ellsberg, *Secrets*, 194–5; James K. Galbraith, "Exit Strategy," *Boston Review*, Oct./Nov. 2003; Howard Jones, *Death of a Generation: How the Assasinations of Diem and JFK Prolonged the Vietnam War* (Oxford: Oxford University Press, 2003), 377, 383. But during the Oct. 2, 1963 meeting to discuss McNamara's recommendations, "The President objected to the phrase 'by the end of this year' in the sentence 'The U.S. program for training Vietnamese should have progressed to the point where 1,000

U.S. military personnel assigned to South Vietnam could be withdrawn.' He believed that if we were not able to take this action by the end of this year, we would be accused of being over optimistic." This suggests he was keeping his options open. *FRUS*, 1961–3, 4: doc. 169. See also Mark J. Selverstone, "It's a Date: Kennedy and the Timetable for a Vietnam Troop Withdrawal," *Diplomatic History*, 34/3 (June 2010), 485–95.

53. On Nov. 20, 1963, McNamara observed: "South Vietnam is under tremendous pressure... We must be prepared to devote enough resources to this job of winning the war to be certain of accomplishing it instead of just hoping to accomplish it." *FRUS*, 1961–3, 4: doc. 32.

54. In the Jan. 1964 coup, General Nguyen Khanh ousted the Nov. coup leader General Duong Van Minh. See Logevall, *Choosing War*, 100–3.

55. Moyar, *Triumph Forsaken*, 360–61. On Chinese policy, see "Discussion between Mao Zedong and Pham Van Dong," Oct. 5, 1964, CWIHP Virtual Archive, Vietnam War Collection; Chen Jian, *Mao's China*, ch. 8; Yang Kuisong, "Changes in Mao Zedong's Attitude," 28–9.

56. Mao said, "*China's armies would not go beyond her borders to fight... Only if the United States attacked China would the Chinese fight.*" (emphasis in original) Mao interview with Snow, Jan. 9, 1965, *Works of Mao Tse-tung*. http://www.marxists.org/reference/archive/mao/selected works.

57. Chen Jian, *Mao's China*, 216. On Chinese warnings, see "Discussion between Zhou, Nguyen Van Hieu and Nguyen Thi Binh," May 16, 1965, CWIHP Virtual Archive, Vietnam War Collection.

58. Chen Jian, *Mao's China*.

59. On this point, see Nguyen Vu Tung, "Interpreting Beijing and Hanoi: A View of Sino-Vietnamese relations, 1965–1970," in "77 Conversations," CWIHP Working Paper no. 22, 43–65.

60. See memo of Zhou–Ho conversation, Mar. 1, 1965; memo of Zhou- Pham Van Dong conversation, Oct. 9, 1965; memo of Zhou conversation with Deng Xiaoping, Kang Shen, Le Duan, and Nguyen Duy Trinh, Apr. 13, 1966; memo of Zhou conversation with Pham Van Dong and Vo Nguyen Giap, Apr. 11, 1967; memo of Zhou- Pham Van Dong conversation, Apr. 19, 1968; memo of Zhou- Pham Hung conversation, June 29, 1968. CWIHP Virtual Archive, Vietnam War Collection. See also Yang Kuisong, "Changes in Mao Zedong's Attitude," 30–3. Soviet-bloc supplies were also shipped by sea.

61. On the U.S. Phoenix and CORDS programs see John Prados, *Safe for Democracy: The Secret Wars of the CIA* (Chicago: Ivan R. Dee, 2006),

207–39. Lewis Sorley documents the success of some pacification efforts after 1968, but this never compensated for the fundamental weaknesses of the Saigon regime and army. See *A Better War: The Unexamined Victories and Final Tragedy of America's Last Years in Vietnam* (Orlando FL: Harcourt, 1999).

62. Moyar, *Triumph Forsaken* (215–16) blames American journalists for undermining Diem by exaggerating the significance of Buddhist protests.

63. Bundy to LBJ, Feb. 7, 1965, *FRUS*, 1964–8, 2: doc. 84.

64. See Robert S. McNamara, *In Retrospect: The Tragedy and Lessons of Vietnam* (New York: Times Books, 1995), ch. 9.

65. See Larry Berman, *Lyndon Johnson's War* (New York: Norton, 1989).

66. In 1965, 1,863 Americans died in Vietnam. In 1966, the figure was 6,143; 1967: 11,153; 1968: 16,592; 1969: 11,616; 1970: 6,081; 1971: 2,357; 1972: 641.

67. Discussion between Zhou and Indonesian Prime Minister Subandrio, May 28, 1965, CWIHP Virtual Archive, Vietnam War Collection. Ho quoted in Pierre Brocheux, *Ho Chi Minh* (Cambridge: Cambridge University Press, 2007), 120.

68. See Herring, *America's Longest War*, 181–2.

69. This 1967 request was now renewed by Westmoreland and the JCS, but Clifford received no assurances that the additional 200,000 would turn the tide, and was told the enemy could match them. Clark Clifford, "A Viet Nam Reappraisal: The Personal History of One Man's View and How It Evolved," *Foreign Affairs*, 47/4 (July 1969), 601–22.

70. Johnson recalled, "For me, the key influence was the change in the situation in Vietnam. But other matters, especially our financial problems, played an important part in that final decision." Lyndon B. Johnson, *The Vantage Point: Perspectives of the Presidency, 1963–1969* (New York: Holt, Rinehart and Winston, 1971), 423.

71. Lodge, Taylor, Abe Fortas, and Amb. Robert Murphy dissented from the majority. See notes of meeting, Mar. 26, 1968, *FRUS*, 1964–68, 4: doc. 158.

72. See Herring, *America's Longest War*, ch. 6; Ellsberg, *Secrets*, 71–2. See also, *Public Papers of the Presidents of the United States: Lyndon B. Johnson, 1968–69*, Book I, 469–76.

73. See Hanhimäki and Westad, eds., *The Cold War*, 230–1; Simon Hall, *Peace and Freedom: The Civil Rights and Antiwar Movements of the 1960s* (Philadelphia: University of Pennsylvania Press, 2005). This is not to denigrate the impact of groups such as the Vietnam Veterans Against the War which emerged later (1971).

74. On contacts between Thieu's ambassador in Washington and the Nixon campaign, revealed in 2001, see Larry Berman, *No Peace, No Honor: Nixon, Kissinger and Betrayal in Vietnam* (New York: Touchstone, 2001), ch. 1.

Chapter 7—The Rise and Decline of Détente, 1969–1977

1. See Michael Harrison, *The Reluctant Ally: France and Atlantic Security* (Baltimore: Johns Hopkins University Press, 1981); Wolfgang Hanrieder, *Germany, America, and Europe: Forty Years of German Foreign Policy* (New Haven: Yale University Press, 1989). See also NATO's Dec. 1967 Harmel Report, www.nato.org. On Nixon's concern, see memo of Nixon–Pompidou conversation, Dec. 13, 1971, in William Burr, ed., *The Kissinger Transcripts: The Top Secret Talks with Beijng and Moscow* (New York: New Press, 1998). 36–7. For Kissinger's worries, see memo of Kissinger–Zhou conversation, Nov. 11, 1973, ibid., 175; Henry A. Kissinger, *White House Years* (Boston: Little, Brown, 1979), 529–30.

2. For Nixon's views, see *Foreign Affairs*, 46/1, Oct. 1967. For Kissinger's see his Oct. 20, 1969 memo to Nixon, *FRUS*, 1969–72, 1: doc. 41.

3. See English, *Russia and the Idea of the West*, 110–14.

4. See Raymond Garthoff, *Détente and Confrontation: American–Soviet Relations from Nixon to Reagan* (Washington: Brookings, 1994), 59, 63.

5. Kissinger, *American Foreign Policy* (New York: Norton, 1969), 58.

6. See David Calleo, *The Imperious Economy* (Cambridge MA: Harvard University Press, 1982).

7. Memo of conversation, Feb. 21, 1972, *FRUS*, 1969–72, 1: doc. 106; Kissinger Background briefing, Dec. 18, 1969. Ibid., doc 47.

8. Kissinger, *A World Restored: Metternich, Castlereagh and the Problems of Peace, 1812–1822* (Boston: Houghton Mifflin, 1957); Nixon, *Six Crises* (Garden City, NY: Doubleday, 1962).

9. On Oct. 12, 1970 Nixon remarked that the future depended "on whether we have the guts, the stamina, the wisdom to exert leadership." *FRUS*, 1969–72, 1: doc. 75, Editorial Note. Signals included Oct. 1969 and Oct. 1973 nuclear alerts, and the bombing campaigns against North Vietnam in May and December 1972. See Jeffrey Kimball, ed., *The Vietnam War Files: Uncovering the Secret History of Nixon Era Strategy* (Lawrence: University Press of Kansas, 2004), ch. 3; William Burr and Jeffery Kimball, "Nixon's Secret Nuclear Alert: Vietnam War Diplomacy and the Joint Chiefs of Staff Readiness Test, October 1969," *Cold War History*, 3/2 (Jan. 2003), 113–6.

10. Nixon stated in a Sept. 16, 1970, briefing, "We hope to work out with the Soviet Union a live-and-let-live attitude." *FRUS*, 1972–6, 1: doc. 71. On June 29, 1971, he said: "We will have a live-and-let-live situation with the Soviet Union" Ibid., doc. 91.

11. Giuseppe Tomasi di Lampedusa, *The Leopard* (New York: William Collins Sons, 1960), 28; Third Annual Report on U.S. Foreign Policy, Feb. 9, 1972, *FRUS*, 1969–72, 1: doc. 104.

12. See Kissinger, *White House* Years, 128–9.

13. See memo of Kissinger conversation with PRC U.N. ambassador Huang Hua, Aug. 4, 1972, in Burr, ed., *The Kissinger Transcripts*, 73; Kissinger, *White House Years*, 763.

14. Memo of Heath–Nixon conversation, Dec. 20, 1971, *FRUS*, 1969–72, 1: doc. 102; Memo of Kissinger conversation with Huang Hua, Aug. 4, 1972, in Burr, ed., *The Kissinger Transcripts*, 73.

15. See Chen Jian, *Mao's China*, ch. 9; Garthoff, *Détente and Confrontation*, 242–70; Kissinger off-the-record briefing, Dec. 9, 1970, *FRUS*, 1969–72, 1: doc. 80.

16. See Chen Jian, *Mao's China*, 269–71; Garthoff, *Détente and Confrontation* 269.

17. See memo of Nixon–Mao conversation, Feb. 21, 1972, in Burr, ed. *The Kissinger Transcripts*, 59–66.

18. The war was precipitated by Pakistan's suppression of the East Pakistan independence movement, leading to Indian intervention and the birth of Bangladesh.

19. The Chinese did not respond to Kissinger's Nov. 1973 bid to establish a hotline providing intelligence on Soviet activity. But a limited degree of co-operation later developed. See Burr, ed., *The Kissinger Transcripts*, 205–6, 269, 286. Robert C. McFarlane and Zofia Smardz *Special Trust: Pride, Principle and Politics inside the White House* (London: Cadell and Davies, 1994). On the Sept. 11, 1969 Zhou–Kosygin meeting, see Zhou letter to Kosygin, Sept. 18, 1969, and Zhou talk to Chinese delegation to border talks, Oct. 7, 1969, in CWIHP Virtual Archive, Sino-Soviet Relations Collection.

20. See memos of Kissinger's conversations with Huang Hua, July 6, 1973, and Deng Xiaoping, Nov. 24, 1974, in Burr, ed., *The Kissinger Transcripts*, 142, 300–1. For Mao's statement see memo of Kissinger conversation with Chinese leaders, Nov. 12, 1973, ibid., 184. See also memos of Kissinger's conversations with Deng, Apr. 14, 1973, ibid., 283, and Nov. 27, 1974, ibid., 309.

21. See transcripts of Kissinger–Deng conversations, Nov. 26 and 27, 1974, ibid., 290, 304, 311.

22. Zhou's remark to Haig quoted in Chen Jian, *Mao's China*, 273. See also memo of Kissinger–Deng conversation, Oct. 20, 1975, in Burr, ed., *The Kissinger Transcripts*, 384.

23. Kissinger, *White House Years*, 776–7.

24. See memo of Nixon–Dobrynin conversation, Oct. 19, 1969, *FRUS*, 1969–72, 1: doc. 40, Editorial Note.

25. Dobrynin, *In Confidence*, 193, 218; Tucker, *Political Culture and Leadership*, 128.

26. Khrushchev's successors changed the name of the Presidium back to Politburo. Zubok, *A Failed Empire*, 205.

27. Dobrynin, *In Confidence*, 193.

28. Zubok, *A Failed Empire*, 223.

29. Western access to the city was definitively guaranteed, but it was acknowledged that West Berlin was not part of the FRG.

30. See Zubok, *A Failed Empire*, 218; Garthoff, *Détente and Confrontation*, 290; Kissinger, *White House Years*, 1163–4.

31. Nixon quoted in Berman, *No Peace, No Honor*, 132.

32. The expression "in the balance" is Dobrynin's, *In Confidence*, 248.

33. Kissinger, *American Foreign Policy*, 97. Robert E. Osgood, "Introduction: The Nixon Doctrine and Strategy," in Osgood, ed. *Retreat From Empire?* (Baltimore: Johns Hopkins University Press, 1973).

34. See Nixon remarks, July 25, 1969. *FRUS*, 1969–72, 1: doc. 29, Editorial Note.

35. For denials, see Kissinger, *White House Years*, 1470. But his handwritten notation, "We want a decent interval," appears in the briefing book for his July 1971 meeting with Zhou. See Kimball, *The Vietnam War Files*, following p. 120. On pessimism, see Thomas Alan Schwartz, "'Henry . . . Winning an Election is Terribly Important': Partisan Politics in the History of U.S. Foreign Relations," *Diplomatic History*, 33/2, Apr. 2009, 174.

36. From Nixon's remarks, Sept. 16, 1970, *FRUS*, 1969–72, 1: doc. 71.

37. Nixon–Kissinger taped conversation, Sept. 21, 1971, quoted in Berman, *No Peace, No Honor*, 98. Nixon remarks at Camp David, *FRUS*, 1969–72, 1: doc. 38, Editorial Note.

38. See Nixon's overview at May 15, 1969 cabinet meeting, *FRUS*, 1969–76, 1: doc 25. Editorial note. The negotiations, begun in Aug. 1969, were disclosed to disarm domestic critics and impress world opinion.

39. During a demonstration against the Cambodian operation, National Guardsmen killed four students at Kent State University in Ohio. See also William Safire, *Before the Fall: An Inside View of the Pre-Watergate White House* (Piscataway, NJ: Transaction Publishers, 2005).

40. One of Nixon's main considerations in making this move was to counter intense domestic pressure to end the war.

41. See Berman, *No Peace, No Honor*, 176.

42. See Kissinger, *White House Years*, 1449.

43. Nixon remarks to cabinet, June 16, 1972, in *FRUS*, 1969–72, 1: doc. 119.

44. Zubok, *A Failed Empire*, 247.

45. Garthoff, *Détente and Confrontation*, 53, and ch. 2 in general.

46. McNamara had defined "assured destruction" as the capacity to destroy one-fourth to one-third of the Soviet population and two-thirds of Soviet industry.

47. With more domestic support and a reliable technology, Nixon might have developed an ABM system, regardless of MAD. See Avis Bohlen, "The Rise and Fall of Strategic Arms Control: What Did It All Mean Anyway?" (unpublished paper, courtesy of author).

48. See Garthoff, *Détente and Confrontation*, 152–8.

49. According to Nitze, Kissinger had prevented his (Nitze's) views from reaching Nixon, and the Watergate scandal then ruled out effective negotiations. *From Hiroshima to Glasnost*, 336–41.

50. See Nitze, "Assuring Strategic Stability in an Era of Détente," *Foreign Affairs*, 54/2, Jan. 1976, 207–32; "Intelligence Community Experiment in Competitive Analysis: Soviet Strategic Objectives, An Alternative View, Report of Team 'B'", Dec. 1976, especially 41–7 (emphasis in original). http://www.foia.cia.gov. See also Anne Hessing Cahn, *Killing Détente: The Right Attacks the CIA* (University Park: Pennsylvania State University Press, 1998).

51. Memo of Kissinger–Deng conversation, Nov. 27, 1974, in Burr, ed. *The Kissinger Transcripts*, 307.

52. See *FRUS*, 1969–72, 1: doc. 116.

53. Garthoff, *Détente and Confrontation*, 333, quoting Soviet commentary.

54. Kissinger Senate testimony, June 15, 1972, in *FRUS*, 1969–72, 1: doc. 118. On the security conference–MBFR trade-off, see Garthoff, *Détente and Confrontation*, 342.

55. See Gaddis, *Strategies of Containment*, ch. 9.

56. Kissinger, *American Foreign Policy*, 57.

57. See Kissinger to Nixon, Oct. 20, 1969, *FRUS*, 1969–72, 1: doc. 41. See also memo of Kissinger–Gromyko conversation, July 11, 1975, in Burr. ed., *The Kissinger Transcripts*, 363.

58. Kissinger briefing of Congressional leaders, May 19, 1972, *FRUS*, 1969–72, doc. 114; Garthoff, *Détente and Confrontation*, 345–46.

59. Kissinger did not renounce U.S. support of German reunification. But he did not see it as likely or particularly desirable.

60. As controversies surrounding détente worsened, Kissinger allowed negotiations to drag on assuming that, as long as they continued, Moscow would not take drastic measures, for example in the Middle East. See Burr, ed., *The Kissinger Transcripts*, 343.

61. See "State Department Summary of Remarks by Sonnenfeldt," *New York Times*, Apr. 6, 1976. The leaked summary became fodder in the 1976 electoral campaign. Kissinger issued a statement correcting Sonnenfeldt, but he does not appear to have disagreed fundamentally. See also Kissinger, *Years of Renewal* (New York: Simon and Schuster, 1999), 862–6.

62. As Garthoff (*Détente and Confrontation*, 410) shows, Moscow had warned of an explosion, but the U.S. had discounted this, assuming war could only be a disaster for Sadat.

63. See Zubok, *A Failed Empire*, 238–40.

64. On the Soviet view, see Garthoff, *Détente and Confrontation*, 442–6. Transcript of Kissinger–Huang Hua conversation, Oct. 25, 1973, Burr, ed., *The Kissinger Transcripts*, 157.

65. On Brezhnev's anger, see, Burr, ed., *The Kissinger Transcripts*, 245–6. The U.S. nuclear alert in Oct. 1973 showed scant regard for a joint "Agreement on the Prevention of Nuclear War" signed at the June 1973 U.S.–Soviet summit, calling for consultation and restraint.

66. See Merle L. Pribbenow, "North Vietnam's Final Offensive: Strategic Endgame Nonpareil," *Parameters*, winter 1999–2000, 58–71.

67. This should not be confused with the temporary Arab embargo of the U.S. and the Netherlands for supporting Israel in the war.

68. See Westad, *The Global Cold War*, ch. 6; Piero Gleijeses, *Conflicting Missions: Havana, Washington, and Africa, 1959–1976* (Chapel Hill: University of North Carolina Press, 2002).

69. See Prados, *Safe for Democracy*, 440–54.

70. Gleijeses, *Conflicting Missions*.

71. See Garthoff, *Détente and Confrontation*, 567.

72. According to Westad (*The Global Cold War*, 231) this included U.S. support for its "homelands" strategy, the end of an arms embargo, and tolerance of Pretoria's nuclear weapons program.

73. See memo of Castro–Todor Zhivkov conversation, Mar. 11, 1976. CWIHP Virtual Archive. Anti-Colonialism in the Cold War Collection. In Apr. 1976, there were 36,000 Cuban troops in Angola.

74. For Castro's assessment, see his conversation with Zhivkov, cited previous note. See also Kissinger, *Years of Upheaval*, ch. 26.

75. For the argument that détente was over-sold, see Burr, ed., *The Kissinger Transcripts:* 470; Cahn, *Killing Détente*, 49, 52.

76. The "NEP" ended the dollar's convertibility into gold and imposed a temporary 10 percent surcharge on imports. The goal was to devalue the dollar and do away with the constraints of the Bretton Woods system, regardless of European and Japanese wishes.

77. These included previously undisclosed illegal domestic operations aimed at dissidents, and plots to kill Castro and Rafael Trujillo.

78. In the reshuffle, George H. W. Bush replaced William Colby as CIA Director and General Brent Scowcroft became national security adviser. See Kissinger, *Years of Renewal*, 834–44.

79. Garthoff, *Détente and Confrontation*, 455; Cahn, *Killing Détente*, 30–1.

80. Pipes led the team evaluating Soviet strategic objectives. His advisory panel included Nitze and Paul Wolfowitz.

81. Dana Allin, *Cold War Illusions: America, Europe, and Soviet Power, 1969–1989* (New York: St Martin's Press, 1997).

82. According to Zubok, *A Failed Empire*, 232–34, Jewish emigration rose from 2,673 in 1969 to 29,821 in 1972. In 1974, the Kremlin secretly assured Kissinger that it would allow some 50,000 Jews to emigrate per year, but did not want a formal, public agreement. Informed by Kissinger, Jackson announced it publicly, leading the Kremlin to withdraw the offer. See Paula Stern, *Water's Edge: Domestic Politics and the Making of American Foreign Policy* (Westport, CT: Greenwood Press, 1979).

83. Memo of Kissinger conversation with staff, Mar. 18, 1974, in Burr, ed., *The Kissinger Transcripts*, 224–5. In September 1973, the USSR had done nothing when the CIA-supported Chilean military deposed the leftist government of Salvador Allende.

84. See memo Kissinger–Gromyko conversation, Jan. 23, 1976, in Burr, ed., *The Kissinger Transcripts*, 462.

85. Brezhnev suffered grand mal seizures during the Vladivostok summit.

86. See Westad, *The Global Cold War* 206, and chs. 5 and 6, in general; Dobrynin, *In Confidence*, 404; Zubok, *A Failed Empire*, 51–252.
87. Soviet aircraft may have been involved before Nov. 11, 1975, but advisers arrived in Luanda the day after.
88. See Dobrynin, *In Confidence*, 405; Westad, *The Global Cold War*, 242, characterizing the Soviet view.
89. See Stephen G. Brooks and William C. Wohlforth, "Power, Globalization, and the End of the Cold War: Reevaluating a Landmark Case for Ideas," *International Security*, 25/3 (winter 2000–1) (5–53), 16–17.
90. See Kissinger, *Years of Renewal*, 868.
91. The Gang, who tried to purge Deng again in Apr. 1976, lost power after Mao's death in September, and were arrested in October 1976.
92. See memo of Kissinger–Deng conversation, July 8, 1975, in Burr, ed., *The Kissinger Transcripts*, 384–5. See also Kissinger memo to Nixon, Mar. 2, 1973, ibid., 115.
93. See Kissinger, *Years of Upheaval*, 122–7, 300–1, 416–17, 979–80.
94. See Ellsberg, *Secrets*, ch. 31.
95. See Kevin Phillips, *Post-Conservative America: People, Politics and Ideology in a Time of Crisis* (New York: Random House, 1982).
96. Kevin Phillips, *The Emerging Republican Majority*, (New Rochelle, NY: Arlington House, 1969).

Chapter 8—To the Panic of '79

1. See Kissinger, "Between the Old Left and the New Right," *Foreign Affairs*, 78/3, May–June 1999, 106. Brezhnev's Jan. 1977 speech quoted in Garthoff, *Détente and Confrontation*, 647, 850. Brezhnev to Carter, Feb. 4, 1977, CWIHP Virtual Archive, U.S.–Soviet Relations Collection.
2. Garthoff, *Détente and Confrontation*, 819–20, notes Soviet dismay after the publication of Kissinger's *White House Years* in 1979.
3. Ford said Kissinger had the thinnest skin of anyone he had known in public life. Bob Woodward, "Ford Disagreed with Bush about Invading Iraq," *Washington Post*, Dec. 28, 2006.
4. See Brzezinski, *Power and Principle: Memoirs of the National Security Adviser, 1977–1981* (London: Weidenfeld and Nicolson, 1983), 148–9.
5. See ibid., 43. See also, Brzezinski, "America in a Hostile World," *Foreign Policy*, 23 (Summer, 1976), 83.

6. Jimmy Carter, *Keeping Faith: Memoirs of a President* (New York: Bantam, 1982), 142, 144.

7. Garthoff, *Détente and Confrontation*, 889–90, Brzezinski, *Power and Principle*, 157–64; Strobe Talbott, *Endgame: The Inside Story of SALT II* (New York: Harper and Row, 1979), 155.

8. For Georgi Arbatov, the proposals confirmed to Moscow that Carter "was not serious." Quoted in Garthoff, *Détente and Confrontation*, 26 n. 8.

9. See Zubok, *A Failed Empire*, 237; Odd Arne Westad, "Beginnings of the End: How the Cold War Crumbled," in Silvio Pons and Federico Romero, eds., *Reinterpreting the End of the Cold War* (London: Frank Cass, 2005).

10. On Brezhnev–Grechko confrontation, see Zubok, *A Failed Empire*, 245.

11. Brezhnev to Carter, Feb. 27, 1977, CWIHP Virtual Archive, U.S.–Soviet Relations Collection. Gromyko–Ustinov–Andropov memo, and Brezhnev's Feb. 27 letter to Carter are quoted in Dobrynin, *In Confidence*, 391–2.

12. See English, *Russia and the Idea of the West*, 150–4.

13. Dobrynin, *In Confidence*, 404–5.

14. This is Westad's judgment, *The Global Cold War*, 271.

15. Memo of Castro–Honecker conversation, Apr. 4, 1977, quoted ibid., 274.

16. See ibid., 261; Garthoff, *Détente and Confrontation*, 698–9, Piero Gleijeses, "Moscow's Proxy? Cuba and Africa, 1975–1988," *Journal of Cold War Studies*, 8/4, fall 2006 (98–146), 108. Cyrus Vance, *Hard Choices* (New York: Simon and Schuster, 1983), 73.

17. Westad, *The Global Cold War*, 276.

18. Brzezinski, *Power and Principle*, 183.

19. The treaties returning sovereignty to Panama were under consideration in spring 1978.

20. See Gleijeses, "Moscow's Proxy?"

21. Brzezinski, *Power and Principle*, ch. 6; Annex I.

22. Ibid., 211.

23. Garthoff, *Détente and Confrontation*, 766–7, 784.

24. Ibid., 767–70, 785.

25. Ibid., 783; Richard Evans, *Deng Xiaoping and the Making of Modern China* (London: Penguin, 1997), ch. 12; Li Lanqing, *Breaking Through: The Birth of China's Opening-up Policy* (Oxford: Oxford University Press, 2009).

26. Garthoff, *Détente and Confrontation*, 869–70; Hoffman, *The Dead Hand*, 23. PD 59 was the latest in a series of refinements begun in 1974 to answer an alleged Soviet war-fighting doctrine.

27. Carter quoted in Garthoff, *Détente and Confrontation*, 1067.
28. Nitze, "Assuring Strategic Stability in an Era of Détente" (Ch. 7 n. 50 above); Allin, *Cold War Illusions*, 59–65.
29. See Garthoff, *Détente and Confrontation*, 857–58.
30. Viktor Starodubov, quoted in Zubok, *A Failed Empire*, 243. Along with the MX, the U.S. was developing the Trident II missile and enhancing the accuracy and power of the already-deployed Minuteman III.
31. For Kennan's argument, see Ch. 2.
32. "Intelligence Community Experiment in Competitive Analysis, Soviet Strategic Objectives: An Alternative View, Report of team 'B' ", 43.
33. Between 1977 and 1982, 243 SS-20s were deployed aimed at Europe, and 108 aimed at China. Garthoff, *Détente and Confrontation*, 973.
34. Allin, *Cold War Illusions*, 84; H. Schmidt, "The 1977 Alastair Buchan Memorial Lecture," *Survival*, 20/1, Jan. 1978, 3–4.
35. On increases, see Garthoff, *Détente and Confrontation*, 936.
36. The "neutron bomb," or Enhanced Radiation Weapon, was an artillery shell thought to be particularly effective against tanks. The administration convinced Schmidt to accept deployment (the weapon was deeply unpopular in Germany), then deferred a decision because of Carter's moral qualms.
37. When the dollar fell, the deutschmark appreciated against European currencies. To stabilize trade relations between the FRG and France, Giscard and Schmidt launched the European Monetary System in 1979.
38. On Moscow's view, see Garthoff, *Détente and Confrontation*, 968–9; Vojtech Mastny, "How Able was Able Archer?", *Journal of Cold War Studies*, 11/1, winter 2009 (108–23), 112.
39. Dobrynin, *In Confidence*, 430–2.
40. Kennan quoted in Allin, *Cold War Illusions*, 112. See also George Kennan, "Zero Options," *New York Review of Books*, May 12, 1983, 3.
41. For Nitze's view see Strobe Talbott, *Deadly Gambits: The Reagan Administration and the Stalemate in Nuclear Arms Control* (New York: Knopf, 1984), 135–6. For Richard Pipes's, see Brzezinski, *Power and Principle*, 309.
42. See the testimony of V. V. Shlykov, a high military intelligence official, in Ellman and Kantorovich, eds., *The Destruction of the Soviet Economic System*, 43–4.
43. See for example Robert W. Tucker, "America in Decline: The Foreign Policy of 'Maturity,'" *Foreign Affairs*, 58/1, Jan. 1980, 474.

44. Soviet doctrine defined the military's role not as encouraging revolution but deterring counter-revolutionary pressure. See Garthoff, *Détente and Confrontation*, 750–1, 876.
45. Quoted in Westad, *The Global Cold War*, 296.
46. Brzezinski, *Power and Principle*, 427; Garthoff, *Détente and Confrontation*, 1050, n. 202. See also Richard N. Haas, *War of Necessity, War of Choice: A Memoir of Two Iraqi Wars* (New York: Simon and Schuster, 2009), 14.
47. See Westad, *The Global Cold War*, ch. 8; Garthoff, *Détente and Confrontation*, ch. 26.
48. Brzezinski, *Power and Principle*, 430.
49. On this point, see Westad, *The Global Cold War*, 323.
50. See "The CIA's Intervention in Afghanistan: Interview with Zbigniew Brzezinski," posted at globalresearch.ca. (translation of interview published by *Le Nouvel Observateur*, Jan. 15–21, 1998.)
51. See transcripts of Politburo meetings, Mar. 17, 18, 19, 1979, CWIHP Virtual Archive, Soviet Invasion of Afghanistan Collection; Westad, *The Global Cold War*, 309.
52. See Garthoff, *Détente and Confrontation*, ch. 24.
53. See Westad, *The Global Cold War*, 319; Zubok, *A Failed Empire*, 262.
54. Andropov personal memo to Brezhnev, Dec. 1, 1979; "Report on events in Afghanistan on Dec. 27–28, 1979," Dec. 31, 1979. CWIHP Virtual Archive, Soviet Invasion of Afghanistan Collection.
55. On the Dec. 8 and 12, 1979 meetings, see Dobrynin, *In Confidence*, 437–8; Zubok, *A Failed Empire*, 262–4.
56. See Calleo, *The Imperious Economy*.
57. Brooks and Wohlforth, "Power, Globalization, and the End of the Cold War," 20.
58. Brzezinski, *Power and Principle*, (quoting from his diary), 189. Carter quoted in Garthoff, *Détente and Confrontation*, 1,067.
59. In addition to the conversion of much of the South to the Republican Party, developments included the population shift from the "Rust-belt" (Northeast and Mid-West) to the "Sun-belt," the more libertarian and conservative West and Southwest. An organized "new right" emerged in the 1970s opposed to liberal social policies, feminism, and gay-rights. The new right overlapped with a "religious right," opposed to an alleged secularist tide threatening traditional values. Wealthy conservatives fostered an intellectual "counter-establishment" housed in Washington-based "think-tanks" like the American Enterprise Institute and the Heritage Foundation.

Chapter 9—Stirrings of Change, 1980–1985

1. Coral Bell, *The Reagan Paradox: American Foreign Policy in the 1980s* (New Brunswick, NJ: Rutgers University Press, 1989); Beth A. Fischer, *The Reagan Reversal: Foreign Policy and the End of the Cold War* (Columbia: University of Missouri Press, 1997).

2. Reagan quoted in James Mann, *The Rebellion of Ronald Reagan: A History of the End of the Cold War* (New York: Viking, 2009), 28–9.

3. Defense spending reached 14.2 percent of GDP in 1953. The highest level under Reagan was 6.2 percent in 1986.

4. See National Security Decision Directive 75, "U.S. Relations with the USSR," Jan. 17, 1983, in McFarlane and Smardz, *Special Trust*, 372–80. See also Jack Matlock, *Reagan and Gorbachev* (New York: Random House, 2004), 76. Then NSC-staffer Matlock cites his notes on goals from a high-level meeting on Nov. 19, 1983. For another view, see Peter Schweizer, *Victory* (New York: Atlantic Monthly Press, 1994).

5. On Feb. 17, 1983, he observed that the U.S. ambassador to El Salvador, "under the direction of the same kind of St. Dept. bureaucrats who made Castro possible are screwing up the situation in El Salvador." See Ronald Reagan, *The Reagan Diaries* (New York: HarperCollins, 2007), 132.

6. This was Nixon's advice to Dobrynin in Nov. 1980. See Dobrynin, *In Confidence*, 465, 491–2.

7. See Lou Cannon, *President Reagan: The Role of a Lifetime* (New York: Public Affairs, 2000), 381; Reagan, *The Reagan Diaries*, entry for June 25, 1982, 90–1.

8. See John Patrick Diggins, *Ronald Reagan: Fate, Freedom, and the Making of History* (New York: Norton, 2007); Mann, *The Rebellion of Ronald Reagan*; Daniel Deudney and G. John Ikenberry "Who Won the Cold War," *Foreign Policy*, 87, summer 1992, 123–38.

9. See Christopher Andrew and Oleg Gordievsky, eds., *Comrade Kryuchkov's Instructions: Top Secret Files on KGB Foreign Operations, 1975–1985* (Stanford, CA: Stanford University Press, 1993), 67.

10. Andropov left the KGB to become Secretary of the CPSU CC in May 1982, six months before succeeding Brezhnev.

11. Gorbachev to his wife Raisa, Mar. 1985. See *Memoirs* (New York: Doubleday, 1995), 165 (italics in original).

12. Tucker, *Political Culture and Leadership*, 108.

13. See Zubok, *A Failed Empire*, 268, 277; English, *Russia and the Idea of the West*, 139, 165; Westad, *The Global Cold War*, 284–7.

14. Andropov's Nov. 1982 statement quoted in English, *Russia and the Idea of the West*, 178. On IEMSS analyst E. Ambartsumov's Nov. 1983 article, see ibid., 178.

15. After the 1970 crisis, Poland's economic strategy was based on heavy borrowing from the West. Between 1971 and 1980, hard-currency debt went from $1.2 billion to $23.5 billion. Ben Slay, *The Polish Economy* (Princeton: Princeton University Press, 1994), 36–49.

16. Andropov quoted in Zubok, *A Failed Empire*, 267. See also the Politburo commission's Special Dossier, Aug. 28, 1980, CWIHP Virtual Archive, Poland in the Cold War Collection.

17. See Vojtech Mastny, "The Soviet Non-Invasion of Poland in 1980/81 and the End of the Cold War," CWIHP Working Paper No. 23, Sept. 1998, especially 8–9, 12–15; Mark Kramer, "The Kuklinski Files and the Polish Crisis of 1980–81: An Analysis of the Newly Released CIA Documents on Ryszard Kuklinski," CWIHP, Working Paper no. 59, Mar. 2009.

18. Session of the the Politburo, Dec. 10, 1981, CWIHP Virtual Archive, Poland in the Cold War Collection. Emphasis added.

19. See Alec Nove, *An Economic History of the USSR*, 389.

20. This is according to the CIA and G. I. Khanin's later calculations. Official figures put growth at about 4 percent. See Brooks and Wohlforth, "Power, Globalization, and the End of the Cold War," 17; Khanin essay in Ellman and Kontorovich, eds., *The Destruction of the Soviet Economic System*, 84–5, 93.

21. These included microelectronics, computers, aerospace, telecommunications, new materials, biotechnology, and chemicals. Brooks and Wohlforth, "Power," 36–7.

22. See Gorbachev, *Memoirs*, 136, 215.

23. See Stephen Kotkin, *Armageddon Averted* (Oxford: Oxford University Press, 2000), 117.

24. Zhores Medvedev, *Andropov* (Oxford: Blackwell, 1983), chs. 8, 15; Tucker *Political Culture and Leadership*, 131. On USSR work-stoppages, see Mark Kramer, "Soviet Deliberations during the Polish Crisis, 1980–81," CWIHP Special Working Paper No. 1, (Apr. 1999), 26.

25. Kosygin died on Dec. 18, 1980, Suslov, Jan. 25, 1982, Brezhnev, Nov. 11, 1982, Andropov, Feb. 9, 1984, Ustinov, Dec. 20, 1984, and Andropov's successor Chernenko, Mar. 10, 1985.

26. Gorbachev quoted in English, *Russia and the Idea of the West*, 181, 220. On Chernyaev's view, see ibid., 183.

27. Andropov Nov. 1982 remark quoted in Dobrynin, *In Confidence*, 513.
28. Ibid., 491–3.
29. See Garthoff, "Foreign Intelligence and the Historiography of the Cold War," 40; Andrew and Gordievsky, eds., *Comrade Kryuchkov's Instructions*, ch. 4. On "Perimeter," tested in 1984 and made operational in 1985, see Hoffman, *The Dead Hand*, ch. 6.
30. See Dobrynin, *In Confidence*, 528; English, *Russia and the Idea of the West*, 173; Cannon, *President Reagan*, 81–2.
31. Andropov quoted in English, *Russia and the Idea of the West*, 173.
32. According to Dobrynin, *In Confidence*, (537), Ustinov talked Andropov (furious with the military) out of a public apology. For Andropov on Reagan, and the official statement, see ibid., 539–40.
33. Quoted in Fischer, *The Reagan Reversal*, 129.
34. After William Clark's departure, Reagan picked McFarlane as a compromise between the hawkish Jeane Kirkpatrick and moderate James Baker. McFarlane interviewed by Fischer, ibid., 133. See also Andrews and Gordievsky, *Comrade Kryuchkov's Instructions*, 85–8; Mastny, "How Able was Able Archer?," 119; Hoffman, *The Dead Hand*, 55.
35. Mastny, "How Able was Able Archer?"
36. On McFarlane and Weinberger, see Fischer, *The Reagan Reversal*, 133–4. On CIA analysis, see Mann, *The Rebellion of Ronald Reagan*, 78. See also George Shultz, *Turmoil and Triumph: My Years as Secretary of State* (New York: Simon and Schuster, 1993) 375, 464.
37. The film depicted the consequences for Lawrence, KA of a limited attack on near-by SAC headquarters. See entry for Oct. 10, 1983, *The Reagan Diaries*, 186.
38. See Fischer, *The Reagan Reversal*, 134–5 (who attributes the phrase "genuine anxiety" to McFarlane).
39. Ronald Reagan, *An American Life* (New York: Simon and Schuster, 1990), 588.
40. *The Reagan Diaries*, entry for Nov. 18, 1983, 199; Cannon, *President Reagan*, 275.
41. Lawrence Wittner, *Toward Nuclear Abolition: A History of the Nuclear Disarmament Movement, 1971–Present*, vol. 3, (Stanford, CA: Stanford University Press, 2003), 261.
42. After seeing the film privately he was unsure of its effects. On Nov. 18, shortly before its public showing, he wrote: "it's 'anti-nuke' propaganda but we're going to take it over & say it shows why we must keep on doing what we're doing." *The Reagan Diaries*, 189, 199.

43. Cannon, *President Reagan*, 447–8.
44. Mondale quoted in Mann, *The Rebellion of Ronald Reagan*, 79. Poll quoted in Cannon, *President Reagan*, 449. The figures also reflected dissatisfaction with policy toward Nicaragua and Lebanon, where 250 marines had died in a terrorist attack.
45. See Cannon, *President Reagan*, ch. 18.
46. See Matlock, *Reagan and Gorbachev*, 80–7.
47. http://www.reagan.utexas.edu/archives/speeches/1984/11684a.htm. On the Soviet reaction, see Matlock, *Reagan and Gorbachev*, 80–7.
48. Dobrynin, *In Confidence*, 555–7.
49. The ABM dispute pitted the Pentagon and McFarlane, favoring a loose interpretation, against Shultz who wanted one restricting SDI development. On rhetoric, see Raymond Garthoff, *The Great Transition: American–Soviet Relations and the End of the Cold War* (Washington: Brookings Institution Press, 1994), 219–20.
50. Anatoly S. Chernyaev, *My Six Years with Gorbachev* (University Park: Pennsylvania State University Press, 2000), 5.
51. Gorbachev quoted in English, *Russia and the Idea of the West*, 189. See also Zubok, *A Failed Empire*, 278.
52. See Dobrynin, *In Confidence*, 565; Gorbachev, *Memoirs*, 166. English (*Russia and the Idea of the West*, 196–7, 322) argues Ustinov might have opposed Gorbachev. See also Chernyaev, *My Six Years*, 19–21.
53. See Dobrynin, *In Confidence*, 571; Gorbachev, *Memoirs*, 162.
54. See Margaret Thatcher, *The Downing Street Years* (London: HarperCollins, 1993), 463; Gorbachev, *Memoirs*, 180. According to Yakovlev, Gromyko had promised to support Gorbachev in return for appointment to chairmanship of the Supreme Soviet. Hoffman, *The Dead Hand*, 186.
55. Chernyaev, *My Six Years*, 22.
56. Gorbachev, *Memoirs*, 167, 217–19.
57. See Ellman and Kontorovich, eds. *The Destruction of the Soviet Economic System;* Nove, *An Economic History of the USSR*, 126–32, 400.
58. Gorbachev, *Memoirs*, 401; Frédéric Bozo et al., eds. *Europe and the End of the Cold War: A Reappraisal* (London: Routledge, 2009), 209–10.
59. Gorbachev, (undated) quoted in Chernyaev, *My Six Years*, 83–84.
60. Chernyaev, *My Six Years*, 32, quoting May 5, 1985 diary entry; Dobrynin, *In Confidence*, 591; Garthoff, *The Great Transition*, 228.
61. Gorbachev, *Memoirs*, 405.

62. Bell, *The Reagan Paradox*, 70–1. Gorbachev cited the $70 billion figure in an interview with *Time*, Sept. 9, 1985, 5.

63. For Gorbachev on the military-industrial complex, see *Memoirs*, 406.

64. On Gorbachev's remarks to Reagan, see ibid., 406–7; Leffler, *Soul of Mankind*, 383. On the Soviet alternative, see also, Chernyaev, *My Six Years*, 90.

65. See Gorbachev's account of his May 1988 exchange with Reagan, *Memoirs*, 455.

66. Yakovlev quoted in Garthoff, *The Great Transition*, 221–2.

67. *Time*, Sept. 9, 1985, 3.

68. See Mann, *The Rebellion of Ronald Reagan*, 82–93. Gorbachev, *Memoirs*, 405; Dobrynin, *In Confidence*, 592.

69. *The Reagan Diaries*, entry for Nov. 22, 1985, 371.

Chapter 10—Putting an End to the Cold War, 1986–1990

1. Chernyaev *My Six Years* (54) described him thus in early 1986.

2. Excerpt from Chernyaev Diary, May 2, 1989, in CWIHP Document Reader, "The End of the Cold War." Not until a July 1991 central committee plenum did Gorbachev explicitly abandon Marxism–Leninism.

3. Chernyaev, *My Six Years*, 144.

4. Zubok, *A Failed Empire*, 330. Michnik quoted in Martin Malia, *The Soviet Tragedy* (New York: Maxwell Macmillan International, 1994), 457.

5. Chernyaev, *My Six Years*, 59; Garthoff, *The Great Transition*, 252–3.

6. Gorbachev quoted in Garthoff, *The Great Transition*, 258–60 (emphasis in original); English, *Russia and the Idea of the West*, 210–13; Chernyaev, *My Six Years*, 57, 75–7.

7. Shultz, *Turmoil and Triumph*, 711.

8. See Garthoff, *The Great Transition*, 270; Cannon, *President Reagan*, ch. 19.

9. Gorbachev (in two separate meetings on Mar. 24, 1986), quoted in Chernyaev, *My Six Years*, 56–7.

10. Zubok, *A Failed Empire*, 288.

11. Ibid., 288. The expression is Chernyaev's, *My Six Years*, 65.

12. Speech quoted in Robert English, "Ideas and the End of the Cold War," in Pons and Romero, eds., *Reinterpreting the End*, 128–9; Zubok, *A Failed Empire*, 299.

13. Chernyaev, *My Six Years*, 80–1.

14. Shultz, *Turmoil and Triumph*, 690, 695. The deficit reached a decade-high $237.9 billion in 1986.
15. See State Dept. "Iceland Chronology," Oct. 14, 1986, Digital National Security Archives (DNSA).
16. State Dept. Memo of Conversation, Oct. 16, 1986 (containing the transcript of sessions on Oct. 12), DNSA.
17. Reagan told Gorbachev that the "so-called right wing" at home was "kicking his brains out" on the SDI issue. Ibid., 13. See also Nitze, *From Hiroshima to Glasnost*, 427–8; Soviet transcript of the Oct. 12 meetings, published by the Foreign Broadcast Information Service, Sept. 20, 1993 (available at the DNSA); Matlock, *Reagan and Gorbachev*, 238. Matlock changed his mind after concluding (oddly) that Gorbachev had *not* agreed to eliminate ballistic missiles.
18. Quoted in Mann, *The Rebellion of Ronald Reagan*, 234.
19. Chernyaev, *My Six Years*, 89–90.
20. See Chernyaev notes taken Oct. 12, 1986, CWIHP Document Reader, "The End".
21. For the view that Reagan had helped Gorbachev, see Mann *The Rebellion of Ronald Reagan*, 101–2.
22. Iran and Iraq had been at war since September 1980.
23. See Cannon, *President Reagan*, chs. 19–20.
24. Ibid., 694.
25. Shultz, *Turmoil and Triumph*, 904.
26. See Mann, *The Rebellion of Ronald Reagan*, chs. 5, 7, 9.
27. See Allin, *Cold War Illusions*, 177.
28. Gorbachev quoted in Chernyaev, *My Six Years*, 92; Malia, *The Soviet Tragedy*, 425.
29. Chernyaev, *My Six Years*, 301; Zubok, *A Failed Empire*, 301.
30. Minutes of Politiburo meeting, Feb. 26, 1987, INF Document Collection, DNSA. Massie's message came from her contact, KGB officer Radomir Bogdanov. The quoted text is from Carlucci's notes of her meeting with Reagan (emphasis in original). Mann, *The Rebellion of Ronald Reagan*, 113.
31. See Mann, Ibid., 113–14; Garthoff, *The Great Transition*, 305, 312; Hoffman, *The Dead Hand*, 278.
32. Gorbachev's chief-of staff Valery Boldin believed that Raisa had convinced her husband the incident had been staged.

33. Chernyaev, *My Six Years*, 116–18. Rust's plane was pursued but higher authorities, probably remembering KAL 007, denied authorization to shoot it down.

34. See Garthoff, *The Great Transition*, 306; Chernayev notes on Politburo session, May 8, 1987, CWIHP Document Reader, "The End." Thatcher visited Moscow, Mar. 28–Apr. 1, 1987.

35. Ronald Reagan (June 12, 1987), *Remarks on East–West Relations in West Berlin at the Brandenburg Gate* available at http://www.reagan.utexas.edu/archives/speeches/1987/061287d.htm. See also Mann, *The Rebellion of Ronald Reagan*, Part III.

36. Ibid., 120, 199–206.

37. Weinberger insisted on converting INF into SRINF and giving them to Germany, while deploying the residual 100 INF permitted by the treaty in Alaska.

38. See Shultz, *Turmoil and Triumph*, 896–7.

39. SFRC report, Sept. 20, 1987, mentioned ibid., 989; Garthoff, *The Great Transition*, 329.

40. Garthoff, *The Great Transition*, 352, 355.

41. Assistant Secretary of State Rozanne Ridgway, quoted in Mann, *The Rebellion of Ronald Reagan*, 310.

42. Malia, *The Soviet Tragedy*, 432.

43. English, "Ideas and the End of the Cold War," 131.

44. This was a classic half-measure, contributing to the economy's break-down.

45. Gorbachev conversation with PCI leader A. Natta, Mar. 1988, quoted in M. P. Rey, "Gorbachev's New Thinking and Europe," in Bozo et al., eds., *Europe and the End of the Cold War*, 29. See by the same author, "'Europe is Our Common Home': A Study of Gorbachev's Diplomatic Concept," *Cold War History*, 4/2 (Jan. 2004), 33–65.

46. Kohl had incurred Gorbachev's wrath by comparing him in 1986 to Joseph Goebbels.

47. From Chernyaev's notes of the Politburo meeting, Nov. 3, 1988, Chernyaev, *My Six Years*, 195.

48. Anonymous "Notes for Presentation at the Politburo session, Dec. 27, 1988," CWIHP Document Reader, "The End."

49. Chernyaev notes, Oct. 31, 1988, CWIHP Document Reader, "The End."

50. Kennan, *Memoirs*, i: 293.

51. Mikhail Gorbachev, Dec. 7, 1988 Speech to the United Nations, available at http://isc.temple.edu/hist249/course/Documents/gorbachev_speech_to_UN.htm

(emphasis added). On Bush's assurances to Gorbachev in Dec. 1987, see Michael Beschloss and Strobe Talbott, *At the Highest Levels: The Inside Story of the End of the Cold War* (Boston: Little, Brown, 1993), 34.

52. Thousands of people gathered at the wall after GDR official Gunter Schabowski, in an impromptu press conference, interpreted the government's new travel policy as applying "immediately." Lacking precise orders except to avoid bloodshed, guards opened the wall around 10:30 P.M. on Nov. 9.

53. See Mary Elise Sarotte, *1989: The Struggle to Create Post-Cold War Europe* (Princeton: Princeton University Press, 2009); Timothy Garton Ash, "1989!" in *New York Review of Books*, 54/17, Nov. 5, 2009, 4–8. The Bulgarian Communists replaced their leader Todor Zhivkov in late 1989 and transformed themselves into a socialist party.

54. Westad ("Beginnings of the End," 75–6) suggests December 1981; Mark Kramer argues for 1989. See his "Gorbachev and the Demise of East European Communism," in Pons and Romero, eds., *Reinterpreting the End of the Cold War*, 180.

55. Communiqué quoted in ibid., 181. Gorbachev quoted in Svetlana Savranskaya, "In the Name of Europe: Soviet withdrawal from Eastern Europe," in Bozo et al., eds., *Europe and the End of the Cold War*, 40–3.

56. See Jacques Lévesque, *The Enigma of 1989: The USSR and the Liberation of Eastern Europe* (Berkeley: University of Calfornia Press, 1997). On the term "velvet revolution," see Timothy Garton Ash, "Velvet Revolution: The Prospects," *New York Review of Books*, 54/19, Dec. 3, 2009, 20.

57. See Feb. 1989 MO memo to Yakovlev, in CWIHP Document Reader, "The End."

58. Zubok, *A Failed Empire*, (318–21) emphasizes this point.

59. Garton Ash, "Velvet Revolution," 20.

60. The quoted words are Savranskaya's, in "In the Name of Europe," 36.

61. Kramer, "Gorbachev and the Demise," 184–5. See also Georgi Shakhnazarov's Oct. 6, 1988 memo to Gorbachev, CWIHP Document Reader, "The End."

62. Kramer, "Gorbachev and the Demise," 187–91.

63. See record of Gorbachev–SED leaderhip conversation, Oct. 7, 1989; Chernyaev Diary excerpt, Oct. 11, 1989; Memo of Krenz-Gorbachev conversation (GDR version), Nov. 1, 1989, in CWIHP Document Reader, "The End."

64. Malia, *The Soviet Tragedy*, 450.

65. See Foreign Ministry memo on Eastern Europe, Feb. 24, 1989, and MO memo to Yakovlev, Feb. 1989, in CWIHP Document Reader, "The End."

66. Memo of Krenz–Gorbachev conversation, Nov. 1, 1989, ibid.

67. Quoted in Rey, "Gorbachev's New Thinking and Europe," 32.

68. MO memo to Yakovlev, Feb. 1989, CWIHP Document Reader, "The End." Kramer, "Gorbachev and the Demise," 189; Jacques Lévesque, "In the Name of Europe's Future," in Bozo et al., eds., *Europe and the End of the Cold War.*

69. Record of Gorbachev–Kohl conversation, June 12, 1989; Record of Gorbachev–Thatcher conversation, Sept. 23, 1989, CWIHP Document Reader, "The End."

70. Don Oberdorfer, "Kissinger offers Bush an East–West Plan on Central Europe," *International Herald Tribune*, Feb. 13, 1989.

71. For example at Governor's Island, N.Y. in Dec. 1988. See Record of the Politiburo meeting, Dec. 27–8, 1988; Bush letter to Gorbachev, Jan. 17, 1989 (delivered by Kissinger), CWIHP Document Reader, "The End."

72. See Chernyaev notes from the Politiburo session, Jan. 21, 1989, where Kissinger's recent visit was discussed. Ibid.

73. See George H. W. Bush and Brent Scowcroft, *A World Transformed* (New York: Knopf, 1998), 53, and James A. Baker, *The Politics of Diplomacy* (New York: Putnam, 1995), 96; George H. W. Bush May 31, 1989 speech, "Remarks to the Citizens of Mainz," available at http://www.presidency.ucsb. edu/ws/index.php?pid=17085.

74. Record of Gorbachev–Thatcher conversation, Sept. 23, 1989, CWIHP Document Reader, "The End."

75. See Condoleeza Rice and Philip Zelikow, *Germany Unified and Europe Transformed* (Cambridge, MA: Harvard University Press, 1997), 107; Christopher Maynard, *Out of the Shadow: George H. W. Bush and the End of the Cold War* (College Station: Texas A&M University Press, 2008), 42.

76. Record of Bush–Kohl tel. conversation, Oct. 23, 1989, CWIHP Document Reader, "The End." On the deal, see Zubok, *A Failed Empire*, 325.

77. Modrow became prime minister on Nov. 13. Record of Gorbachev–Kohl tel. conversation, Nov. 11, 1989, CWIHP Document Reader, "The End."

78. The message was conveyed to Teltschik by Falin's associate Nikolai Portugalov. See Horst Teltschik, *329 Tage. Innenansichten der Einigung* (Berlin: Siedler, 1991); Rice and Zelikow, *Germany Unified*, 118; Andrei Grachev, *Gorbachev's Gamble: Soviet Foreign Policy and the End of the Cold War* (London: Wiley, 2008).

79. For the ten points, see Rice and Zelikow, *Germany Unified*, 120.
80. Kohl followed up with a visit to Dresden on Dec. 19, 1989. His enthusiastic reception there drove home to him that the population was eager for reunification.
81. Record of Gorbachev–Thatcher conversation, Sept. 23, 1989, CWIHP Document Reader, "The End." Gorbachev quoted in Angela Stent, *Russia and Germany Reborn: Unification, the Soviet Collapse, and the New Europe* (Princeton: Princeton University Press, 1999), 93, 101.
82. Record of Gorbachev–Genscher conversation, Dec. 5, 1989. CWIHP Document Reader, "The End." See also Lévesque, "In the Name of Europe's Future," 96.
83. Stent, *Russia and Germany*, 106. The SED had renamed itself the Party of Democratic Socialism. Art. 23 provided for outright annexation rather than writing a new constitution.
84. Two plus Four meant involving the two Germanies and four occupying powers.
85. Quoted in Hannes Adomeit, "Gorbachev's Consent to United Germany's Membership of NATO," in Bozo et al., eds., *Europe and the End of the Cold War*, 111.
86. Ibid., 112–13.
87. See Hans Jürgen Küsters, ed., "The Kohl–Gorbachev Meetings in Moscow and the Caucasus, 1990," *Cold War History*, 2/2, (Jan. 2002) 195–235.
88. See Malin, *The Soviet Tragedy*, 463; Mark Kramer, "The Collapse of East European Communism and the Repercussions within the Soviet Union" (Parts 1–3), *Journal of Cold War Studies*, 5/2, 2003, 178–256; 6/4, 2004, 3–64; 7/1, 2005, 3–96.
89. Dobrynin, *In Confidence*, 630–5; Chernyaev, *My Six Years*, 233–4.
90. Stent, *Russia and Germany*, 135, 142.
91. France had left the integrated military structure but remained an alliance member. See Rey, "Europe is our Common Home," 57; Frédéric Bozo, " 'Winners' and 'Losers': France, the United States and the End of the Cold War," *Diplomatic History*, 33/ 5, Nov. 2009, 927–56.
92. Stent, *Russia and Germany*, 113–14.
93. Assurances included German reaffirmation of no nuclear, biological or chemical weapons, Bundeswehr cuts, a promise to redefine NATO strategy, a pledge not to station NATO troops in the former GDR for a transition period, a proposal to institutionalize the CSCE and make it a

pan-European organization, and German aid to the USSR. Ibid., 128–9. See also the London Declaration, July 6, 1990, www.nato.int/doc/basictxt.

94. See Adomeit, "Gorbachev's consent," 116–17.

95. These were the Treaty on Good Neighborliness, Partnership and Cooperation, and a Treaty on Developing Comprehensive Cooperation on the Economy, Industry, Science and Technology.

96. See Treaty on Conventional Forces in Europe, www.fas.org/nuke/control. The treaty required far deeper cuts by the Warsaw Pact.

97. This is Zubok's view, *A Failed Empire* (330).

Conclusion

1. For Nitze's persistent view, see his "Deterring our Deterrent," *Foreign Policy*, 25 (Winter 1976/7), 195–206.

2. Vadim Medvedev, quoted in Ellman and Kontorovich, eds., *The Destruction of the Soviet Economic System*, 96; Gromyko quoted in Geir Lundestad, "'Imperial Overstretch', Mikhail Gorbachev, and the End of the Cold War," in *Cold War History*, 1/1, Aug. 2000, 6.

3. Aron, *On War*, 24.

4. Iván Berend, *From the Soviet Bloc to the European Union: The Economic and Social Transformation of Central and Eastern Europe since 1973* (Cambridge: Cambridge University Press, 2009).

5. A point made by David Unger.

6. Djilas, *Conversations with Stalin*, 187.

7. Kennan, "America's Duty to the Wide World Starts at Home," *International Herald Tribune*, Mar. 14, 1994, 4; *Memoirs*, i., 365; "The Sources of Soviet Conduct."

8. This is according to an IMEMO estimate cited in Lundestad, "Imperial Overstretch," 3.

9. Quoted in J.-R. Tournoux, *La Tragédie du Général* (Paris: Plon, 1967), 167.

10. De Gaulle, press conference, July 23, 1964, *Discours et Messages*, Vol. 5 (Paris: Plon, 1970–1), 227.

11. Kennan lecture, "Russia and the U.S.," May 27, 1950, Kennan Papers, box 2.

12. Kennan lecture (untitled), May 31, 1948, Kennan Papers, box 17.

13. See Documentary Traces.

14. President George W. Bush speech at West Point, NY, June 1, 2002.

15. The Bush administration National Security Strategy, Sept. 2002.

SELECT BIBLIOGRAPY

PRIMARY SOURCES

Acheson, Dean. *Present at the Creation: My Years at the State Department.* New York: Norton, 1969.

Andrew, Christopher and Oleg Gordievsky, eds. *Comrade Kryuchkov's Instructions: Top Secret Files on KGB Foreign Operations, 1975–1985.* Stanford, CA: Stanford University Press, 1993.

Baker, James A. *The Politics of Diplomacy: Revolution, War, and Peace, 1989–1992.* New York: Putnam's, 1995.

Beschloss, Michael R., ed. *Taking Charge: The Johnson White House Tapes 1963–1964.* New York: Simon and Schuster, 1997.

Blight, James G. and David A. Welch, eds. *On the Brink: Americans and Soviets Reexamine the Cuban Missile Crisis.* New York: Hill and Wang, 1989.

Bohlen, Charles E. *Witness to History, 1929–1969.* New York: Norton, 1973.

Brzezinski, Zbigniew. *Power and Principle: Memoirs of the National Security Adviser, 1977–1981.* London: Weidenfeld and Nicolson, 1983.

Burr, William, ed. *The Kissinger Transcripts: The Top Secret Talks with Beijing and Moscow.* New York: New Press, 1998.

Bush, George H. W. and Brent Scowcroft. *A World Transformed.* New York: Knopf, 1998.

Byrnes, James. *Speaking Frankly.* New York: Harper & Brothers, 1947.

Carter, Jimmy. *Keeping Faith: Memoirs of a President.* New York: Bantam, 1982.

Chernyaev, Anatoly S. *My Six Years with Gorbachev.* University Park: Pennsylvania State University Press, 2000.

Cold War International History Project.
   1956 Hungarian Revolution Collection
   Anti-Colonialism in the Cold War Collection
   Cuban Missile Crisis Collection
   Document Reader: The End of the Cold War

Germany in the Cold War Collection

Poland in the Cold War Collection

Sino-Soviet Relations Collection

Soviet Invasion of Afghanistan Collection

The Cold War in Africa Collection

The Vietnam (Indochina) War(s) Collection

U.S.–Soviet Relations Collection

De Gaulle, Charles. *Discours et messages: pour l'effort août 1962–décembre 1965.* Paris: Plon, 1970–1.

Digital National Security Archives.

The Cuban Missile Crisis Collection

Foreign Broadcast Information Service Transcripts

INF Document Collection

The Kissinger Telephone Conversations

The Reykjavik File

Djilas, Milovan. *Conversations with Stalin.* New York: Harcourt Brace, 1962.

Dobrynin, Anatoly. *In Confidence: Moscow's Ambassador to America's Six Cold War Presidents (1962–1986).* New York: Times Books, 1995.

Ellman, Michael and Vladimir Kontorovich, eds. *The Destruction of the Soviet Economic System: An Insiders' History.* London: M. E. Sharpe, 1998.

Etzold, Thomas H. and John Lewis Gaddis, eds. *Containment: Documents on American Policy and Strategy, 1945–1950.* New York: Columbia University Press, 1978.

Foreign Office Records. Public Record Office. Kew, UK.

Foreign Relations of the United States (FRUS). Various vols. Washington: Government Printing Office.

Gorbachev, Mikhail Sergeyevich. *Memoirs.* New York: Doubleday, 1996.

Hanhimäki, Jussi and Odd Arne Westad, eds. *The Cold War: A History in Documents and Eyewitness Accounts.* Oxford: Oxford University Press, 2003.

Johnson, Lyndon B. *Public Papers of the Presidents of the United States: Lyndon B. Johnson, 1968–1969.* Book I. Washington: Government Printing Office.

——*The Vantage Point: Perspectives of the Presidency, 1963–1969.* New York: Holt, Rinehart and Winston, 1971.

Kennan, George F. *Memoirs.* 2 vols. Boston: Little Brown, 1967–72.

Kennan Papers, Seeley G. Mudd Manuscript Library, Princeton University.

Khrushchev, Nikita. *Khrushchev Remembers.* Boston: Little, Brown, 1970.

——*Memoirs of Nikita Khrushchev.* University Park: Pennsylvania State University Press, 2004–7.

Kimball, Jeffrey, ed. *The Vietnam War Files: Uncovering the Secret History of Nixon Era Strategy*. Lawrence: University Press of Kansas, 2004.

Kimball, Warren F., ed. *Churchill and Roosevelt: Their Complete Correspondence*. 3 vols. Princeton: Princeton University Press, 1984.

Kissinger, Henry A. *White House Years*. Boston: Little, Brown, 1979.

—— *Years of Renewal*. New York: Simon and Schuster, 1999.

—— *Years of Upheaval*. Boston: Little, Brown, 1982.

Küsters, Hans Jürgen, ed. "The Kohl–Gorbachev Meetings in Moscow and the Caucasus, 1990" (with documents). *Cold War History*, 2/2 (Jan. 2002): 195–235.

Lenin, V. I. *Collected Works*. Moscow: Progress Publishers, 1965.

Levering, Ralph B., et al. *Debating the Origins of the Cold War: American and Russian Perspectives*. London: Rowman and Littlefield, 2002.

McFarlane, Robert C. and Zofia Smardz. *Special Trust: Pride, Principle and Politics inside the White House*. London: Cadell and Davies, 1994.

McNamara, Robert S. *In Retrospect: The Tragedy and Lessons of Vietnam*. New York: Times Books, 1995.

Malin, V. *Notes of Presidium Meetings*. Kremlin Decision-Making Project. Miller Center, University of Virginia.

Mao Zedong. *Selected Works of Mao Tse-tung: The First and Second Revolutionary Civil War Period*. Honolulu: University Press of the Pacific, 2001.

May, Ernest R. and Philip D. Zelikow, eds. *The Kennedy Tapes: Inside the White House during the Cuban Missile Crisis*. Cambridge, MA: Harvard University Press, 1997.

Molotov, Viachleslav. *Molotov Remembers: Inside Kremlin Politics. Conversations with Felix Chuev*. London: Ivan Dee, 1991.

Nitze, Paul H., with Steven L. Rearden and Ann M. Smith. *From Hiroshima to Glasnost: At the Center of Decision*. New York: Grove Weidenfeld, 1989.

The Pentagon Papers: The Defense Department History of United States Decisionmaking in Vietnam. The Senator Gravel ed. 5 vols. Boston: Beacon, 1971–2.

Reagan, Ronald. *An American Life*. New York: Simon and Schuster, 1990.

—— *The Reagan Diaries*. New York: HarperCollins, 2007.

Records of the Joint Chiefs of Staff. National Archives. Washington.

Rzheshevsky, Oleg A., ed. *War and Diplomacy: The Making of the Grand Alliance. Documents from Stalin's Archives edited with a Commentary*. Amsterdam: Harwood, 1996.

Schecter, Jerrold L. and Viacheslav V. Luchkov, *Khrushchev Remembers: The Glasnost Tapes*. Boston: Little, Brown, 1990

Schlesinger, Jr., Arthur M. *Journals 1952–2000*. New York: Penguin, 2007.

Shevardnadze, Eduard. *The Future Belongs to Freedom*. New York: Free Press, 1991.

Shultz, George P. *Turmoil and Triumph: My Years as Secretary of State*. New York: Simon and Schuster, 1993.

Soviet–American Relations: The Détente Years, 1969–1972. Washington: Government Printing Office, 2007.

Stalin, J. V., *Problems of Leninism*. Beijing: Foreign Languages Press, 1976.

Teltschik, Horst. *329 Tage. Innenansichten der Einigung*. Berlin: Siedler, 1991.

Truman, Harry S. *Memoirs*. 2 vols. Garden City, NY: Doubleday, 1955.

Vance, Cyrus R. *Hard Choices: Critical Years in America's Foreign Policy*. New York: Simon and Schuster, 1983.

Vandenberg, Jr., Arthur H. *The Private Papers of Senator Vandenberg*. Boston: Houghton Mifflin, 1952.

BOOKS

Allin, Dana. *Cold War Illusions: America, Europe, and Soviet Power, 1969–1989*. New York: St. Martin's Press, 1997.

Alperowitz, Gar. *Atomic Diplomacy: Hiroshima and Potsdam*. New York: Simon and Schuster, 1965.

Ambrose, Stephen E. and Günter Bischof, eds. *Eisenhower, a Centenary Assessment*. Baton Rouge: Louisiana State University Press, 1995.

Asselin, Pierre. *A Bitter Peace: Washington, Hanoi, and the Making of the Paris Agreement*. Chapel Hill: University of North Carolina Press, 2002.

Aron, Raymond. *Le Grand Schisme*. Paris: Gallimard, 1948.

——*On War*. New York: Norton, 1968.

Barraclough, Geoffrey. *An Introduction to Contemporary History*. London: Penguin, 1990 (first published in 1964).

Bell, Coral. *The Reagan Paradox: American Foreign Policy in the 1980s*. New Brunswick, NJ: Rutgers University Press, 1989.

Beisner, Robert. *Dean Acheson: A Life in the Cold War*. Oxford: Oxford University Press, 2006.

Berman, Larry. *Lyndon Johnson's War: The Road to Stalemate in Vietnam*. New York: Norton, 1989.

——*No Peace, No Honor: Nixon, Kissinger and Betrayal in Vietnam*. New York: Touchstone, 2001.

Beschloss, Michael and Strobe Talbott. *At the Highest Levels: The Inside Story of the End of the Cold War.* Boston: Little, Brown, 1993.

Blum, Robert M. *Drawing the Line: The Origin of the American Containment Policy in East Asia.* New York: Norton, 1982.

Bowie, Robert and Richard Immerman. *Waging Peace: How Eisenhower Shaped an Enduring Cold War Strategy.* Oxford: Oxford University Press, 1998.

Bozo, Frédéric. *Mitterrand, the End of the Cold War, and German Unification.* Oxford: Berghahn Books, 2009.

——N. Pier Ludlow, Leopoldo Nuti, and Marie-Pierre Rey, eds. *Europe and the End of the Cold War: A Reappraisal.* London: Routledge, 2009.

Brocheux, Pierre. *Ho Chi Minh: A Biography.* Cambridge: Cambridge University Press, 2007.

Brown, Archie. *The Gorbachev Factor.* Oxford: Oxford University Press, 1996.

Bullock, Alan. *Ernest Bevin: Foreign Secretary, 1945–1951.* New York: Norton, 1983.

Cahn, Anne Hessing. *Killing Détente: The Right Attacks the CIA.* University Park: Pennsylvania State University Press, 1998.

Calleo, David. *The Imperious Economy.* Cambridge, MA: Harvard University Press, 1982.

Cannon, Lou. *President Reagan: The Role of a Lifetime.* New York: Public Affairs, 2000.

Chen, Jian. *Mao's China and the Cold War.* Chapel Hill: University of North Carolina Press, 2001.

Cousins, Norman. *Improbable Triumvirate: John F. Kennedy, Pope John, Nikita Khruschev.* New York: Norton, 1972.

Craig, Campbell and Fredrik Logevall. *America's Cold War: The Politics of Insecurity.* Cambridge MA: Harvard University Press, 2009.

Cumings, Bruce. *The Origins of the Korean War.* 2 vols. Princeton: Princeton University Press, 1981–90.

Dallek, Robert. *An Unfinished Life: John F. Kennedy, 1917–1963.* Boston: Little, Brown, 2003.

Darling, Arthur B. *The Central Intelligence Agency: An Instrument of Government, to 1950.* University Park: Pennsylvania State University Press, 1990.

Diggins, John Patrick. *Ronald Reagan: Fate, Freedom, and the Making of History.* New York: Norton, 2007.

Ellwood, David W. *Rebuilding Europe: Western Europe, America, and Postwar Reconstruction.* London: Longman, 1992.

Engel, Jeffrey A., ed. *The Fall of the Berlin Wall: The Revolutionary Legacy of 1989*. Oxford: Oxford University Press, 2009.

English, Robert D. *Russia and the Idea of the West: Gorbachev, Intellectuals and the End of the Cold War*. New York: Columbia University Press, 2000.

Evans, Richard. *Deng Xiaoping and the Making of Modern China*. London: Penguin, 1997.

Feis, Herbert. *Churchill–Roosevelt–Stalin: The War they Waged and the Peace they Sought*. Princeton: Princeton University Press, 1957.

Fischer, Beth A. *The Reagan Reversal: Foreign Policy and the End of the Cold War*. Columbia: University of Missouri Press, 1997.

Fitzgerald, Frances. *Way Out There in the Blue: Reagan, Star Wars, and the End of the Cold War*. New York: Simon and Schuster, 2000.

Fleming, Denna Frank. *The Cold War and its Origins, 1917–1960*. 2 vols. Garden City: Doubleday, 1961.

Fontaine, André. *History of the Cold War from the October Revolution to the Korean War, 1917–1950*. New York: Pantheon, 1968.

Foot, Rosemary. *The Wrong War: American Policy and the Dimensions of the Korean Conflict, 1950–1953*. Ithaca, NY: Cornell University Press, 1985.

Freedman, Lawrence. *Kennedy's Wars*. Oxford: Oxford University Press, 2000.

—— *The Evolution of Nuclear Strategy*. New York: Palgrave, 2003.

Freeland, Richard M. *The Truman Doctrine and the Origins of McCarthyism*. New York: Knopf, 1972.

Fursenko, Aleksandr and Timothy Naftali. *Khrushchev's Cold War: The Inside Story of an American Adversary*. New York: Norton, 2006.

—— *"One Hell of a Gamble": Khrushchev, Castro and Kennedy, 1958–1964*. New York: Norton, 1997.

Gaddis, John Lewis. *Strategies of Containment: A Critical Appraisal of American National Security Policy during the Cold War*. New York: Oxford University Press, 2005.

—— *The Cold War: A New History*. New York: Penguin, 2005.

—— *The United States and the Origins of the Cold War, 1941–1947*. New York: Columbia University Press, 1972.

—— *We Now Know: Rethinking Cold War History*. Oxford: Oxford University Press, 1997.

Gardner, Lloyd C. *Architects of Illusion: Men and Ideas in American Foreign Policy, 1941–1949*. Chicago: Quadrangle, 1970.

—— Arthur M. Schlesinger, Jr., and Hans Morgenthau. *The Origins of the Cold War*. Lexington, MA: Xerox Books, 1970.

Garthoff, Raymond. *Détente and Confrontation: American–Soviet Relations from Nixon to Reagan.* Washington: Brookings Institution Press, 1994.

——*The Great Transition: American–Soviet Relations and the End of the Cold War.* Washington: Brookings Institution Press, 1994.

Gati, Charles. *Failed Illusions: Moscow, Washington, Budapest, and the 1956 Hungarian Revolt.* Washington: Wilson Center Press, 2006.

Gilman, Nils. *Mandarins of the Future: Modernization Theory in Cold War America.* Baltimore: Johns Hopkins University Press, 2003.

Gleijeses, Piero. *Conflicting Missions: Havana, Washington, and Africa, 1959–1976.* Chapel Hill: University of North Carolina Press, 2002.

Goldstein, Gordon M. *Lessons in Disaster: McGeorge Bundy and the Path to War in Vietnam.* New York: Holt, 2010.

Goncharov, Sergei, John Lewis and Xue Litai. *Uncertain Partners: Stalin, Mao, and the Korean War.* Stanford, CA: Stanford University Press, 1993.

Gorlitzki, Yoram and Oleg Khlevniuk. *Cold Peace: Stalin and the Soviet Ruling Circle, 1945–1953.* Oxford: Oxford University Press, 2004.

Gorodetsky, Gabriel. *Grand Delusion: Stalin and the German Invasion of Russia.* New Haven: Yale University Press, 1999.

Grachev, Andrei. *Gorbachev's Gamble: Soviet Foreign Policy and the End of the Cold War.* London: Wiley, 2008.

Grinevsky, Oleg. *Tysyacha I Odin den' Nikity Sergeyevicha* (A Thousand and One Days of Nikita Khrushchev). Moscow: Vagrius, 1998.

Guhin, Michael. *John Foster Dulles: A Statesman and His Times.* New York: Columbia University Press, 1972.

Halle, Louis J. *The Cold War as History.* New York: Harper and Row, 1967.

Halliday, Fred. *The Making of the Second Cold War.* London: Verso, 1983.

Hanrieder, Wolfram. *Germany, America, and Europe: Forty Years of German Foreign Policy.* New Haven: Yale University Press, 1989.

Harbutt, Fraser J. *The Iron Curtain: Churchill, America, and the Origins of the Cold War.* Oxford: Oxford University Press, 1986.

Harper, John Lamberton. *America and the Reconstruction of Italy, 1945–1948.* Cambridge: Cambridge University Press, 1986.

——*American Visions of Europe: Franklin D. Roosevelt, George F. Kennan, and Dean G. Acheson.* Cambridge: Cambridge University Press, 1994.

Harrison, Hope. *Driving the Soviets up the Wall: Soviet–East German Relations, 1953–1961.* Princeton: Princeton University Press, 2003.

Hasegawa, Tsuyoshi. *Racing the Enemy: Stalin, Truman, and the Surrender of Japan.* Cambridge, MA: Harvard University Press, 2005.

Haynes, John Earl, Harvey Klehr, and Alexander Vassiliev. *Spies: The Rise and Fall of the KGB in America.* New Haven: Yale University Press, 2009.

Herken, Gregg. *The Winning Weapon: The Atomic Bomb in the Cold War, 1945–1950.* New York: Vintage, 1981.

Herring, George C. *America's Longest War: The United States and Vietnam, 1950–1975.* New York: John Wiley, 1979.

Hoffman, David E. *The Dead Hand: The Untold Story of the Cold War Arms Race and its Dangerous Legacy.* New York: Doubleday, 2009.

Hogan, Michael. *A Cross of Iron: Harry S. Truman and the Origins of the National Security State, 1945–1954.* Cambridge: Cambridge University Press, 1998.

—— *The Marshall Plan.* Cambridge: Cambridge University Press, 1987.

Holloway, David. *Stalin and the Bomb: The Soviet Union and Atomic Energy, 1939–1956.* New Haven: Yale University Press, 1994.

Hoopes, Townsend. *The Devil and John Foster Dulles.* Boston: Little, Brown, 1973.

Immerman, Richard H., ed. *John Foster Dulles and the Diplomacy of the Cold War.* Princeton: Princeton University Press, 1990.

Issacson, Walter. *Kissinger: A Biography.* New York: Simon and Schuster, 1992.

Jones, Howard. *Death of a Generation: How the Assassinations of Diem and JFK Prolonged the Vietnam War.* Oxford: Oxford University Press, 2003.

Kahin, George McT. *Intervention: How America Became Involved in Vietnam.* New York: Knopf, 1986.

Kennan, George F. *Russia and the West under Lenin and Stalin.* London: Hutchinson, 1961.

Knight, Amy. *Beria: Stalin's First Lieutenant.* Princeton: Princeton University Press, 1993.

Koen, Ross Y. *The China Lobby in American Politics.* New York: Macmillan, 1960.

Kolko, Gabriel and Joyce Kolko. *The Limits of Power: The World and United States Foreign Policy, 1945–1954.* New York: Praeger, 1972.

Kotkin, Stephen. *Armageddon Averted: The Soviet Collapse, 1970–2000.* Oxford: Oxford University Press, 2001.

Kuniholm, Bruce R. *The Origins of the Cold War in the Near East: Great Power Conflict and Diplomacy in Iran, Turkey, and Greece.* Princeton: Princeton University Press, 1979.

Kyle, Keith. *Suez: Britain's End of Empire in the Middle East.* London: Tauris, 2003.

Larres, K. and K. Osgood, eds. *The Cold War after Stalin's Death: A Missed Opportunity for Peace?* Lanham, MD: Rowman and Littlefield, 2006.

Latham, Michael E. *Modernization as Ideology: American Social Science and Nation-Building in the Kennedy Era.* Chapel Hill: University of North Carolina Press, 2000.

Lawrence, John. *A History of Russia.* New York: Meridian, 1993.

Lawrence, Mark A. and Fredrik Logevall, eds. *The First Vietnam War: Colonial Conflict and Cold War Crisis.* Cambridge, MA: Harvard University Press, 2007.

Leffler, Melvin P. *A Preponderance of Power: National Security, the Truman Administration, and the Cold War.* Stanford, CA: Stanford University Press, 1992.

——*For the Soul of Mankind: The United States, the Soviet Union, and the Cold War.* New York: Hill and Wang, 2007.

——and Odd Arne Westad, eds. *The Cambridge History of the Cold War.* 3 vols. Cambridge: Cambridge University Press, 2009.

Lévesque, Jacques. *The Enigma of 1989: The USSR and the Liberation of Eastern Europe.* Berkeley: University of California Press, 1997.

Lippmann, Walter. *The Cold War: A Study in U.S. Foreign Policy.* New York: Harper and Bros., 1947.

——*U.S. Foreign Policy: Shield of the Republic.* Boston: Little, Brown, 1943.

Logevall, Fredrik. *Choosing War: The Lost Chance for Peace and the Escalation of War in Vietnam.* Berkeley: University of California Press, 1999.

Loth, Wilfred. *Stalin's Unwanted Child: The Soviet Union, the German Question, and the Founding of the GDR.* New York: St. Martin's Press, 1998.

Lukacs, John. *A New History of the Cold War.* Garden City, NY: Anchor, 1966.

Lüthi, Lorenz M. *The Sino-Soviet Split: Cold War in the Communist World.* Princeton: Princeton University Press, 2008.

Mackinder, Halford. *Democratic Ideals and Reality: With Additional Papers* (1919). New York: Norton, 1962.

McMaster, H. R. *Dereliction of Duty: Lyndon Johnson, Robert McNamara, the Joint Chiefs of Staff, and the Lies that Led to Vietnam.* New York: HarperPerennial, 1997.

Malia, Martin. *The Soviet Tragedy: A History of Socialism in Russia.* New York: Simon and Schuster, 1995.

Mandelbaum, Michael. *The Nuclear Question: The United States and Nuclear Weapons, 1946–1976.* Cambridge: Cambridge University Press, 1979.

Mann, James. *The Rebellion of Ronald Reagan: A History of the End of the Cold War.* New York: Viking, 2009.

Mastny, Vojtech. *Russia's Road to the Cold War: Diplomacy, Warfare and the Politics of Communism.* New York: Columbia University Press, 1979.

———*The Cold War and Soviet Insecurity: The Stalin Years.* Oxford: Oxford University Press, 1996.

———Sven G. Holtsmark, and Andreas Wenger, eds. *War Plans and Alliances in the Cold War: Threat Perceptions in the East and West.* New York: Routledge, 2006.

Matlock, Jack F. *Reagan and Gorbachev: How the Cold War Ended.* New York: Random House, 2004.

Maynard, Christopher. *Out of the Shadow: George H. W. Bush and the End of the Cold War.* College Station: Texas A&M University Press, 2008.

Medvedev, Zhores. *Andropov.* Oxford: Basil Blackwell, 1983.

Mee, Charles. *Meeting at Potsdam.* New York: M. Evans, 1975.

Messer, Robert. *The End of an Alliance: James Byrnes, Roosevelt, Truman and the Origins of the Cold War.* Chapel Hill: University of North Carolina Press, 1982.

Meyer, Michel. *Histoire Secrète de la Chute du Mur de Berlin.* Paris: Odile Jacob, 2009.

Mills, C. Wright. *The Causes of World War Three.* New York: Simon and Schuster, 1958.

Miscamble, Wilson D. *From Roosevelt to Truman: Potsdam, Hiroshima, and the Cold War.* Cambridge: Cambridge University Press, 2007.

Mitrovich, Gregory. *Undermining the Kremlin: America's Strategy to Subvert the Soviet Bloc, 1947–1956.* Ithaca, NY: Cornell University Press, 2000.

Moyar, Mark. *Triumph Forsaken: The Vietnam War, 1954–1965.* Cambridge: Cambridge University Press, 2006.

Niebuhr, Reinhold. *The Irony of American History.* New York: Scribner, 1952.

Nove, Alec. *An Economic History of the USSR, 1917–1991.* London: Penguin Books, 1992.

Odom, William E. *The Collapse of the Soviet Military.* New Haven: Yale University Press, 1998.

Osgood, Robert Endicott, ed. *Retreat From Empire? The First Nixon Administration.* Baltimore: Johns Hopkins University Press, 1973.

Pons, Silvio and Federico Romero, eds. *Reinterpreting the End of the Cold War: Issues, Interpretations, Periodizations.* London: Frank Cass, 2005.

Prados, John. *Safe for Democracy: The Secret Wars of the CIA.* Chicago: Ivan R. Dee, 2006.

——*Vietnam: The History of an Unwinnable War, 1945–1975.* Lawrence: University Press of Kansas, 2009.

Rabe, Stephen G. *Eisenhower and Latin America: The Foreign Policy of Anti-Communism.* Chapel Hill: University of North Carolina Press, 1988.

——*The Most Dangerous Area in the World: John F. Kennedy Confronts Communist Revolution in Latin America.* Chapel Hill: The University of North Carolina Press, 1999.

Rice, Condoleeza and Philip Zelikow. *Germany Unified and Europe Transformed: A Study in Statecraft.* Cambridge, MA: Harvard University Press, 1995.

Roberts, Geoffrey. *Stalin's Wars: From World War to Cold War, 1939–1953.* New Haven: Yale University Press, 2006.

Rostow, Walt W. *The Stages of Economic Growth: A Non-Communist Manifesto.* Cambridge: Cambridge University Press, 1960.

Sarotte, Mary Elise. *1989: The Struggle to Create Post-Cold War Europe.* Princeton: Princeton University Press, 2009.

Saul, Norman E. *War and Revolution: The United States and Russia, 1914–1921.* Lawrence: University Press of Kansas, 2001.

Sebestyen, Victor. *Revolution 1989: The Fall of the Soviet Empire.* London: Pantheon, 2009.

Sherry, Michael S. *Preparing for the Next War: American Plans for Postwar Defense, 1941–45.* New Haven: Yale University Press, 1977.

Sherwin, Martin. *A World Destroyed: The Atomic Bomb and the Grand Alliance.* New York: Random House, 1977.

Statler, Kathryn C. *Replacing France: The Origins of American Intervention in Vietnam.* Lexington: University Press of Kentucky, 2007.

Steel, Ronald. *Walter Lippmann and the American Century.* New Brunswick, NJ: Transaction, 1999.

Steininger, Ralf. *The German Question and the Stalin Note of 1952.* New York: Columbia University Press, 1992.

Stent, Angela. *Russia and Germany Reborn: Unification, the Soviet Collapse, and the New Europe.* Princeton: Princeton University Press, 1999.

Stern, Paula. *Water's Edge: Domestic Politics and the Making of American Foreign Policy.* Westport, CT: Greenwood Press, 1979.

Stueck, William. *The Korean War: An International History.* Princeton: Princeton University Press, 1995.

Suri, Jeremi. *Power and Protest: Global Revolution and the Rise of Détente.* Cambridge MA: Harvard University Press, 2003.

Taubman, William. *Khrushchev: The Man and his Era*. New York: Norton, 2003.

Trachtenberg, Marc. *A Constructed Peace: The Making of the European Settlement 1945–1963*. Princeton: Princeton University Press, 1999.

Tucker, Nancy B. *Patterns in the Dust: Chinese–American Relations and the Recognition Controversy, 1949–1950*. New York: Columbia University Press, 1983.

Tucker, Robert C. *Political Culture and Leadership in Soviet Russia: From Lenin to Gorbachev*. New York: Norton, 1988.

Tuveson, Ernest Lee. *Redeemer Nation: The Idea of America's Millennial Role*. Chicago: University of Chicago Press, 1968.

Ulam, Adam. *Stalin: The Man and his Era*. New York: Viking Press, 1973.

Van Ree, Erik. *The Political Thought of Joseph Stalin*. London: Routledge, 2002.

Volkogonov, Dimitri. *Stalin: Triumph and Tragedy*. New York: Grove Weidenfeld, 1991.

Westad, Odd Arne. *The Global Cold War: Third World Interventions and the Making of our Times*. Cambridge: Cambridge University Press, 2005.

Williams, William Appleman. *The Tragedy of American Diplomacy*. Cleveland: World Publishing, 1959.

Wittner, Lawrence S. *The Struggle Against the Bomb: iii. Toward Nuclear Abolition: A History of the Nuclear Disarmament Movement, 1971-Present*. Stanford: Stanford University Press, 2003.

Yergin, Daniel. *Shattered Peace: The Origins of the Cold War and the National Security State*. Boston: Houghton Mifflin, 1977.

Young, Marilyn B. *The Vietnam Wars, 1945–1990*. New York: HarperCollins, 1991.

Zubok, Vladislav M. *A Failed Empire: The Soviet Union in the Cold War from Stalin to Gorbachev*. Chapel Hill: University of North Carolina Press, 2007.

——and Constantine Pleshakov. *Inside the Kremlin's Cold War: From Stalin to Khrushchev*. Cambridge, MA: Harvard University Press, 1996.

ARTICLES AND WORKING PAPERS

Allyn, Bruce J., James G. Blight, and David A. Welch. "Essence of Revision: Moscow, Havana, and the Cuban Missile Crisis." *International Security*, 14/4 (winter 1989/90): 136–2.

Bernstein, Barton. "Roosevelt, Truman and the Atomic Bomb: A Reinterpretation." *Political Science Quarterly*, 90/1 (spring 1973): 23–40.

Brooks, Stephen G. and William C. Wohlforth. "Power, Globalization, and the End of the Cold War: Reevaluating a Landmark Case for Ideas." *International Security*, 25/3 (winter 2000–1): 5–53.

Burr, William and Jeffery Kimball. "Nixon's Secret Nuclear Alert: Vietnam War Diplomacy and the Joint Chiefs of Staff Readiness Test, October 1969." *Cold War History*, 3/2 (Jan. 2003): 113–56.

Chapman, Jessica M. "Staging Democracy: South Vietnam's 1955 Referendum to Depose Bao Dai." *Diplomatic History*, 30/4 (Sept. 2006): 671–703.

Chen, Jian. "The Sino-Soviet Alliance and China's Entry into the Korean War." Working Paper no. 1. CWIHP (June 1992).

Ellsberg, Daniel. "The Quagmire Myth and the Stalemate Machine." *Public Policy*, 19/2 (spring 1971): 217–74.

Gaddis, John Lewis. "The Emerging Post-Revisionist Synthesis on the Origins of the Cold War." *Diplomatic History*, 7/3 (summer 1983): 171–90.

Galbraith, James K. "Exit Strategy." *Boston Review*, 28/5 (Oct./Nov. 2003): 29–34.

Garthoff, Raymond L. "Foreign Intelligence and the Historiography of the Cold War." *Journal of Cold War Studies*, 6/2 (spring 2004): 21–56.

Garton Ash, Timothy. "1989!" *New York Review of Books* 56/17 (Nov. 5, 2009): 4–8.

——"Velvet Revolution: The Prospects." *New York Review of Books*, 55/19 (Dec. 3, 2009): 20–3.

Gleijeses, Piero. "Moscow's Proxy? Cuba and Africa, 1975–1988." *Journal of Cold War Studies*, 8/4 (fall 2006): 98–146.

Harper, John L. "Anatomy of a Habit: America's Unnecessary Wars." *Survival*, 47/2 (summer 2005): 57–86.

——"Henry Stimson and the Origin of America's Attachment to Atomic Weapons." *SAIS Review* 5/2 (summer–fall 1985): 17–28.

Iatrides, John O. "Revolution or Self-Defense? Communist Goals, Strategy, and Tactics in the Greek Civil War." *Journal of Cold War Studies*, 7/3 (summer 2005): 3–33.

Kaplan, Fred. "JFK's First-Strike Plan." *Atlantic Monthly*. Oct. 2001, 81–6.

Kennan, George F. "The Gorbachev Prospect." *New York Review of Books*, 21 (Jan. 21, 1988).

Kramer, Mark. "Soviet Deliberations during the Polish Crisis, 1980–81." Special Working Paper no. 1. CWIHP (April 1999).

——"The Collapse of East European Communism and the Repercussions within the Soviet Union" (Part 1). *Journal of Cold War Studies*, 5/4 (2003): 178–256.

—— "The Collapse of East European Communism and the Repercussions within the Soviet Union" (Part 2). *Journal of Cold War Studies*, 6/4 (2004): 3–64.

—— "The Collapse of East European Communism and the Repercussions within the Soviet Union" (Part 3). *Journal of Cold War Studies*, 7/1 (2005): 3–96.

—— "The Kuklinski Files and the Polish Crisis of 1980–81: An Analysis of the Newly Released CIA Documents on Ryszard Kuklinski." Working Paper no. 59. CWIHP (March 2009).

Kuisong, Yang. "Changes in Mao Zedong's Attitude toward the Indochina War, 1949–1973." Working Paper no. 34. CWIHP (Feb. 2002).

Leffler, Melvyn. "The Cold War: What do we Now Know?" *American Historical Review*, 104 (April 1999): 501–24.

Louis, William Roger. "American Anti-colonialism and the Dissolution of the British Empire." *International Affairs* 61/3 (summer 1985): 395–420.

Lundestad, Geir. "Empire by Invitation? The United States and Western Europe, 1945–1952." *Journal of Peace Research*, 23 (Sept. 1986): 263–77.

Maier, Charles S. "The Marshall Plan and the Division of Europe." *Journal of Cold War Studies*, 7/1 (winter 2005): 168–74.

Mark, Eduard. "American Policy toward Eastern Europe and the Origins of the Cold War, 1941–1946: An Alternative Interpretation." *Journal of American History*, 68/2 (Sept. 1981): 313–36.

—— "Charles E. Bohlen and the Acceptable Limits of Soviet Hegemony in Eastern Europe: A memorandum of 18 October 1945." *Diplomatic History* 3 (spring 1979): 201–13.

—— "Revolution by Degrees: Stalin's National Front Strategy for Europe, 1941–1947." Working Paper no. 31. CWIHP (Feb. 2001).

—— "The War Scare of 1946 and Its Consequences." *Diplomatic History*, 21/3 (summer 1997): 383–415.

Mastny, Vojtech. "NATO in the Beholder's Eye: Soviet Perceptions and Policies, 1949–1956." Working Paper no. 35. CWIHP (Mar. 2002).

—— "The Soviet Non-Invasion of Poland in 1980/81 and the End of the Cold War." Working Paper no. 23. CWIHP (Sept. 1998).

Miller, Edward. "Vision, Power and Agency: The Ascent of Ngo Dinh Diem: 1945–54." *Journal of Southeast Asian Studies*, 35/3 (Oct. 2004): 433–58.

Miller, James E. "Taking the Gloves Off: The United States and the Italian Elections of 1948." *Diplomatic History*, 7 (1983): 35–55.

Mistry, Kaeten. "The Case for Political Warfare: Strategy, Organization and US Involvement in the 1948 Italian Election." *Cold War History*, 6/3 (Aug. 2006): 301–29.

Naimark, Norman. "Stalin and Europe in the Postwar Period, 1945–53: Issues and Problems." *Journal of Modern European History* 2 (2004): 28–56.

Pechatnov, Vladimir O. "'The Allies are Pressing on you to Break your Will . . .' Foreign Policy Correspondence Between Stalin and Molotov and other Politburo Members, September 1945–December 1946." Working Paper No. 26. CWIHP (Sept. 1999).

——— "The Big Three after World War II: New Documents on Soviet Thinking about Post War Relations with the United States and Great Britain." Working Paper no. 13. CWIHP (May 1995).

Pons, Silvio. "Stalin, Togliatti, and the Origins of the Cold War in Europe." *Journal of Cold War Studies*, 3/2 (spring 2001): 3–27.

Pribbenow, Merle L. "North Vietnam's Final Offensive: Strategic Endgame Nonpareil." *Parameters* (winter 1999–2000): 58–71.

Rey, M.-P. " 'Europe is Our Common Home': A Study of Gorbachev's Diplomatic Concept." *Cold War History*, 4/2 (Jan. 2004): 33–65.

Richter, James. "Reexamining Soviet Policy towards Germany during the Beria Interregnum." Working Paper no. 3. CWIHP (June 1992).

Roberts, Geoffrey. "Litvinov's Lost Peace, 1941–1946." *Journal of Cold War Studies*, 4/2 (spring 2002): 23–54.

——— "A Chance for Peace? The Soviet Campaign to end the Cold War, 1953–1955." Working Paper no. 57. CWIHP (Dec. 2008).

——— "Sexing Up the Cold War: New Evidence on the Molotov–Truman Talks of April 1945." *Cold War History*, 4/3 (Apr. 2004): 105–5.

Schwartz, Alan. " 'Henry . . . Winning an Election is Terribly Important': Partisan Politics in the History of U.S. Foreign Relations." *Diplomatic History*, 33/2 (April 2009): 173–90.

See, Jennifer W. "An Uneasy Truce: John F. Kennedy and Soviet–American Détente, 1963." *Cold War History*' 2/2 (Jan. 2002): 161–94.

Sfikas, Thanasis D. "War and Peace in the Strategy of the Communist Party of Greece, 1945–1949." *Journal of Cold War Studies*, 3/3 (fall 2001): 5–30.

Shepley, James. "How Dulles Averted War." *Life* 40 (Jan. 16, 1956): 70–80.

Van Dijk, Ruud. "The 1952 Stalin Note Debate: Myth or Missed Opportunity for German Unification?" Working Paper no. 14. CWIHP (May 1996).

Warner, M. "The CIA's Office of Policy Coordination: From NSC 10/2 to NSC 68." *International Journal of Intelligence and Counterintelligence*, 11/2 (summer 1998): 211–20.

Weathersby, Kathryn. "'Should We Fear This?' Stalin and the Danger of War with America." Working Paper no. 39. CWIHP (July 2002).

—— "Soviet Aims in Korea and the Origins of the Korean War: New Evidence from Russian Archives." Working Paper no. 8. CWIHP (Nov. 1993).

Westad, Odd Arne. "The Sino-Soviet Alliance and the United States: War, Politics, and Perceptions, 1950–1961." Paper presented to CWIHP conference on "The Cold War and Asia." Hong Kong, Jan. 1996.

—— Chen Jian, Stein Tonnessen, Nguyen Vu Tungand, and James G. Hershberg, eds. "77 Conversations Between Chinese and Foreign Leaders on the Wars in Indochina, 1964–1977." Working Paper no. 22. CWIHP (May 1998).

Wolff, David. " 'One Finger's Worth of Historical Events': New Russian and Chinese Evidence on the Sino-Soviet Alliance and Split, 1948–1959." Working Paper no. 30. CWIHP (Aug. 2005).

Zhihua, Shen. "Sino-Soviet Relations and the Origins of the Korean War: Stalin's Strategic Goals in the Far East." *Journal of Cold War Studies*, 2/ 2 (spring 2000): 44–68.

INDEX

Lightning Source UK Ltd.
Milton Keynes UK
UKOW06f0428281115

263691UK00002B/4/P